the pages in this book were cre-
ɪd—and are printed here—in Japanese
GHT-to-LEFT format. No artwork has
en reversed or altered, so you can
ɪd the stories the way the creators
ɪant for them to be read.

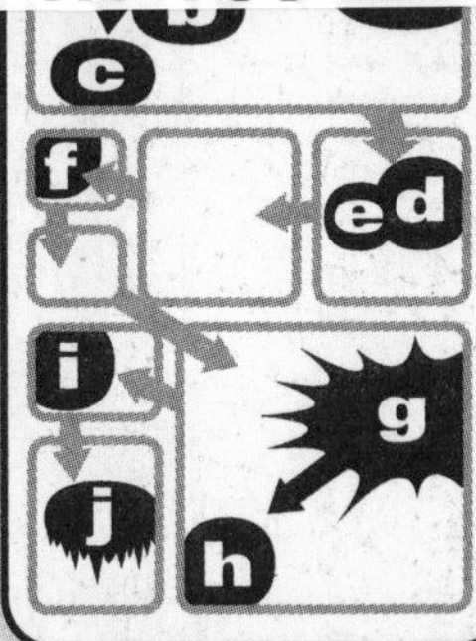

b
c
f
ed
i
g
j
h

FLIP IT!

RIGHT TO LEFT?!

Traditional Japanese manga starts at the upper right-hand corner, and moves right-to-left as it goes down the page. Follow this guide for an easy understanding.

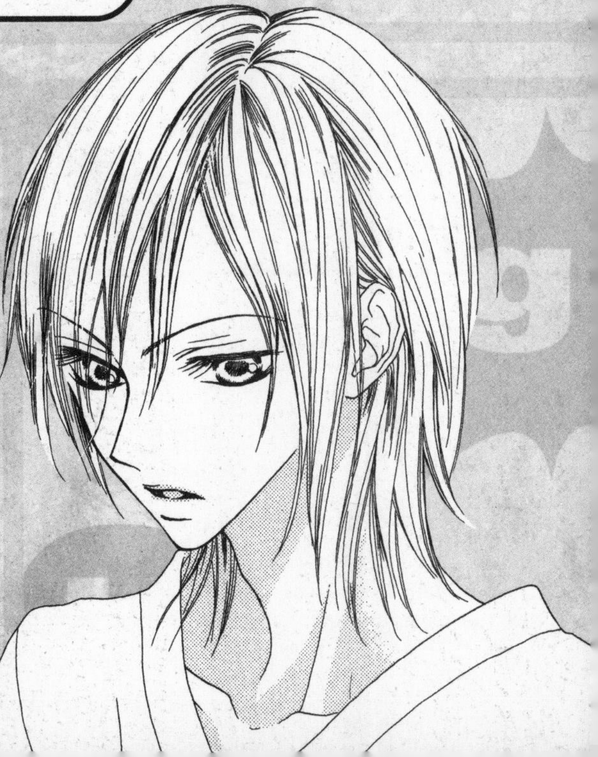

more information and sneak
views, visit cmxmanga.com.
l 1-888-COMIC BOOK for the
arest comics shop or
ɪd to your local book store.

CMX

VENUS CAPRICCIO by Mai Nishikata © 2006 Mai Nishikata. All rights reserved.
First published in Japan in 2006 by HAKUSENSHA, INC. Tokyo.

VENUS CAPRICCIO Volume 1, published by WildStorm Productions, an imprint of DC
Comics, 888 Prospect St. #240, La Jolla, CA 92037. English Translation © 2009. All Rights
Reserved. English translation rights in U.S.A. And Canada arranged with HAKUSENSHA,
INC., through Tuttle-Mori Agency, Inc., Tokyo. CMX is a trademark of DC Comics. The
stories, characters, and incidents mentioned in this magazine are entirely fictional. Printed
on recyclable paper. WildStorm does not read or accept unsolicited submissions of ideas,
stories or artwork. Printed in Canada.

DC Comics, a Warner Bros. Entertainment Company.

This book is manufactured at a facility holding chain-of-custody certification.
This paper is made with sustainably managed North American fiber.

Sheldon Drzka – Translation and Adaptation
MPS Ad Studio – Lettering & Retouching
Larry Berry – Design
Sarah Farber – Assistant Editor
Jim Chadwick – Editor   ISBN: 978-1-4012-2061-7

AKIRA AND TAKAMI ENTER A CONTEST AS COMPETITORS IN AUGUST!

By Mai Nishikata. Takami gets a part-time waitressing job at Club Blue. She is insulted when Akira decides to work there, too, but he just might have other motives than what she suspects. Then when the Aoyama piano school gets a new teacher, Akira is less than thrilled...and the new teacher's incessant flirting with Takami is only part of it. Later, Takami and Akira both enter the same contest. Will their friendship prove to be greater than their musical rivalry?

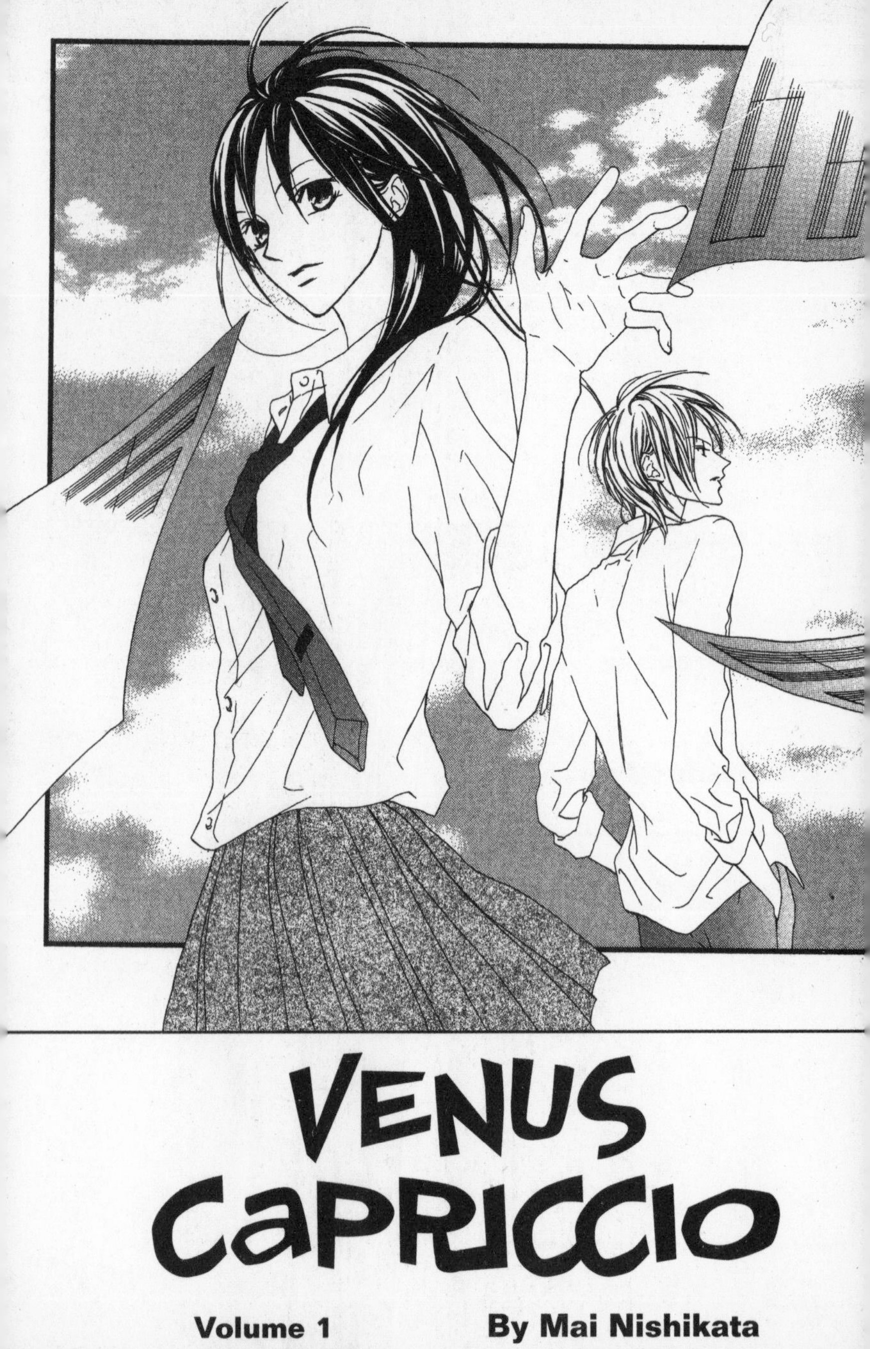

VENUS CAPRICCIO

Volume 1

By Mai Nishikata

CONTENTS

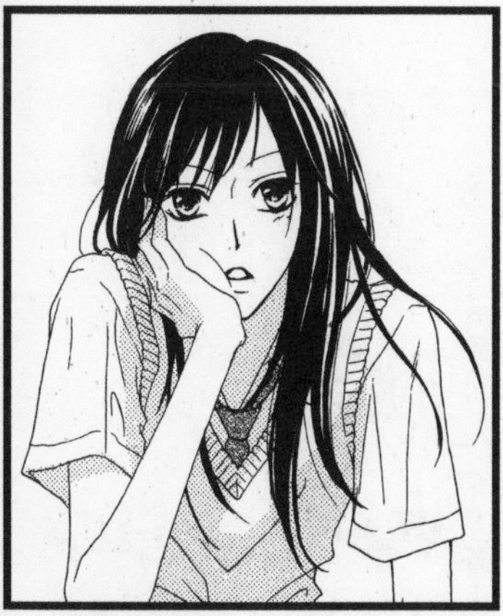

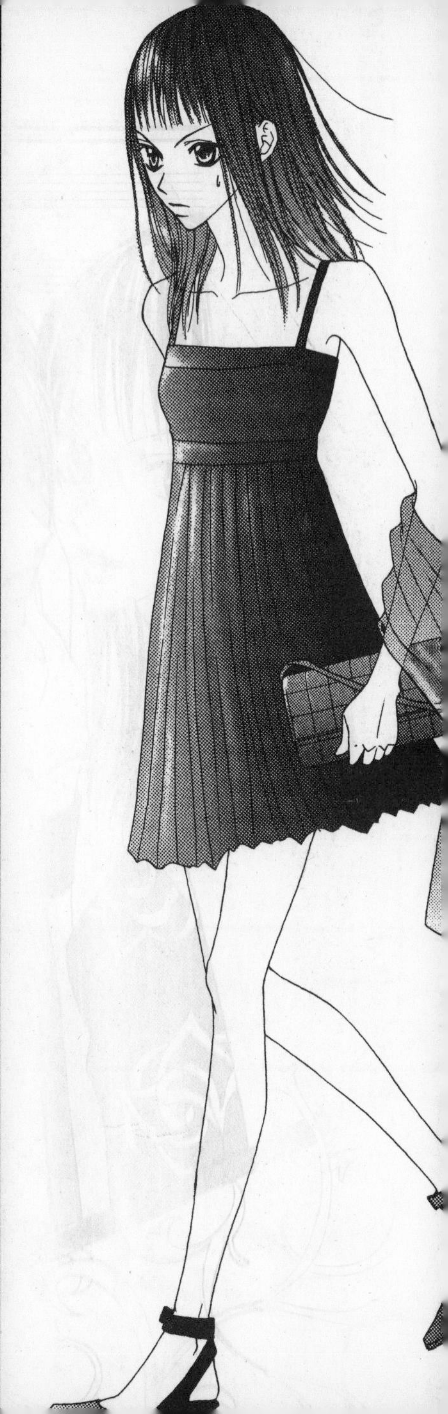

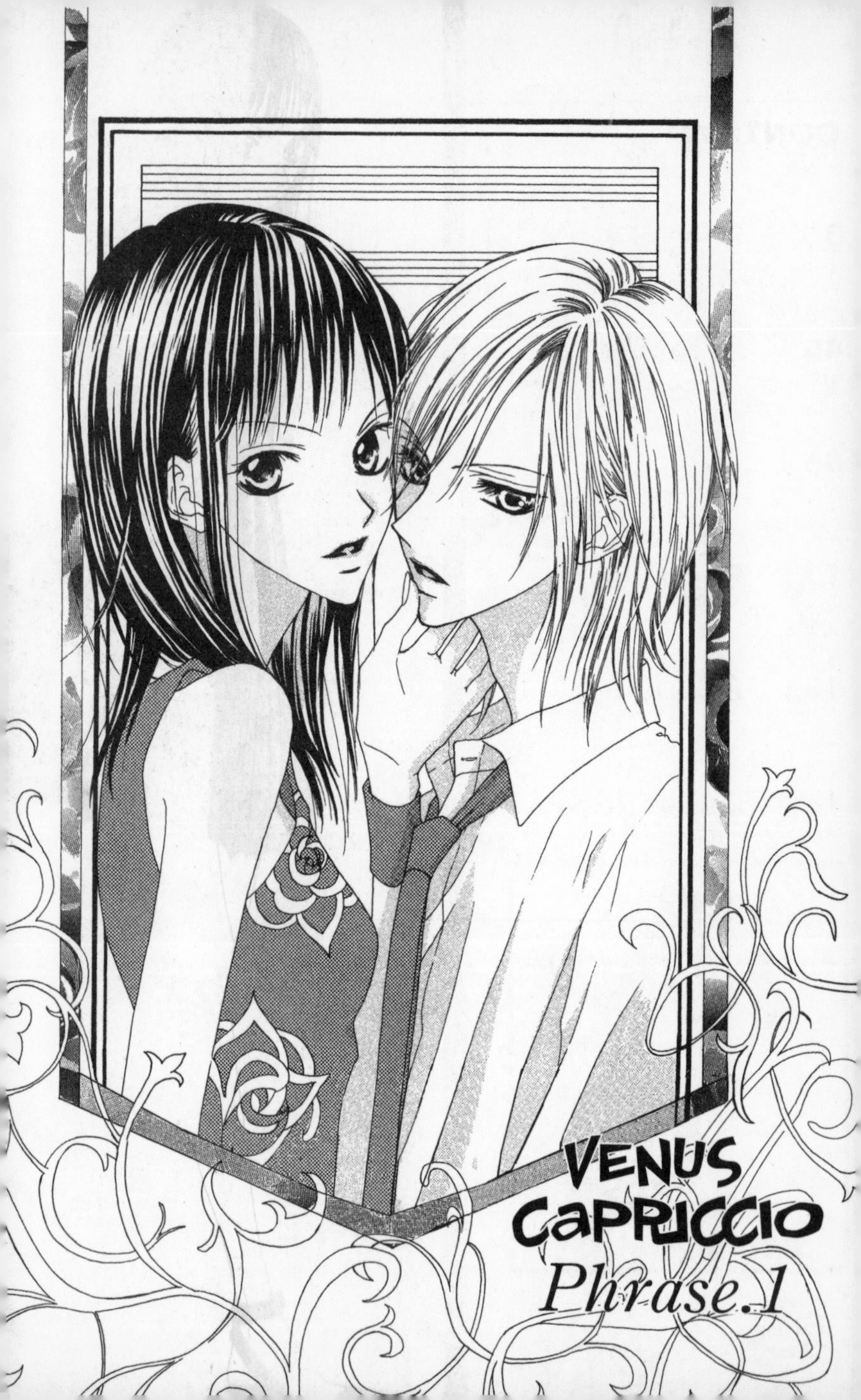
VENUS
CAPRICCIO
Phrase.1

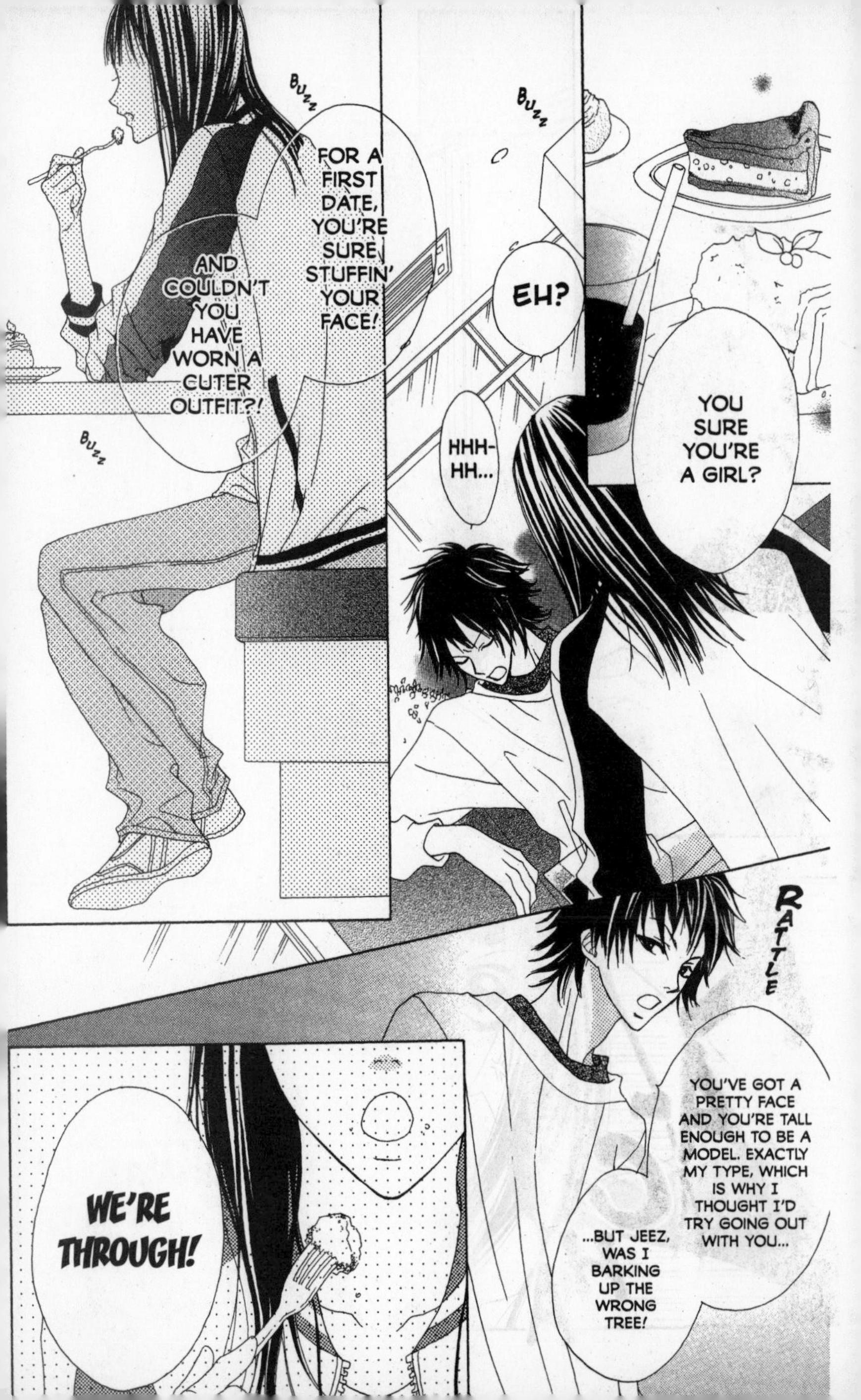
BUZZ
EH?
YOU SURE YOU'RE A GIRL?
HHH-HH...
BUZZ
FOR A FIRST DATE, YOU'RE SURE STUFFIN' YOUR FACE!
AND COULDN'T YOU HAVE WORN A CUTER OUTFIT?!
BUZZ
RATTLE
YOU'VE GOT A PRETTY FACE AND YOU'RE TALL ENOUGH TO BE A MODEL. EXACTLY MY TYPE, WHICH IS WHY I THOUGHT I'D TRY GOING OUT WITH YOU...
...BUT JEEZ, WAS I BARKING UP THE WRONG TREE!
WE'RE THROUGH!

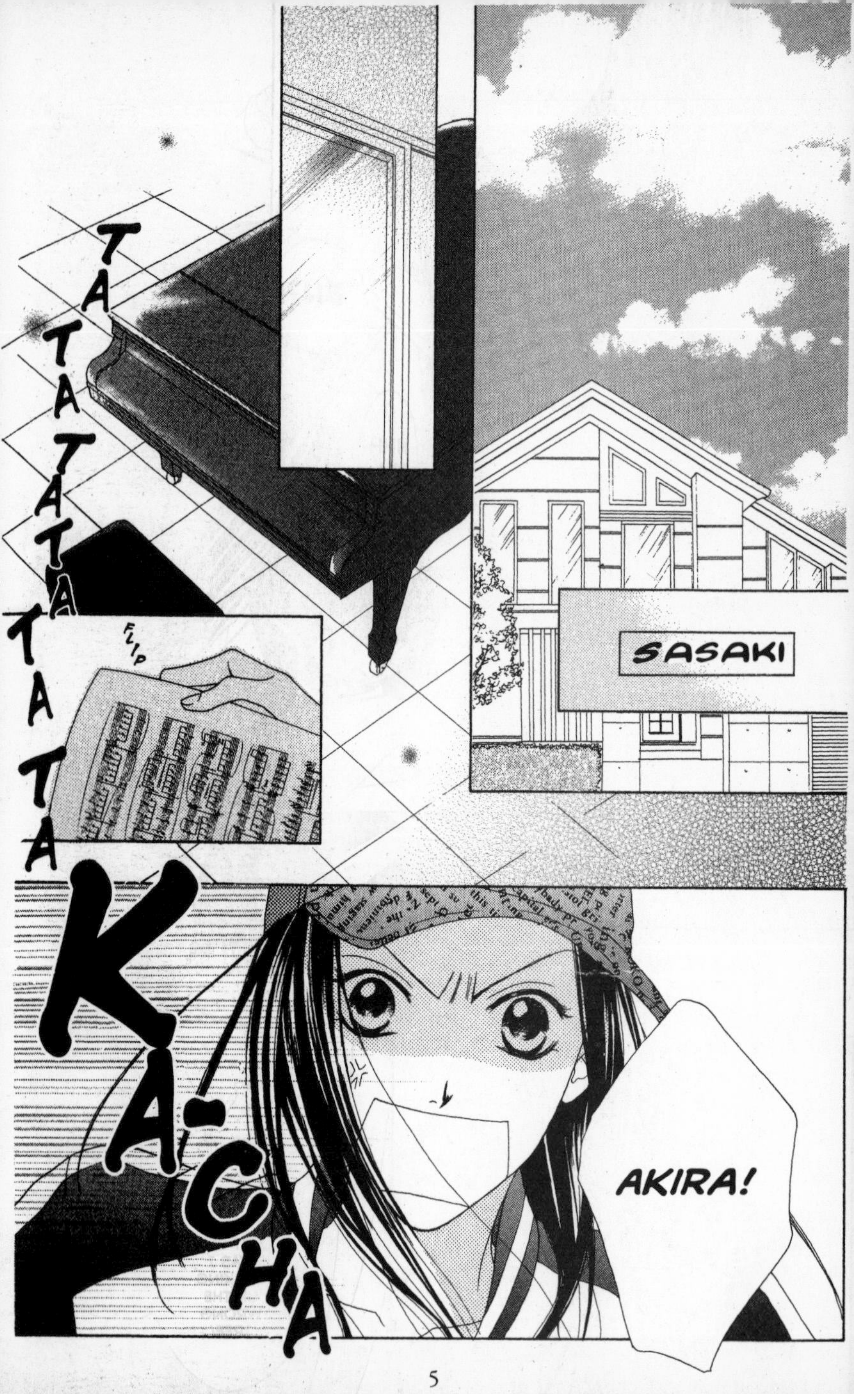
SASAKI
TATATATATA
TA TA TA
FLIP
KACHA
AKIRA!

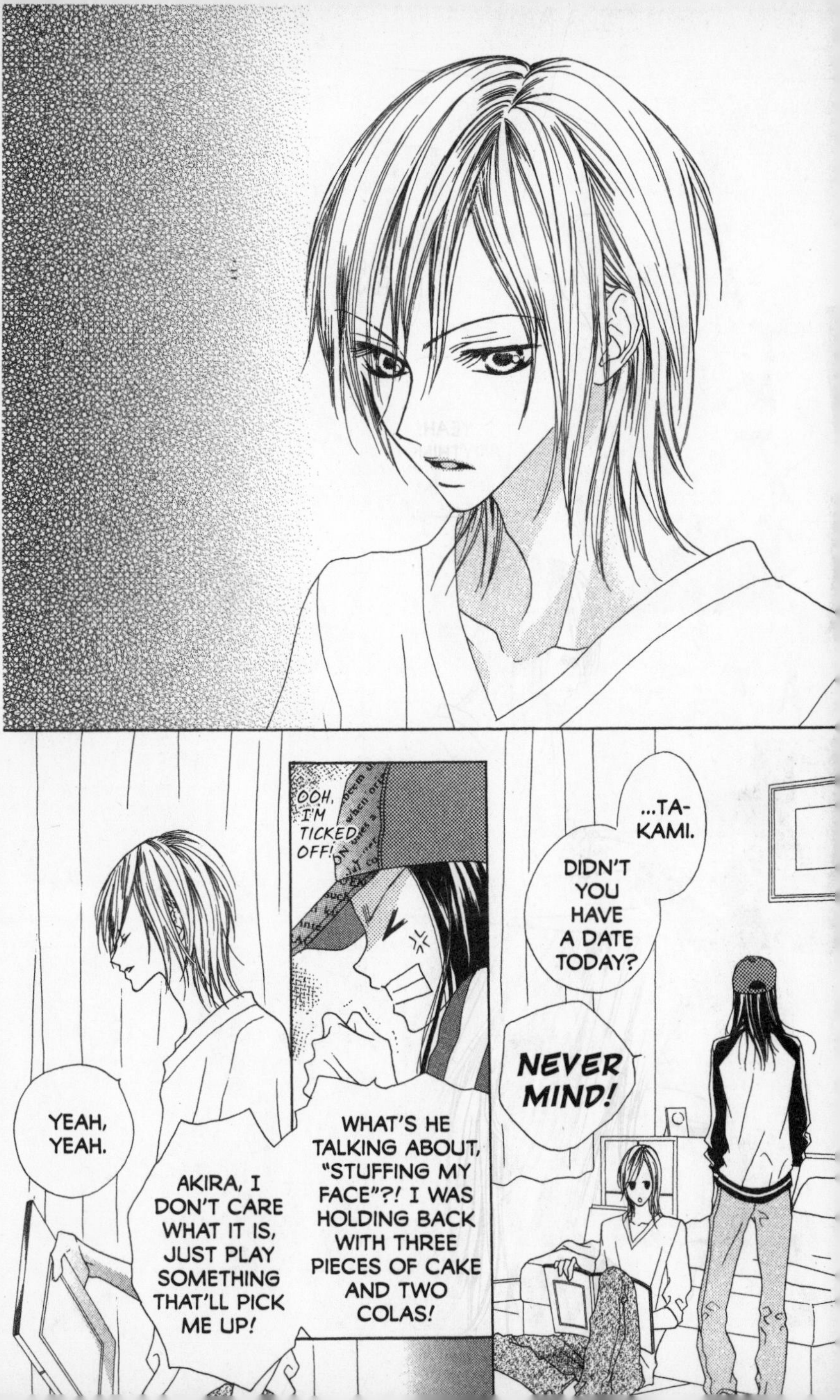
...TA-KAMI.
DIDN'T YOU HAVE A DATE TODAY?
NEVER MIND!
OOH, I'M TICKED OFF!
WHAT'S HE TALKING ABOUT, "STUFFING MY FACE"?! I WAS HOLDING BACK WITH THREE PIECES OF CAKE AND TWO COLAS!
AKIRA, I DON'T CARE WHAT IT IS, JUST PLAY SOMETHING THAT'LL PICK ME UP!
YEAH, YEAH.

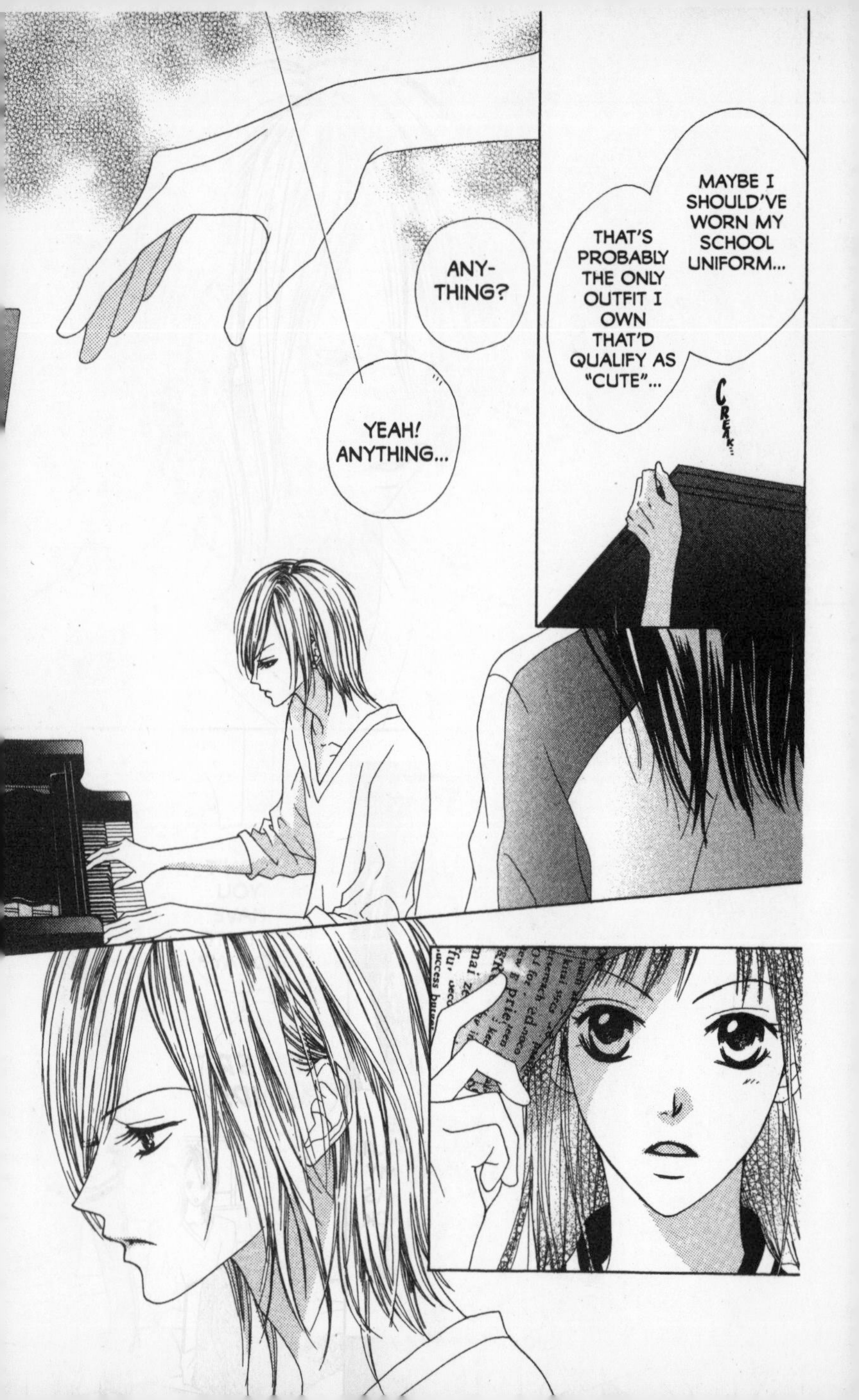
MAYBE I SHOULD'VE WORN MY SCHOOL UNIFORM...
THAT'S PROBABLY THE ONLY OUTFIT I OWN THAT'D QUALIFY AS "CUTE"...
CREAK...
ANY-THING?
YEAH! ANYTHING...

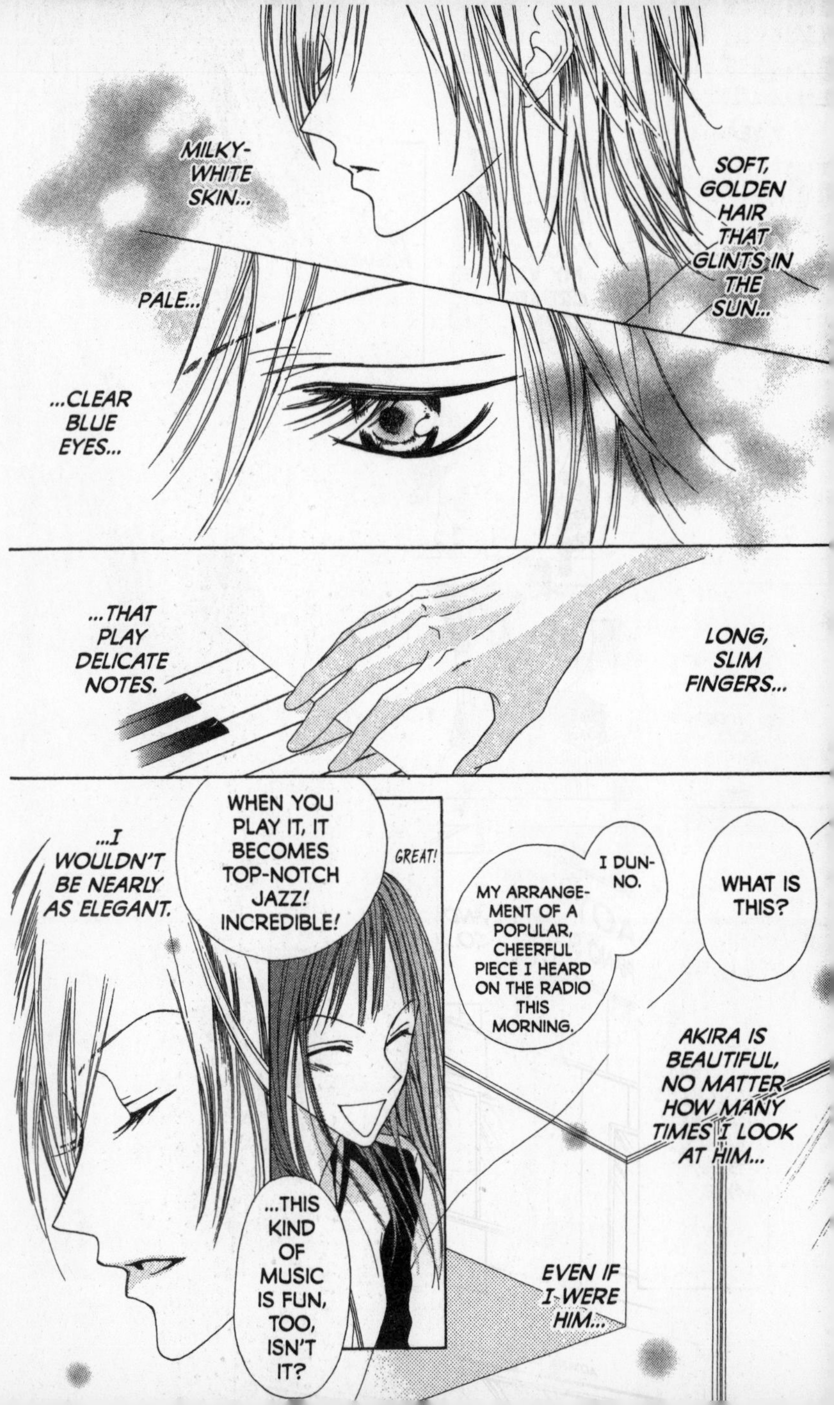
SOFT, GOLDEN HAIR THAT GLINTS IN THE SUN...
MILKY-WHITE SKIN...
PALE...
...CLEAR BLUE EYES...
LONG, SLIM FINGERS...
...THAT PLAY DELICATE NOTES.
WHAT IS THIS?
I DUN-NO.
MY ARRANGEMENT OF A POPULAR, CHEERFUL PIECE I HEARD ON THE RADIO THIS MORNING.
AKIRA IS BEAUTIFUL, NO MATTER HOW MANY TIMES I LOOK AT HIM...
EVEN IF I WERE HIM...
...THIS KIND OF MUSIC IS FUN, TOO, ISN'T IT?
GREAT!
WHEN YOU PLAY IT, IT BECOMES TOP-NOTCH JAZZ! INCREDIBLE!
...I WOULDN'T BE NEARLY AS ELEGANT.

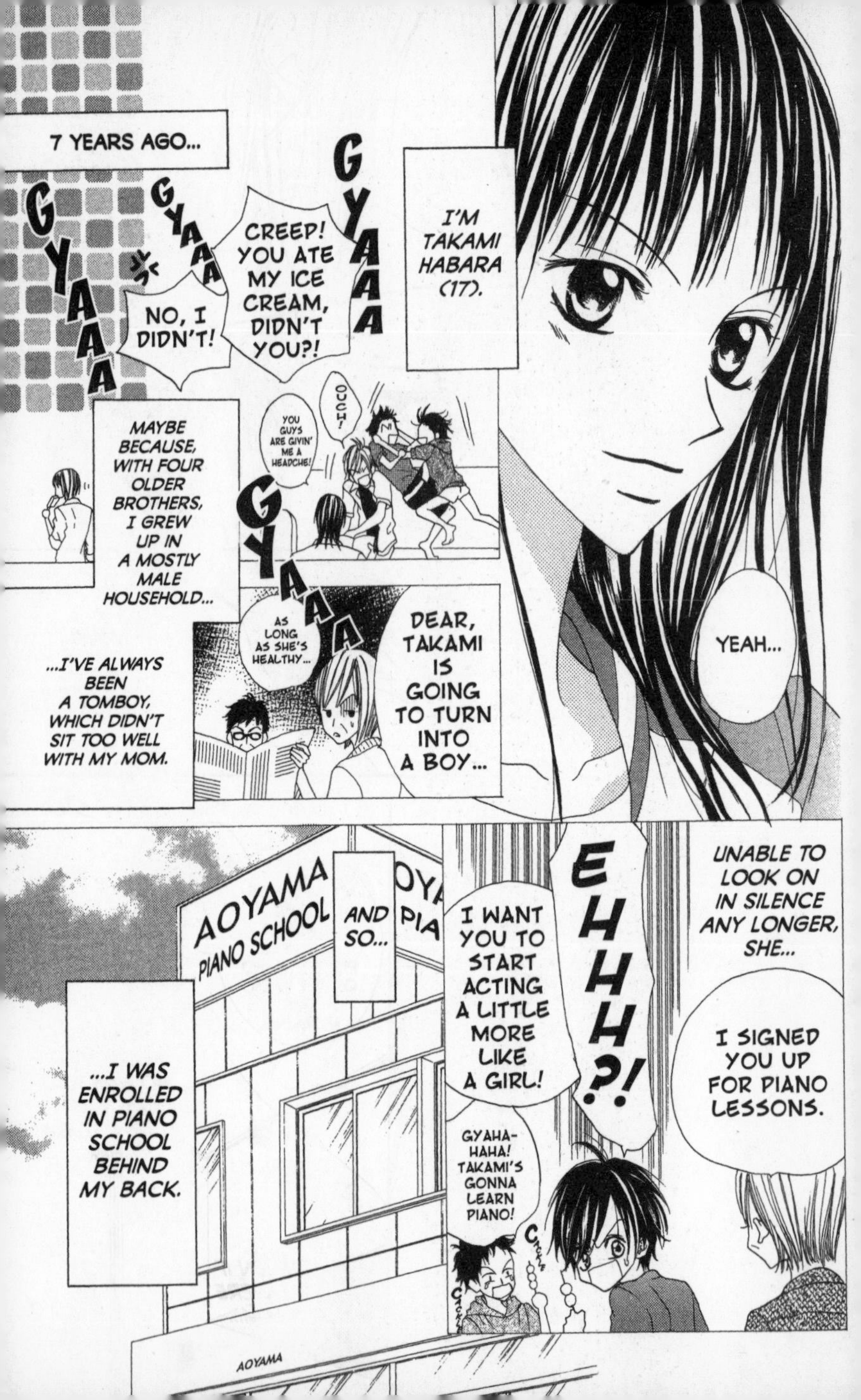
I'M TAKAMI HABARA (17).
YEAH...
7 YEARS AGO...
GYAAA
CREEP! YOU ATE MY ICE CREAM, DIDN'T YOU?!
GYAAA
NO, I DIDN'T!
GYAAA
OUCH!
YOU GUYS ARE GIVIN' ME A HEADCHE!
GYAAA
MAYBE BECAUSE, WITH FOUR OLDER BROTHERS, I GREW UP IN A MOSTLY MALE HOUSEHOLD...
DEAR, TAKAMI IS GOING TO TURN INTO A BOY...
AS LONG AS SHE'S HEALTHY...
...I'VE ALWAYS BEEN A TOMBOY, WHICH DIDN'T SIT TOO WELL WITH MY MOM.
UNABLE TO LOOK ON IN SILENCE ANY LONGER, SHE...
I SIGNED YOU UP FOR PIANO LESSONS.
EHHH?!
I WANT YOU TO START ACTING A LITTLE MORE LIKE A GIRL!
GYAHAHA! TAKAMI'S GONNA LEARN PIANO!
AND SO...
AOYAMA PIANO SCHOOL
...I WAS ENROLLED IN PIANO SCHOOL BEHIND MY BACK.
AOYAMA

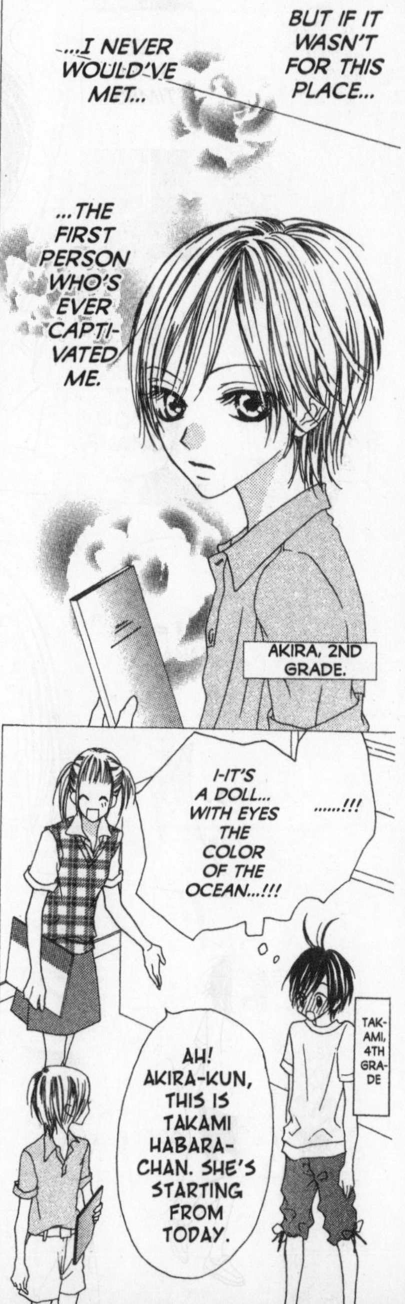
BUT IF IT WASN'T FOR THIS PLACE...
...I NEVER WOULD'VE MET...
...THE FIRST PERSON WHO'S EVER CAPTIVATED ME.
AKIRA, 2ND GRADE.
......!!!
I-IT'S A DOLL... WITH EYES THE COLOR OF THE OCEAN...!!!
TAKAMI, 4TH GRADE
AH! AKIRA-KUN, THIS IS TAKAMI HABARA-CHAN. SHE'S STARTING FROM TODAY.
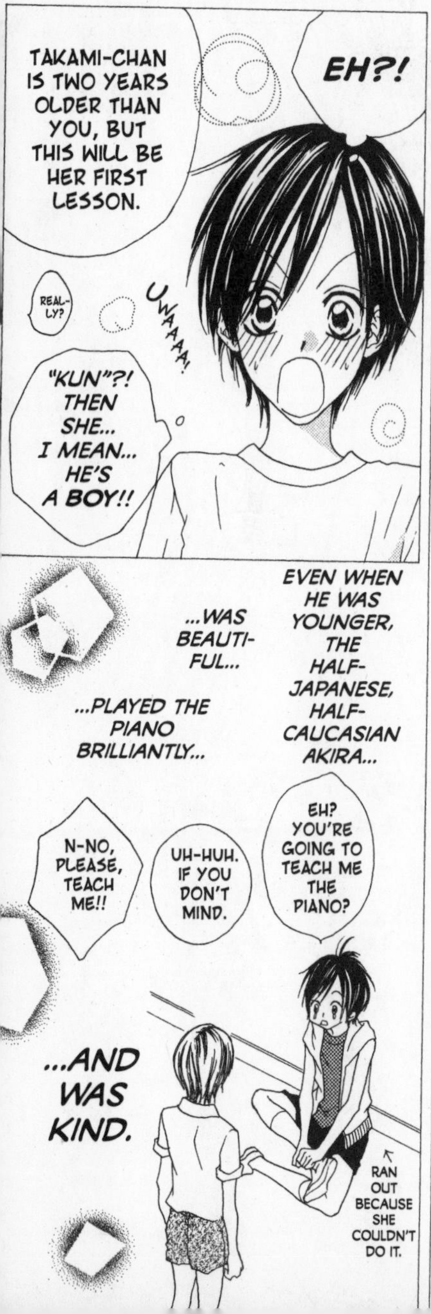
EH?!
TAKAMI-CHAN IS TWO YEARS OLDER THAN YOU, BUT THIS WILL BE HER FIRST LESSON.
UWAAAA!
REALLY?
"KUN"?! THEN SHE... I MEAN... HE'S A BOY!!
EVEN WHEN HE WAS YOUNGER, THE HALF-JAPANESE, HALF-CAUCASIAN AKIRA...
...WAS BEAUTIFUL...
...PLAYED THE PIANO BRILLIANTLY...
EH? YOU'RE GOING TO TEACH ME THE PIANO?
UH-HUH. IF YOU DON'T MIND.
N-NO, PLEASE, TEACH ME!!
RAN OUT BECAUSE SHE COULDN'T DO IT.
...AND WAS KIND.

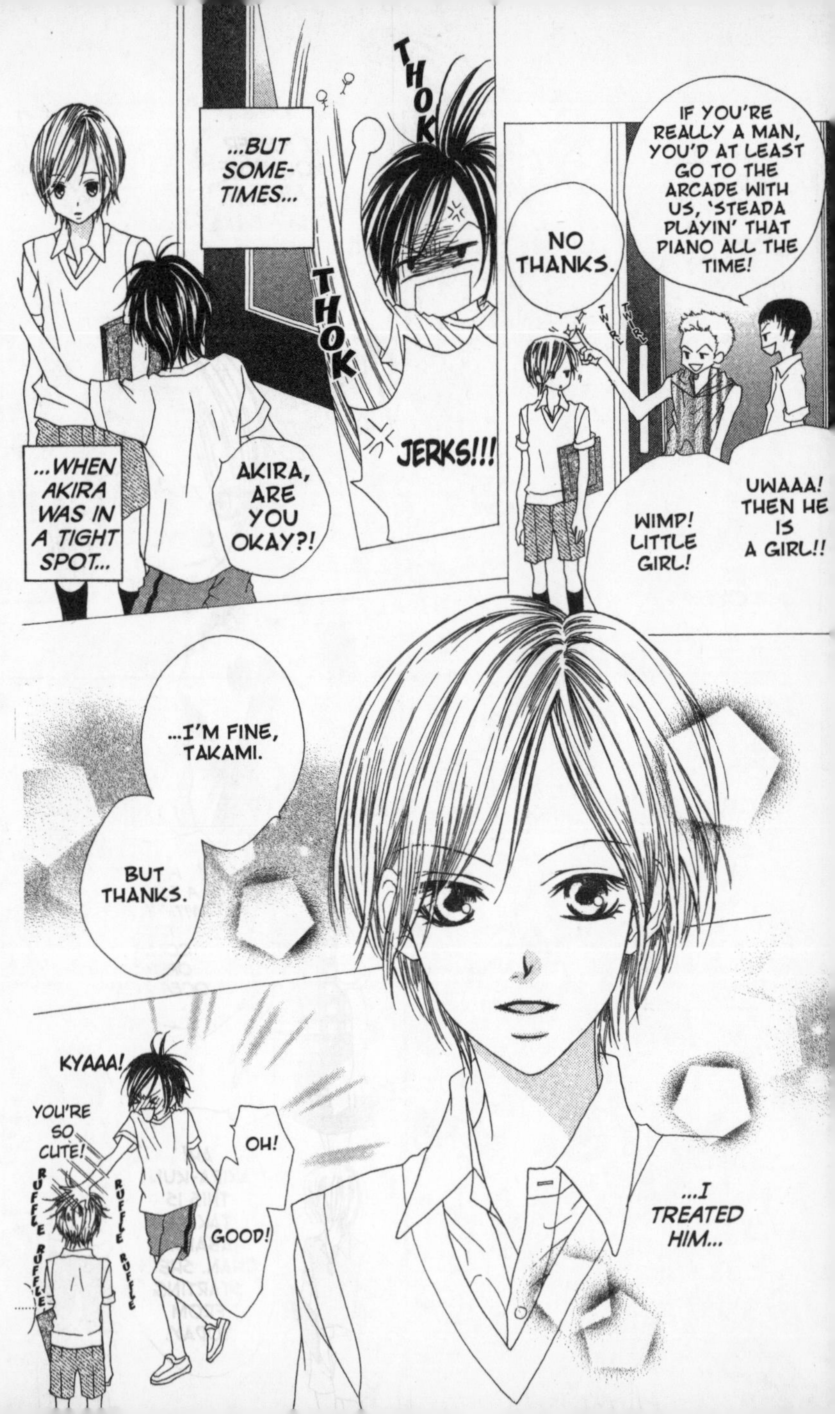
IF YOU'RE REALLY A MAN, YOU'D AT LEAST GO TO THE ARCADE WITH US, 'STEADA PLAYIN' THAT PIANO ALL THE TIME!
NO THANKS.
TWIRL TWIRL
UWAAA! THEN HE IS A GIRL!!
WIMP! LITTLE GIRL!
...BUT SOMETIMES...
THOK THOK
JERKS!!!
AKIRA, ARE YOU OKAY?!
...WHEN AKIRA WAS IN A TIGHT SPOT...
...I'M FINE, TAKAMI.
BUT THANKS.
...I TREATED HIM...
OH!
GOOD!
KYAAA!
YOU'RE SO CUTE!
RUFFLE RUFFLE
RUFFLE RUFFLE

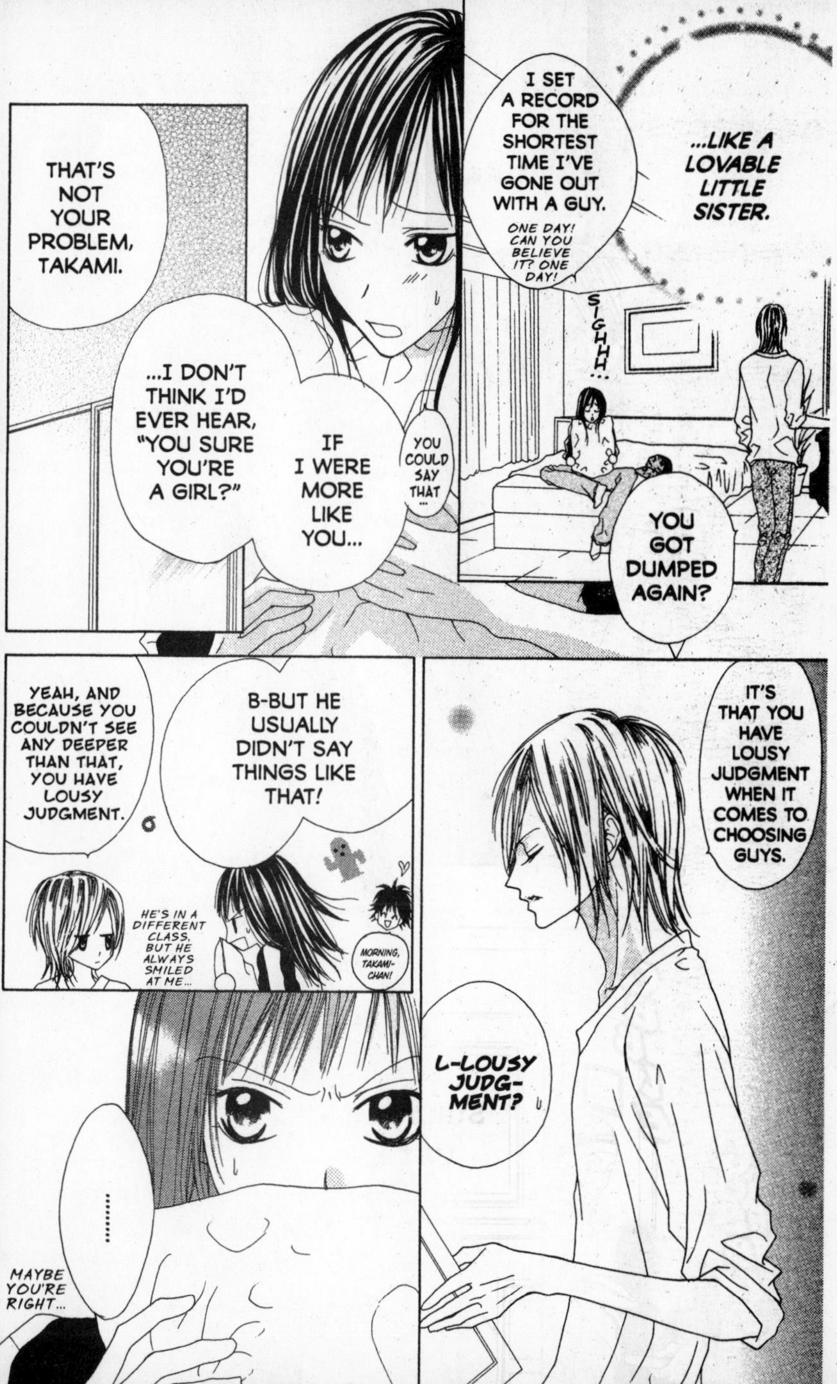
...LIKE A LOVABLE LITTLE SISTER.
I SET A RECORD FOR THE SHORTEST TIME I'VE GONE OUT WITH A GUY.
ONE DAY! CAN YOU BELIEVE IT? ONE DAY!
SIGHHH...
YOU GOT DUMPED AGAIN?
YOU COULD SAY THAT...
IF I WERE MORE LIKE YOU...
...I DON'T THINK I'D EVER HEAR, "YOU SURE YOU'RE A GIRL?"
THAT'S NOT YOUR PROBLEM, TAKAMI.
IT'S THAT YOU HAVE LOUSY JUDGMENT WHEN IT COMES TO CHOOSING GUYS.
L-LOUSY JUDGMENT?
B-BUT HE USUALLY DIDN'T SAY THINGS LIKE THAT!
YEAH, AND BECAUSE YOU COULDN'T SEE ANY DEEPER THAN THAT, YOU HAVE LOUSY JUDGMENT.
HE'S IN A DIFFERENT CLASS, BUT HE ALWAYS SMILED AT ME...
MORNING, TAKAMI-CHAN!
....
MAYBE YOU'RE RIGHT...

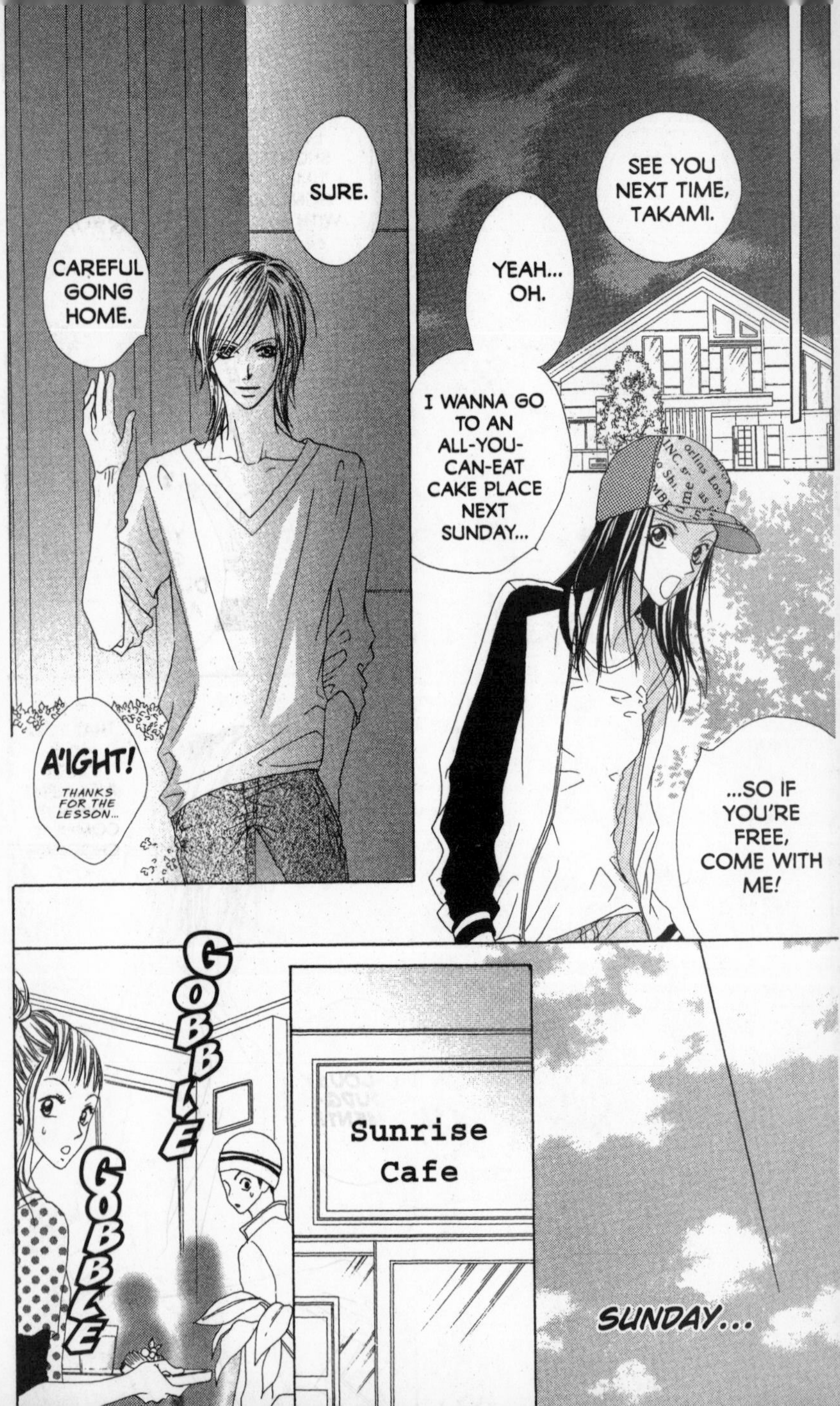
SEE YOU NEXT TIME, TAKAMI.
YEAH... OH.
I WANNA GO TO AN ALL-YOU-CAN-EAT CAKE PLACE NEXT SUNDAY...
...SO IF YOU'RE FREE, COME WITH ME!
SURE.
CAREFUL GOING HOME.
A'IGHT!
THANKS FOR THE LESSON...
SUNDAY...
Sunrise Cafe
GOBBLE
GOBBLE

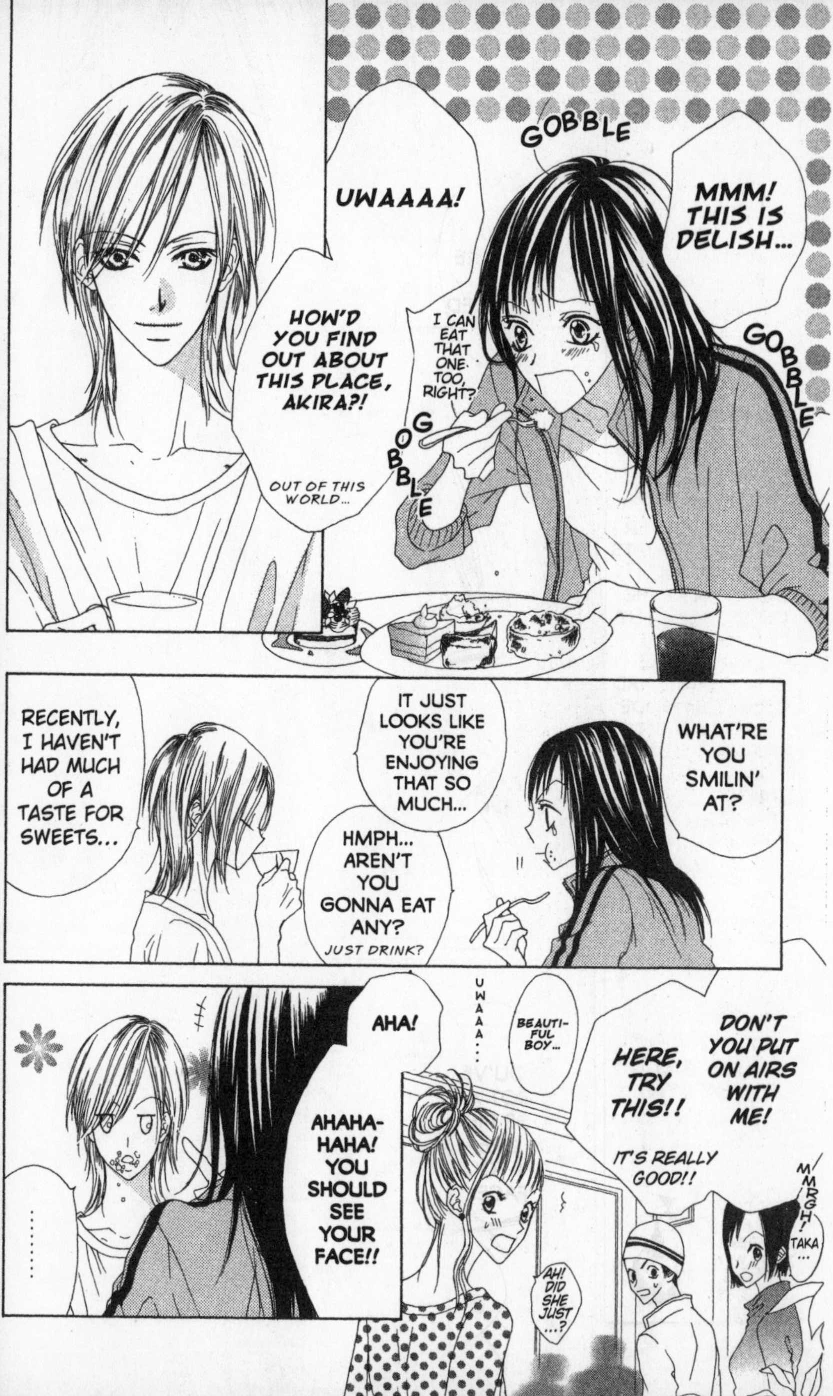
GOBBLE
MMM! THIS IS DELISH...
GOBBLE
UWAAAA!
I CAN EAT THAT ONE TOO, RIGHT?
GOBBLE
HOW'D YOU FIND OUT ABOUT THIS PLACE, AKIRA?!
OUT OF THIS WORLD...
WHAT'RE YOU SMILIN' AT?
IT JUST LOOKS LIKE YOU'RE ENJOYING THAT SO MUCH...
!!
HMPH... AREN'T YOU GONNA EAT ANY?
JUST DRINK?
RECENTLY, I HAVEN'T HAD MUCH OF A TASTE FOR SWEETS...
DON'T YOU PUT ON AIRS WITH ME!
HERE, TRY THIS!!
IT'S REALLY GOOD!!
MMRGH!
TAKA...
AH! DID SHE JUST...?
BEAUTIFUL BOY...
UWAAAA...
AHA!
AHAHAHAHA! YOU SHOULD SEE YOUR FACE!!
......

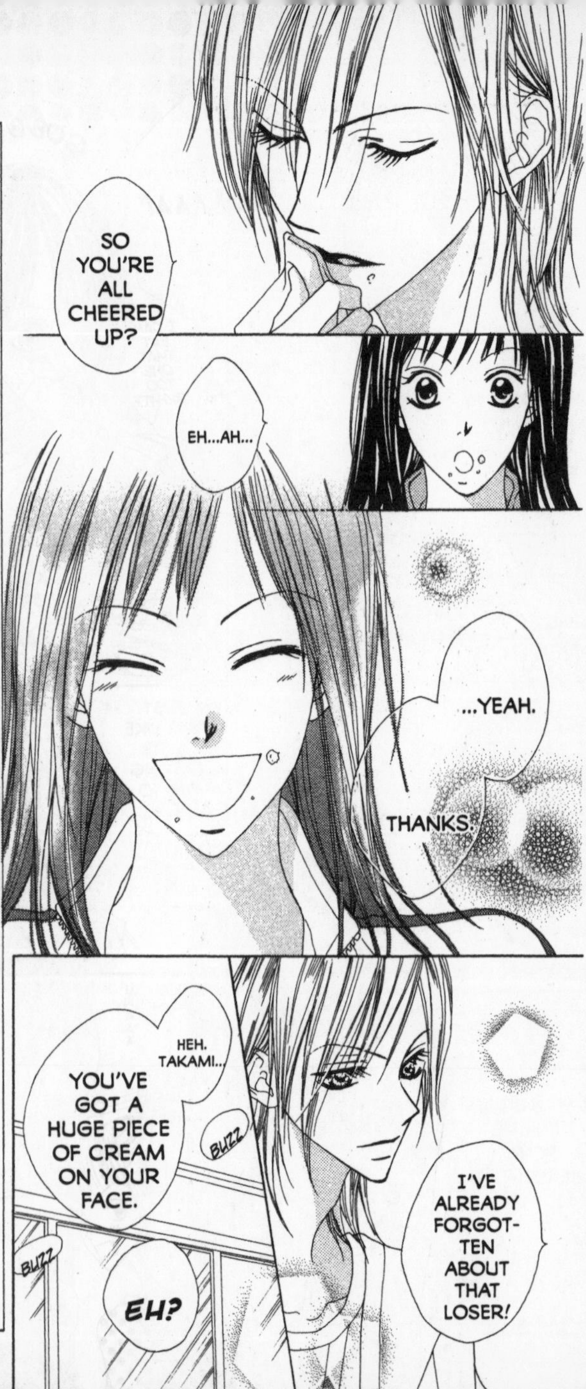
SO YOU'RE ALL CHEERED UP?
EH...AH...
...YEAH.
THANKS.
I'VE ALREADY FORGOT-TEN ABOUT THAT LOSER!
BUZZ
HEH. TAKAMI...
YOU'VE GOT A HUGE PIECE OF CREAM ON YOUR FACE.
BUZZ
EH?

1

HELLO! NICE TO MEET YOU. MY NAME IS MAI NISHIKATA.

THANK YOU SO MUCH FOR GETTING "VENUS CAPRICCIO", MY VERY FIRST COLLECTED SERIES!!

I LOOKED OVER THE MANUSCRIPTS TO GET THEM READY FOR THE COLLECTION, BUT IT HAD BEEN EXACTLY ONE YEAR SINCE I HAD DRAWN EPISODE ONE. THE ART HAD CHANGED SO MUCH FROM EPISODE ONE AND THE FOLLOWING EPISODES THAT IT MADE ME DIZZY.

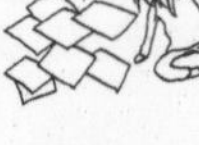

ANYWAY, I HOPE YOU ENJOY IT!

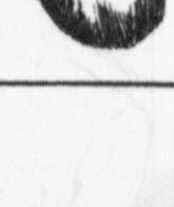

NOT THAT THIS HAS ANYTHING TO DO WITH ANYTHING, BUT HERE'S MY CAT!

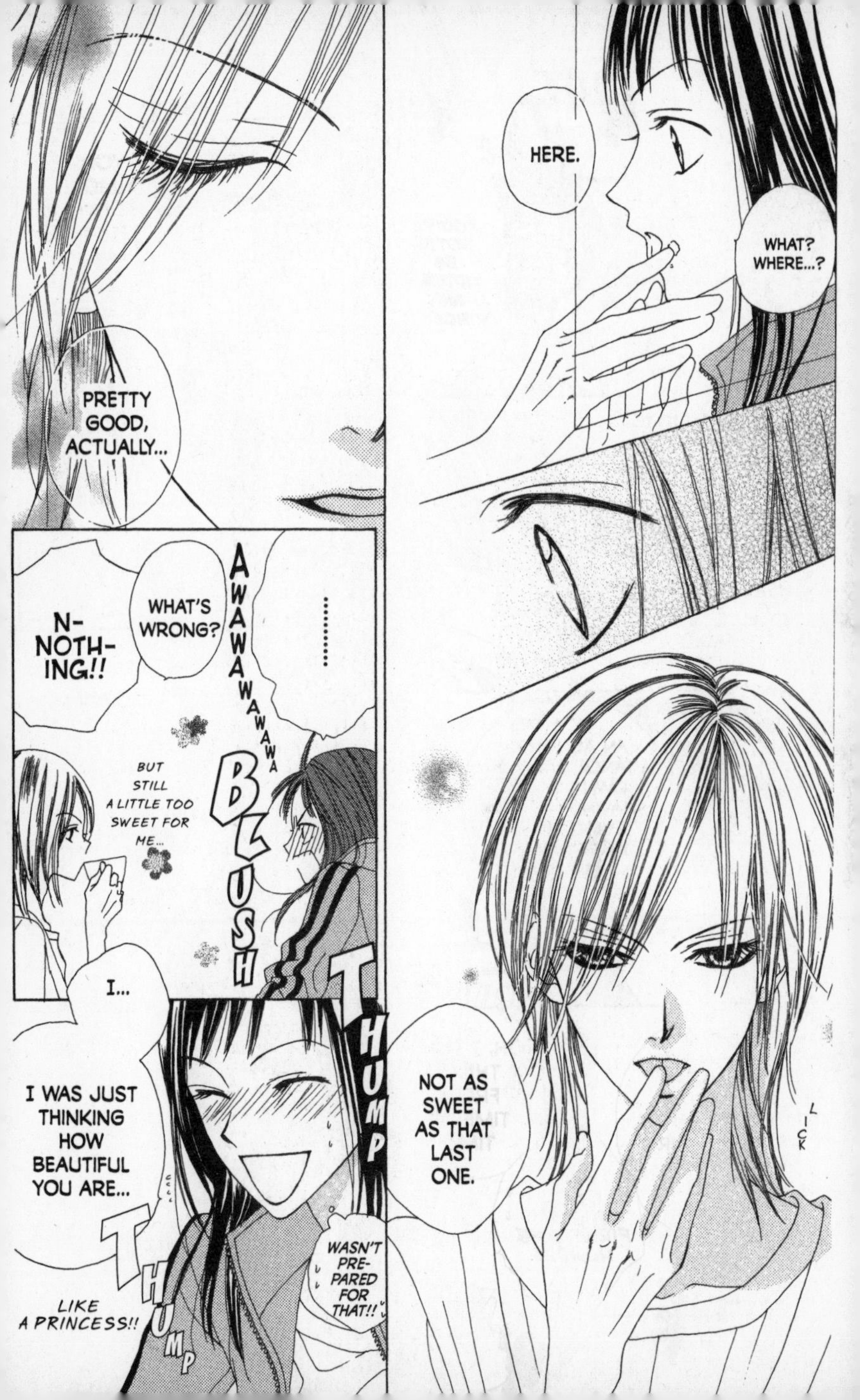
WHAT? WHERE...?
HERE.
NOT AS SWEET AS THAT LAST ONE.
LICK
PRETTY GOOD, ACTUALLY...
......
WHAT'S WRONG?
AWAWAWAWAWAWA
N-NOTHING!!
BLUSH
BUT STILL A LITTLE TOO SWEET FOR ME...
THUMP
I...
I WAS JUST THINKING HOW BEAUTIFUL YOU ARE...
WASN'T PREPARED FOR THAT!!
LIKE A PRINCESS!!
THUMP

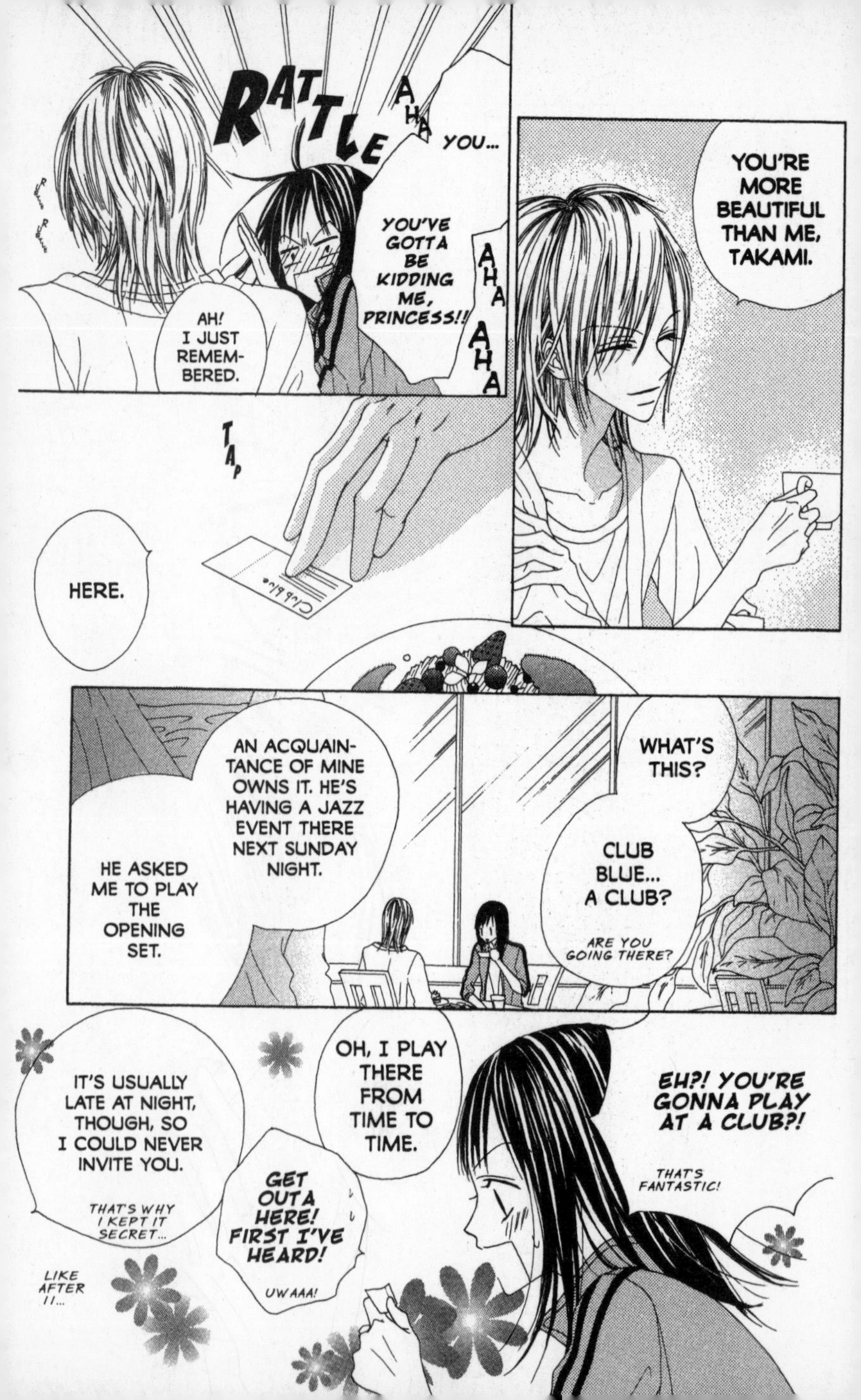
YOU'RE MORE BEAUTIFUL THAN ME, TAKAMI.
RATTLE
AHA
YOU...
YOU'VE GOTTA BE KIDDING ME, PRINCESS!!
AHA
AHA
AHA
AH! I JUST REMEMBERED.
TAP
HERE.
WHAT'S THIS?
CLUB BLUE... A CLUB?
ARE YOU GOING THERE?
AN ACQUAINTANCE OF MINE OWNS IT. HE'S HAVING A JAZZ EVENT THERE NEXT SUNDAY NIGHT.
HE ASKED ME TO PLAY THE OPENING SET.
EH?! YOU'RE GONNA PLAY AT A CLUB?!
THAT'S FANTASTIC!
OH, I PLAY THERE FROM TIME TO TIME.
GET OUTA HERE! FIRST I'VE HEARD!
UWAAA!
IT'S USUALLY LATE AT NIGHT, THOUGH, SO I COULD NEVER INVITE YOU.
THAT'S WHY I KEPT IT SECRET...
LIKE AFTER 11...

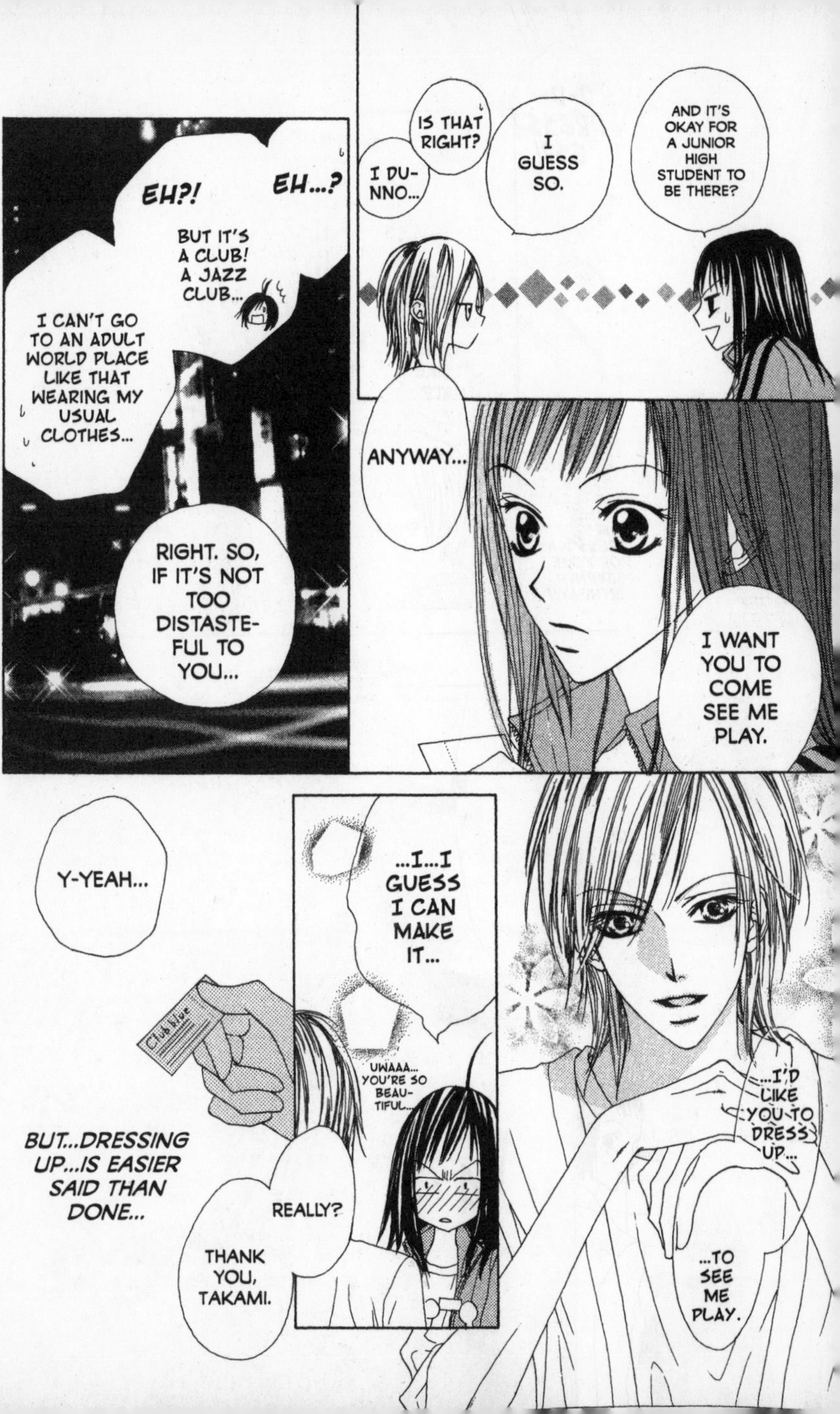
AND IT'S OKAY FOR A JUNIOR HIGH STUDENT TO BE THERE?
I GUESS SO.
IS THAT RIGHT?
I DU-NNO...
ANYWAY...
I WANT YOU TO COME SEE ME PLAY.
EH...?
EH?!
BUT IT'S A CLUB! A JAZZ CLUB...
I CAN'T GO TO AN ADULT WORLD PLACE LIKE THAT WEARING MY USUAL CLOTHES...
RIGHT. SO, IF IT'S NOT TOO DISTASTE-FUL TO YOU...
...I'D LIKE YOU TO DRESS UP...
...TO SEE ME PLAY.
...I...I GUESS I CAN MAKE IT...
UWAAA... YOU'RE SO BEAU-TIFUL...
Club blue
REALLY?
THANK YOU, TAKAMI.
Y-YEAH...
BUT...DRESSING UP...IS EASIER SAID THAN DONE...

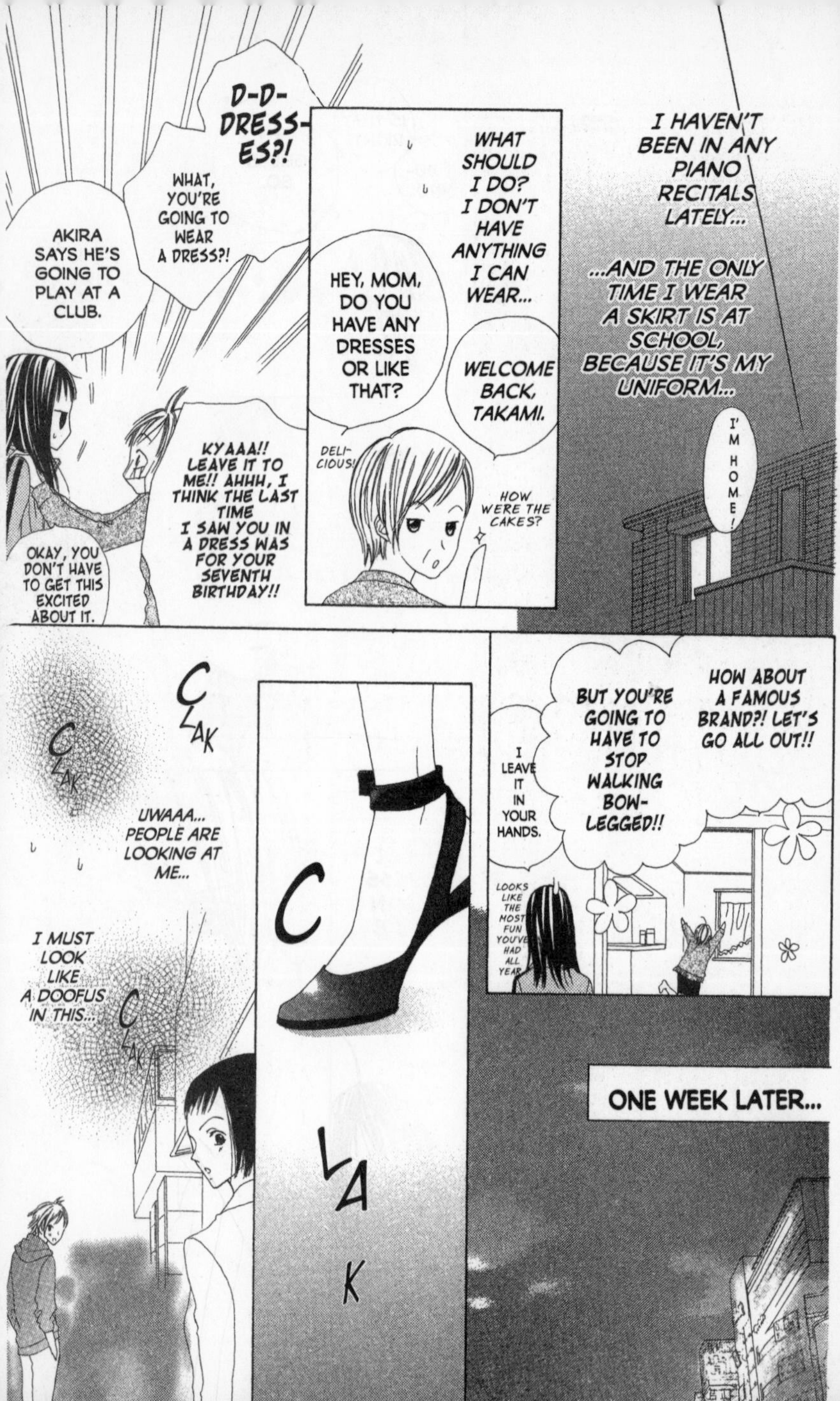

I HAVEN'T BEEN IN ANY PIANO RECITALS LATELY...
...AND THE ONLY TIME I WEAR A SKIRT IS AT SCHOOL, BECAUSE IT'S MY UNIFORM...
I'M HOME!
WHAT SHOULD I DO? I DON'T HAVE ANYTHING I CAN WEAR...
WELCOME BACK, TAKAMI.
HOW WERE THE CAKES?
HEY, MOM, DO YOU HAVE ANY DRESSES OR LIKE THAT?
DELI-CIOUS!
D-D-DRESS-ES?!
WHAT, YOU'RE GOING TO WEAR A DRESS?!
AKIRA SAYS HE'S GOING TO PLAY AT A CLUB.
KYAAA!! LEAVE IT TO ME!! AHHH, I THINK THE LAST TIME I SAW YOU IN A DRESS WAS FOR YOUR SEVENTH BIRTHDAY!!
OKAY, YOU DON'T HAVE TO GET THIS EXCITED ABOUT IT.
HOW ABOUT A FAMOUS BRAND?! LET'S GO ALL OUT!!
BUT YOU'RE GOING TO HAVE TO STOP WALKING BOW-LEGGED!!
I LEAVE IT IN YOUR HANDS.
LOOKS LIKE THE MOST FUN YOU'VE HAD ALL YEAR
ONE WEEK LATER...
CLAK
CLAK
CLAK
UWAAA... PEOPLE ARE LOOKING AT ME...
I MUST LOOK LIKE A DOOFUS IN THIS...
CLAK

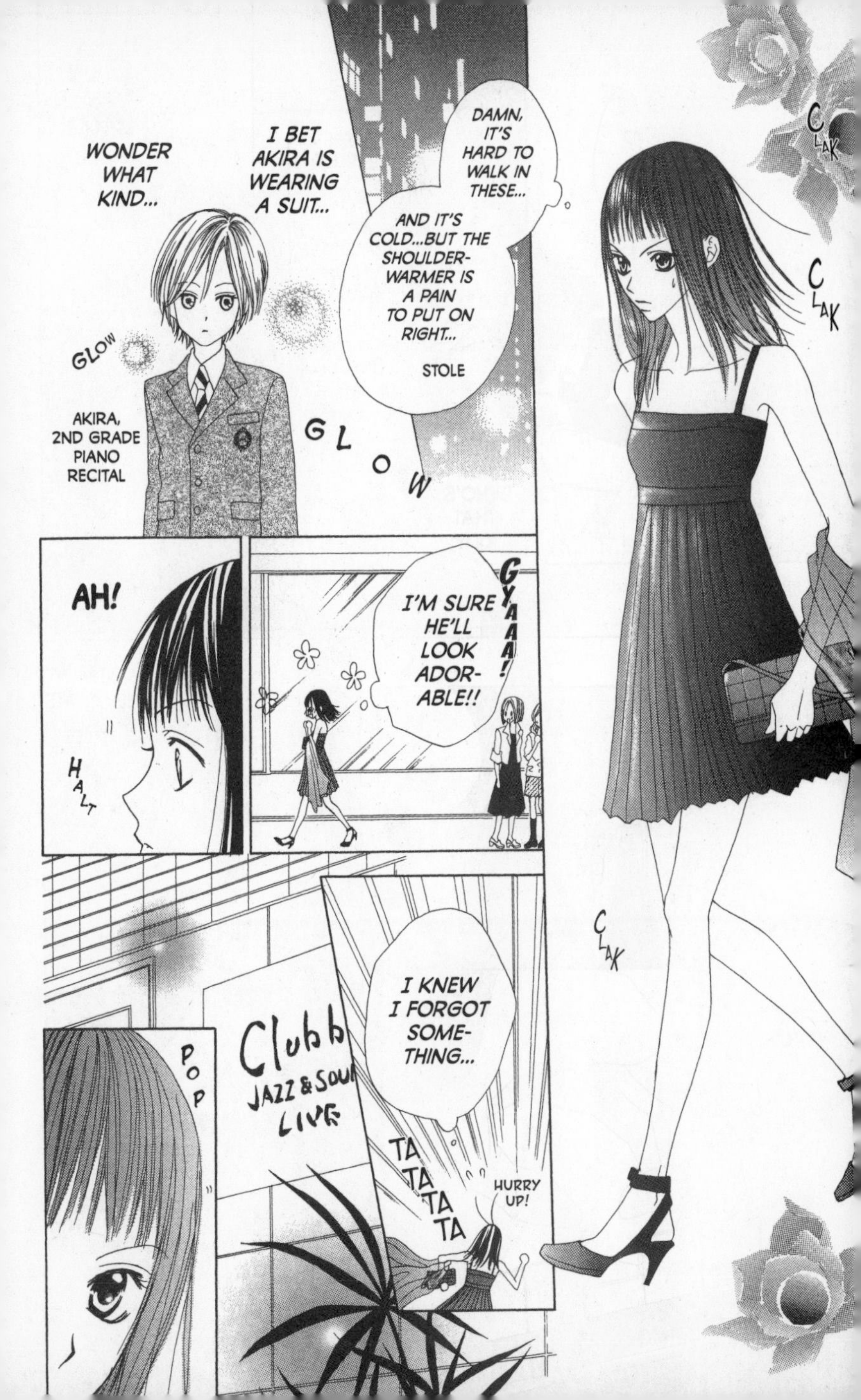
CLAK
CLAK
CLAK
DAMN, IT'S HARD TO WALK IN THESE...
AND IT'S COLD...BUT THE SHOULDER-WARMER IS A PAIN TO PUT ON RIGHT...
STOLE
I BET AKIRA IS WEARING A SUIT...
WONDER WHAT KIND...
GLOW
GLOW
AKIRA, 2ND GRADE PIANO RECITAL
GYAAAA!
I'M SURE HE'LL LOOK ADORABLE!!
AH!
HALT
I KNEW I FORGOT SOMETHING...
TA TA TA TA
HURRY UP!
POP
Clubb
JAZZ & SOU
LIVE

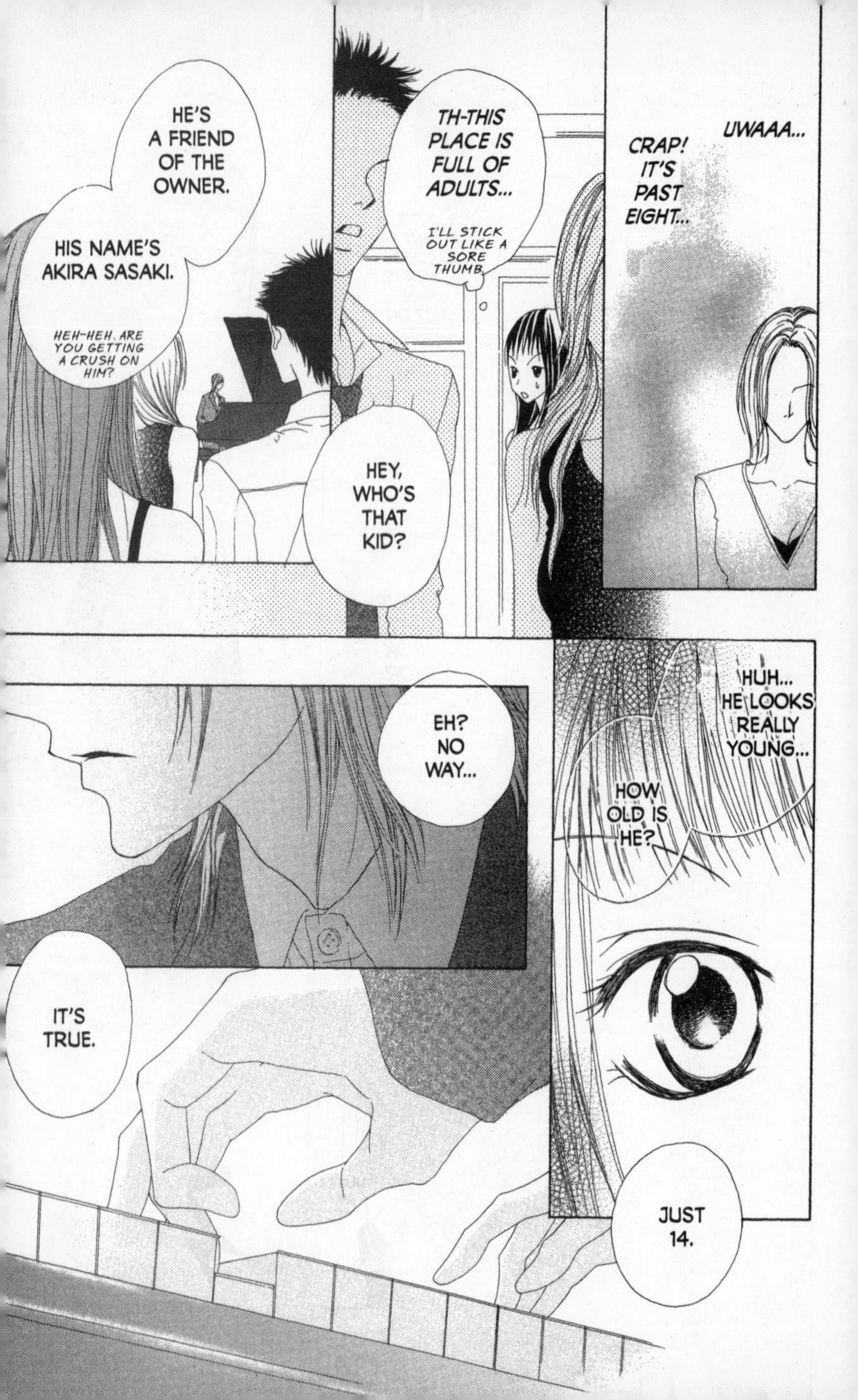
UWAAA...
CRAP! IT'S PAST EIGHT...
TH-THIS PLACE IS FULL OF ADULTS...
I'LL STICK OUT LIKE A SORE THUMB.
HEY, WHO'S THAT KID?
HE'S A FRIEND OF THE OWNER.
HIS NAME'S AKIRA SASAKI.
HEH-HEH. ARE YOU GETTING A CRUSH ON HIM?
HUH... HE LOOKS REALLY YOUNG...
HOW OLD IS HE?
EH? NO WAY...
IT'S TRUE.
JUST 14.

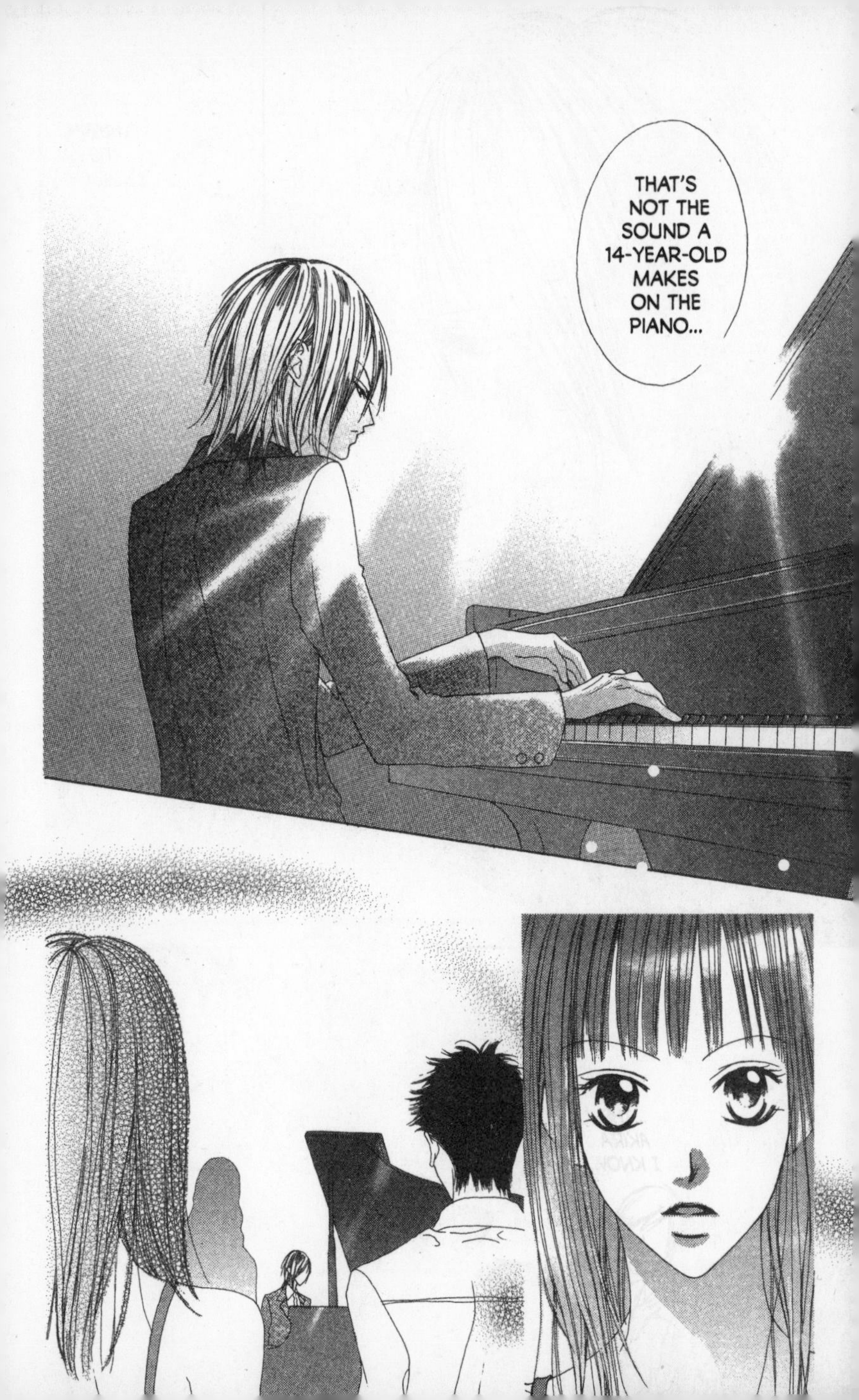
THAT'S NOT THE SOUND A 14-YEAR-OLD MAKES ON THE PIANO...

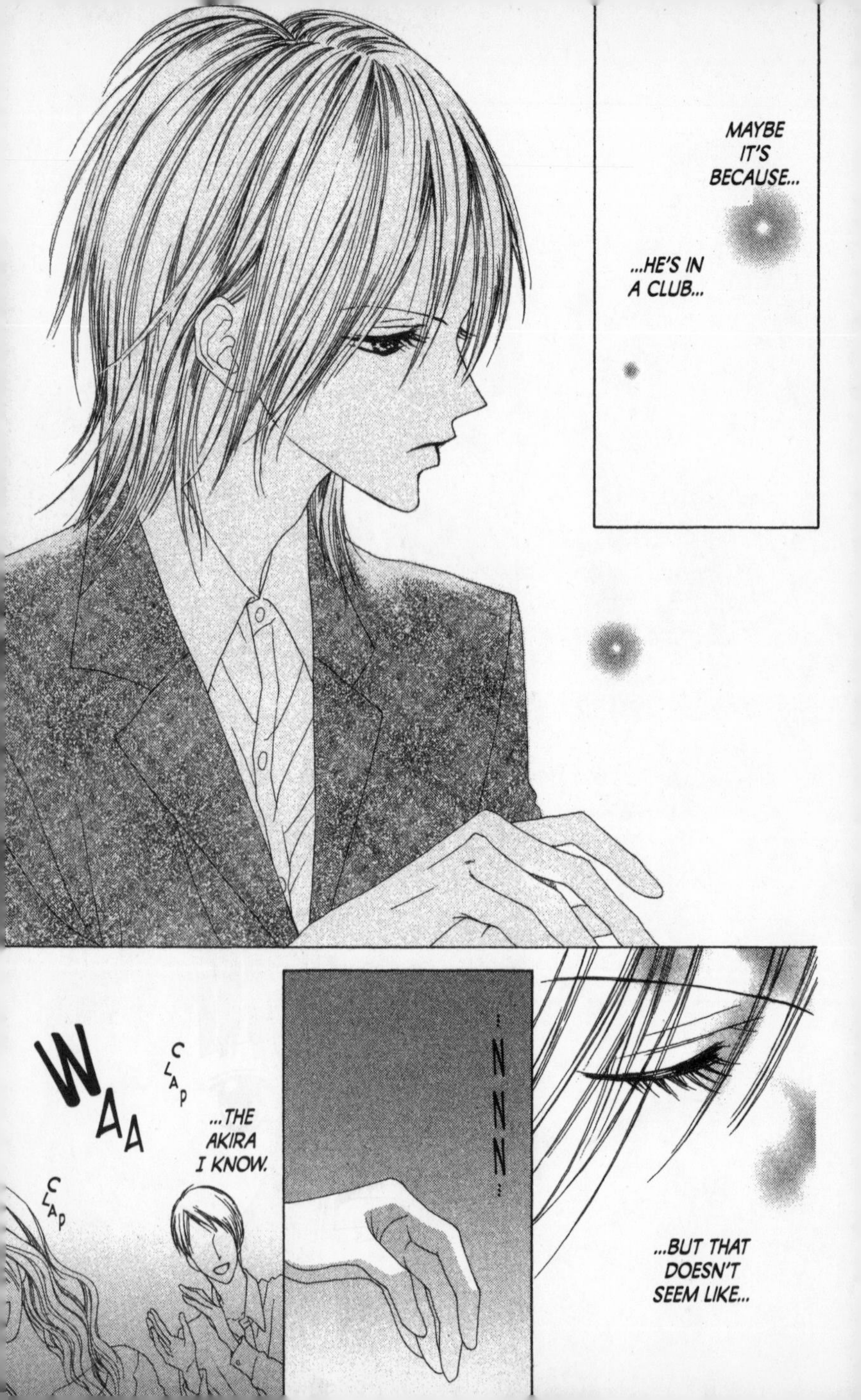
MAYBE IT'S BECAUSE...
...HE'S IN A CLUB...
...BUT THAT DOESN'T SEEM LIKE...
...NNN...
...THE AKIRA I KNOW.
CLAP
WAA
CLAP

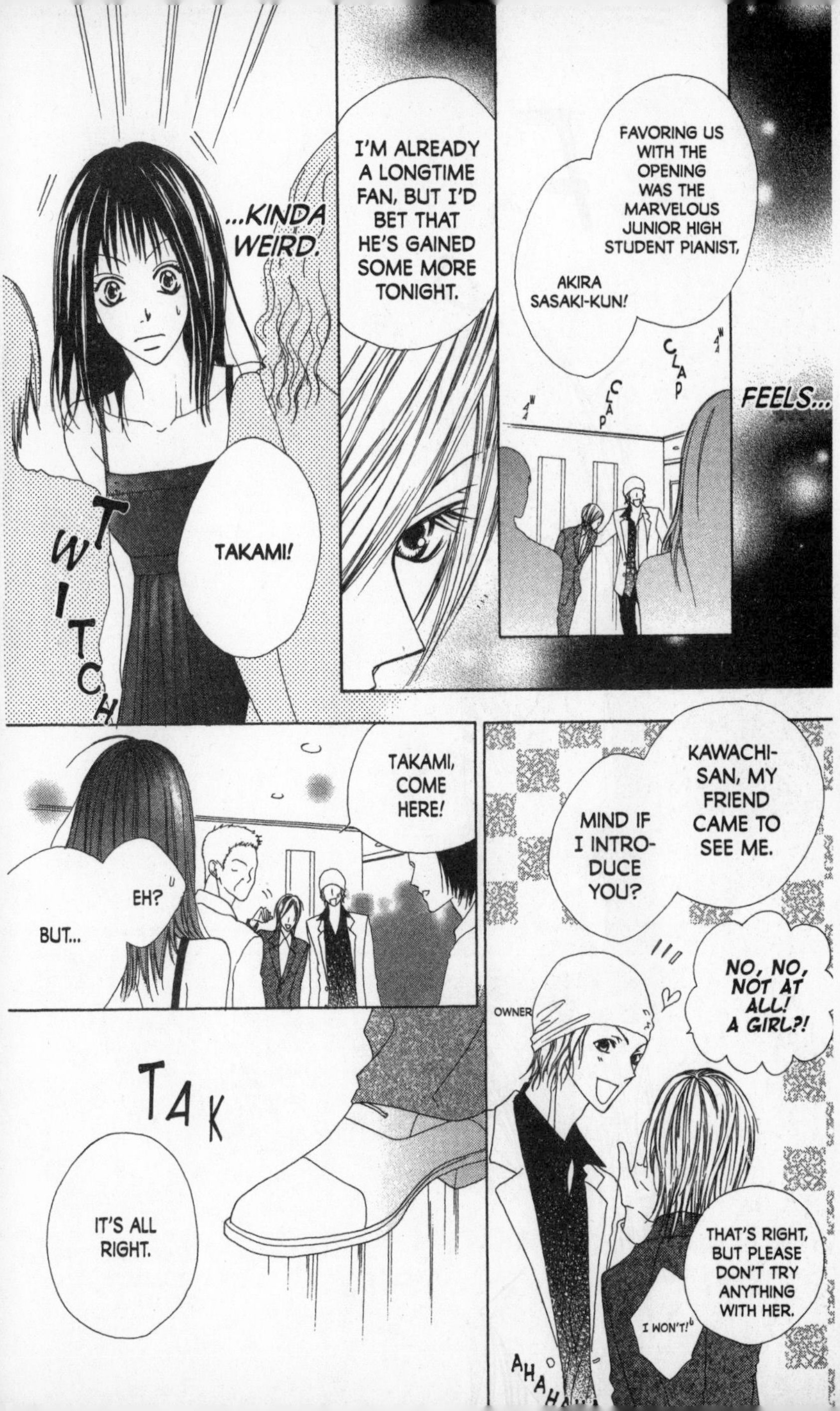
FAVORING US WITH THE OPENING WAS THE MARVELOUS JUNIOR HIGH STUDENT PIANIST,
AKIRA SASAKI-KUN!
CLAP
CLAP
FEELS...
I'M ALREADY A LONGTIME FAN, BUT I'D BET THAT HE'S GAINED SOME MORE TONIGHT.
...KINDA WEIRD.
TAKAMI!
TWITCH
KAWACHI-SAN, MY FRIEND CAME TO SEE ME.
MIND IF I INTRODUCE YOU?
NO, NO, NOT AT ALL! A GIRL?!
OWNER
THAT'S RIGHT, BUT PLEASE DON'T TRY ANYTHING WITH HER.
I WON'T!
AHAHA...
TAKAMI, COME HERE!
EH?
BUT...
TAK
IT'S ALL RIGHT.

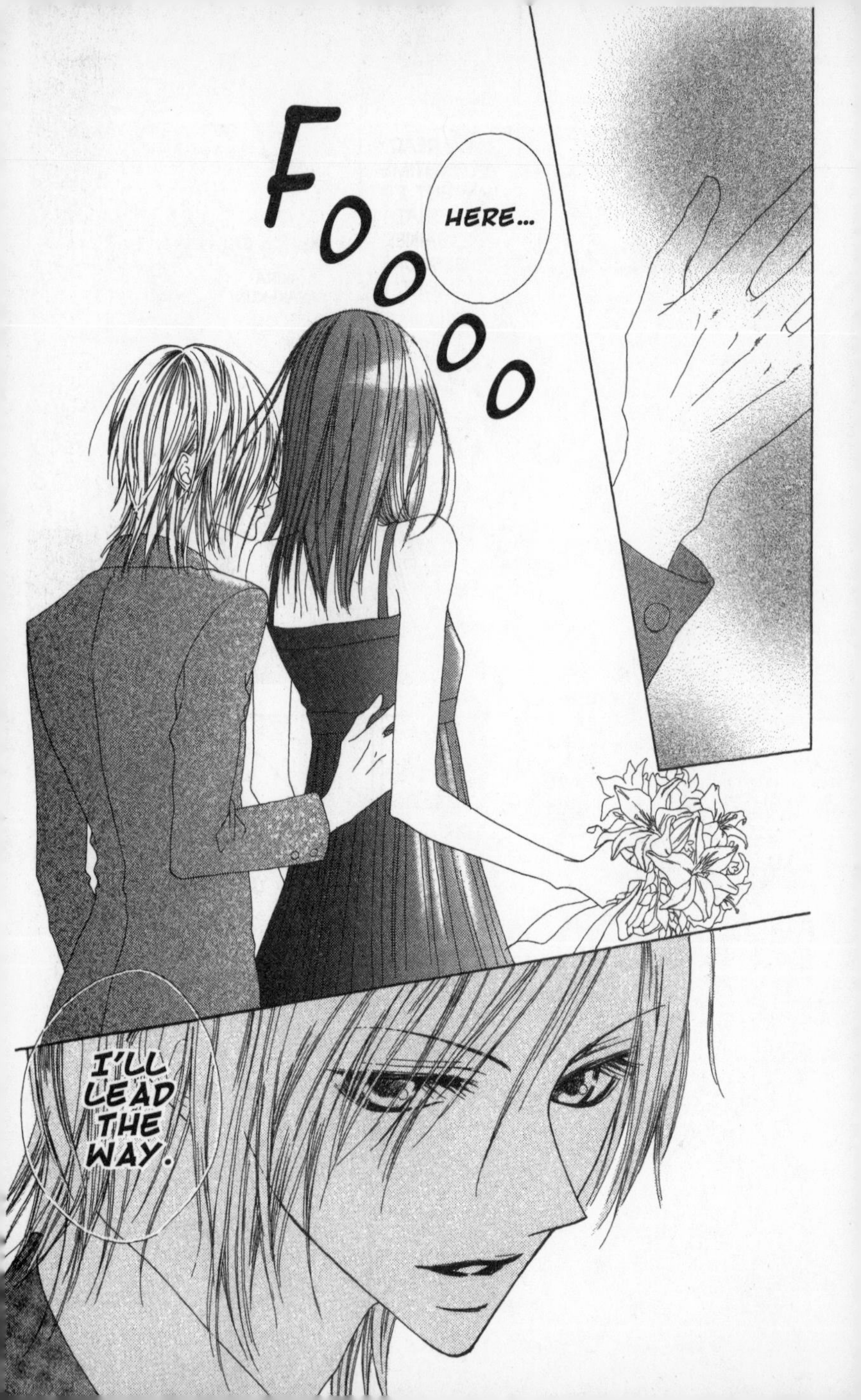
HERE...
FOOOOO
I'LL LEAD THE WAY.

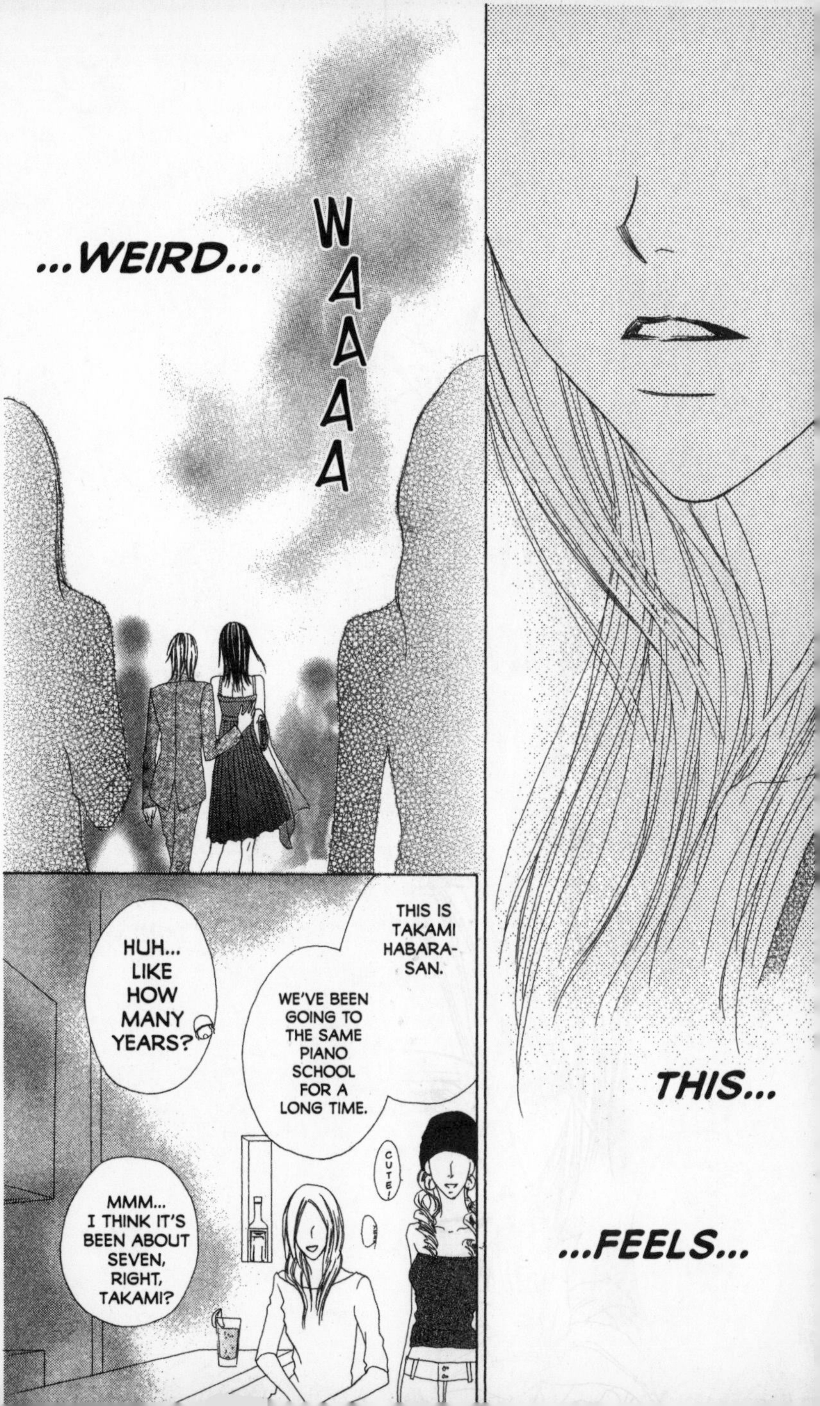
THIS...
...FEELS...
...WEIRD...
WAAAAA
THIS IS TAKAMI HABARA-SAN.
WE'VE BEEN GOING TO THE SAME PIANO SCHOOL FOR A LONG TIME.
HUH... LIKE HOW MANY YEARS?
CUTE!
MMM... I THINK IT'S BEEN ABOUT SEVEN, RIGHT, TAKAMI?

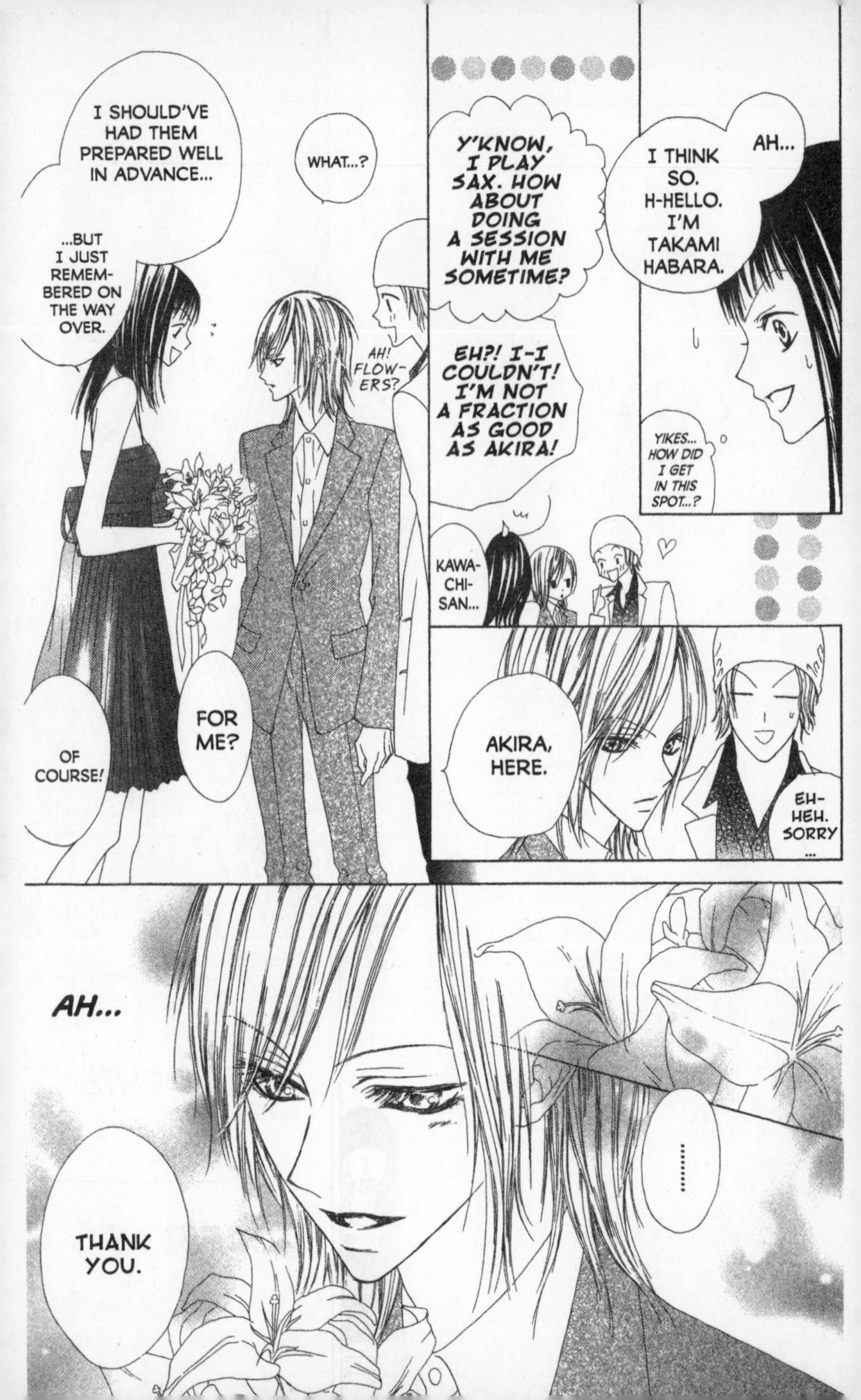
AH...
I THINK SO. H-HELLO. I'M TAKAMI HABARA.
YIKES... HOW DID I GET IN THIS SPOT...?
Y'KNOW, I PLAY SAX. HOW ABOUT DOING A SESSION WITH ME SOMETIME?
EH?! I-I COULDN'T! I'M NOT A FRACTION AS GOOD AS AKIRA!
KAWA-CHI-SAN...
AKIRA, HERE.
EH-HEH. SORRY...
WHAT...?
AH! FLOWERS?
I SHOULD'VE HAD THEM PREPARED WELL IN ADVANCE...
...BUT I JUST REMEMBERED ON THE WAY OVER.
FOR ME?
OF COURSE!
......
AH...
THANK YOU.

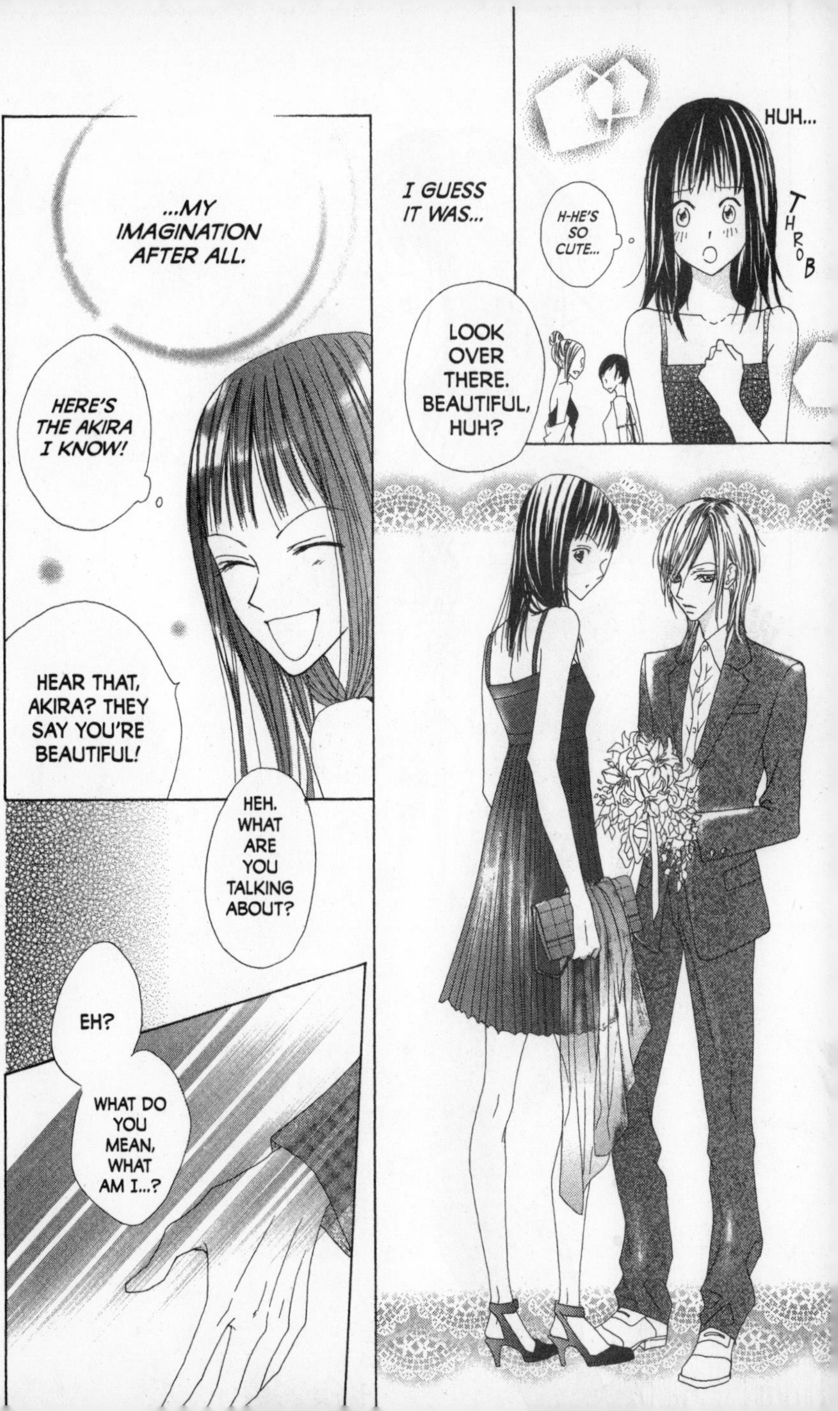
HUH...
THROB
H-HE'S SO CUTE...
LOOK OVER THERE. BEAUTIFUL, HUH?
I GUESS IT WAS...
...MY IMAGINATION AFTER ALL.
HERE'S THE AKIRA I KNOW!
HEAR THAT, AKIRA? THEY SAY YOU'RE BEAUTIFUL!
HEH. WHAT ARE YOU TALKING ABOUT?
EH?
WHAT DO YOU MEAN, WHAT AM I...?

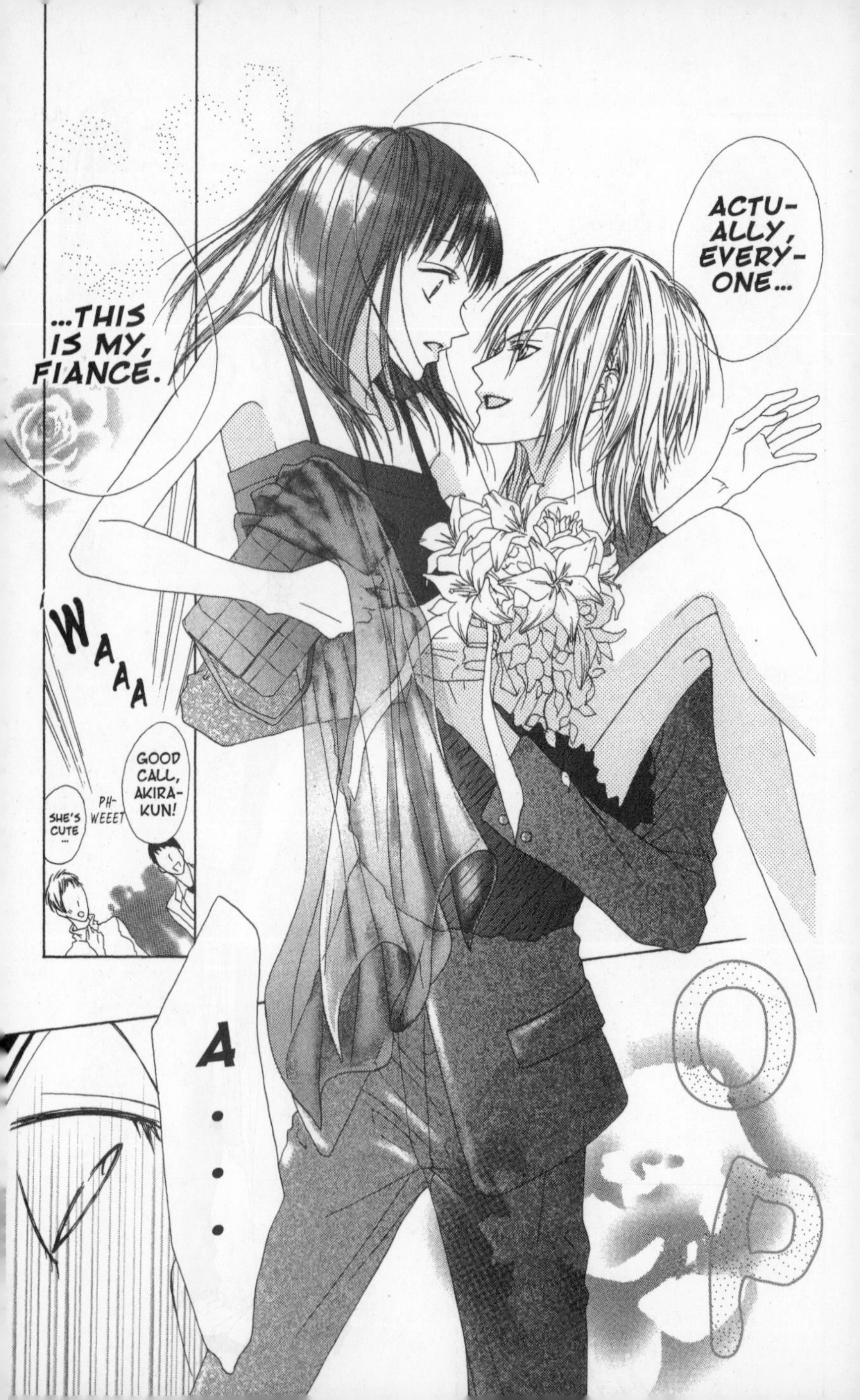
ACTU-ALLY, EVERY-ONE...
...THIS IS MY, FIANCE.
WAAAA
GOOD CALL, AKIRA-KUN!
PH-WEEET
SHE'S CUTE...
A...

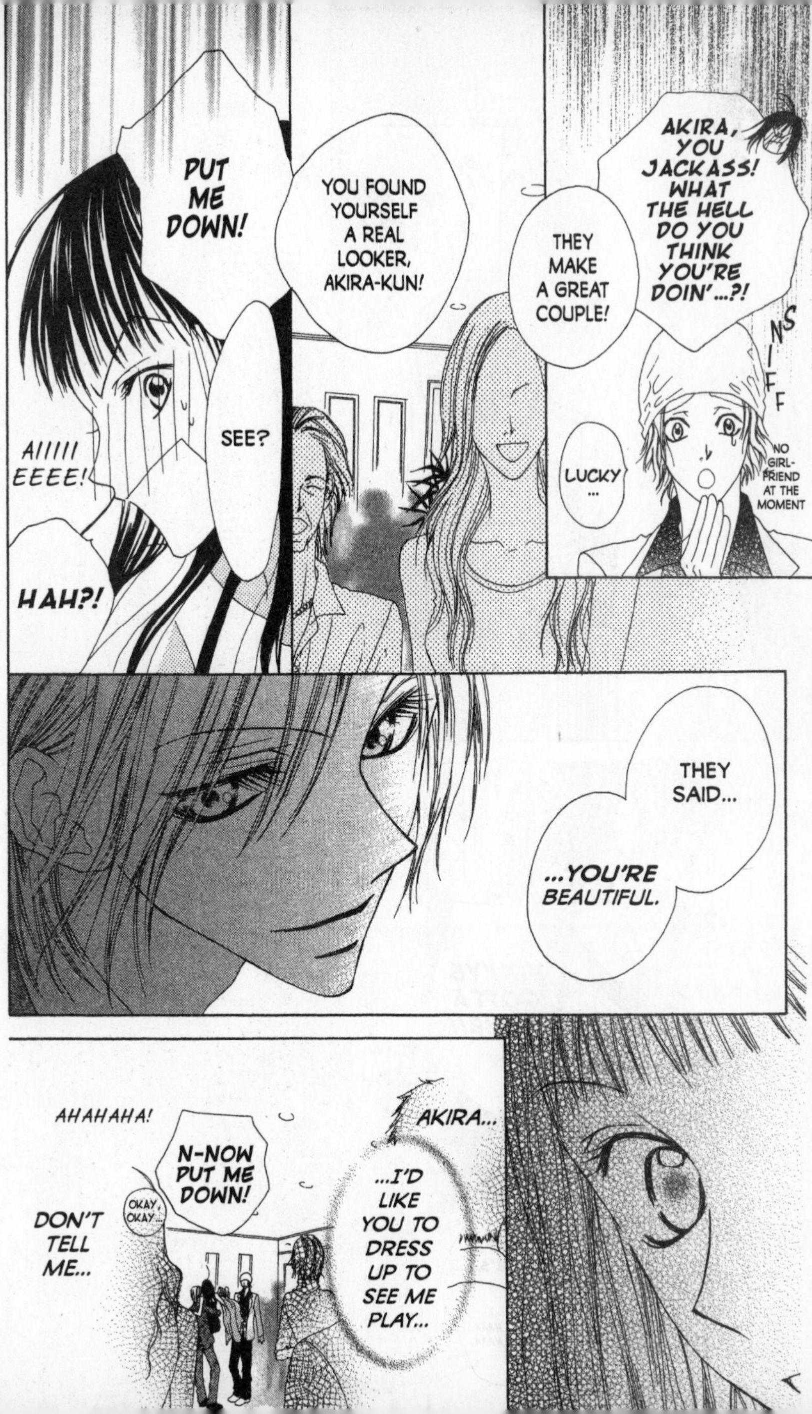
AKIRA, YOU JACKASS! WHAT THE HELL DO YOU THINK YOU'RE DOIN'...?!
SNIFF
LUCKY...
NO GIRL-FRIEND AT THE MOMENT
THEY MAKE A GREAT COUPLE!
YOU FOUND YOURSELF A REAL LOOKER, AKIRA-KUN!
PUT ME DOWN!
SEE?
AIIIIII EEEE!
HAH?!
THEY SAID...
...YOU'RE BEAUTIFUL.
AKIRA...
...I'D LIKE YOU TO DRESS UP TO SEE ME PLAY...
AHAHAHA!
N-NOW PUT ME DOWN!
OKAY, OKAY...
DON'T TELL ME...

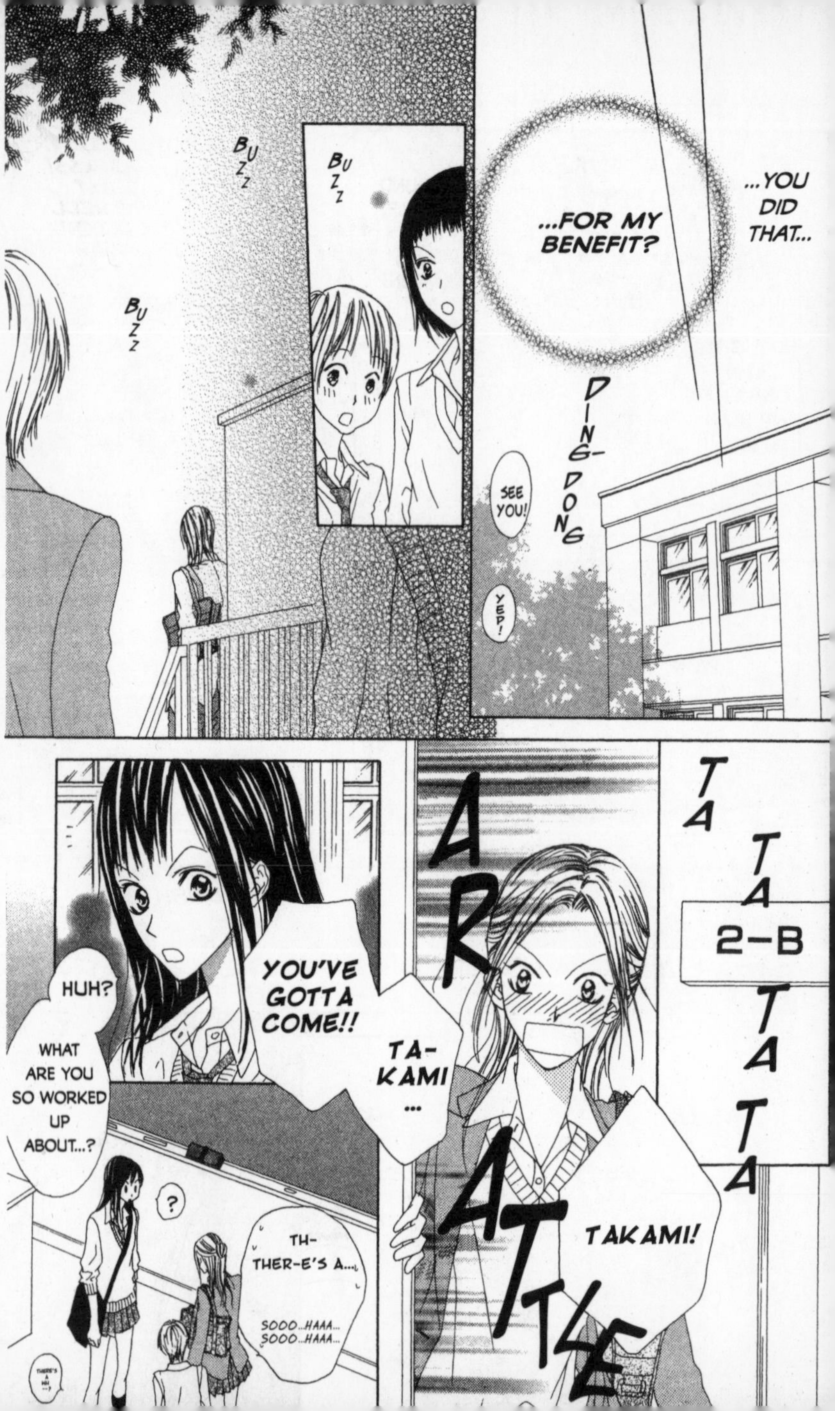
...YOU DID THAT...
...FOR MY BENEFIT?
DING-DONG
SEE YOU!
YEP!
BUZZ
BUZZ
BUZZ
TA TA TA
2-B
TA TA TA
RATTLE
TAKAMI!
TA-KAMI...
YOU'VE GOTTA COME!!
HUH?
WHAT ARE YOU SO WORKED UP ABOUT...?
?
TH-THER-E'S A...
SOOO..HAAA... SOOO..HAAA...

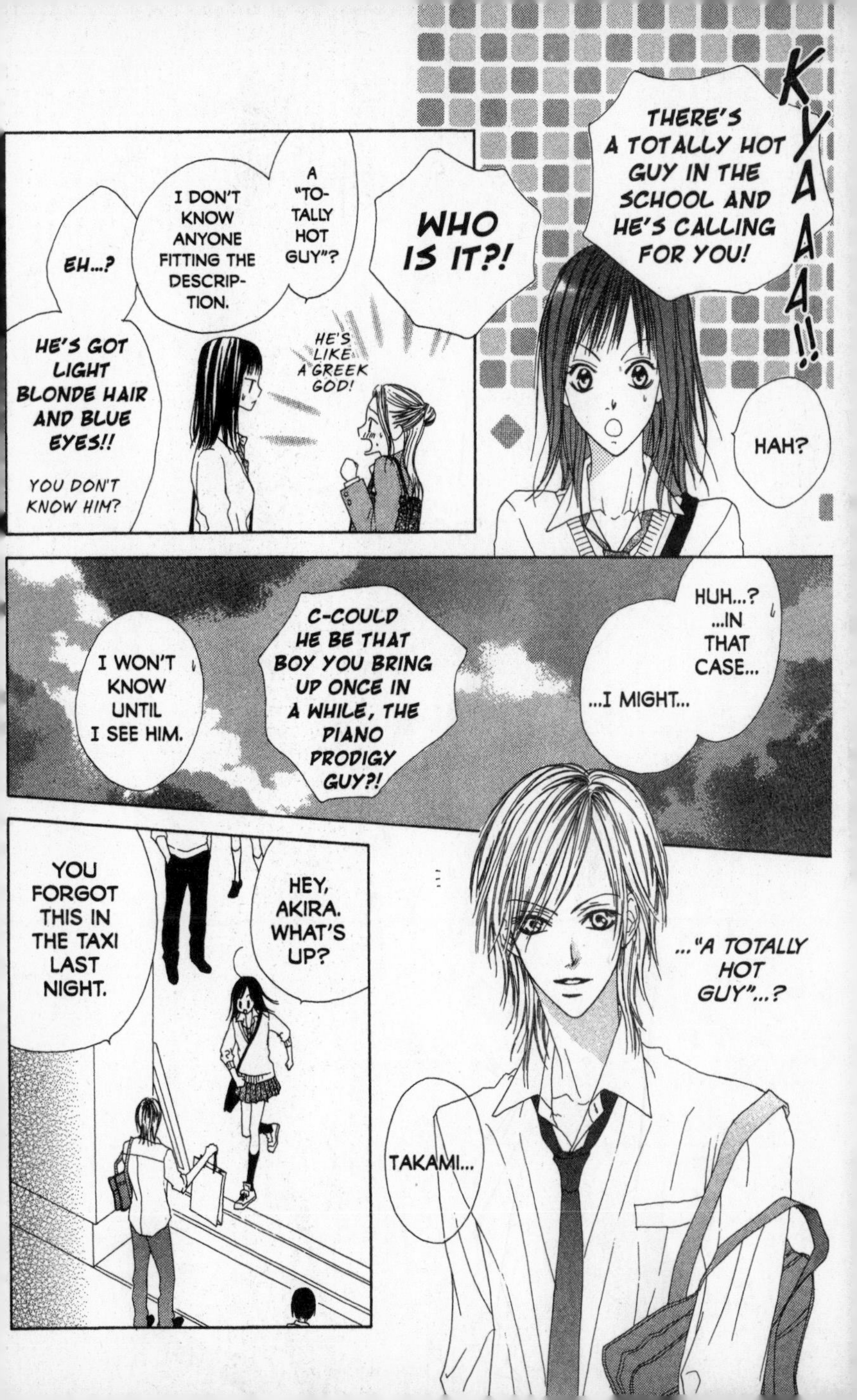
KYAAA!!
THERE'S A TOTALLY HOT GUY IN THE SCHOOL AND HE'S CALLING FOR YOU!
HAH?
WHO IS IT?!
A "TO-TALLY HOT GUY"?
I DON'T KNOW ANYONE FITTING THE DESCRIP-TION.
EH...?
HE'S LIKE A GREEK GOD!
HE'S GOT LIGHT BLONDE HAIR AND BLUE EYES!!
YOU DON'T KNOW HIM?
HUH...? ...IN THAT CASE...
...I MIGHT...
C-COULD HE BE THAT BOY YOU BRING UP ONCE IN A WHILE, THE PIANO PRODIGY GUY?!
I WON'T KNOW UNTIL I SEE HIM.
..."A TOTALLY HOT GUY"...?
TAKAMI...
HEY, AKIRA. WHAT'S UP?
YOU FORGOT THIS IN THE TAXI LAST NIGHT.

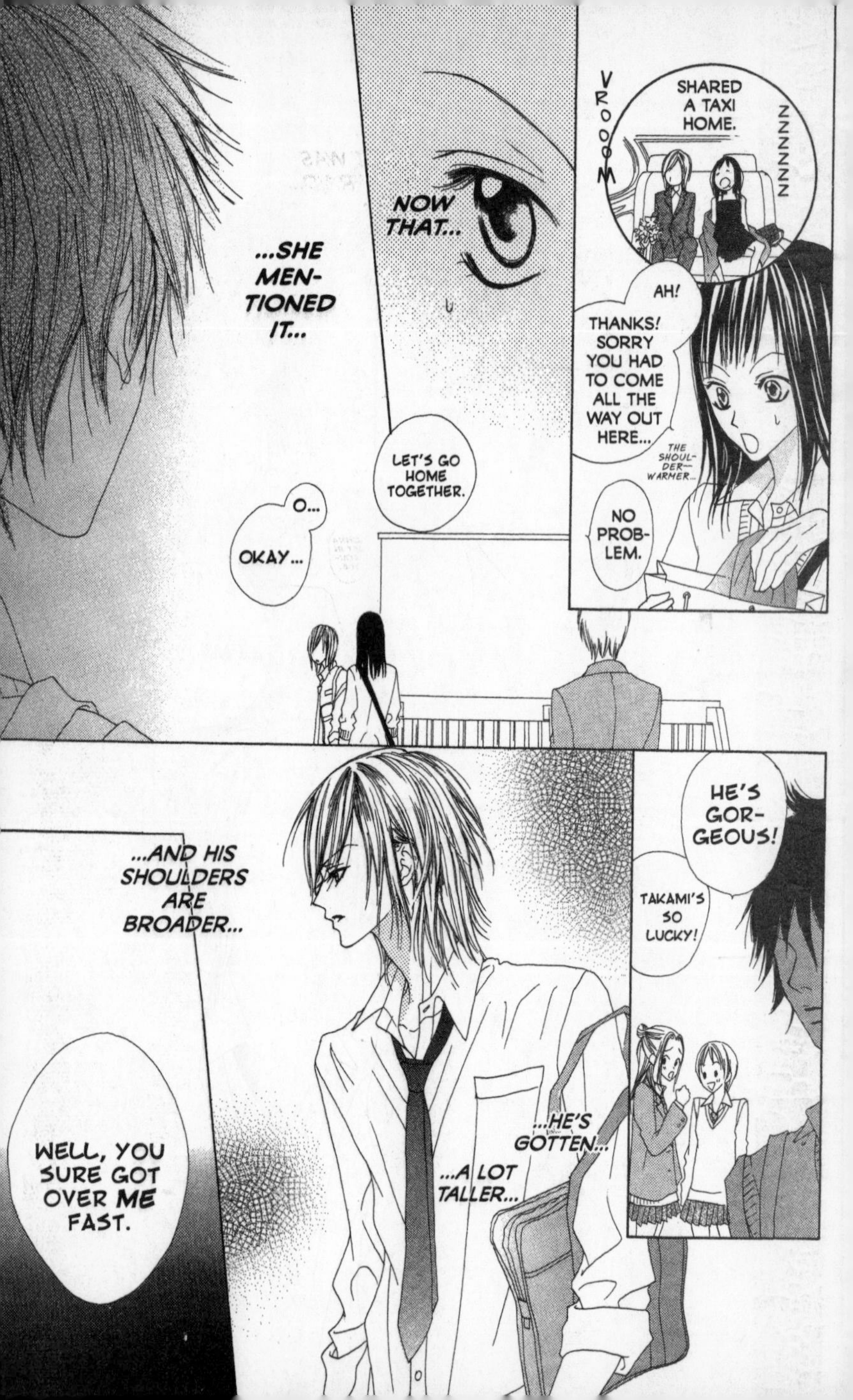

VROOOM
SHARED A TAXI HOME.
ZZZZZZ
AH!
THANKS! SORRY YOU HAD TO COME ALL THE WAY OUT HERE...
THE SHOULDER-WARMER...
NO PROBLEM.
NOW THAT...
...SHE MENTIONED IT...
LET'S GO HOME TOGETHER.
O... OKAY...
HE'S GORGEOUS!
TAKAMI'S SO LUCKY!
...HE'S GOTTEN...
...A LOT TALLER...
...AND HIS SHOULDERS ARE BROADER...
WELL, YOU SURE GOT OVER ME FAST.

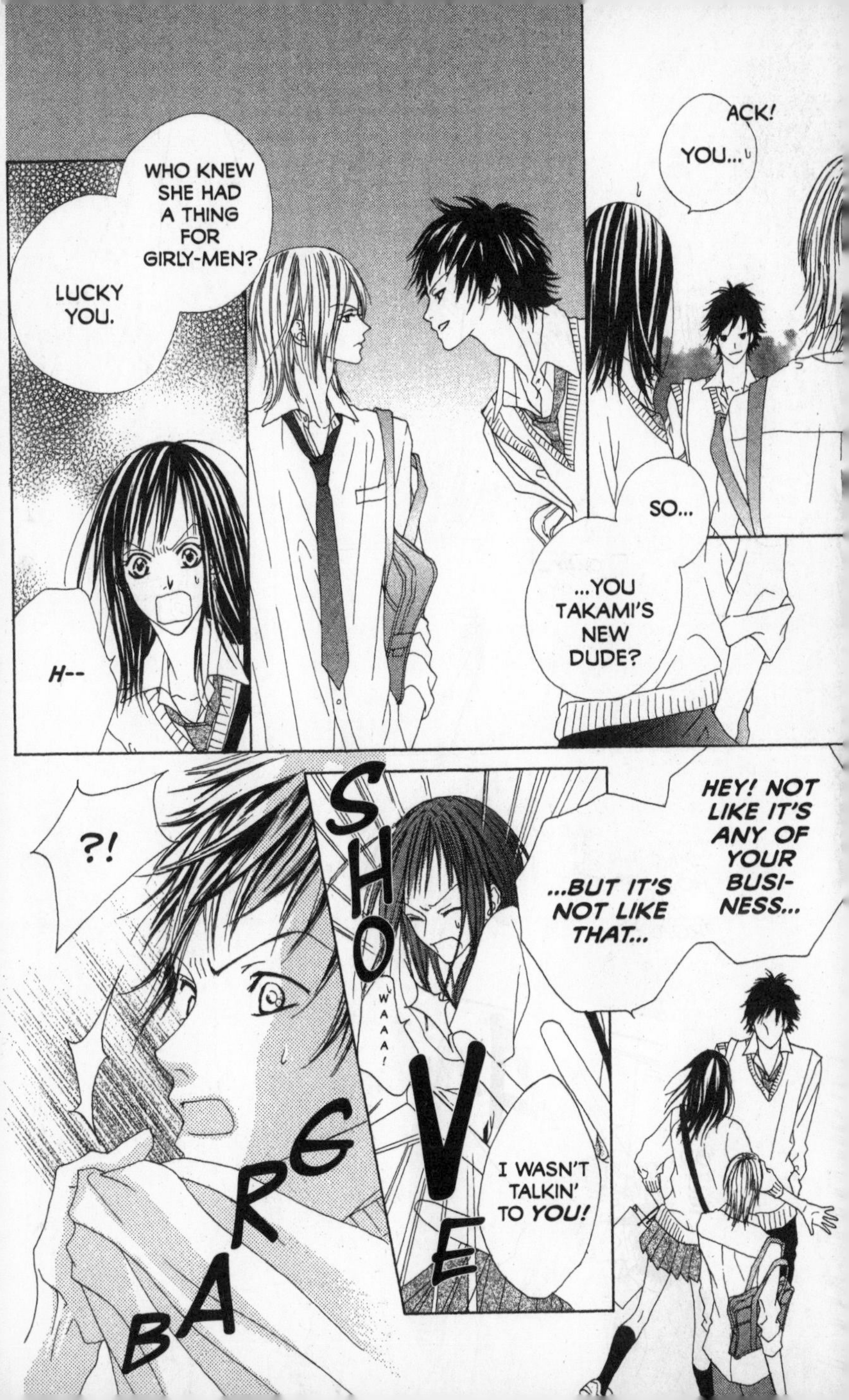
ACK! YOU...
SO...
...YOU TAKAMI'S NEW DUDE?
WHO KNEW SHE HAD A THING FOR GIRLY-MEN?
LUCKY YOU.
H--
HEY! NOT LIKE IT'S ANY OF YOUR BUSI- NESS...
...BUT IT'S NOT LIKE THAT...
SHOVE
WAAAA!
I WASN'T TALKIN' TO YOU!
?!
BARRG

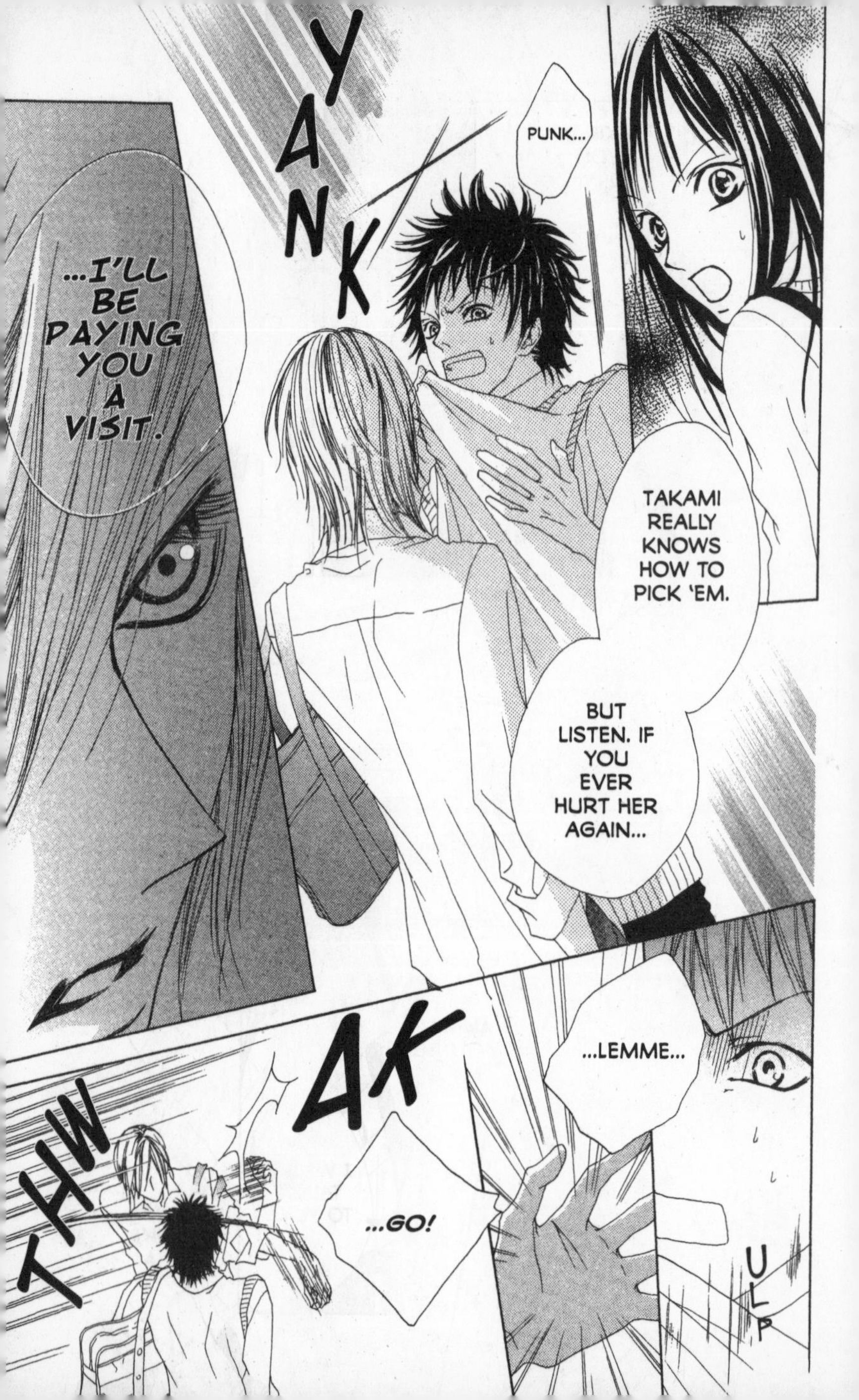
YANK
PUNK...
TAKAMI REALLY KNOWS HOW TO PICK 'EM.
BUT LISTEN. IF YOU EVER HURT HER AGAIN...
...I'LL BE PAYING YOU A VISIT.
...LEMME...
ULP
...GO!
THWAK

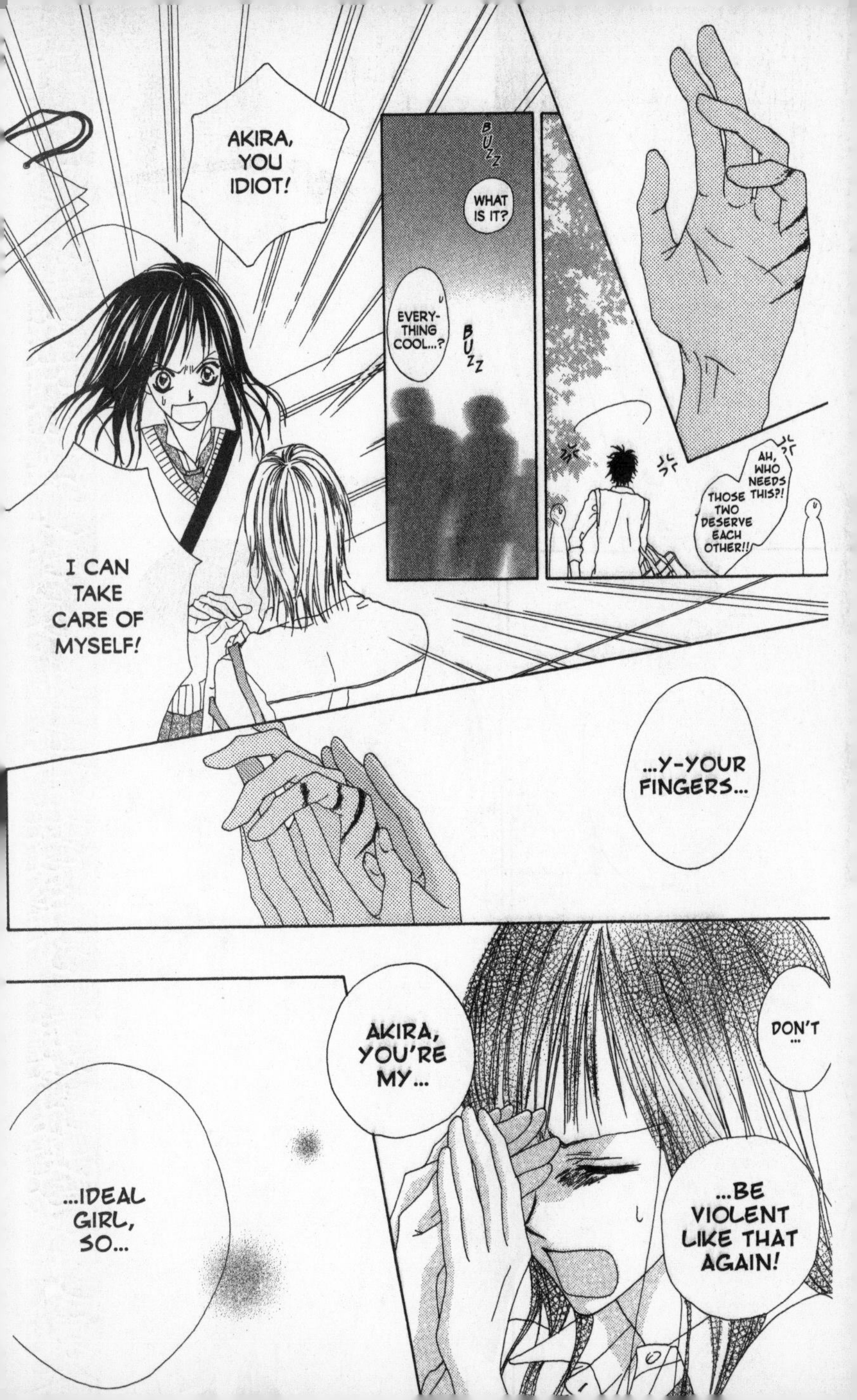
AH, WHO NEEDS THIS?!
THOSE TWO DESERVE EACH OTHER!!
BUZZ
WHAT IS IT?
EVERYTHING COOL...?
BUZZ
AKIRA, YOU IDIOT!
I CAN TAKE CARE OF MYSELF!
...Y-YOUR FINGERS...
DON'T...
...BE VIOLENT LIKE THAT AGAIN!
AKIRA, YOU'RE MY...
...IDEAL GIRL, SO...

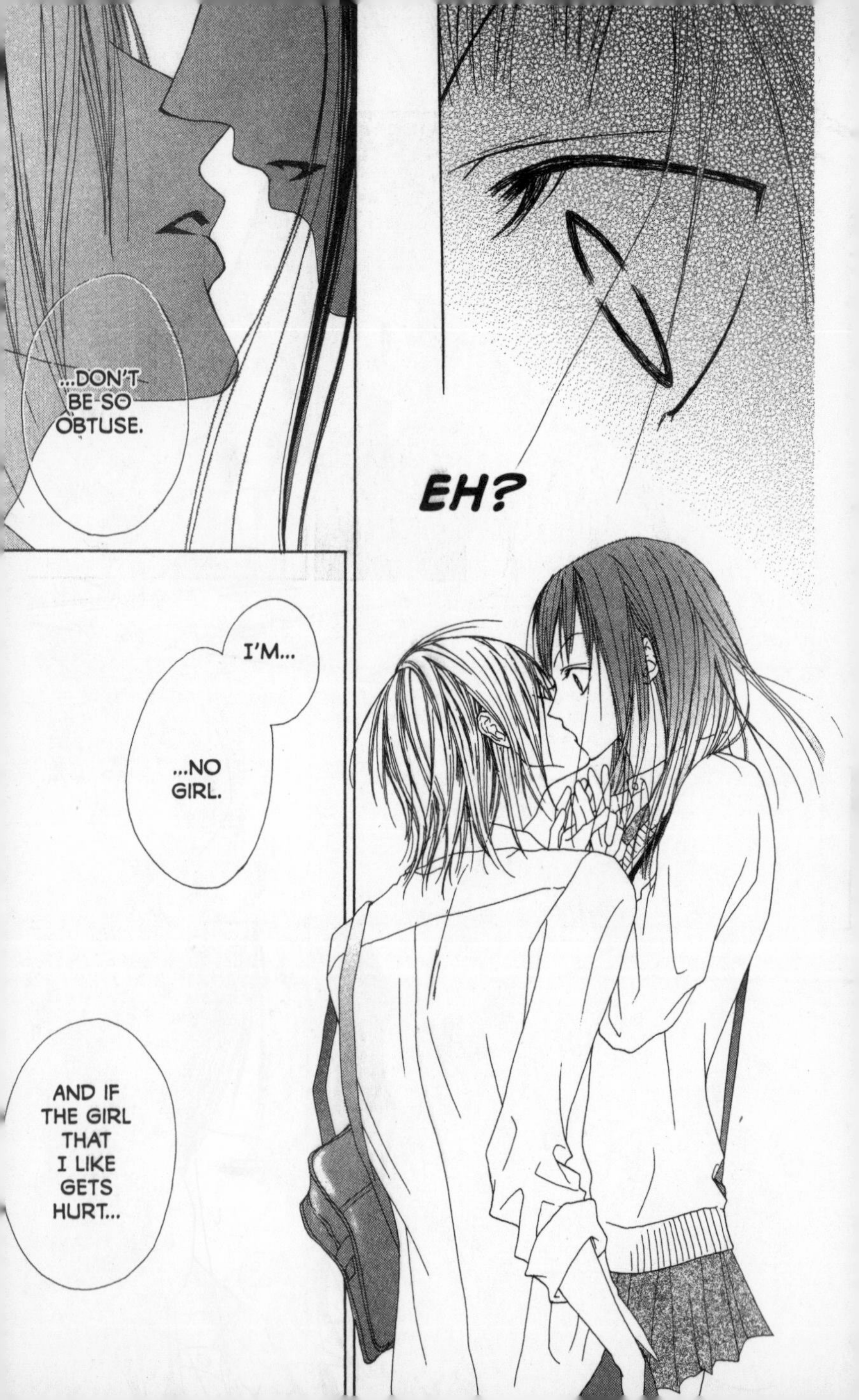
EH?
...DON'T BE SO OBTUSE.
I'M...
...NO GIRL.
AND IF THE GIRL THAT I LIKE GETS HURT...

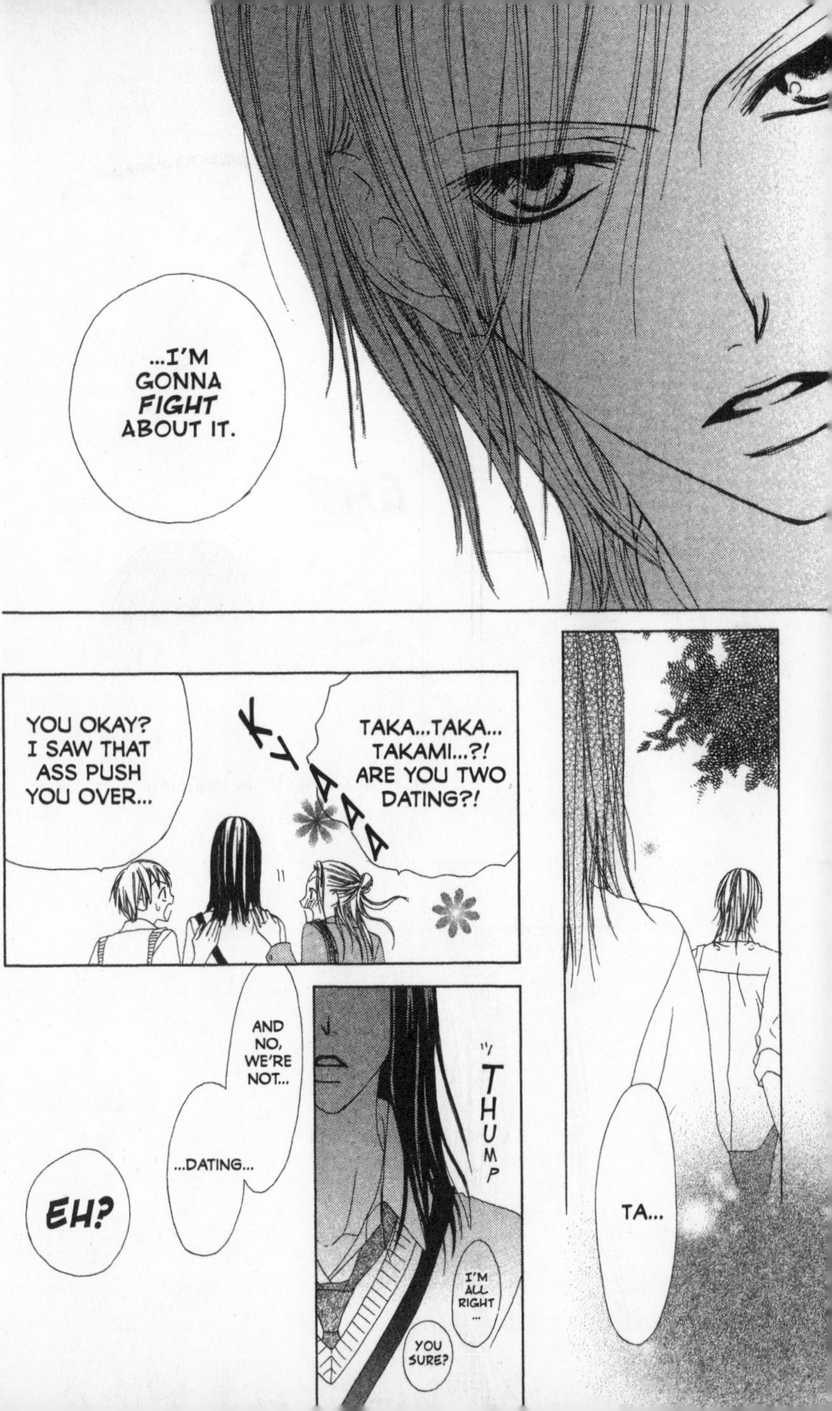
...I'M GONNA *FIGHT* ABOUT IT.
TA...
TAKA...TAKA... TAKAMI...?! ARE YOU TWO DATING?!
KYAAAA
YOU OKAY? I SAW THAT ASS PUSH YOU OVER...
THUMP
AND NO, WE'RE NOT...
...DATING...
I'M ALL RIGHT...
YOU SURE?
EH?

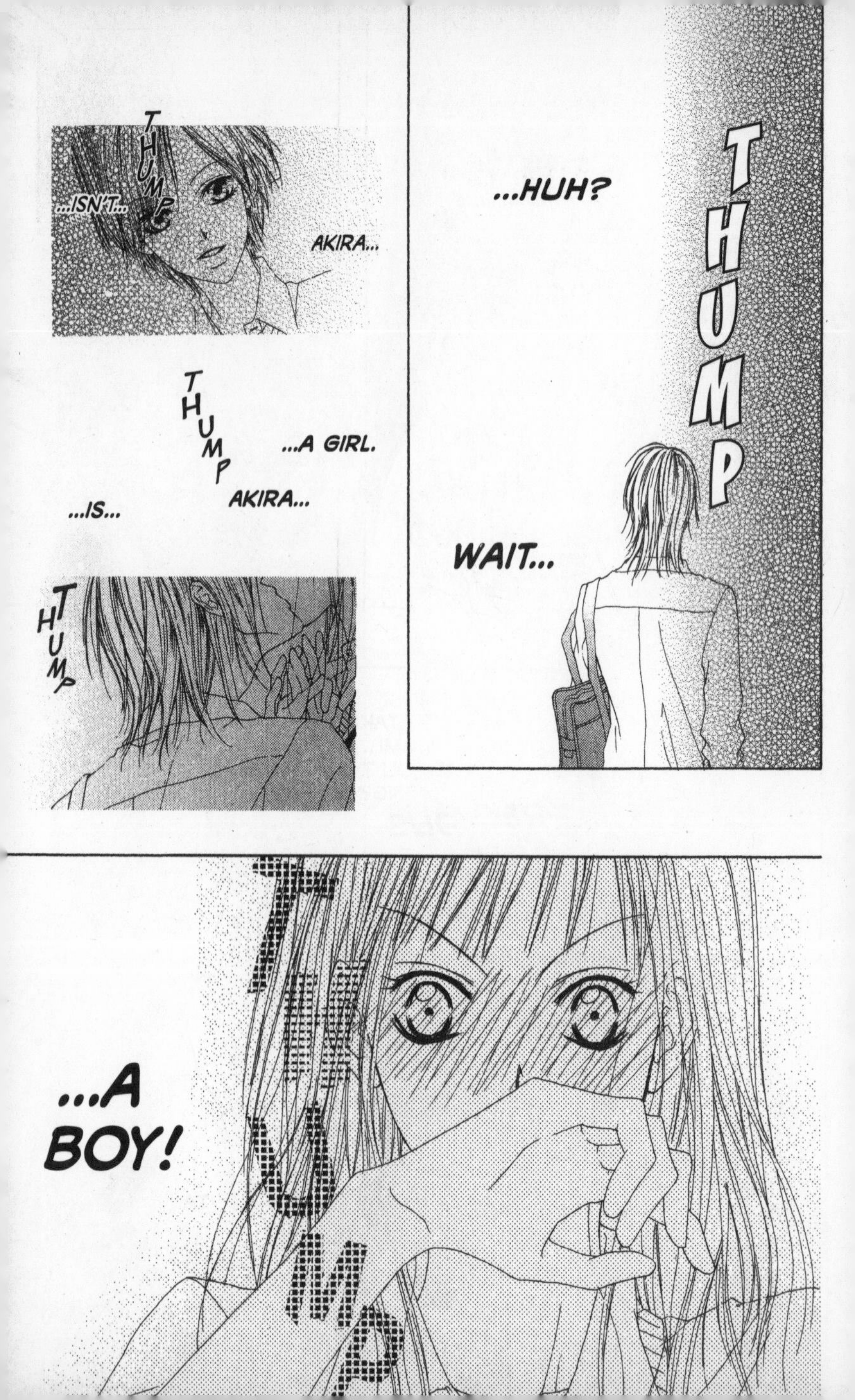
THUMP
...HUH?
WAIT...
THUMP
AKIRA...
...ISN'T...
...A GIRL.
THUMP
AKIRA...
...IS...
THUMP
THUMP
...A BOY!

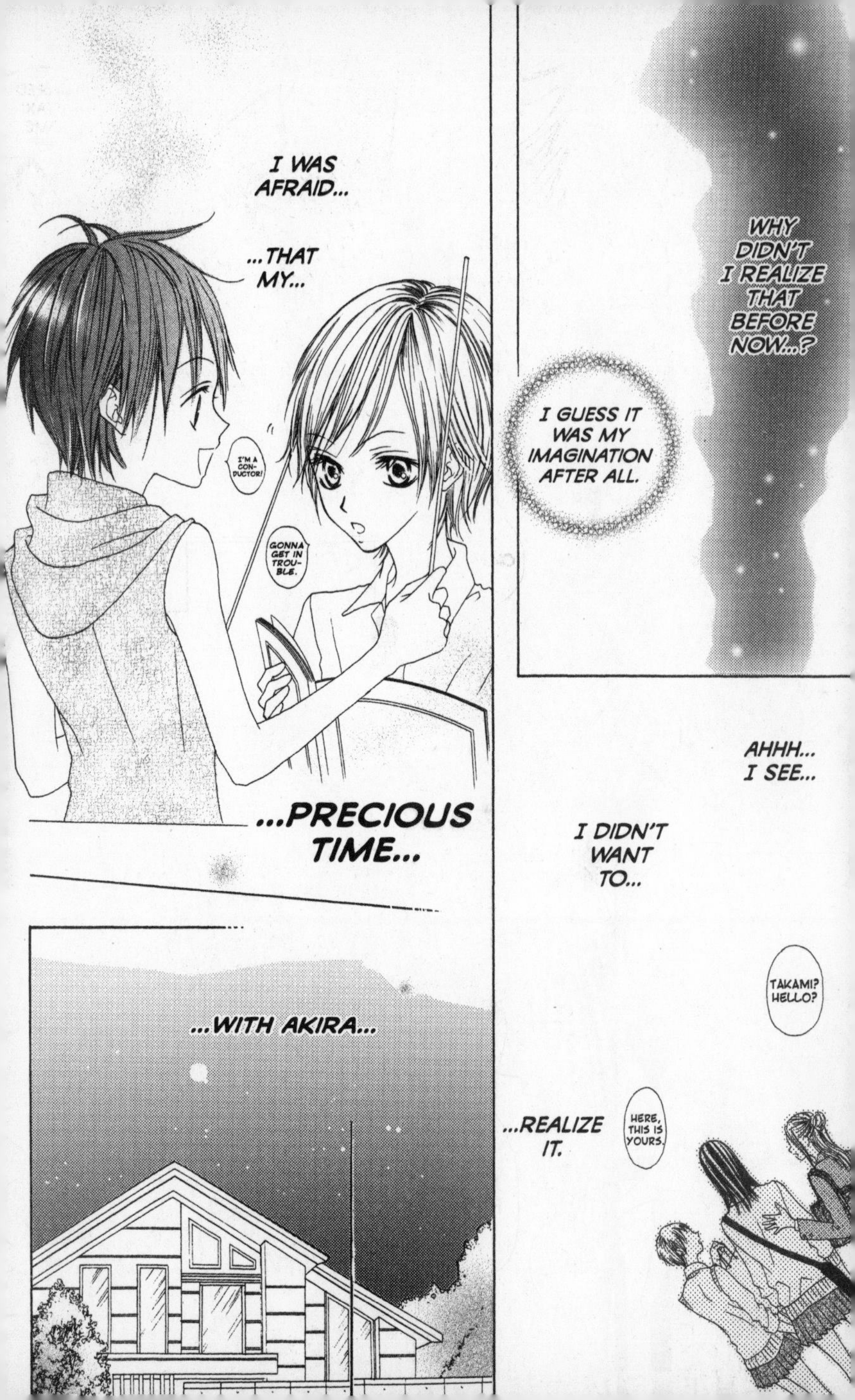
WHY DIDN'T I REALIZE THAT BEFORE NOW...?
I GUESS IT WAS MY IMAGINATION AFTER ALL.
AHHH... I SEE...
I DIDN'T WANT TO...
TAKAMI? HELLO?
HERE, THIS IS YOURS.
...REALIZE IT.
I WAS AFRAID...
...THAT MY...
I'M A CONDUCTOR!
GONNA GET IN TROUBLE.
...PRECIOUS TIME...
...WITH AKIRA...

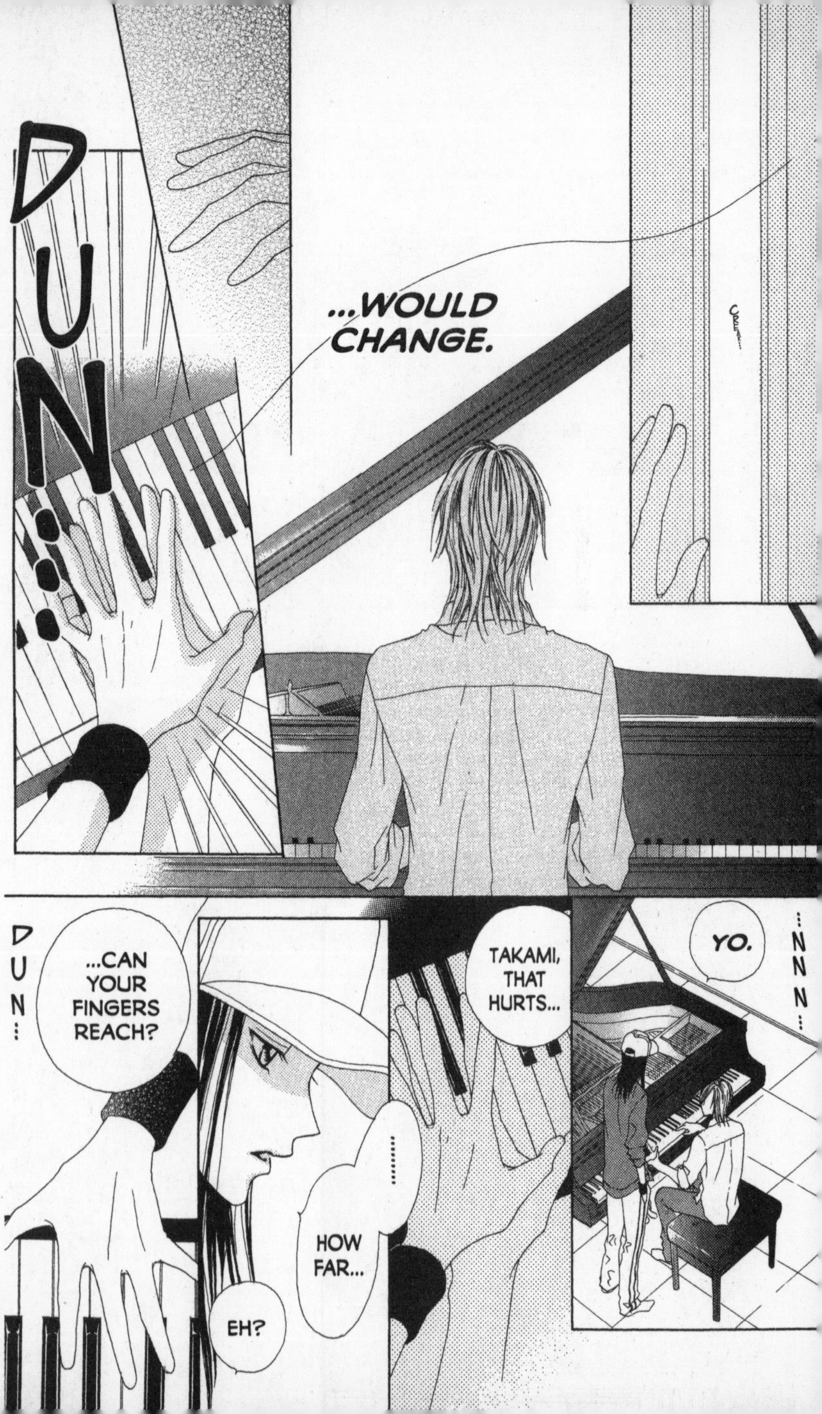
CREAK...
...WOULD CHANGE.
DUN...
...NNN...
YO.
TAKAMI, THAT HURTS...
......
HOW FAR...
EH?
...CAN YOUR FINGERS REACH?
DUN...

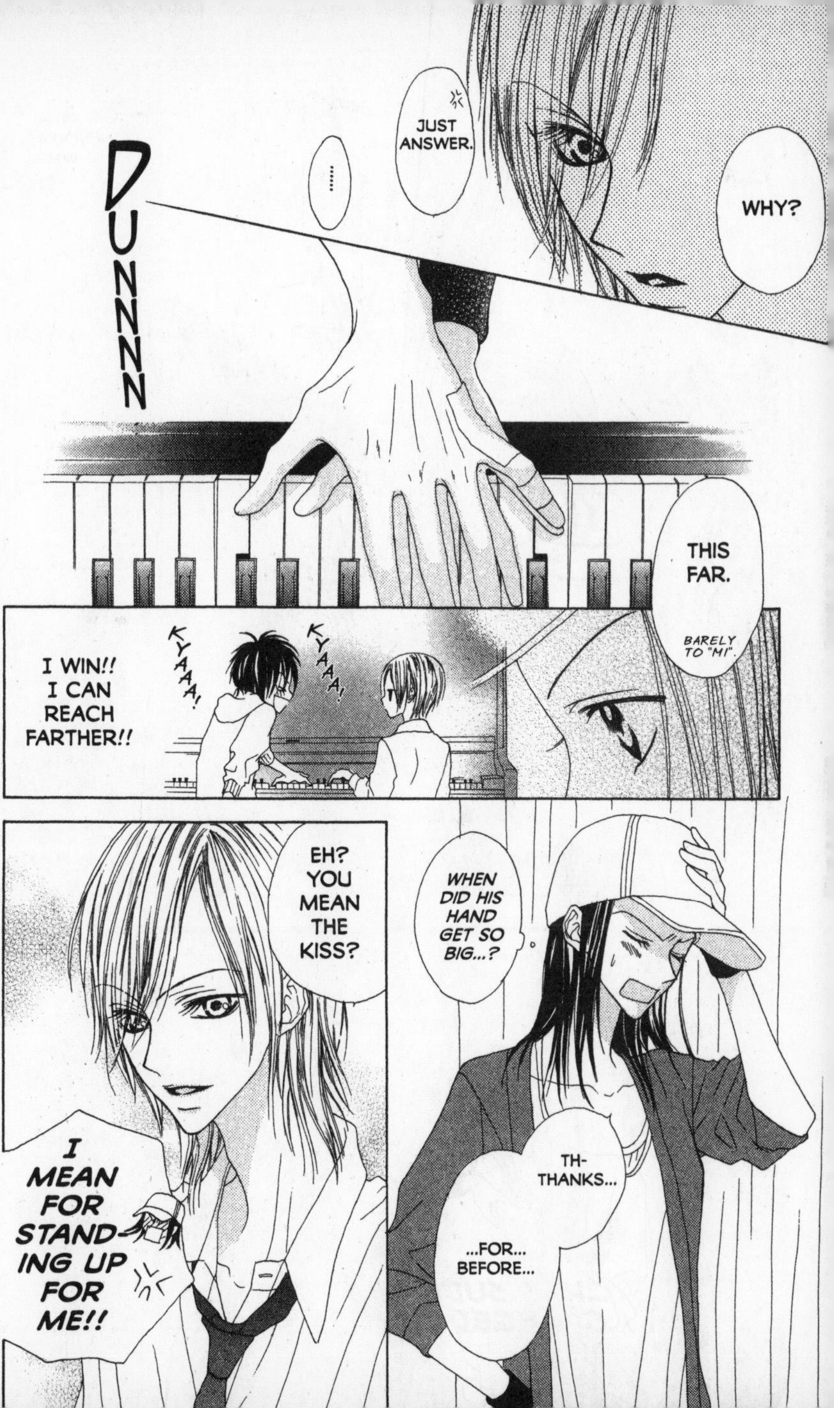
WHY?
JUST ANSWER.
......
DUNNNN
THIS FAR.
BARELY TO "MI".
KYAAA!
KYAAA!
I WIN!! I CAN REACH FARTHER!!
WHEN DID HIS HAND GET SO BIG...?
TH- THANKS...
...FOR... BEFORE...
EH? YOU MEAN THE KISS?
I MEAN FOR STAND-ING UP FOR ME!!

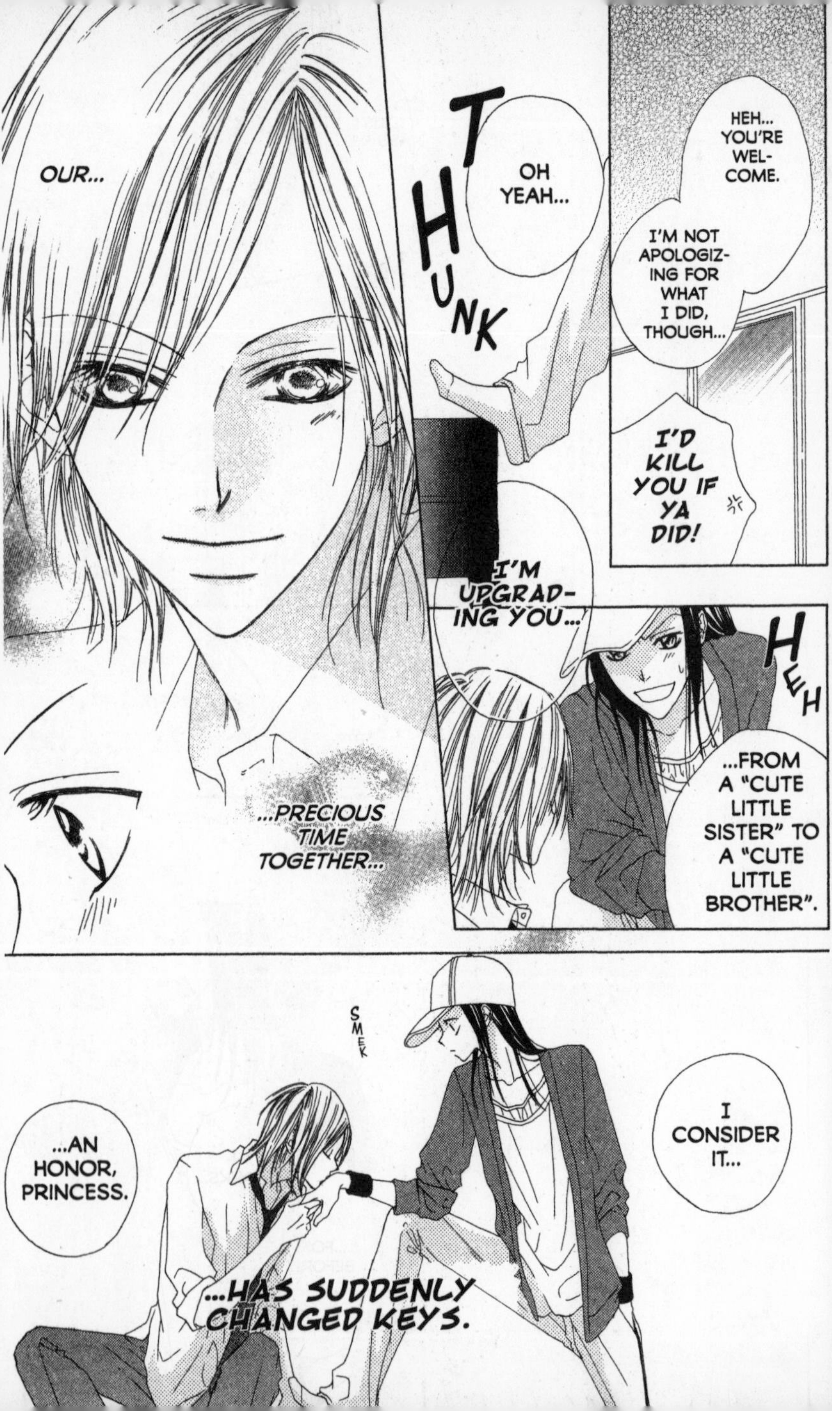
HEH... YOU'RE WEL-COME.
I'M NOT APOLOGIZ-ING FOR WHAT I DID, THOUGH...
I'D KILL YOU IF YA DID!
OH YEAH...
THUNK
I'M UPGRAD-ING YOU...
HEH
...FROM A "CUTE LITTLE SISTER" TO A "CUTE LITTLE BROTHER".
OUR...
...PRECIOUS TIME TOGETHER...
I CONSIDER IT...
SMEK
...AN HONOR, PRINCESS.
...HAS SUDDENLY CHANGED KEYS.

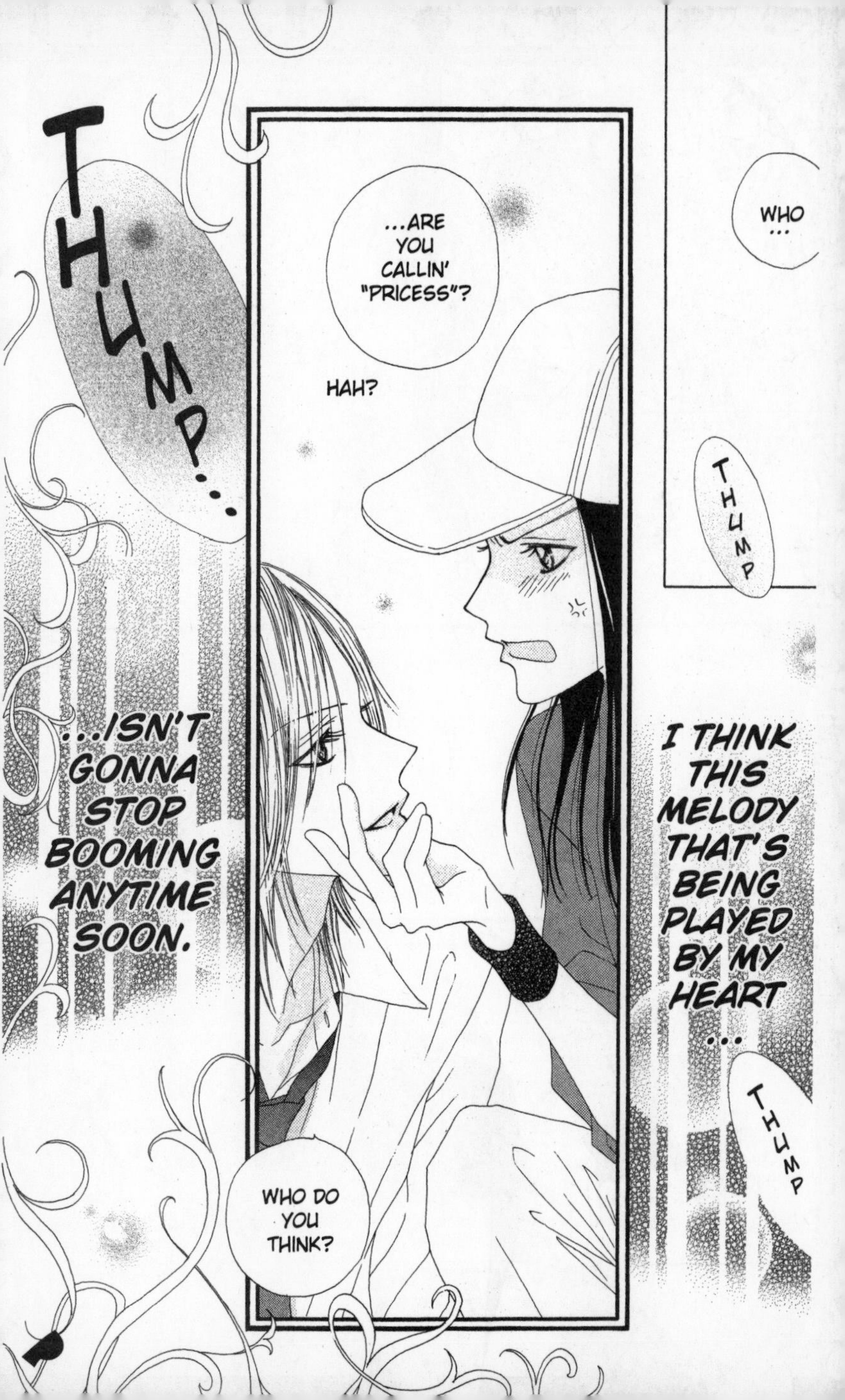
WHO...
THUMP
...ARE YOU CALLIN' "PRICESS"?
HAH?
WHO DO YOU THINK?
I THINK THIS MELODY THAT'S BEING PLAYED BY MY HEART...
THUMP
THUMP...
...ISN'T GONNA STOP BOOMING ANYTIME SOON.

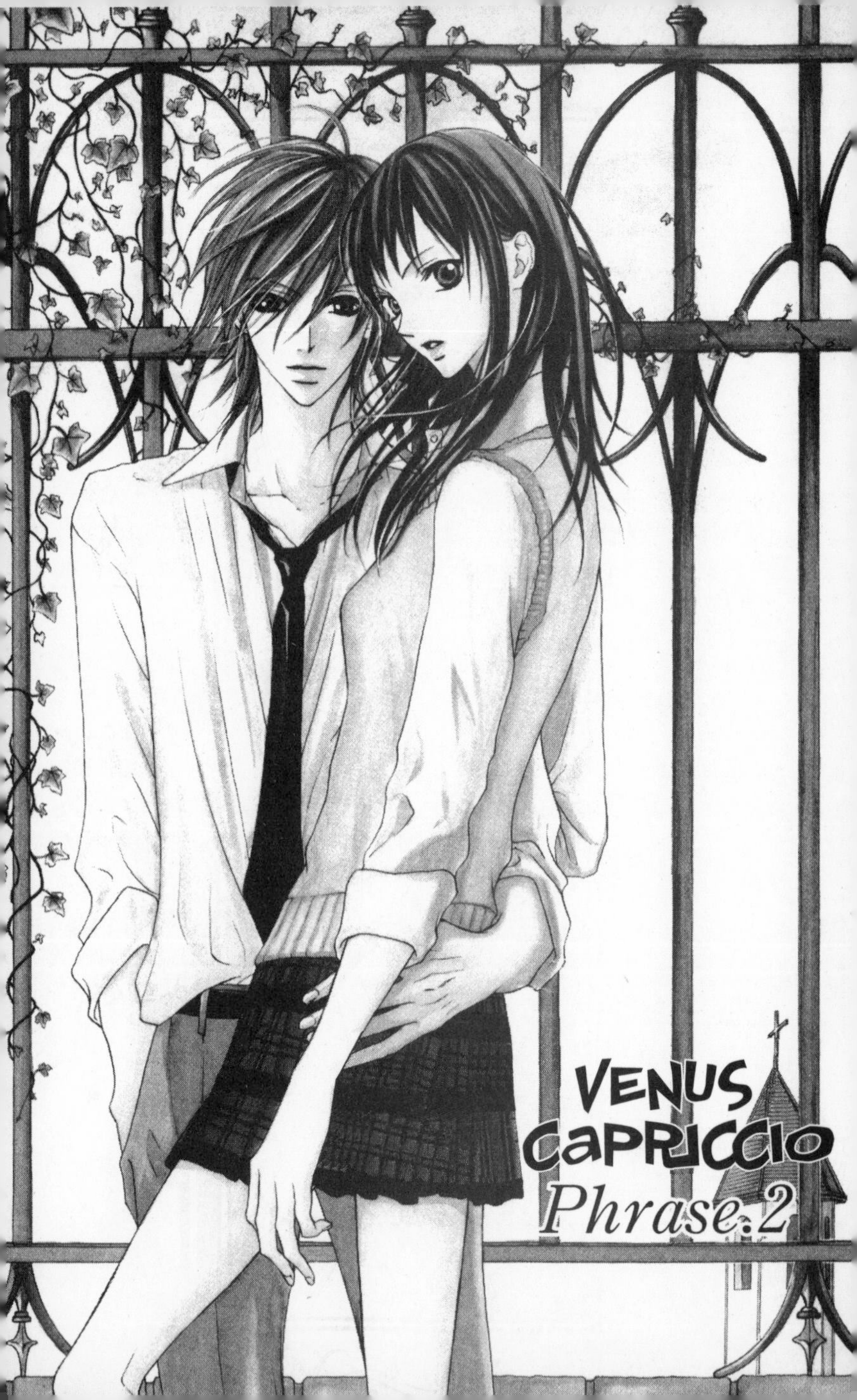
VENUS
CAPRICCIO
Phrase.2

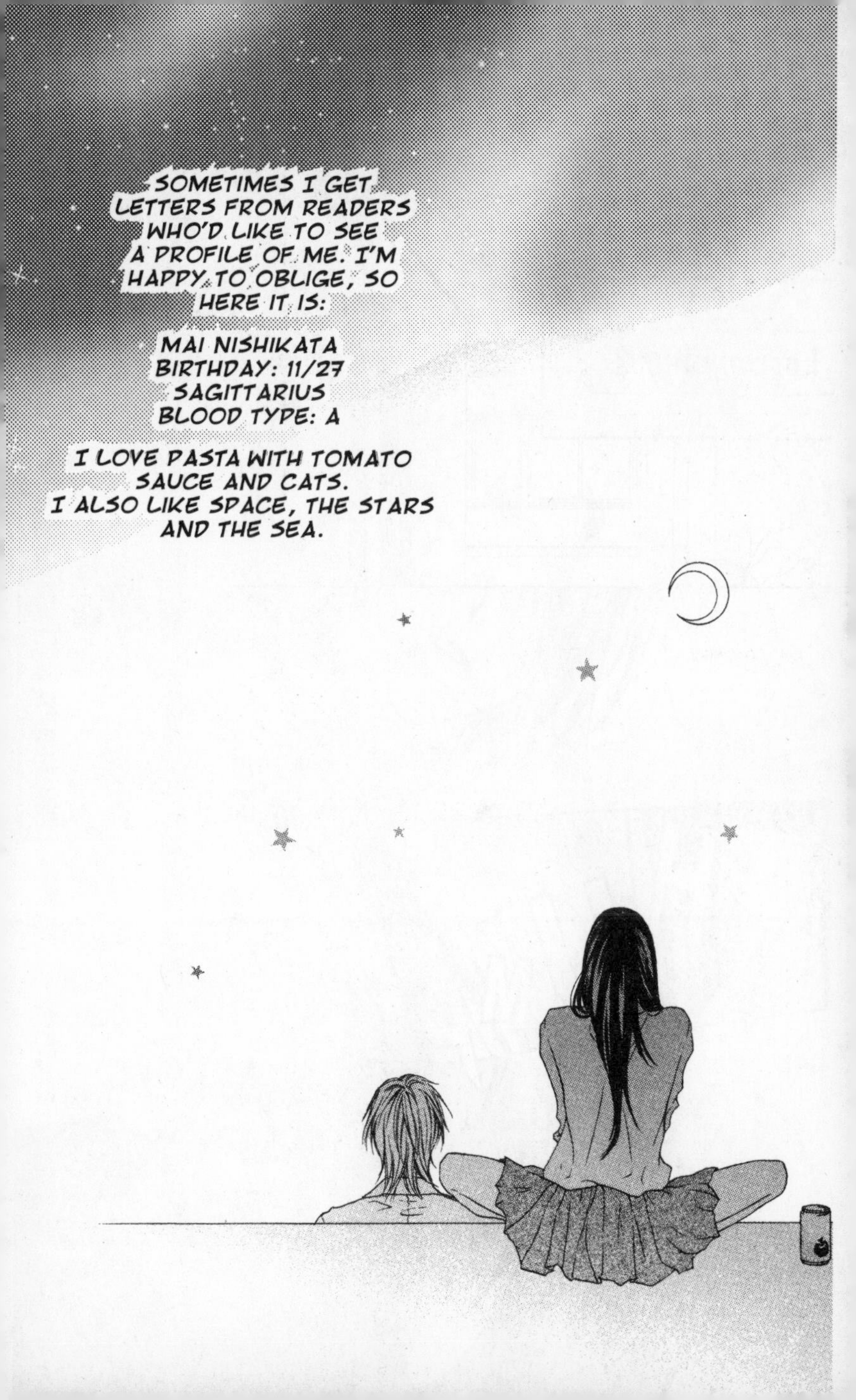
SOMETIMES I GET LETTERS FROM READERS WHO'D LIKE TO SEE A PROFILE OF ME. I'M HAPPY TO OBLIGE, SO HERE IT IS:
MAI NISHIKATA
BIRTHDAY: 11/27
SAGITTARIUS
BLOOD TYPE: A
I LOVE PASTA WITH TOMATO SAUCE AND CATS.
I ALSO LIKE SPACE, THE STARS AND THE SEA.

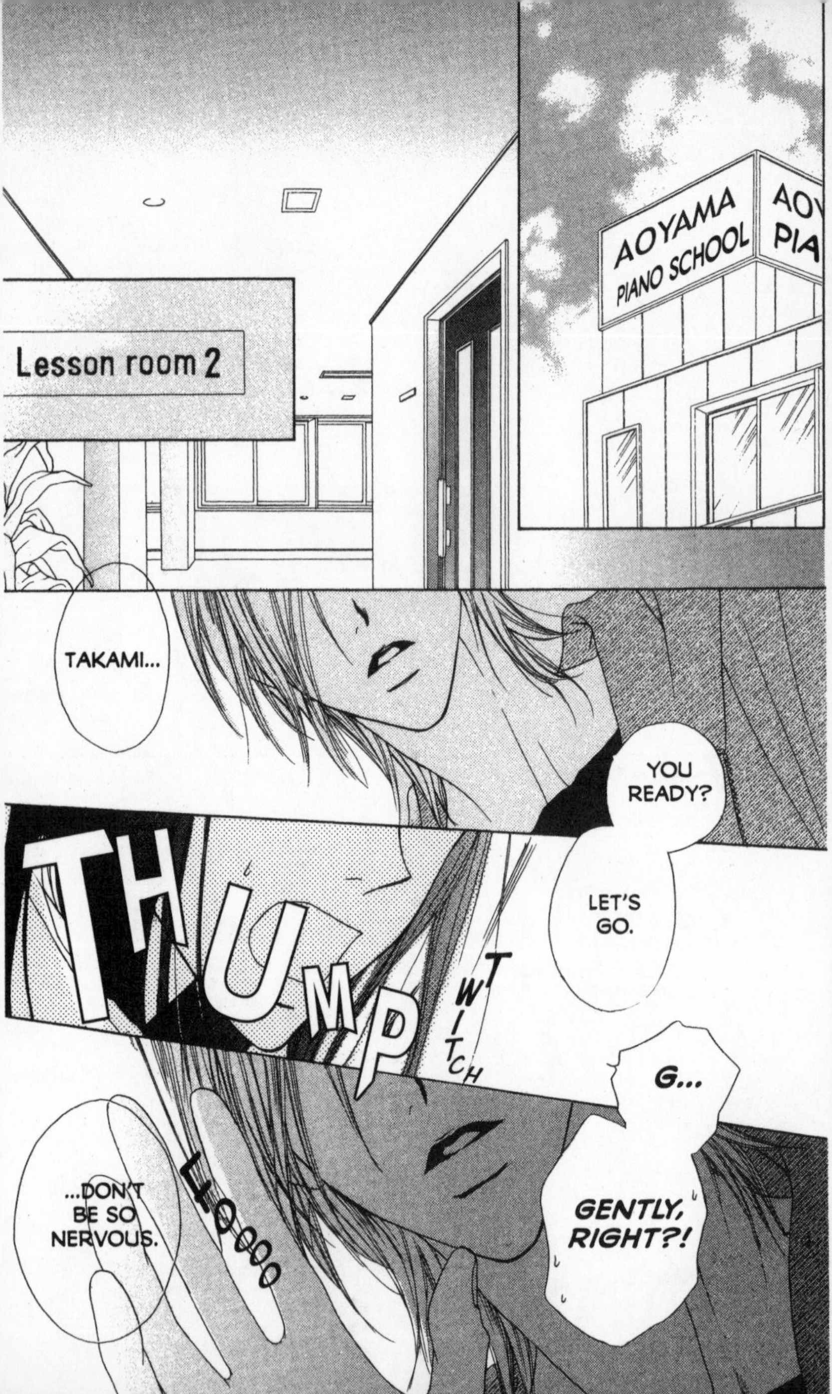
AOYAMA PIANO SCHOOL
AOY PIA
Lesson room 2
TAKAMI...
YOU READY?
LET'S GO.
THUMP
TWITCH
G...
GENTLY, RIGHT?!
...DON'T BE SO NERVOUS.

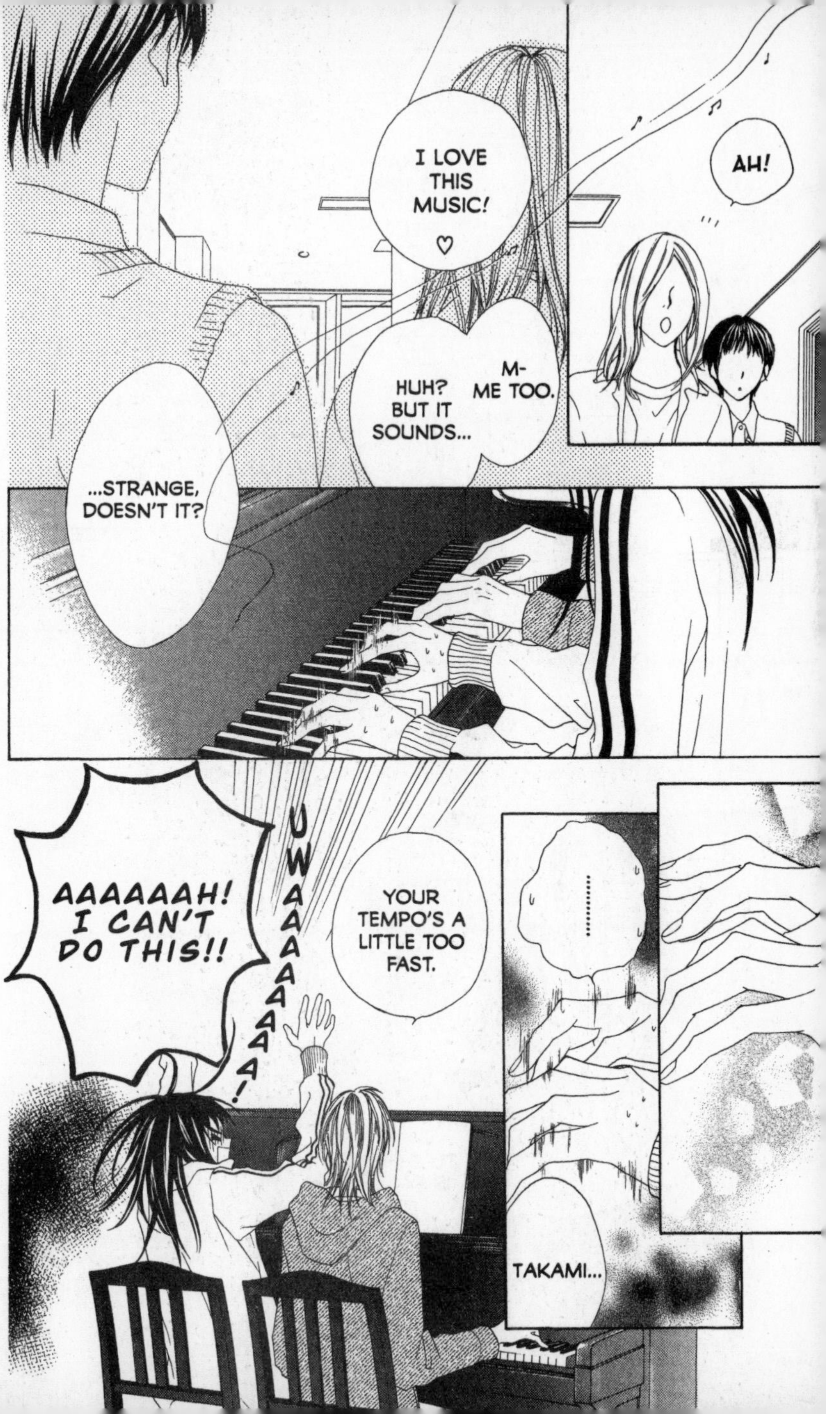
AH!
I LOVE THIS MUSIC! ♡
M- ME TOO.
HUH? BUT IT SOUNDS...
...STRANGE, DOESN'T IT?
......
TAKAMI...
YOUR TEMPO'S A LITTLE TOO FAST.
UWAAAAAAAAAA!
AAAAAAH! I CAN'T DO THIS!!

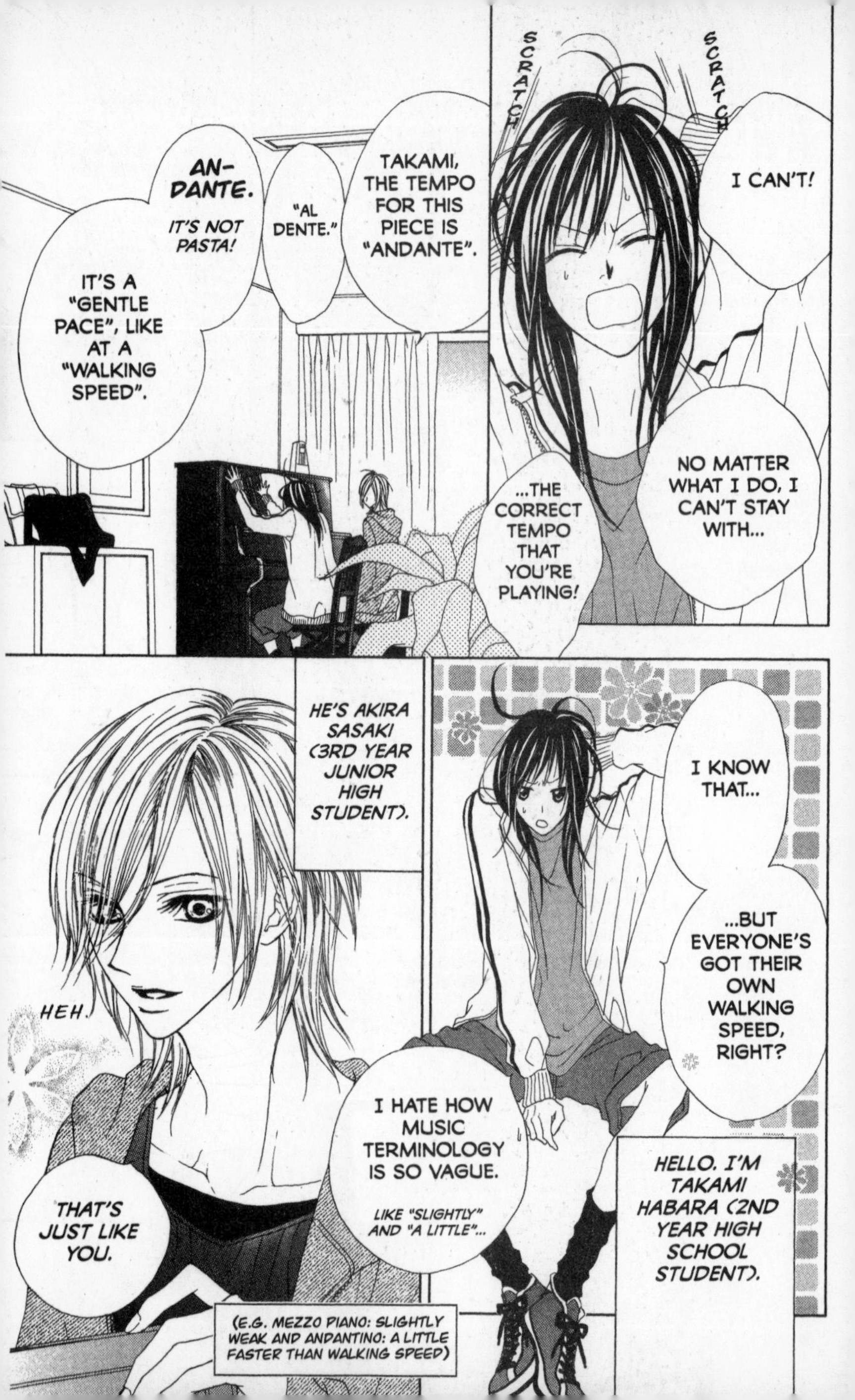
SCRATCH
SCRATCH
I CAN'T!
NO MATTER WHAT I DO, I CAN'T STAY WITH...
...THE CORRECT TEMPO THAT YOU'RE PLAYING!
TAKAMI, THE TEMPO FOR THIS PIECE IS "ANDANTE".
"AL DENTE."
AN-DANTE.
IT'S NOT PASTA!
IT'S A "GENTLE PACE", LIKE AT A "WALKING SPEED".
I KNOW THAT...
...BUT EVERYONE'S GOT THEIR OWN WALKING SPEED, RIGHT?
HELLO. I'M TAKAMI HABARA (2ND YEAR HIGH SCHOOL STUDENT).
I HATE HOW MUSIC TERMINOLOGY IS SO VAGUE.
LIKE "SLIGHTLY" AND "A LITTLE"...
(E.G. MEZZO PIANO: SLIGHTLY WEAK AND ANDANTINO: A LITTLE FASTER THAN WALKING SPEED)
HE'S AKIRA SASAKI (3RD YEAR JUNIOR HIGH STUDENT).
HEH.
THAT'S JUST LIKE YOU.

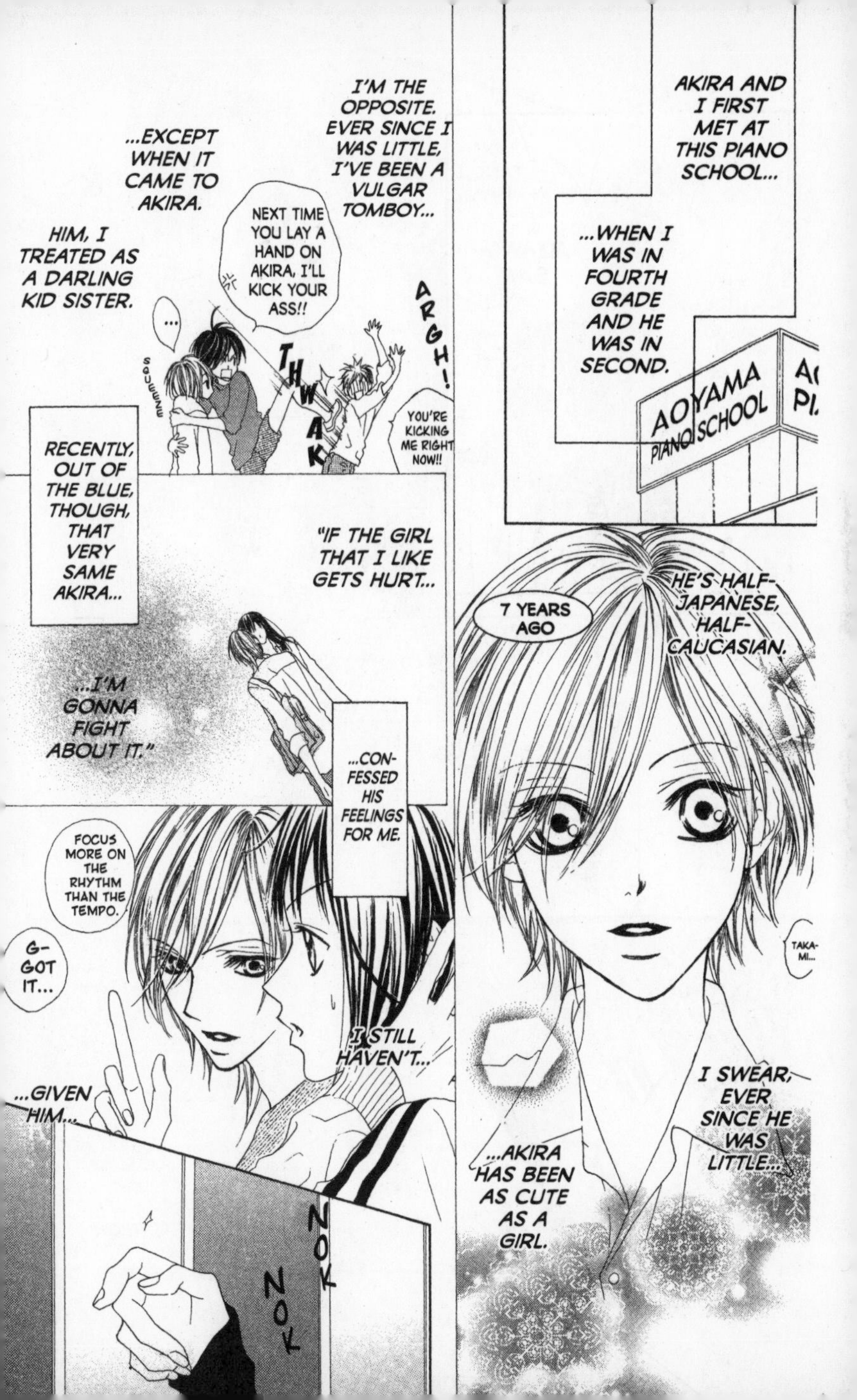
AKIRA AND I FIRST MET AT THIS PIANO SCHOOL...
...WHEN I WAS IN FOURTH GRADE AND HE WAS IN SECOND.
AOYAMA PIANO SCHOOL
7 YEARS AGO
HE'S HALF-JAPANESE, HALF-CAUCASIAN.
TAKA-MI...
I SWEAR, EVER SINCE HE WAS LITTLE...
...AKIRA HAS BEEN AS CUTE AS A GIRL.
I'M THE OPPOSITE. EVER SINCE I WAS LITTLE, I'VE BEEN A VULGAR TOMBOY...
...EXCEPT WHEN IT CAME TO AKIRA.
HIM, I TREATED AS A DARLING KID SISTER.
ARGH!
NEXT TIME YOU LAY A HAND ON AKIRA, I'LL KICK YOUR ASS!!
YOU'RE KICKING ME RIGHT NOW!!
THWAK
...
SQUEEZE
"IF THE GIRL THAT I LIKE GETS HURT...
RECENTLY, OUT OF THE BLUE, THOUGH, THAT VERY SAME AKIRA...
...I'M GONNA FIGHT ABOUT IT."
...CON-FESSED HIS FEELINGS FOR ME.
I STILL HAVEN'T...
FOCUS MORE ON THE RHYTHM THAN THE TEMPO.
G-GOT IT...
...GIVEN HIM...
NOK
NOK

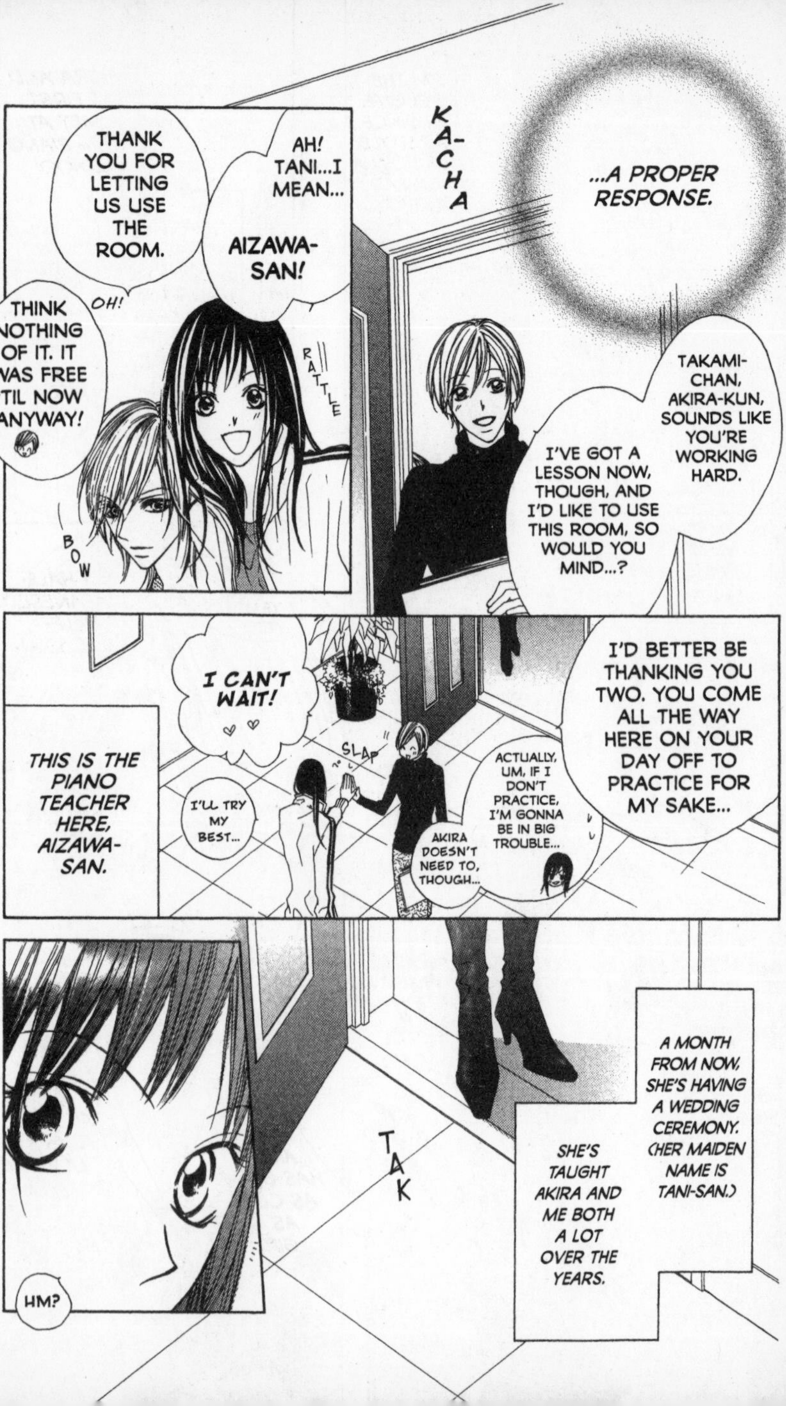
...A PROPER RESPONSE.
KA-CHA
TAKAMI-CHAN, AKIRA-KUN, SOUNDS LIKE YOU'RE WORKING HARD.
I'VE GOT A LESSON NOW, THOUGH, AND I'D LIKE TO USE THIS ROOM, SO WOULD YOU MIND...?
AH! TANI...I MEAN... AIZAWA-SAN!
RATTLE
THANK YOU FOR LETTING US USE THE ROOM.
OH!
THINK NOTHING OF IT. IT WAS FREE 'TIL NOW ANYWAY!
BOW
I'D BETTER BE THANKING YOU TWO. YOU COME ALL THE WAY HERE ON YOUR DAY OFF TO PRACTICE FOR MY SAKE...
ACTUALLY, UM, IF I DON'T PRACTICE, I'M GONNA BE IN BIG TROUBLE...
AKIRA DOESN'T NEED TO, THOUGH...
I CAN'T WAIT!
SLAP
I'LL TRY MY BEST...
THIS IS THE PIANO TEACHER HERE, AIZAWA-SAN.
A MONTH FROM NOW, SHE'S HAVING A WEDDING CEREMONY. (HER MAIDEN NAME IS TANI-SAN.)
SHE'S TAUGHT AKIRA AND ME BOTH A LOT OVER THE YEARS.
TAK
HM?

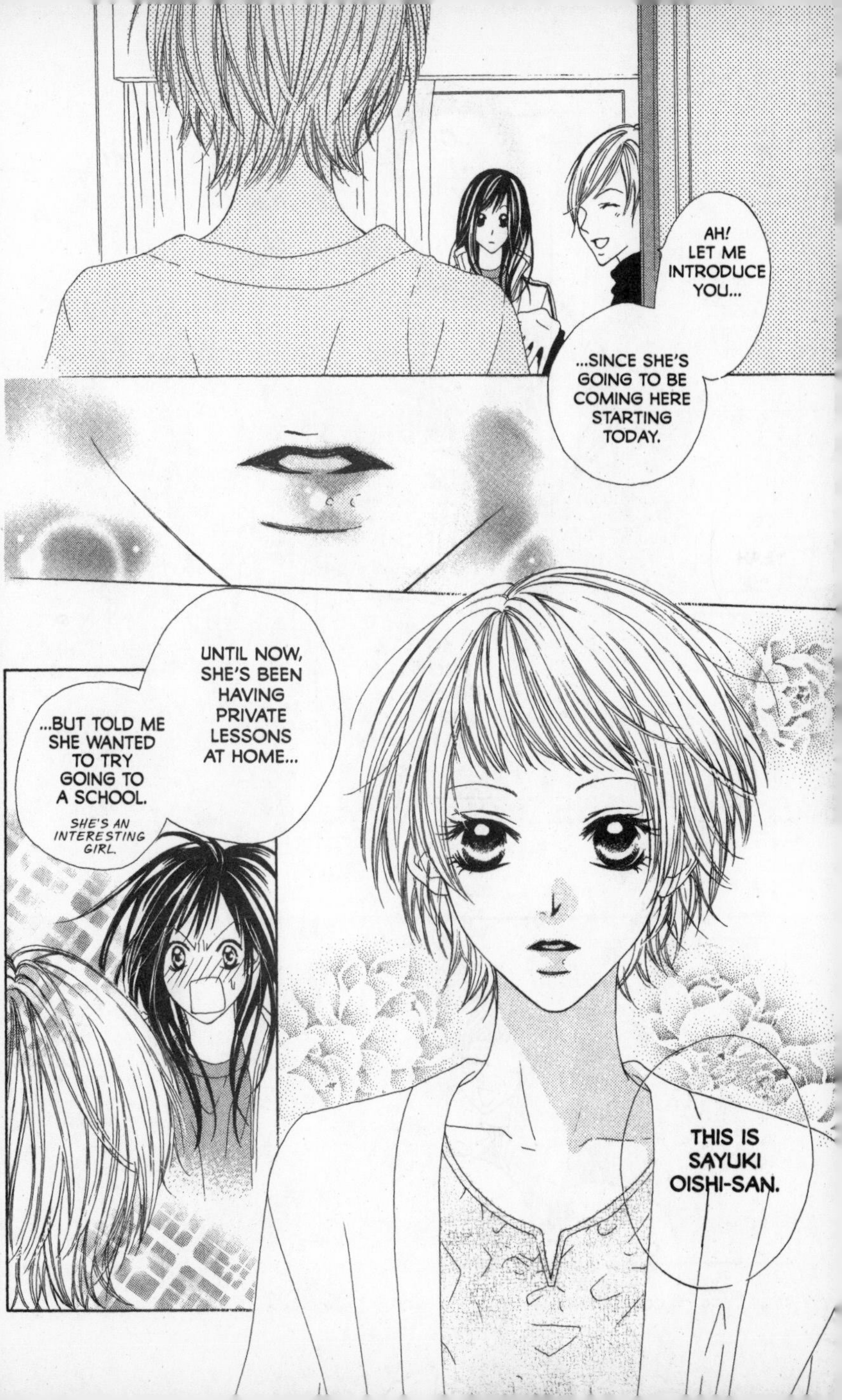
AH! LET ME INTRODUCE YOU...
...SINCE SHE'S GOING TO BE COMING HERE STARTING TODAY.
THIS IS SAYUKI OISHI-SAN.
UNTIL NOW, SHE'S BEEN HAVING PRIVATE LESSONS AT HOME...
...BUT TOLD ME SHE WANTED TO TRY GOING TO A SCHOOL.
SHE'S AN INTERESTING GIRL.

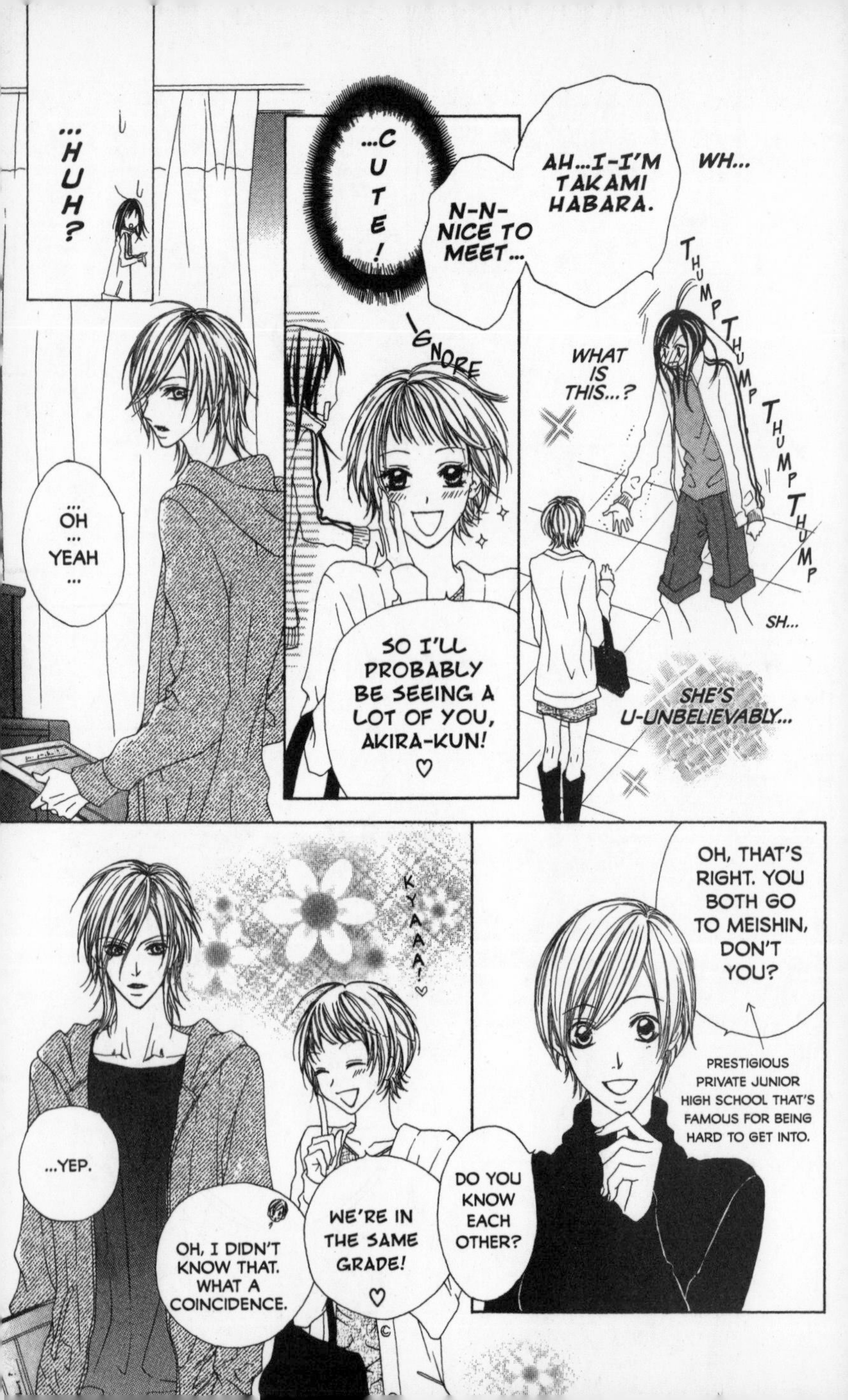
WH...
AH...I-I'M TAKAMI HABARA.
THUMP THUMP THUMP THUMP
WHAT IS THIS...?
SH...
SHE'S U-UNBELIEVABLY...
...CUTE!
N-N-NICE TO MEET...
IGNORE
SO I'LL PROBABLY BE SEEING A LOT OF YOU, AKIRA-KUN! ♡
...HUH?
...OH...YEAH...
OH, THAT'S RIGHT. YOU BOTH GO TO MEISHIN, DON'T YOU?
PRESTIGIOUS PRIVATE JUNIOR HIGH SCHOOL THAT'S FAMOUS FOR BEING HARD TO GET INTO.
DO YOU KNOW EACH OTHER?
KYAAA! ♡
WE'RE IN THE SAME GRADE! ♡
OH, I DIDN'T KNOW THAT. WHAT A COINCIDENCE.
...YEP.

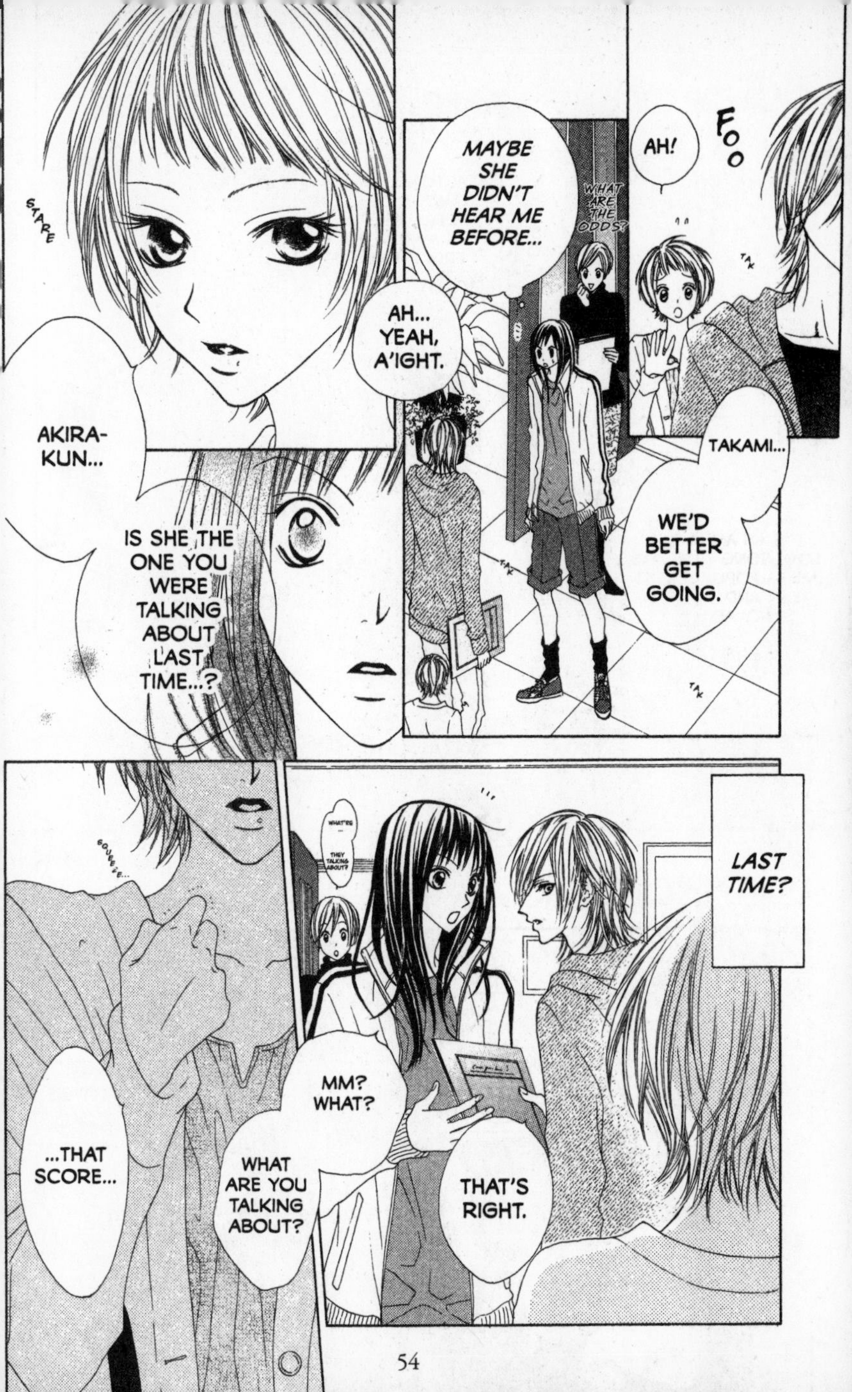
AH!
FOO
TAK
TAKAMI...
WE'D BETTER GET GOING.
TAK
TAK
STARE
AKIRA-KUN...
MAYBE SHE DIDN'T HEAR ME BEFORE...
WHAT ARE THE ODDS?
AH... YEAH, A'IGHT.
IS SHE THE ONE YOU WERE TALKING ABOUT LAST TIME...?
LAST TIME?
WHAT'RE ... THEY TALKING ABOUT?
MM? WHAT?
THAT'S RIGHT.
WHAT ARE YOU TALKING ABOUT?
SQUEEZE...
...THAT SCORE...

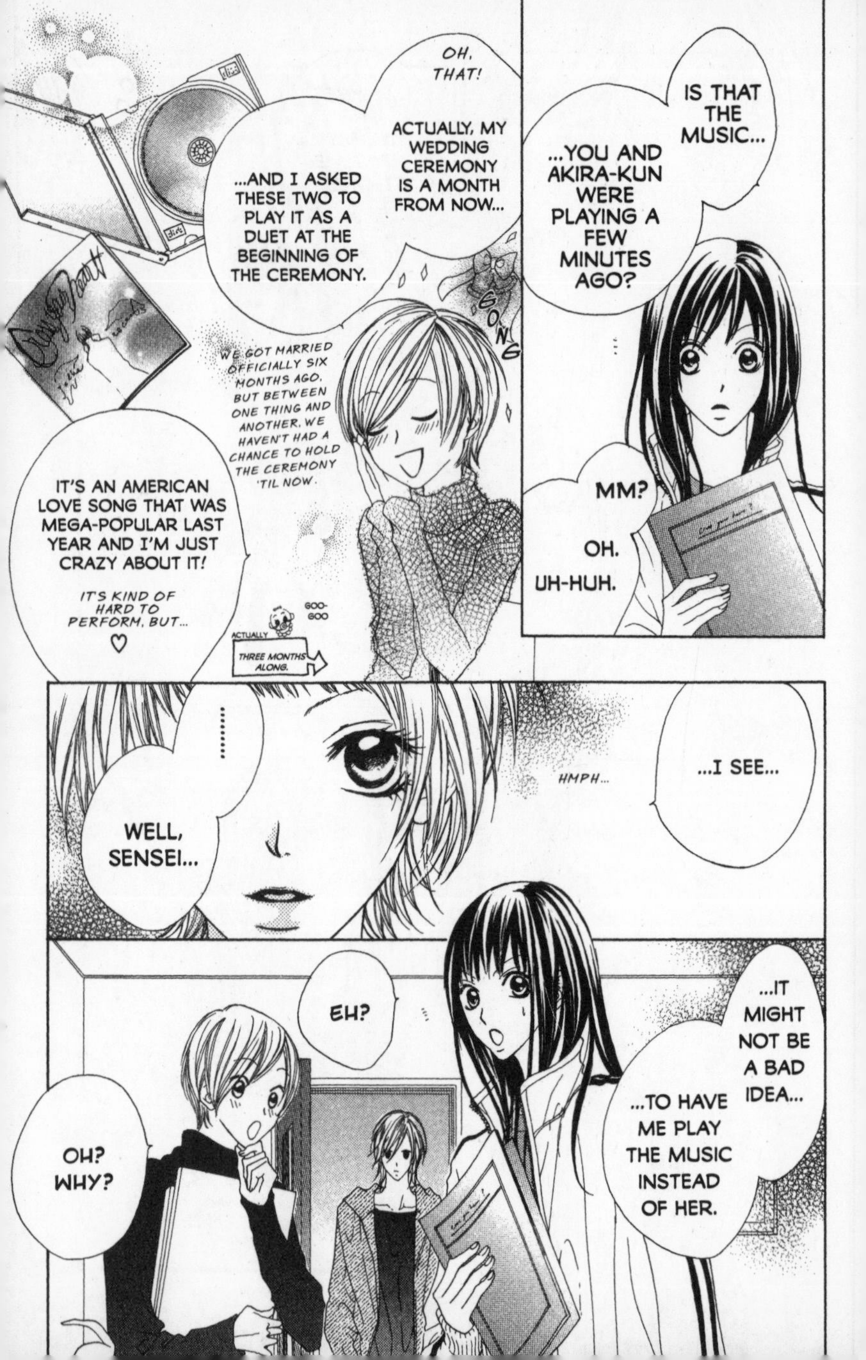
IS THAT THE MUSIC...
...YOU AND AKIRA-KUN WERE PLAYING A FEW MINUTES AGO?
MM?
OH.
UH-HUH.
OH, THAT!
ACTUALLY, MY WEDDING CEREMONY IS A MONTH FROM NOW...
...AND I ASKED THESE TWO TO PLAY IT AS A DUET AT THE BEGINNING OF THE CEREMONY.
GONG
WE GOT MARRIED OFFICIALLY SIX MONTHS AGO, BUT BETWEEN ONE THING AND ANOTHER, WE HAVEN'T HAD A CHANCE TO HOLD THE CEREMONY 'TIL NOW.
IT'S AN AMERICAN LOVE SONG THAT WAS MEGA-POPULAR LAST YEAR AND I'M JUST CRAZY ABOUT IT!
IT'S KIND OF HARD TO PERFORM, BUT... ♡
GOO-GOO
ACTUALLY
THREE MONTHS ALONG.
...I SEE...
HMPH...
....
WELL, SENSEI...
...IT MIGHT NOT BE A BAD IDEA...
...TO HAVE ME PLAY THE MUSIC INSTEAD OF HER.
EH?
OH? WHY?

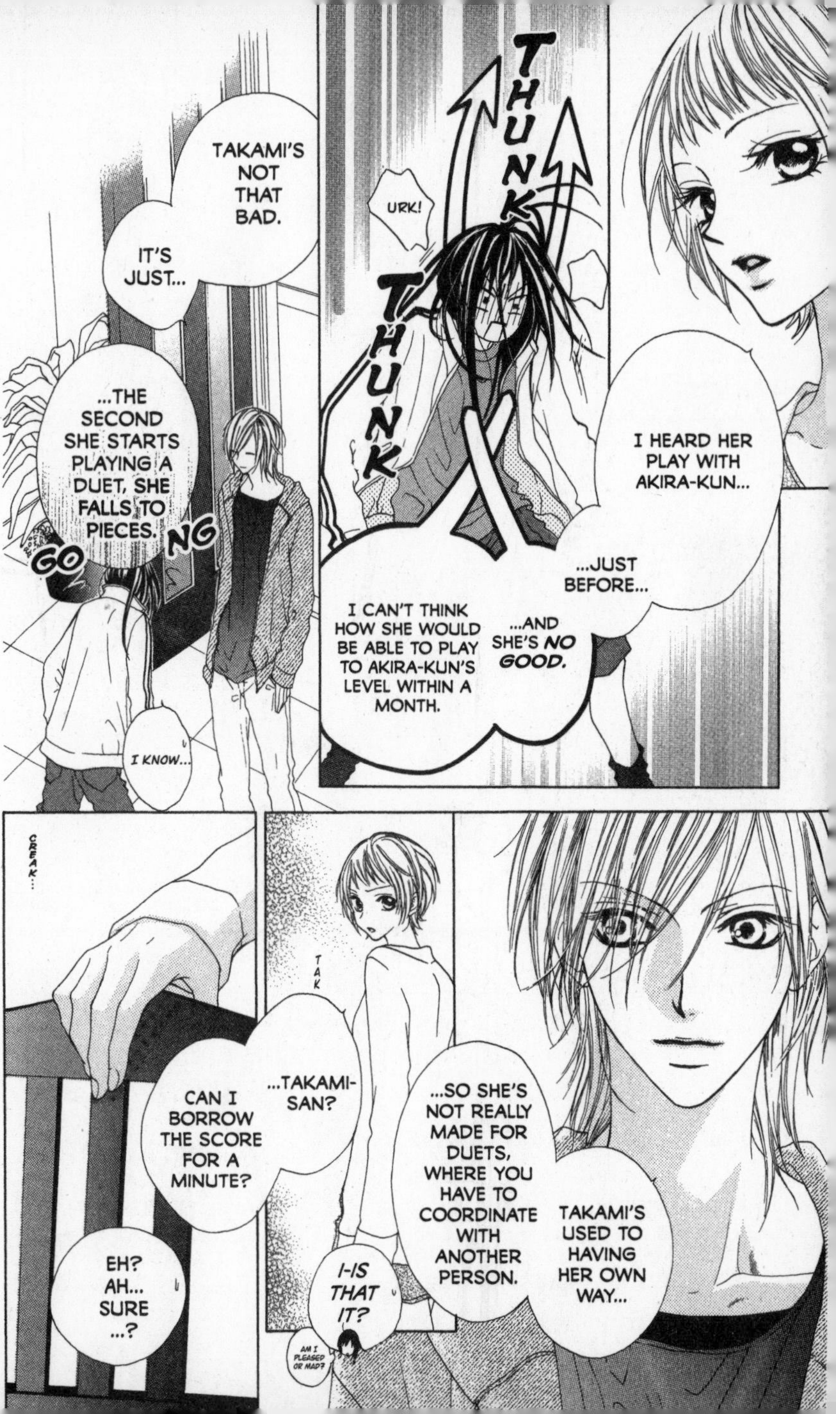
I HEARD HER PLAY WITH AKIRA-KUN...
...JUST BEFORE...
...AND SHE'S NO GOOD.
I CAN'T THINK HOW SHE WOULD BE ABLE TO PLAY TO AKIRA-KUN'S LEVEL WITHIN A MONTH.
THUNK
THUNK
URK!
TAKAMI'S NOT THAT BAD.
IT'S JUST...
...THE SECOND SHE STARTS PLAYING A DUET, SHE FALLS TO PIECES.
GONG
I KNOW...
TAKAMI'S USED TO HAVING HER OWN WAY...
...SO SHE'S NOT REALLY MADE FOR DUETS, WHERE YOU HAVE TO COORDINATE WITH ANOTHER PERSON.
TAK
I-IS THAT IT?
AM I PLEASED OR MAD?
...TAKAMI-SAN?
CAN I BORROW THE SCORE FOR A MINUTE?
CREAK...
EH? AH... SURE ...?

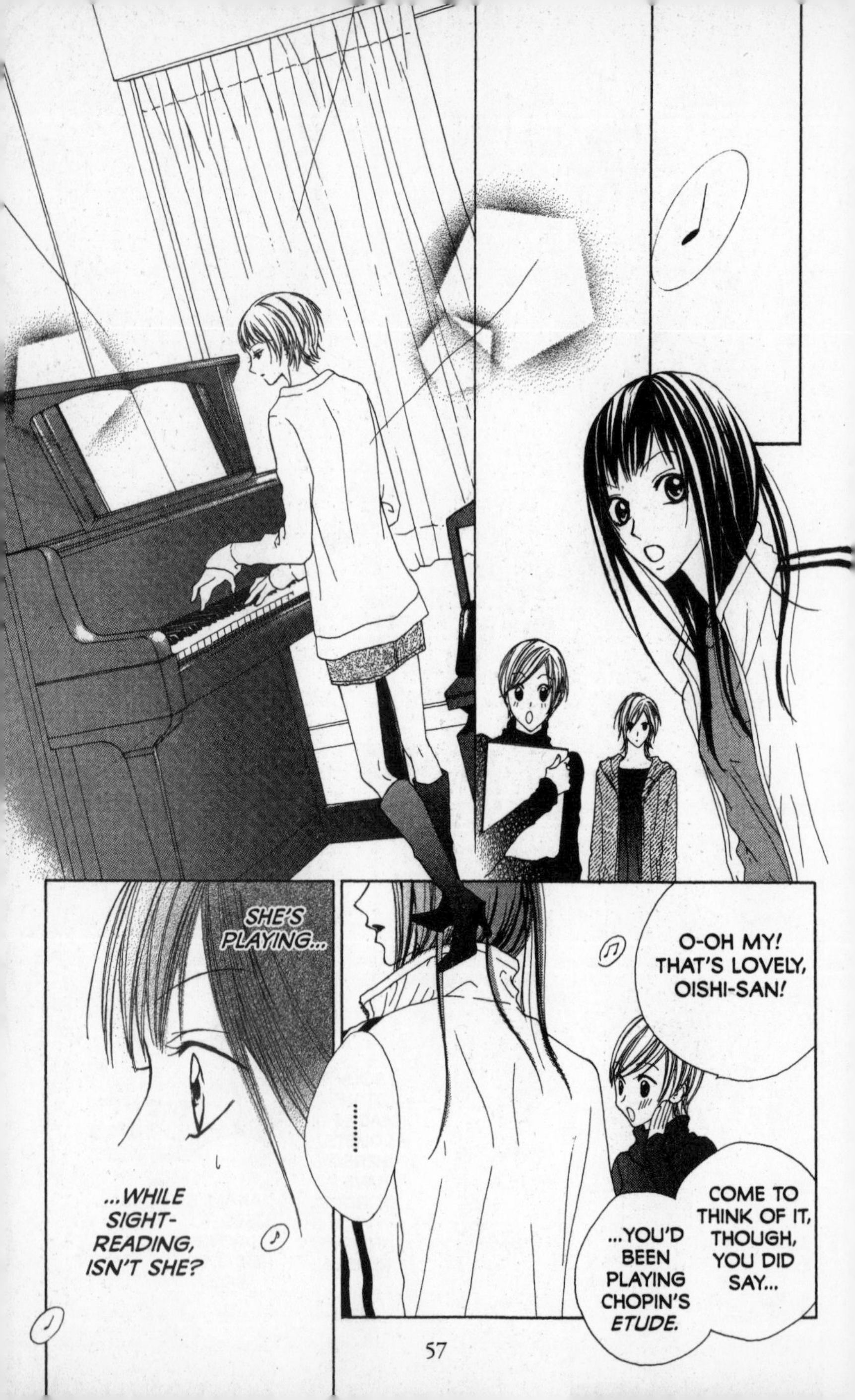
O-OH MY! THAT'S LOVELY, OISHI-SAN!
COME TO THINK OF IT, THOUGH, YOU DID SAY...
...YOU'D BEEN PLAYING CHOPIN'S *ETUDE.*
......
SHE'S PLAYING...
...WHILE SIGHT-READING, ISN'T SHE?

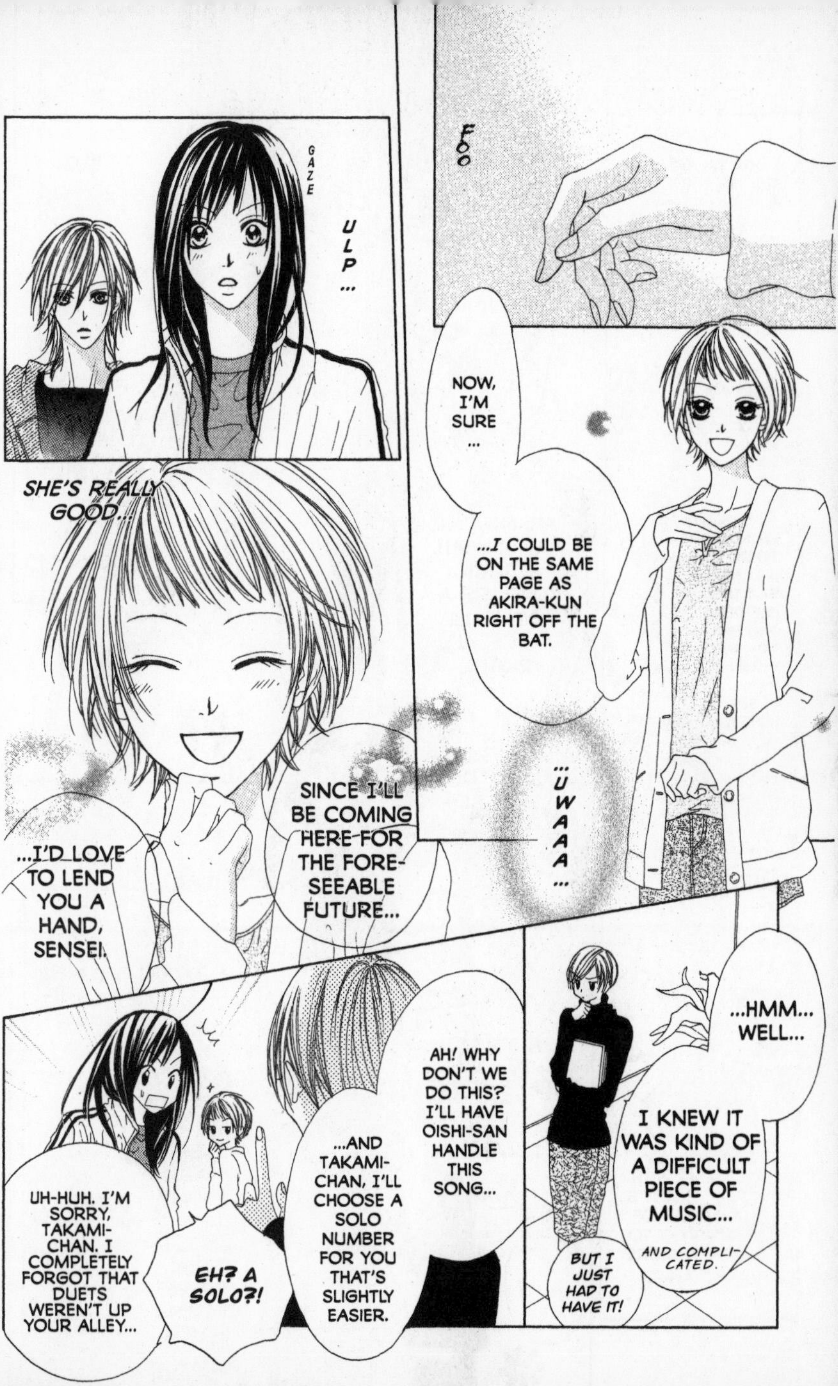
FOO
GAZE
ULP...
NOW, I'M SURE...
...I COULD BE ON THE SAME PAGE AS AKIRA-KUN RIGHT OFF THE BAT.
...UWAAAA...
SHE'S REALLY GOOD...
SINCE I'LL BE COMING HERE FOR THE FORE-SEEABLE FUTURE...
...I'D LOVE TO LEND YOU A HAND, SENSEI.
...HMM... WELL...
I KNEW IT WAS KIND OF A DIFFICULT PIECE OF MUSIC...
AND COMPLI-CATED.
BUT I JUST HAD TO HAVE IT!
AH! WHY DON'T WE DO THIS? I'LL HAVE OISHI-SAN HANDLE THIS SONG...
...AND TAKAMI-CHAN, I'LL CHOOSE A SOLO NUMBER FOR YOU THAT'S SLIGHTLY EASIER.
EH? A SOLO?!
UH-HUH. I'M SORRY, TAKAMI-CHAN. I COMPLETELY FORGOT THAT DUETS WEREN'T UP YOUR ALLEY...

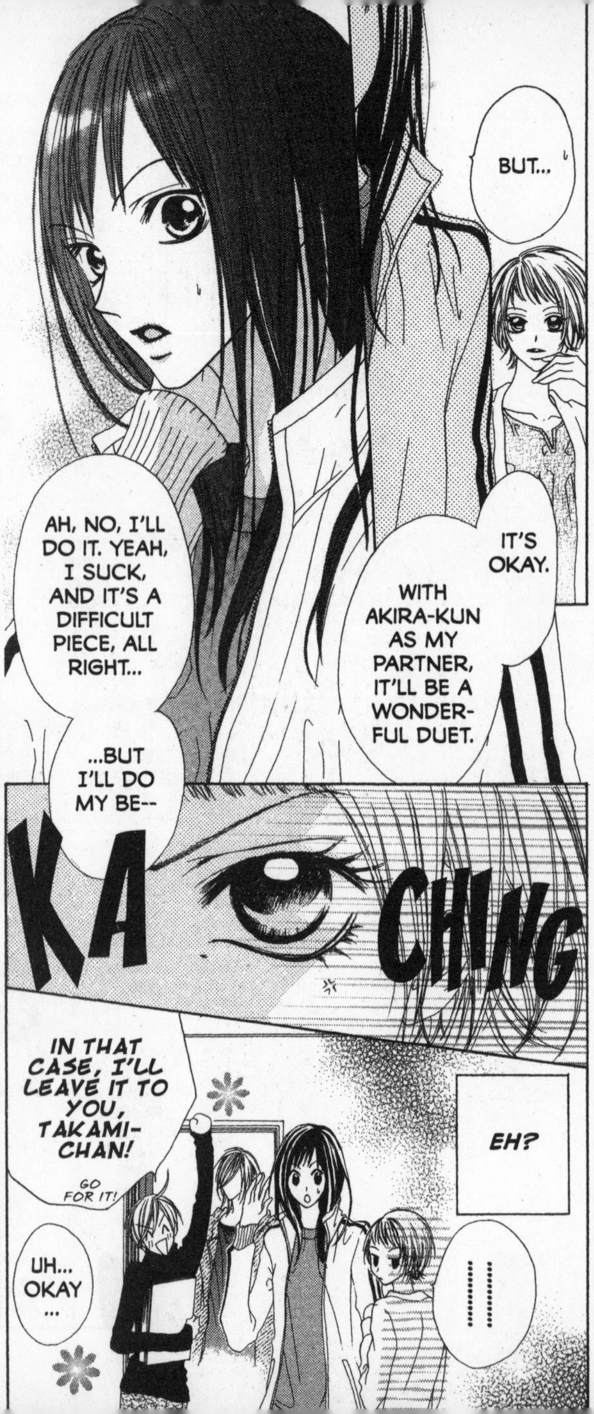
BUT...
IT'S OKAY.
WITH AKIRA-KUN AS MY PARTNER, IT'LL BE A WONDER-FUL DUET.
AH, NO, I'LL DO IT. YEAH, I SUCK, AND IT'S A DIFFICULT PIECE, ALL RIGHT...
...BUT I'LL DO MY BE--
KA CHING
IN THAT CASE, I'LL LEAVE IT TO YOU, TAKAMI-CHAN!
GO FOR IT!
EH?
!!......
UH... OKAY ...

2

I WAS THRILLED THE FIRST TIME I GOT TO WORK IN COLOR (THE PREVIEW CUT), BUT IT'D BEEN YEARS SINCE I PAINTED WITH COLORS, SO I WAS ALSO PRETTY NERVOUS. THE ART TOOLS I'D USED BACK IN JUNIOR HIGH (AND STILL HAD) WERE KIND OF HARDENED AFTER YEARS OF NON-USE, SO I WONDERED WHAT TO DO (DUH...GO BUY NEW STUFF), BUT THEN I SUDDENLY REMEMBERED MY YOUNGER SISTER HAD NICE, NEWER PAINTING SUPPLIES. I BORROW THEM, PAINTED...AND THEN HELD ON TO THE PAINTS.(HEY!) IN FACT, I USED THESE PAINTS TO COLOR THE ART ON THE INSIDE FLAP. THE NEXT DAY, MY EDITOR, WHO FELT SORRY FOR ME, CALLED TO SAY...

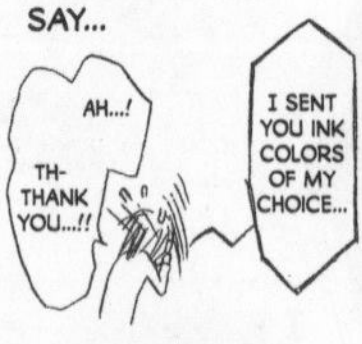
I SENT YOU INK COLORS OF MY CHOICE...
AH...!
TH-THANK YOU...!!

IT'S REALLY DIFFICULT WORKING WITH COLOR, BUT IT'S ALSO A LOT OF FUN. I WANT TO PRACTICE MORE WITH IT.

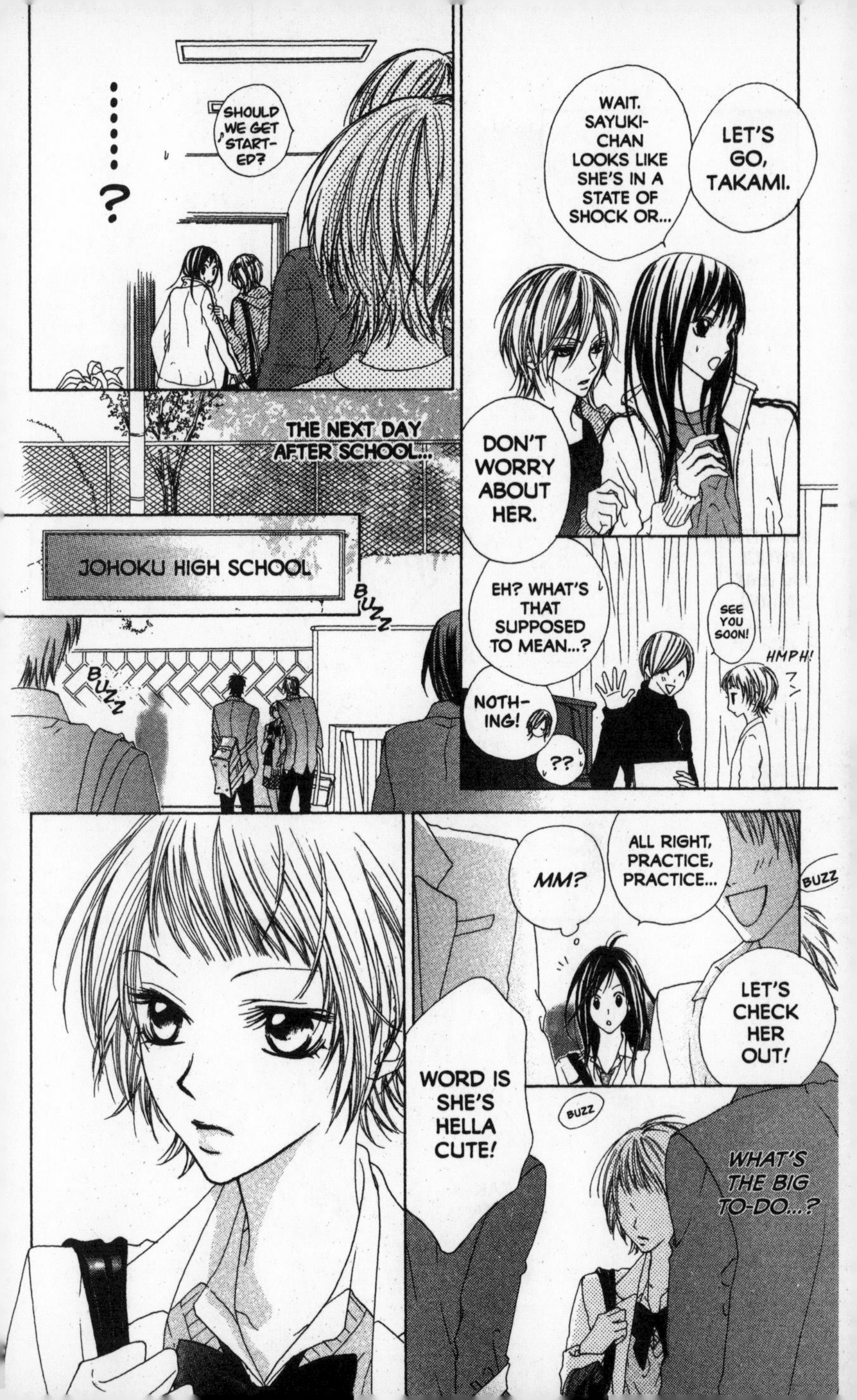
LET'S GO, TAKAMI.
WAIT. SAYUKI-CHAN LOOKS LIKE SHE'S IN A STATE OF SHOCK OR...
DON'T WORRY ABOUT HER.
EH? WHAT'S THAT SUPPOSED TO MEAN...?
SEE YOU SOON!
HMPH!
NOTHING!
??
SHOULD WE GET STARTED?
......?
THE NEXT DAY AFTER SCHOOL...
JOHOKU HIGH SCHOOL
BUZZ
BUZZ
BUZZ
ALL RIGHT, PRACTICE, PRACTICE...
MM?
LET'S CHECK HER OUT!
WORD IS SHE'S HELLA CUTE!
BUZZ
WHAT'S THE BIG TO-DO...?

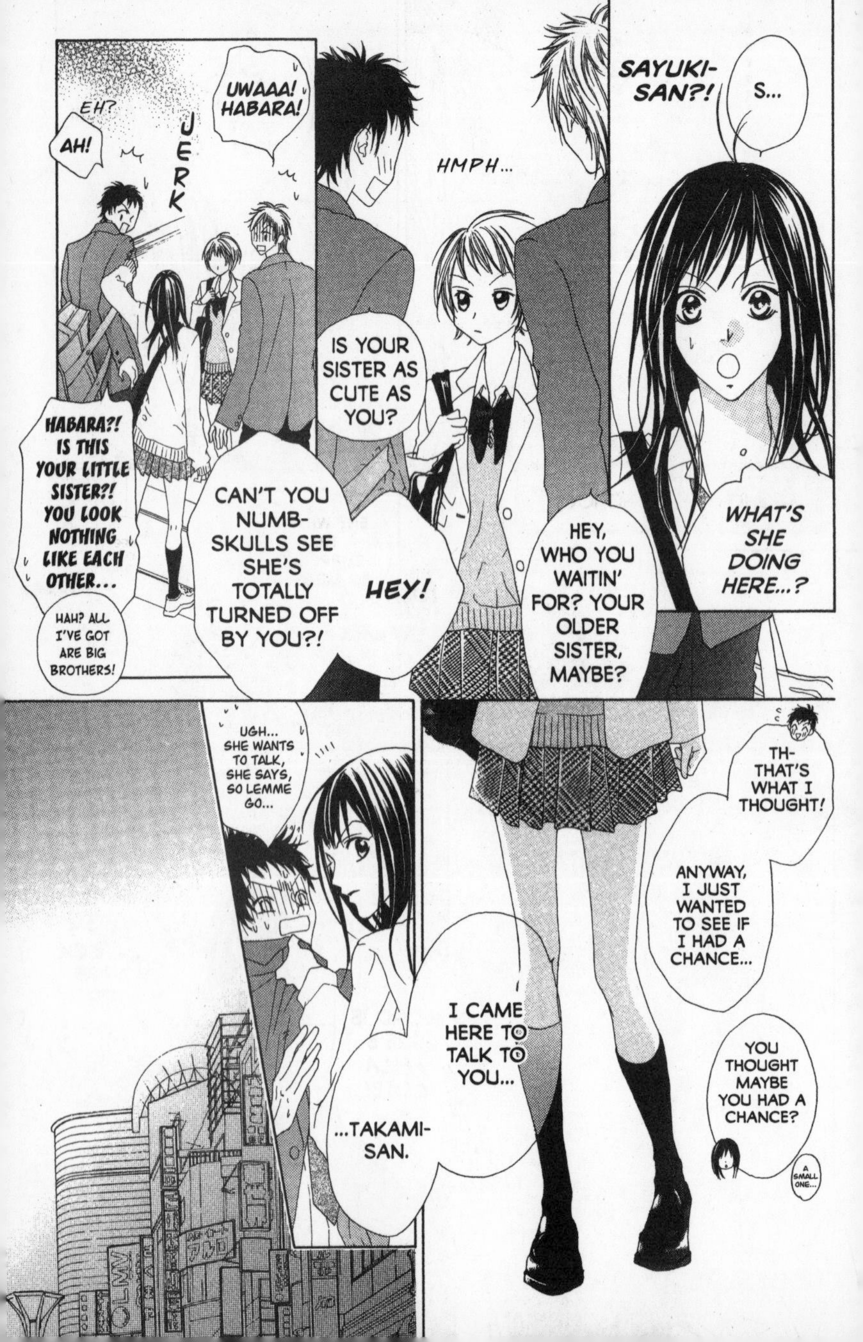
S...
SAYUKI-SAN?!
WHAT'S SHE DOING HERE...?
HMPH...
HEY, WHO YOU WAITIN' FOR? YOUR OLDER SISTER, MAYBE?
IS YOUR SISTER AS CUTE AS YOU?
HEY!
CAN'T YOU NUMB-SKULLS SEE SHE'S TOTALLY TURNED OFF BY YOU?!
UWAAA! HABARA!
JERK
EH?
AH!
HABARA?! IS THIS YOUR LITTLE SISTER?! YOU LOOK NOTHING LIKE EACH OTHER...
HAH? ALL I'VE GOT ARE BIG BROTHERS!
TH-THAT'S WHAT I THOUGHT!
ANYWAY, I JUST WANTED TO SEE IF I HAD A CHANCE...
YOU THOUGHT MAYBE YOU HAD A CHANCE?
A SMALL ONE...
I CAME HERE TO TALK TO YOU...
...TAKAMI-SAN.
UGH... SHE WANTS TO TALK, SHE SAYS, SO LEMME GO...

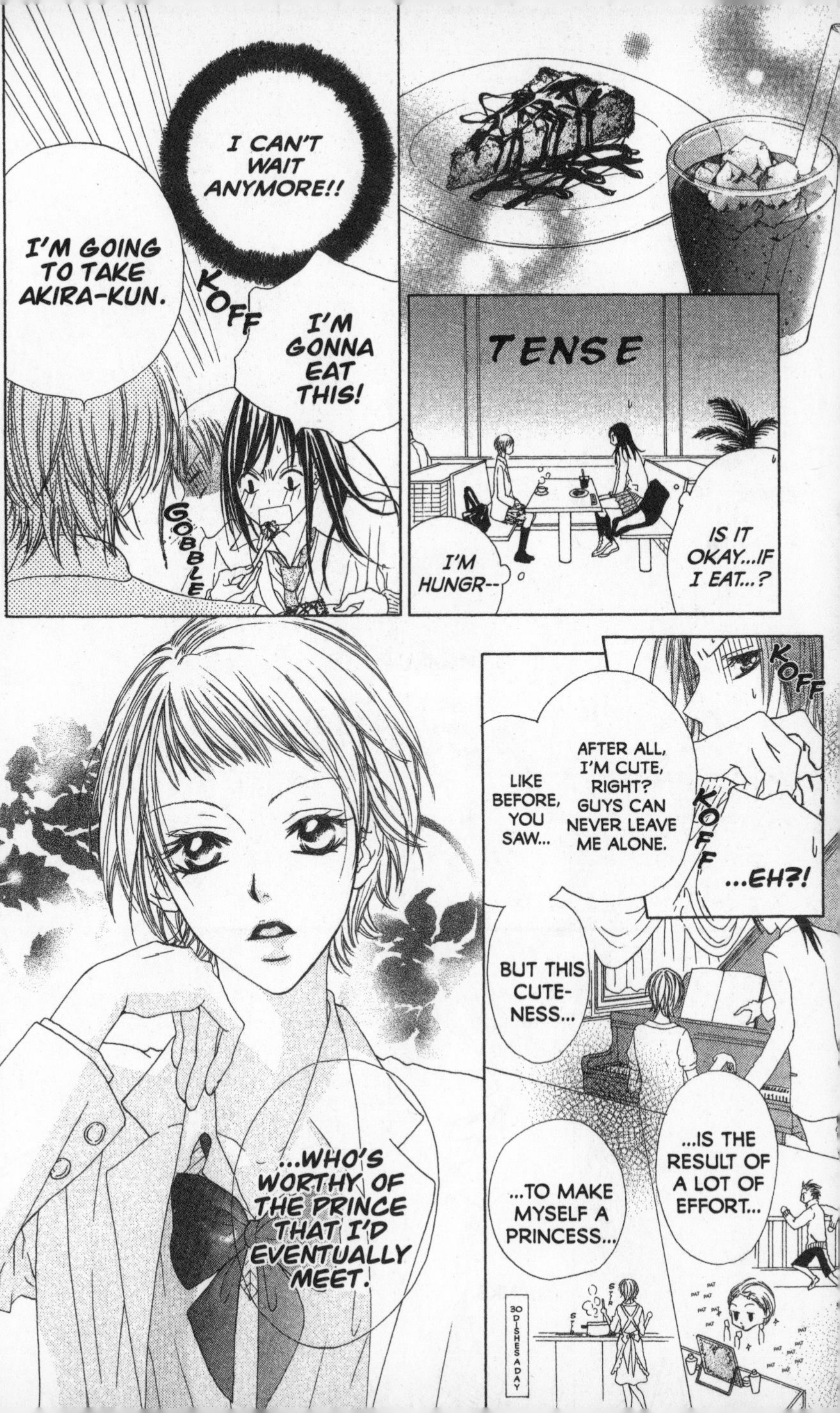
TENSE
IS IT OKAY...IF I EAT...?
I'M HUNGR--
I CAN'T WAIT ANYMORE!!
I'M GONNA EAT THIS!
KOFF
I'M GOING TO TAKE AKIRA-KUN.
GOBBLE
KOFF
KOFF
...EH?!
AFTER ALL, I'M CUTE, RIGHT? GUYS CAN NEVER LEAVE ME ALONE.
LIKE BEFORE, YOU SAW...
BUT THIS CUTENESS...
...IS THE RESULT OF A LOT OF EFFORT...
...TO MAKE MYSELF A PRINCESS...
30 DISHES A DAY
...WHO'S WORTHY OF THE PRINCE THAT I'D EVENTUALLY MEET.

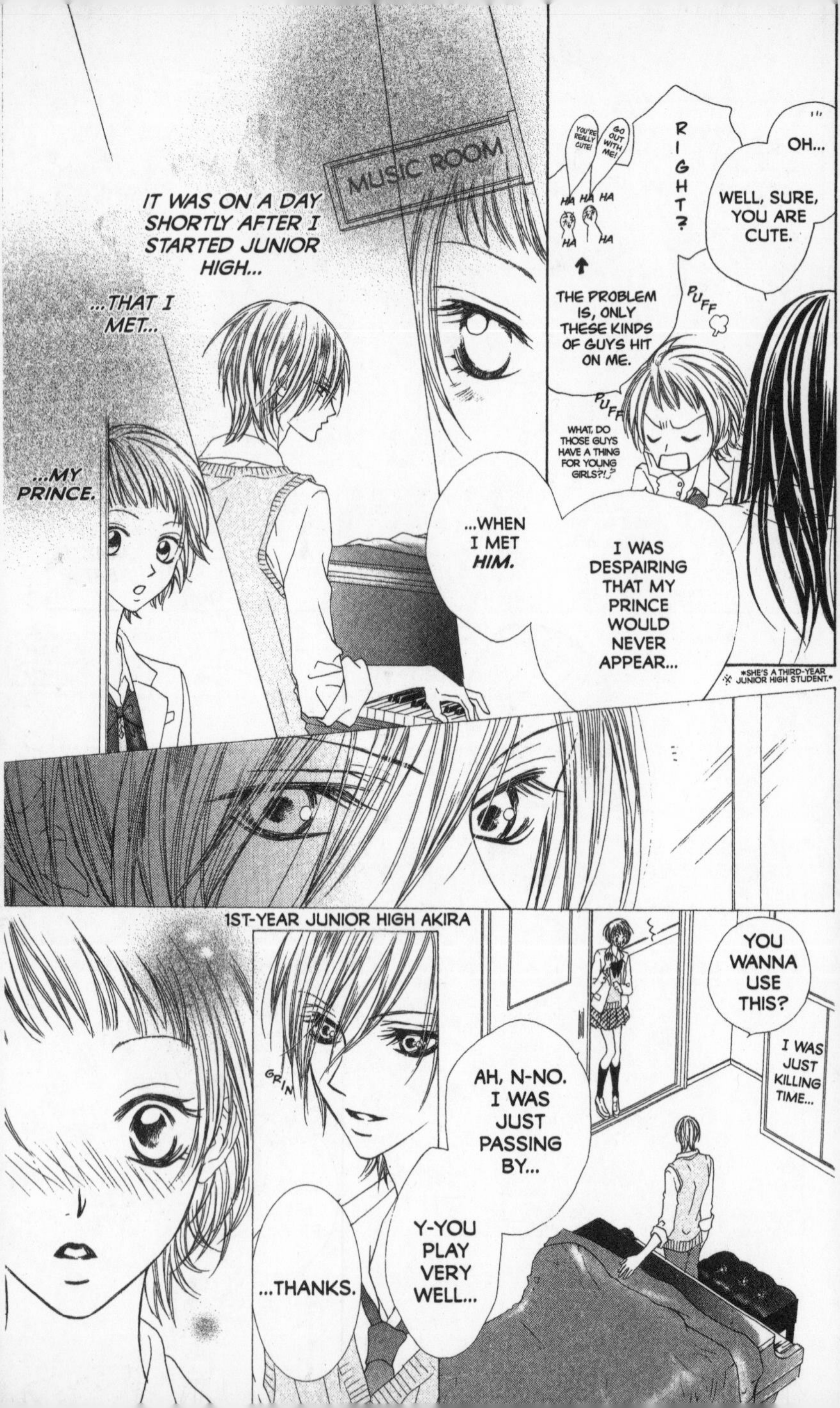
OH...
WELL, SURE, YOU ARE CUTE.
RIGHT?
PUFF
GO OUT WITH ME!
YOU'RE REALLY CUTE!
HA HA HA
HA HA
THE PROBLEM IS, ONLY THESE KINDS OF GUYS HIT ON ME.
PUFF
WHAT, DO THOSE GUYS HAVE A THING FOR YOUNG GIRLS?!
SHE'S A THIRD-YEAR JUNIOR HIGH STUDENT.
I WAS DESPAIRING THAT MY PRINCE WOULD NEVER APPEAR...
...WHEN I MET HIM.
MUSIC ROOM
IT WAS ON A DAY SHORTLY AFTER I STARTED JUNIOR HIGH...
...THAT I MET...
...MY PRINCE.
YOU WANNA USE THIS?
I WAS JUST KILLING TIME...
AH, N-NO. I WAS JUST PASSING BY...
Y-YOU PLAY VERY WELL...
1ST-YEAR JUNIOR HIGH AKIRA
GRIN
...THANKS.

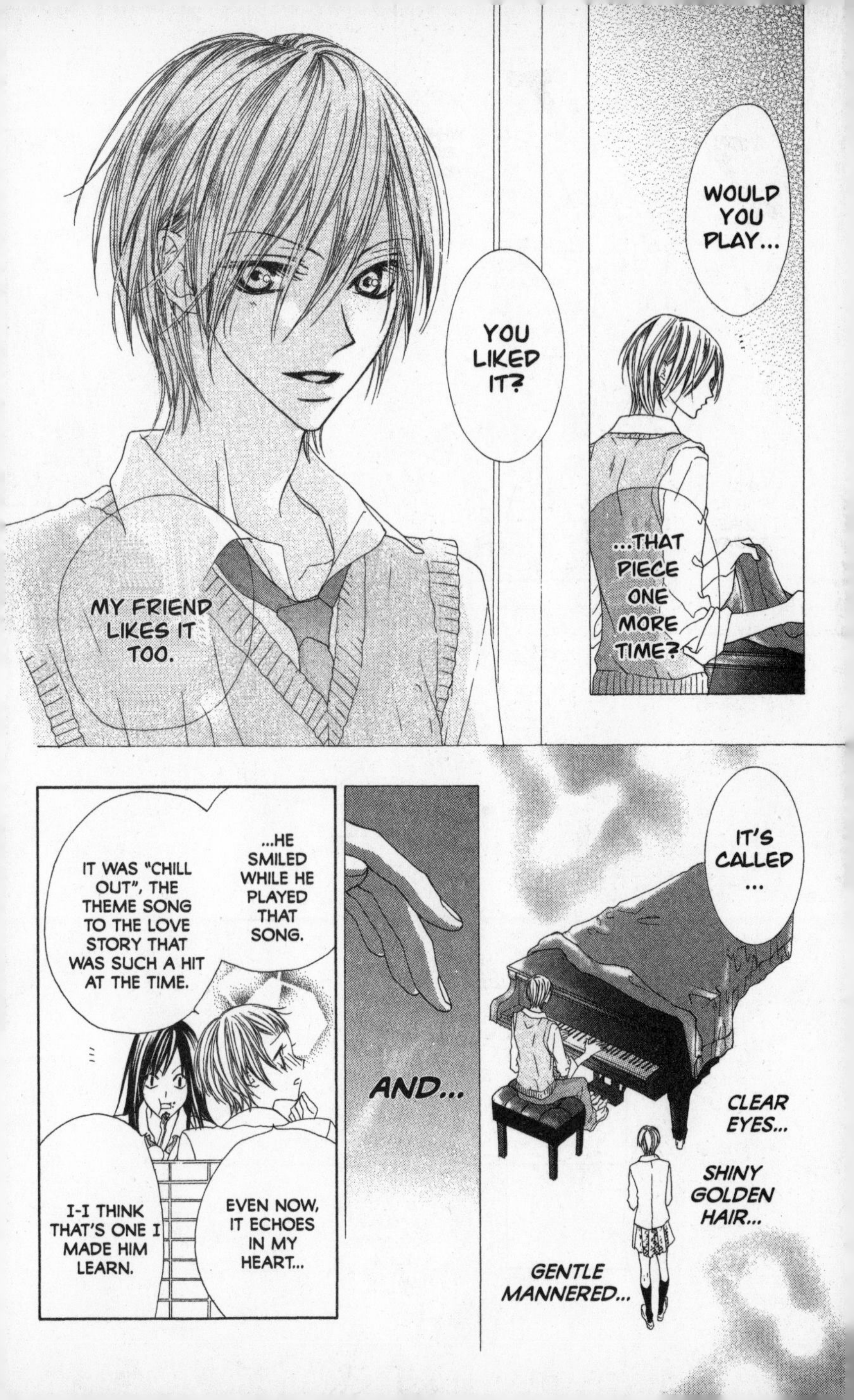
WOULD YOU PLAY...
...THAT PIECE ONE MORE TIME?
YOU LIKED IT?
MY FRIEND LIKES IT TOO.
IT'S CALLED ...
CLEAR EYES...
SHINY GOLDEN HAIR...
GENTLE MANNERED...
AND...
...HE SMILED WHILE HE PLAYED THAT SONG.
IT WAS "CHILL OUT", THE THEME SONG TO THE LOVE STORY THAT WAS SUCH A HIT AT THE TIME.
EVEN NOW, IT ECHOES IN MY HEART...
I-I THINK THAT'S ONE I MADE HIM LEARN.

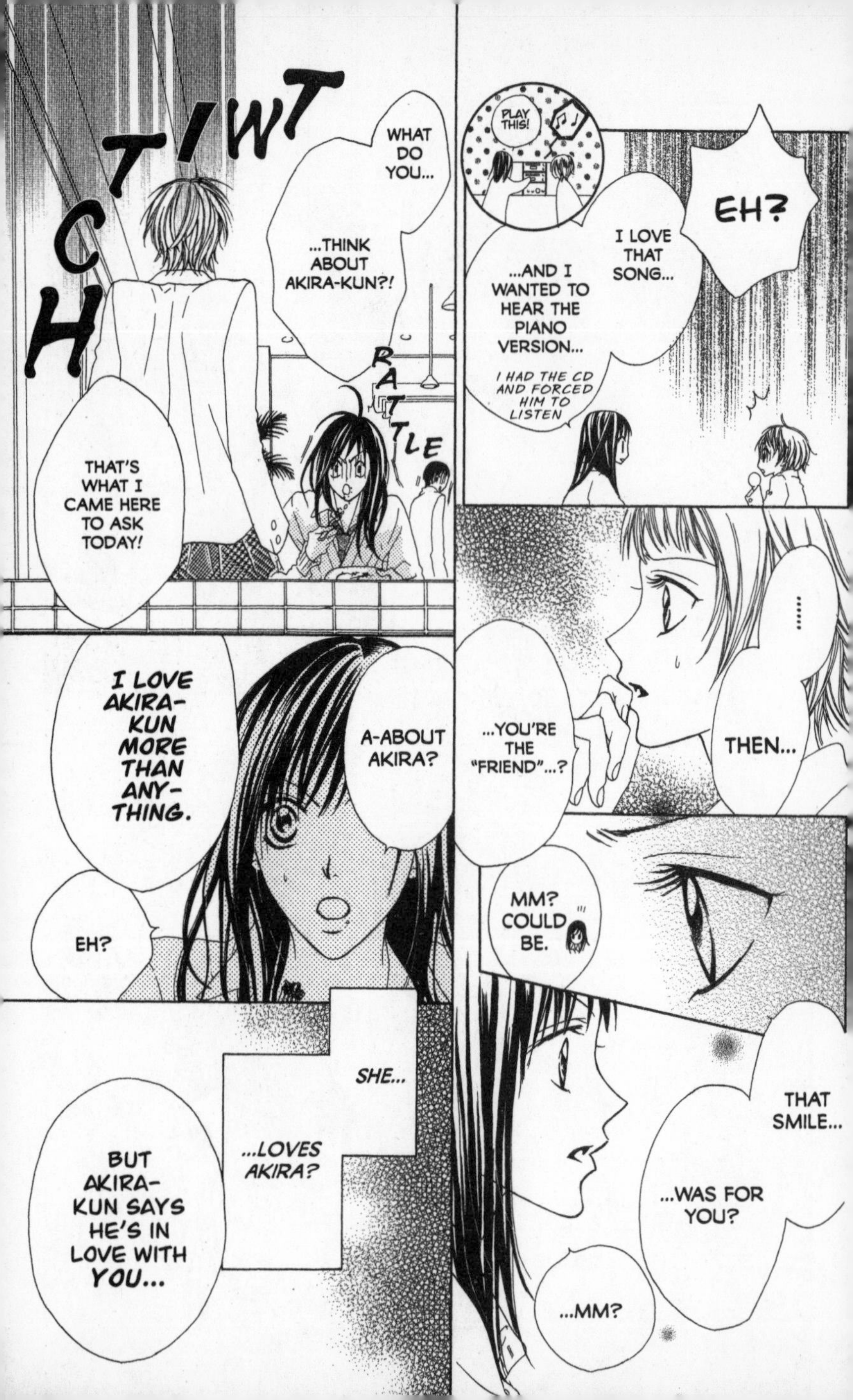
EH?
PLAY THIS!
I LOVE THAT SONG...
...AND I WANTED TO HEAR THE PIANO VERSION...
I HAD THE CD AND FORCED HIM TO LISTEN
......
THEN...
...YOU'RE THE "FRIEND"...?
MM? COULD BE.
THAT SMILE...
...WAS FOR YOU?
...MM?
TWITCH
WHAT DO YOU...
...THINK ABOUT AKIRA-KUN?!
RATTLE
THAT'S WHAT I CAME HERE TO ASK TODAY!
A-ABOUT AKIRA?
I LOVE AKIRA-KUN MORE THAN ANYTHING.
EH?
SHE...
...LOVES AKIRA?
BUT AKIRA-KUN SAYS HE'S IN LOVE WITH YOU...

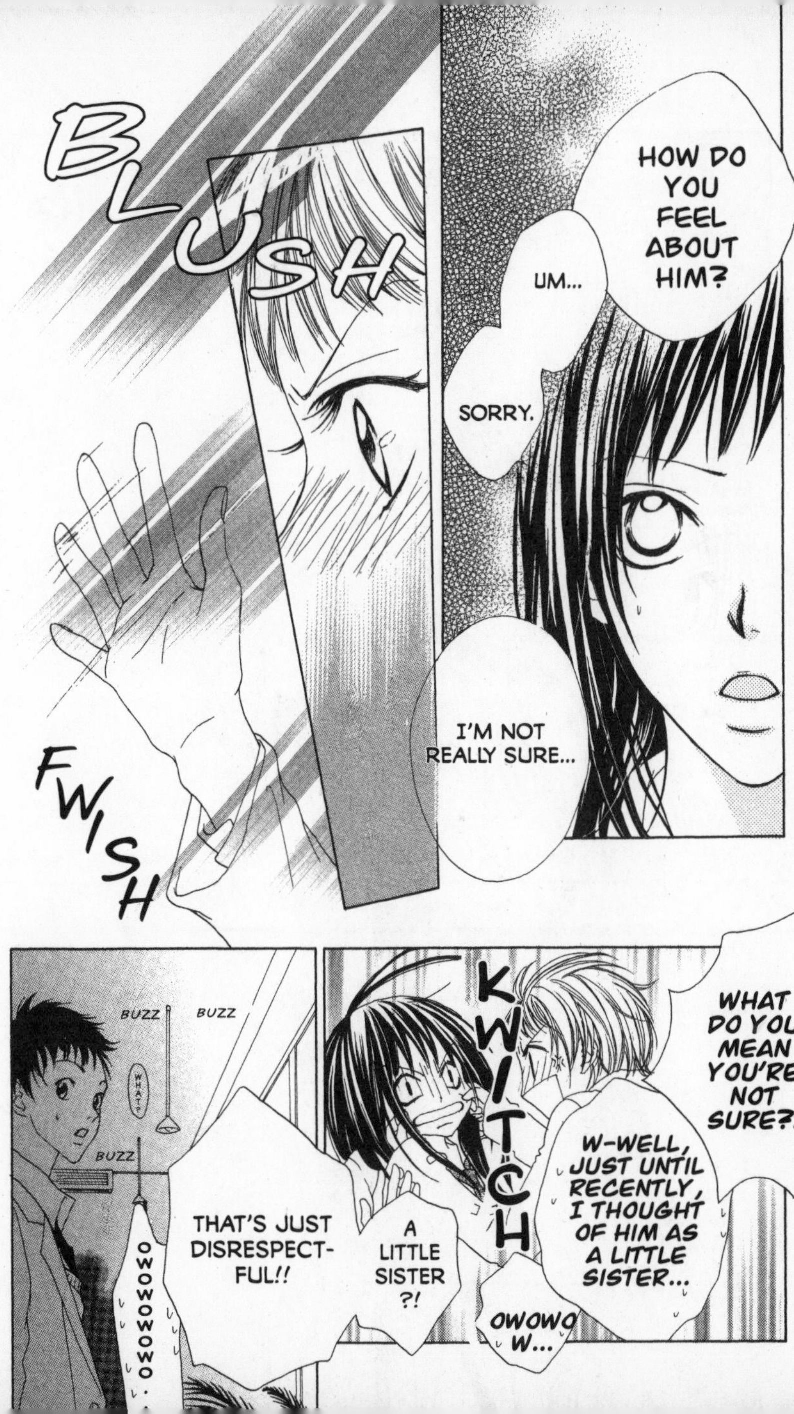
HOW DO YOU FEEL ABOUT HIM?
UM...
SORRY.
I'M NOT REALLY SURE...
BLUSH
FWISH
WHAT DO YOU MEAN YOU'RE NOT SURE?!
KWITCH
W-WELL, JUST UNTIL RECENTLY, I THOUGHT OF HIM AS A LITTLE SISTER...
A LITTLE SISTER?!
OWOWOW...
THAT'S JUST DISRESPECT-FUL!!
BUZZ
BUZZ
WHAT?
BUZZ
OWOWOWOWOWO...

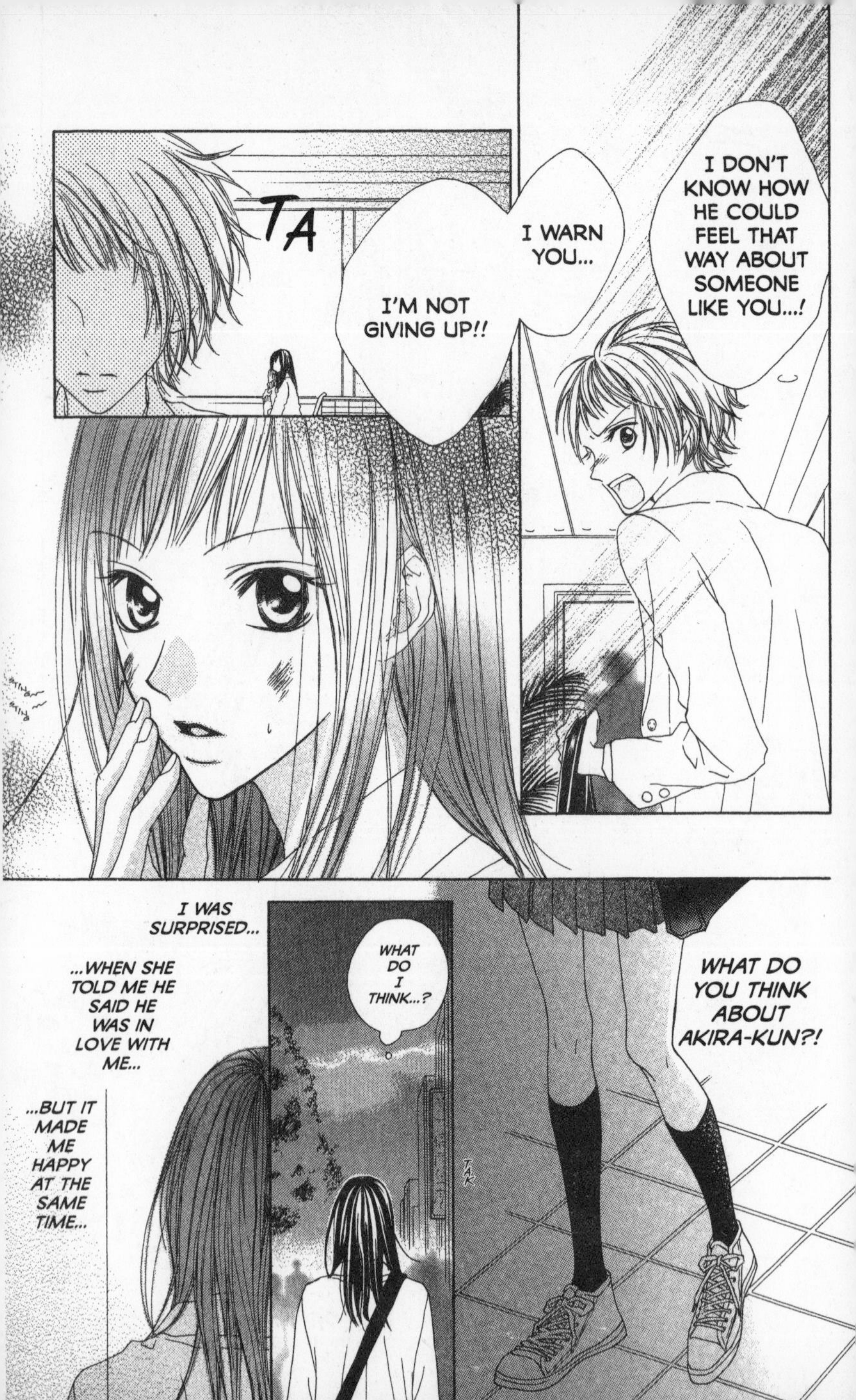
I DON'T KNOW HOW HE COULD FEEL THAT WAY ABOUT SOMEONE LIKE YOU...!
I WARN YOU...
I'M NOT GIVING UP!!
TA
WHAT DO YOU THINK ABOUT AKIRA-KUN?!
TAK
WHAT DO I THINK...?
I WAS SURPRISED...
...WHEN SHE TOLD ME HE SAID HE WAS IN LOVE WITH ME...
...BUT IT MADE ME HAPPY AT THE SAME TIME...

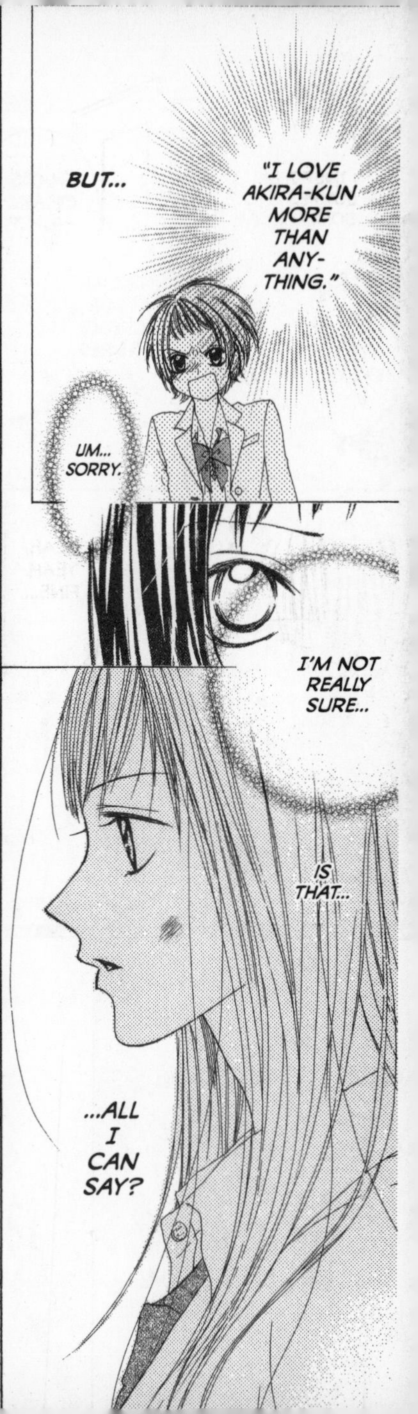
"I LOVE AKIRA-KUN MORE THAN ANY-THING."
BUT...
UM... SORRY.
I'M NOT REALLY SURE...
IS THAT...
...ALL I CAN SAY?
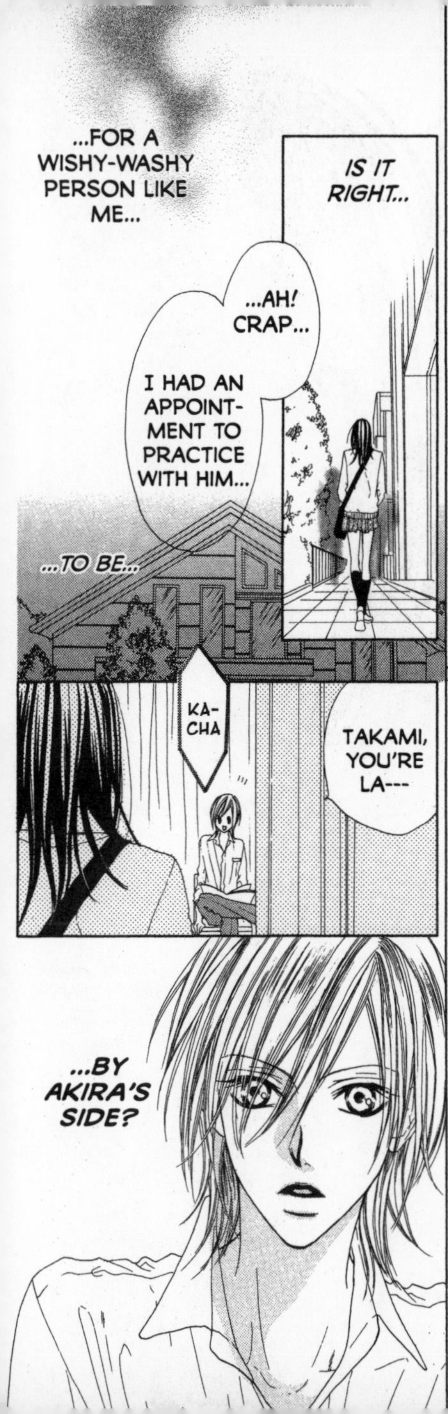
IS IT RIGHT...
...AH! CRAP...
I HAD AN APPOINT-MENT TO PRACTICE WITH HIM...
...FOR A WISHY-WASHY PERSON LIKE ME...
...TO BE...
KA-CHA
TAKAMI, YOU'RE LA---
...BY AKIRA'S SIDE?

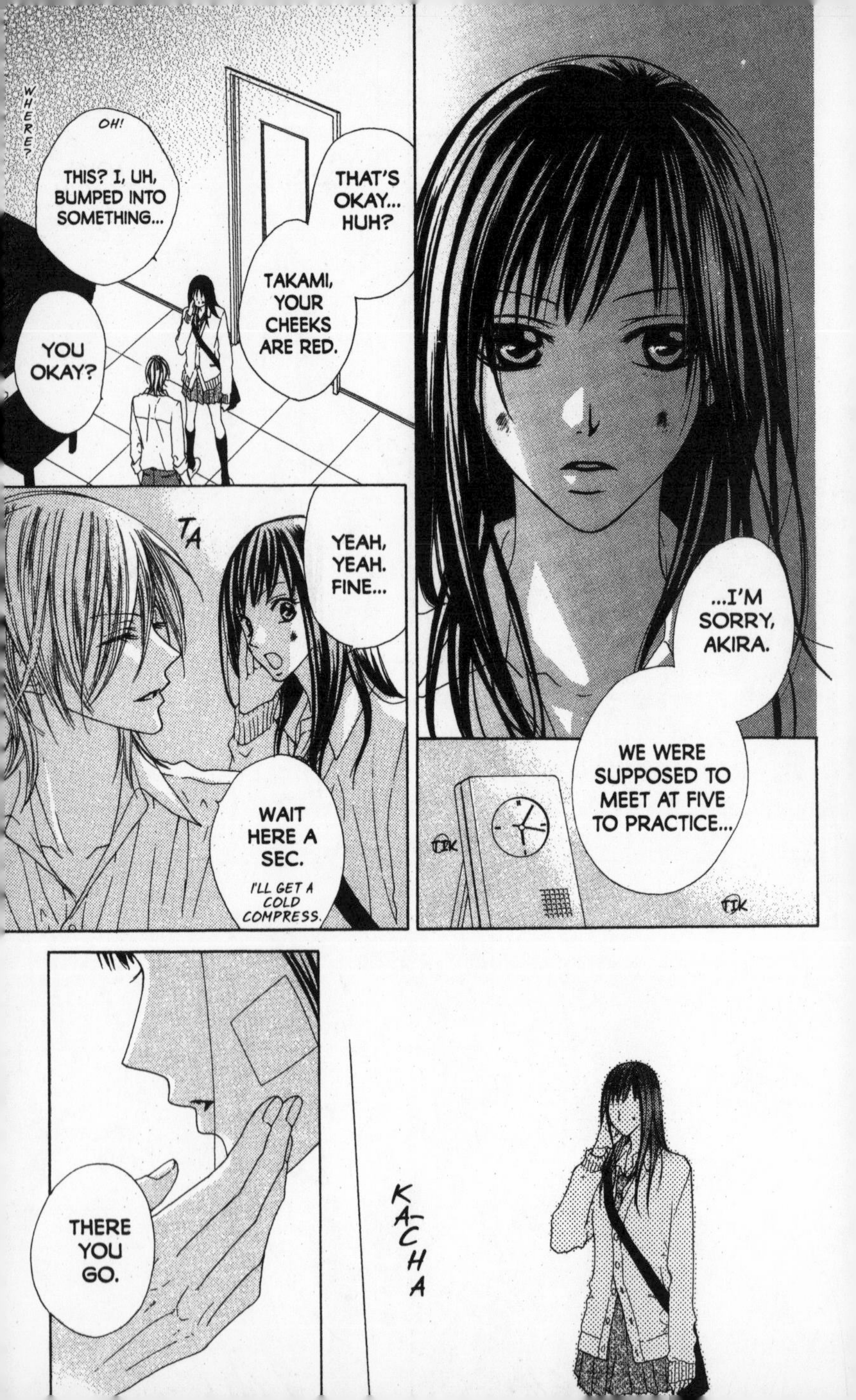
...I'M SORRY, AKIRA.
WE WERE SUPPOSED TO MEET AT FIVE TO PRACTICE...
TIK
TIK
THAT'S OKAY... HUH?
TAKAMI, YOUR CHEEKS ARE RED.
OH!
WHERE?
THIS? I, UH, BUMPED INTO SOMETHING...
YOU OKAY?
YEAH, YEAH. FINE...
TA
WAIT HERE A SEC.
I'LL GET A COLD COMPRESS.
KA-CHA
THERE YOU GO.

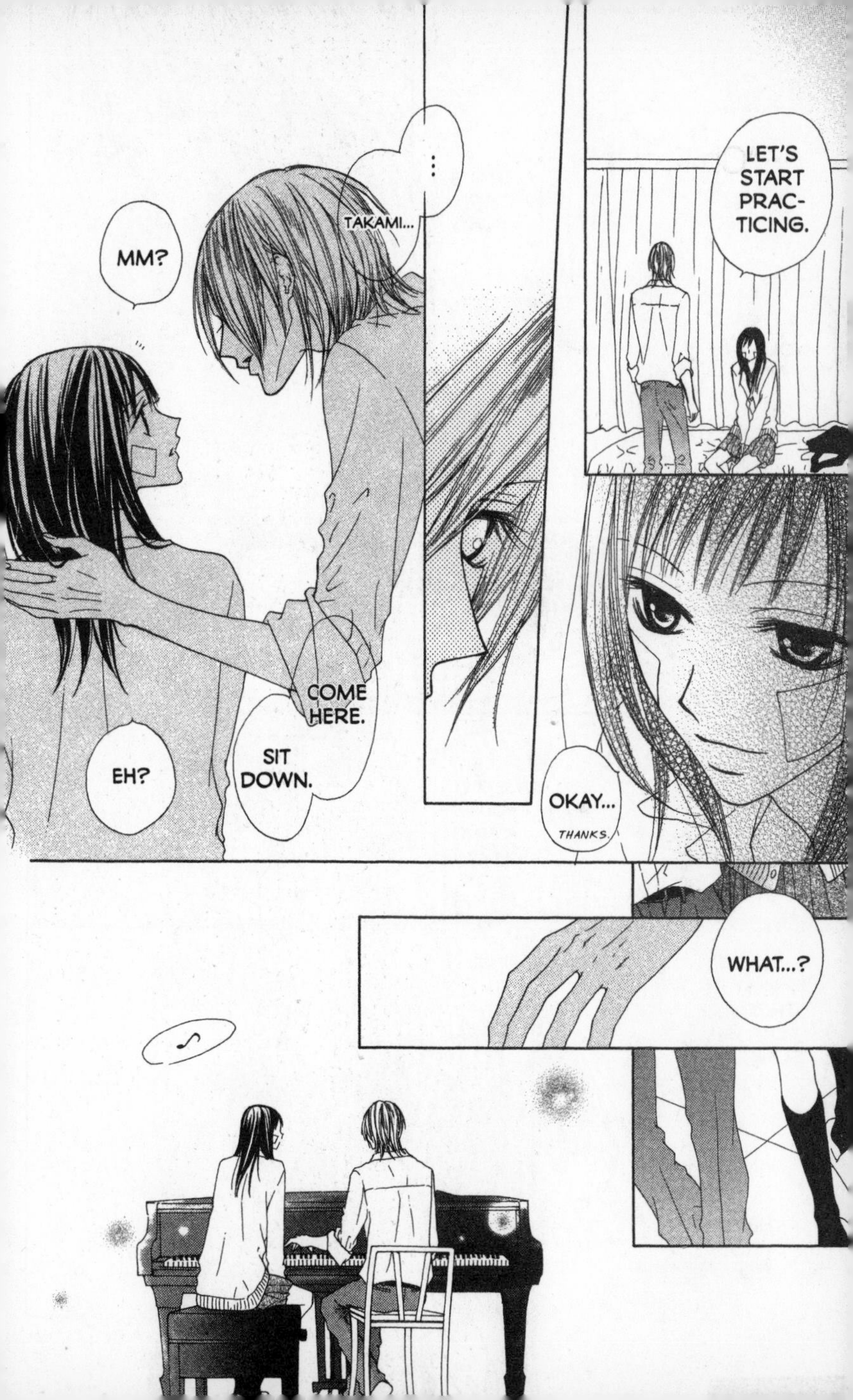
LET'S START PRAC-TICING.
OKAY...
THANKS.
...
TAKAMI...
MM?
COME HERE.
SIT DOWN.
EH?
WHAT...?

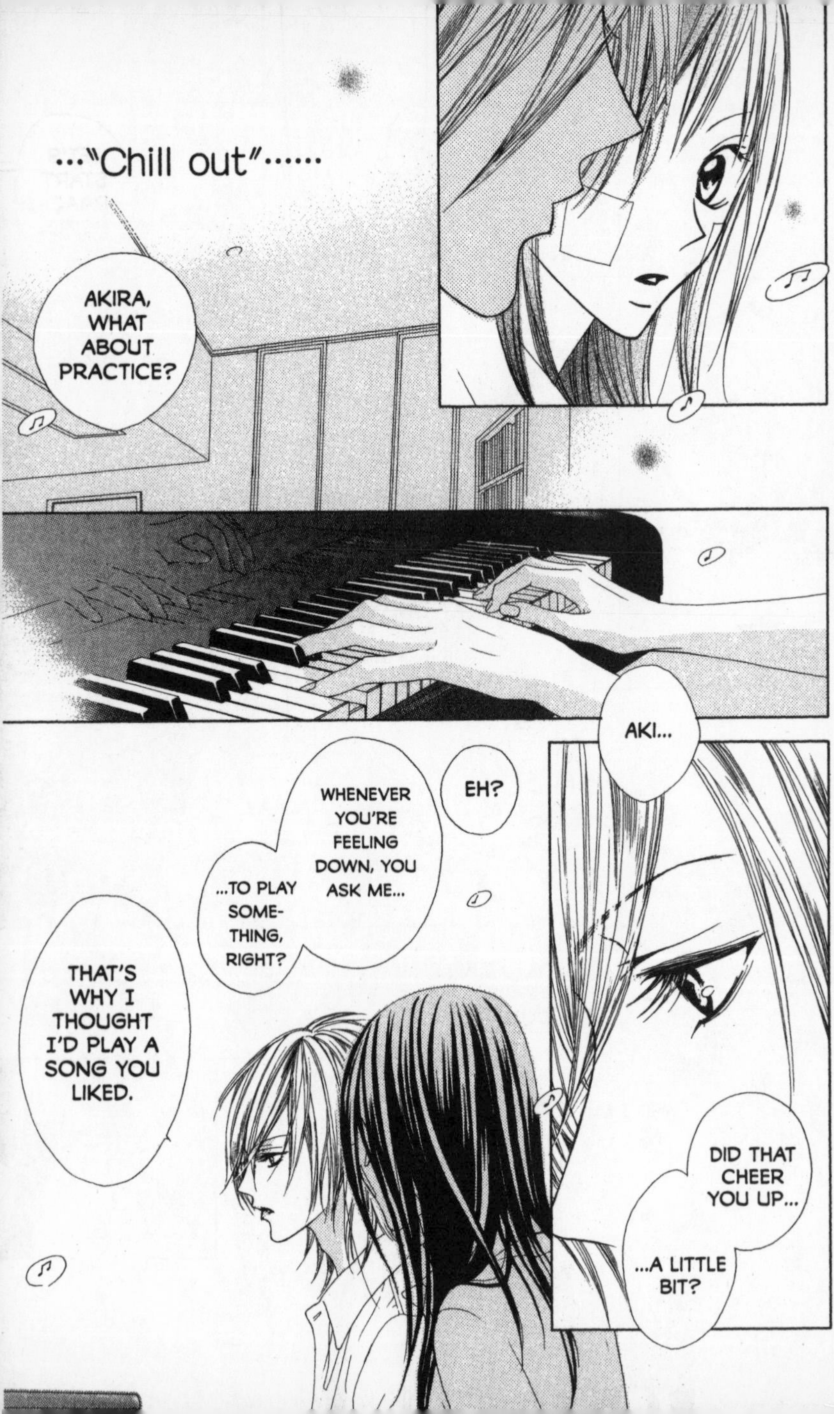
...“Chill out”......
AKIRA, WHAT ABOUT PRACTICE?
AKI...
EH?
WHENEVER YOU'RE FEELING DOWN, YOU ASK ME...
...TO PLAY SOME-THING, RIGHT?
THAT'S WHY I THOUGHT I'D PLAY A SONG YOU LIKED.
DID THAT CHEER YOU UP...
...A LITTLE BIT?

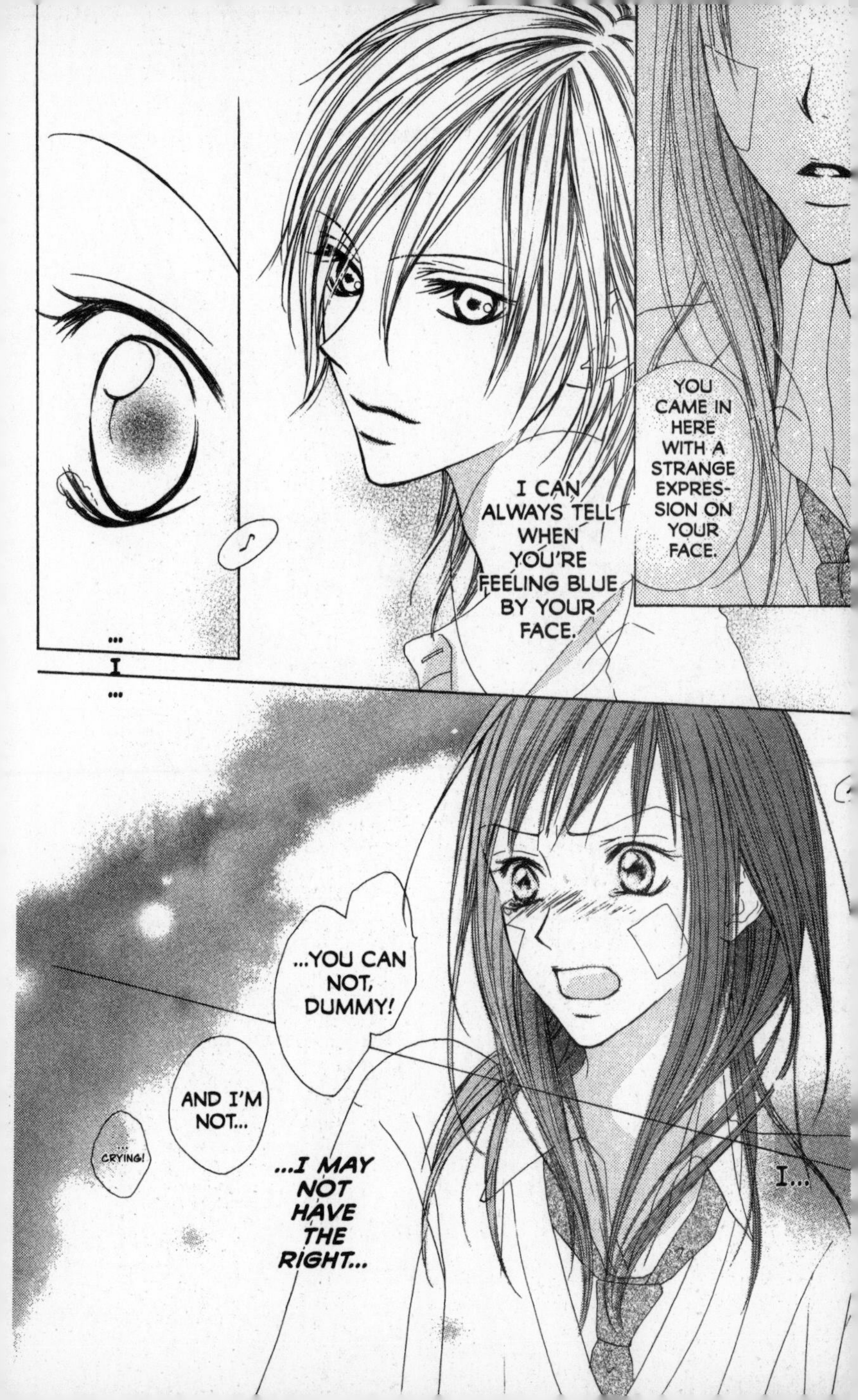
YOU CAME IN HERE WITH A STRANGE EXPRESSION ON YOUR FACE.
I CAN ALWAYS TELL WHEN YOU'RE FEELING BLUE BY YOUR FACE.
...I...
I...
...YOU CAN NOT, DUMMY!
...I MAY NOT HAVE THE RIGHT...
AND I'M NOT...
...CRYING!

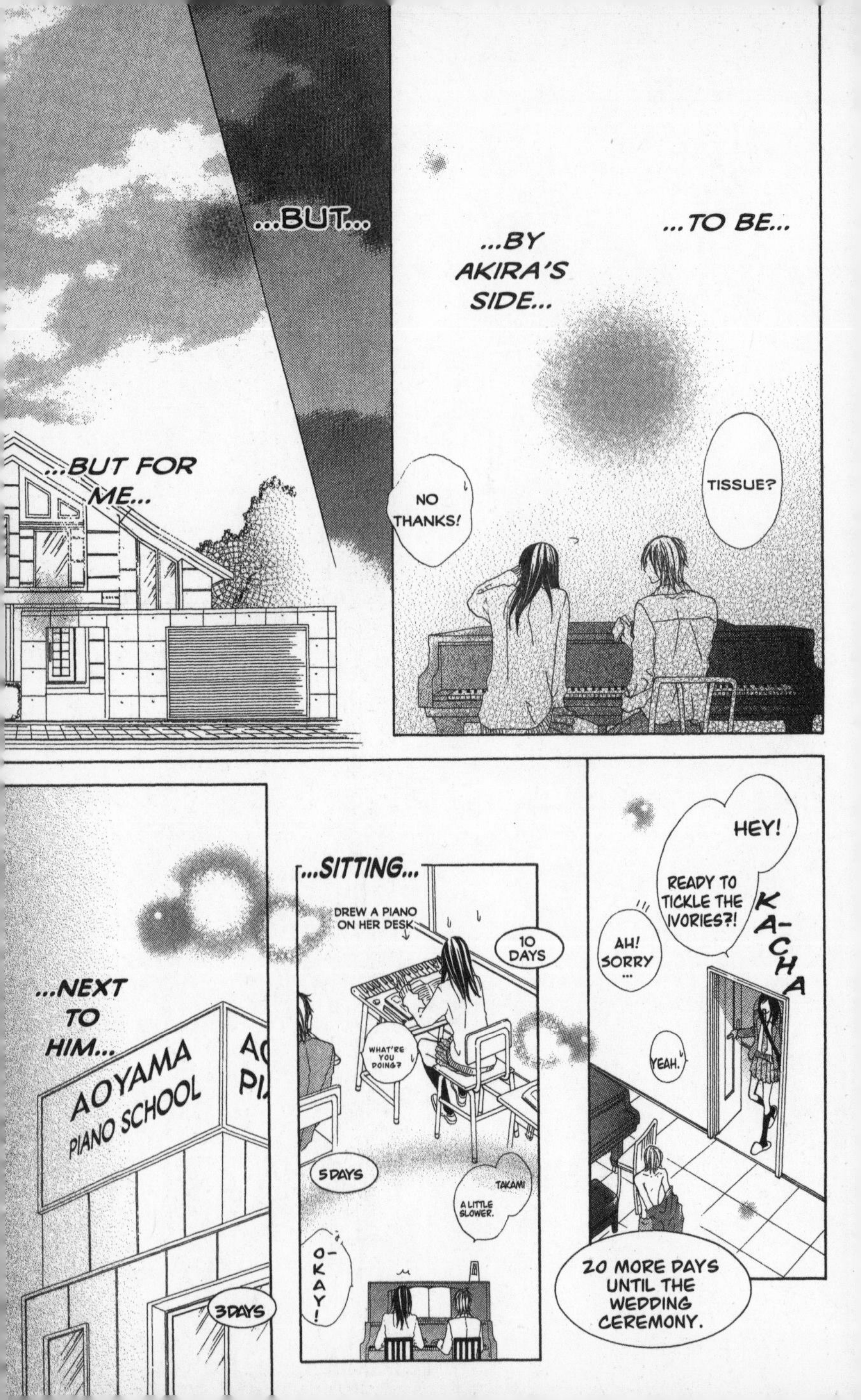
...TO BE...
...BY AKIRA'S SIDE...
TISSUE?
NO THANKS!
...BUT...
...BUT FOR ME...
HEY!
READY TO TICKLE THE IVORIES?!
KACHA
AH! SORRY...
YEAH.
20 MORE DAYS UNTIL THE WEDDING CEREMONY.
...SITTING...
DREW A PIANO ON HER DESK
10 DAYS
WHAT'RE YOU DOING?
5 DAYS
TAKAMI
A LITTLE SLOWER.
O-KAY!
...NEXT TO HIM...
AOYAMA PIANO SCHOOL
3 DAYS

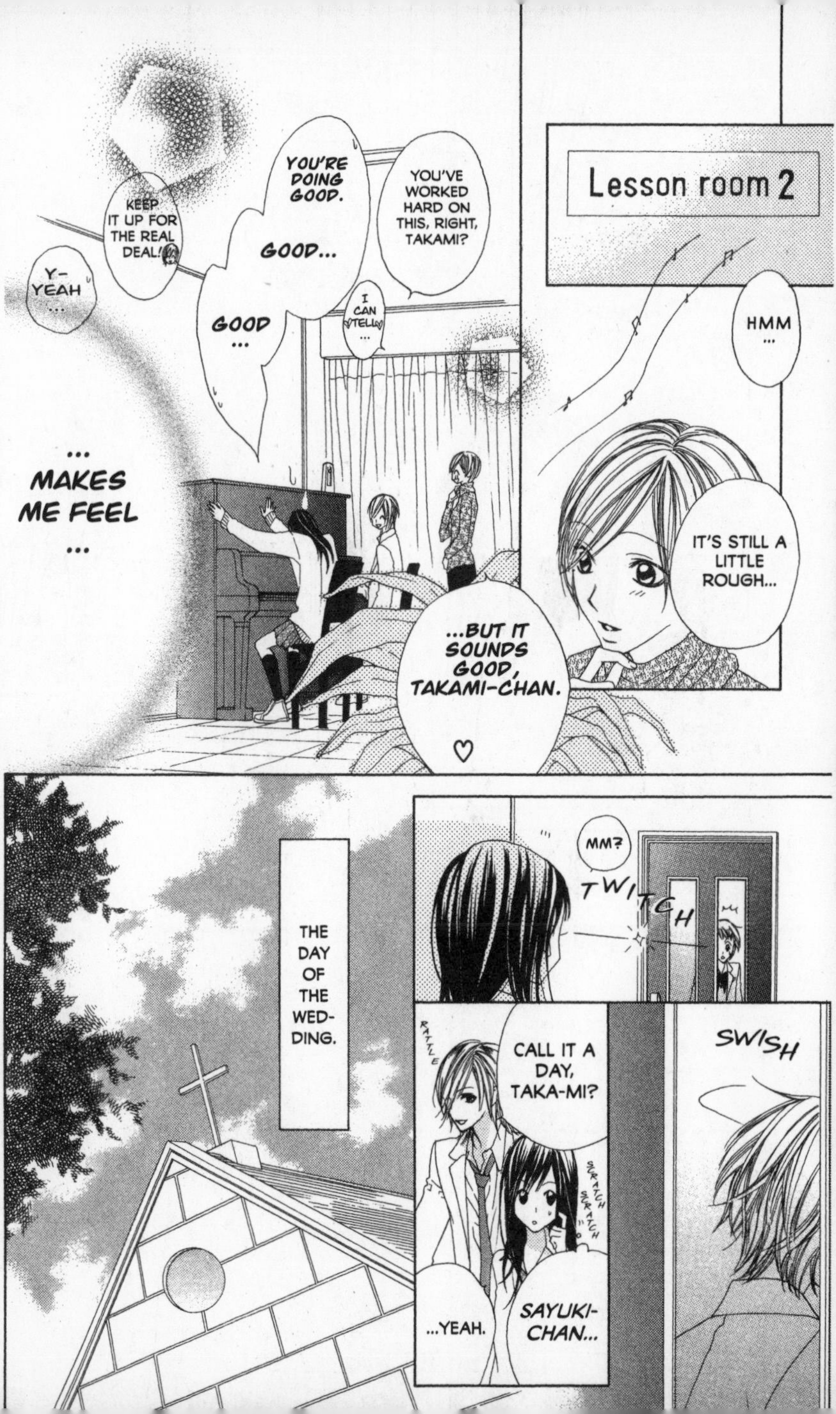

Lesson room 2
HMM...
IT'S STILL A LITTLE ROUGH...
...BUT IT SOUNDS GOOD, TAKAMI-CHAN. ♡
YOU'VE WORKED HARD ON THIS, RIGHT, TAKAMI?
I CAN TELL...
YOU'RE DOING GOOD.
GOOD...
GOOD...
KEEP IT UP FOR THE REAL DEAL!
Y-YEAH...
...MAKES ME FEEL...
MM?
TWITCH
SWISH
CALL IT A DAY, TAKA-MI?
RATTLE
SCRATCH SCRATCH
SAYUKI-CHAN...
...YEAH.
THE DAY OF THE WEDDING.

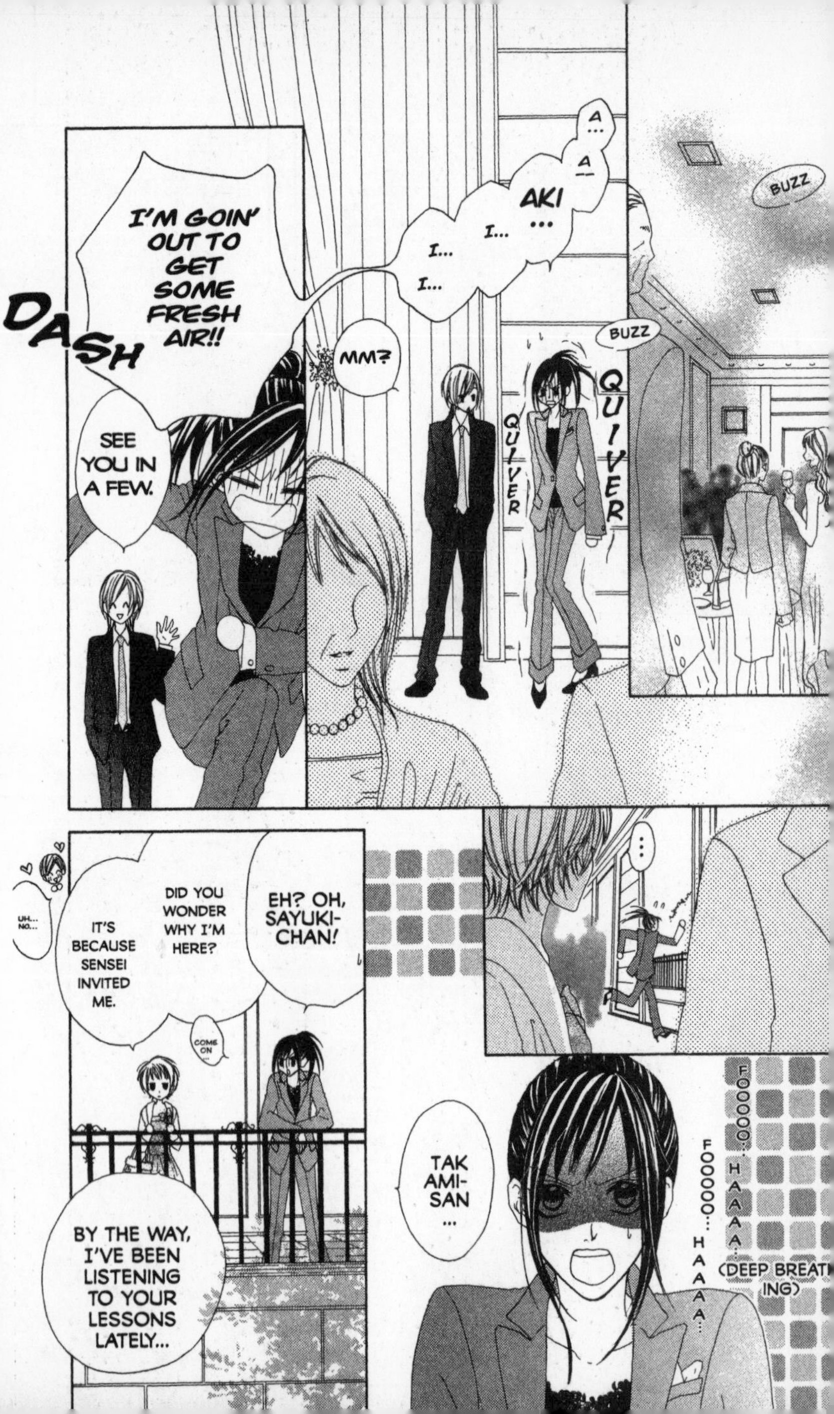
BUZZ
BUZZ
A...
A...
AKI...
I...
I...
I...
QUIVER
QUIVER
MM?
I'M GOIN' OUT TO GET SOME FRESH AIR!!
DASH
SEE YOU IN A FEW.
...
FOOOOO... HAAAA...
FOOOOO... HAAAA...
(DEEP BREATHING)
TAKAMI-SAN...
EH? OH, SAYUKI-CHAN!
DID YOU WONDER WHY I'M HERE?
IT'S BECAUSE SENSEI INVITED ME.
UH... NO...
COME ON
BY THE WAY, I'VE BEEN LISTENING TO YOUR LESSONS LATELY...

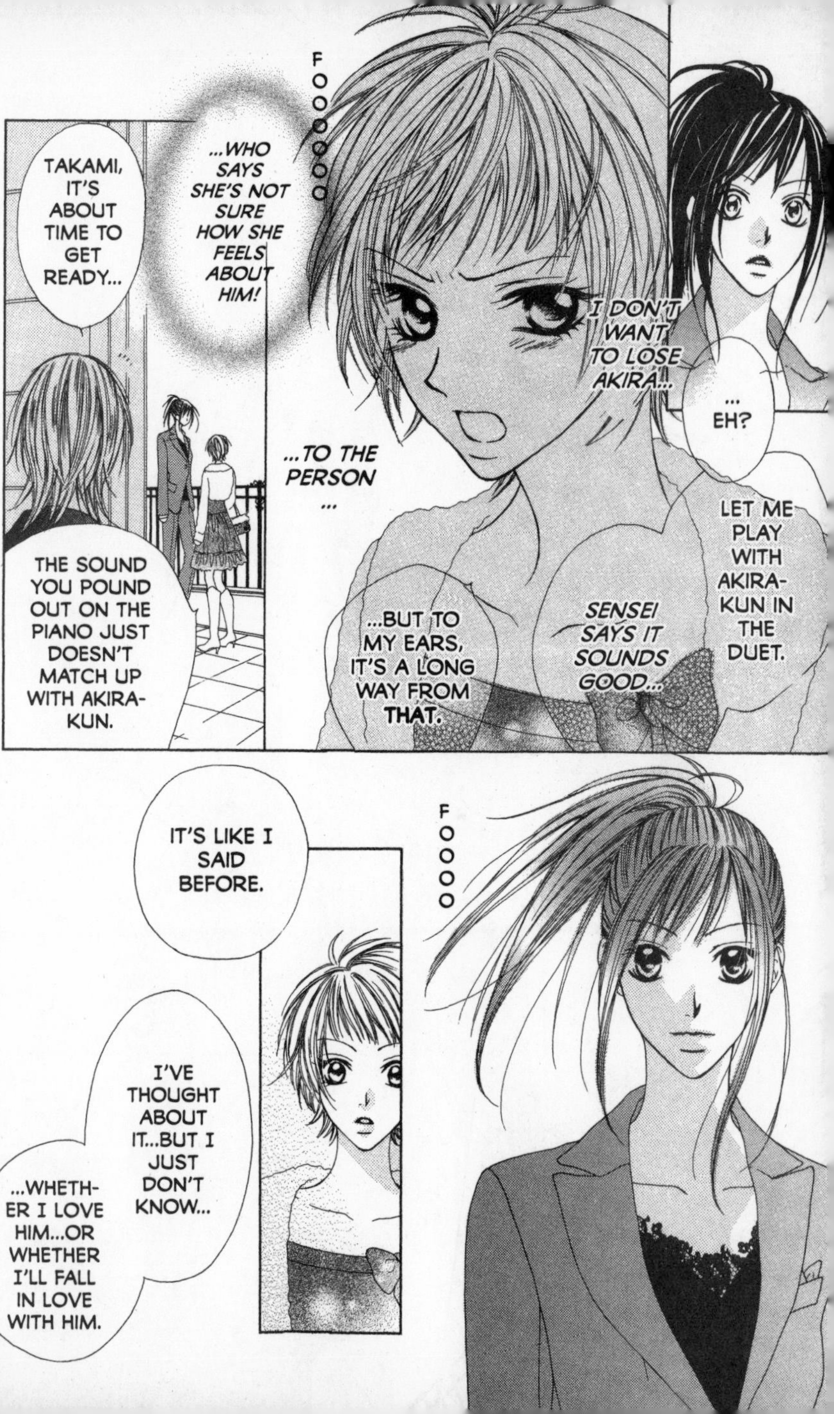
LET ME PLAY WITH AKIRA-KUN IN THE DUET.
... EH?
I DON'T WANT TO LOSE AKIRA...
SENSEI SAYS IT SOUNDS GOOD...
...BUT TO MY EARS, IT'S A LONG WAY FROM THAT.
...TO THE PERSON ...
...WHO SAYS SHE'S NOT SURE HOW SHE FEELS ABOUT HIM!
FOOOOOOO
TAKAMI, IT'S ABOUT TIME TO GET READY...
THE SOUND YOU POUND OUT ON THE PIANO JUST DOESN'T MATCH UP WITH AKIRA-KUN.
FOOOO
IT'S LIKE I SAID BEFORE.
I'VE THOUGHT ABOUT IT...BUT I JUST DON'T KNOW...
...WHETHER I LOVE HIM...OR WHETHER I'LL FALL IN LOVE WITH HIM.

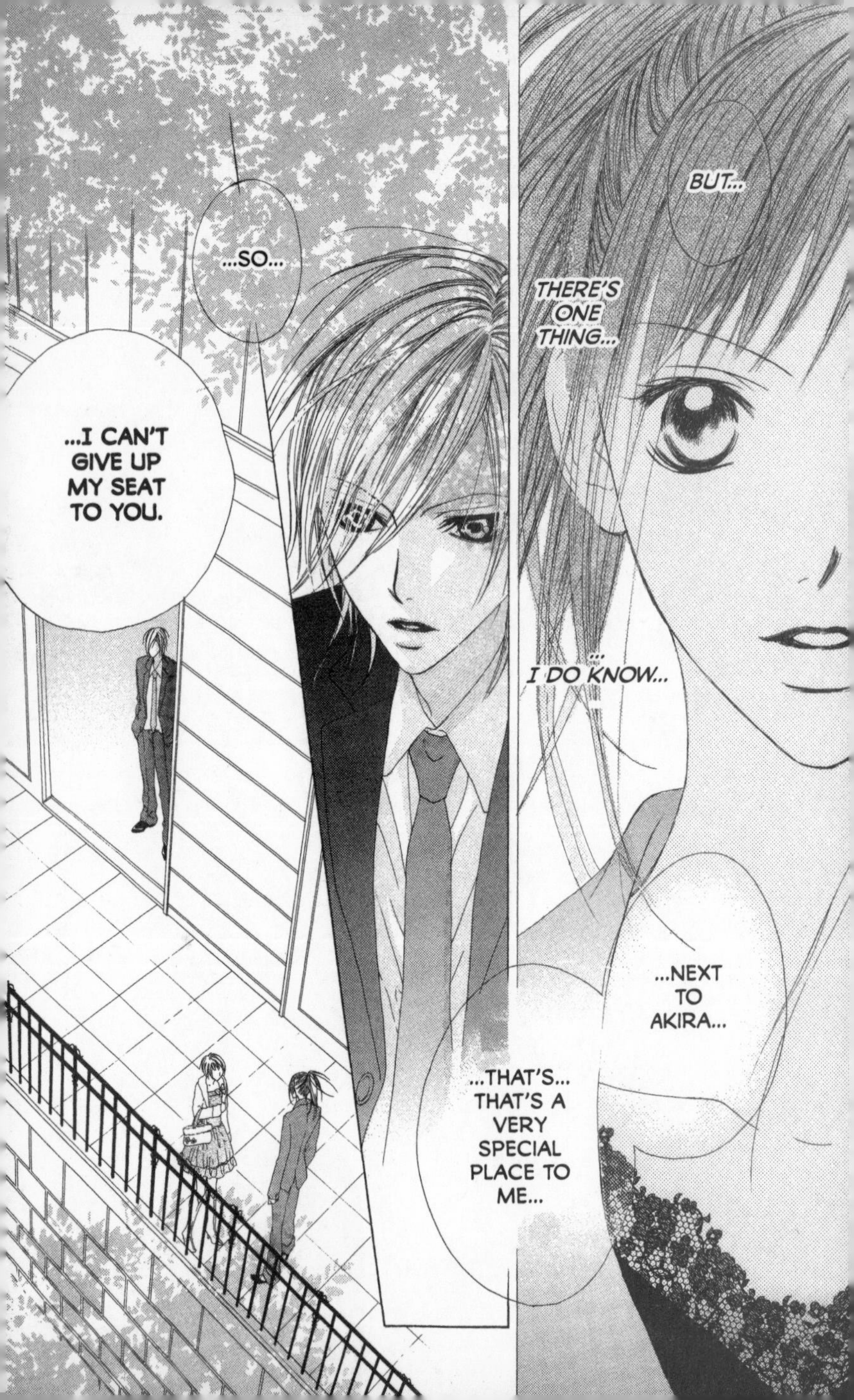
BUT...
THERE'S ONE THING...
...I DO KNOW...
...NEXT TO AKIRA...
...THAT'S... THAT'S A VERY SPECIAL PLACE TO ME...
...SO...
...I CAN'T GIVE UP MY SEAT TO YOU.

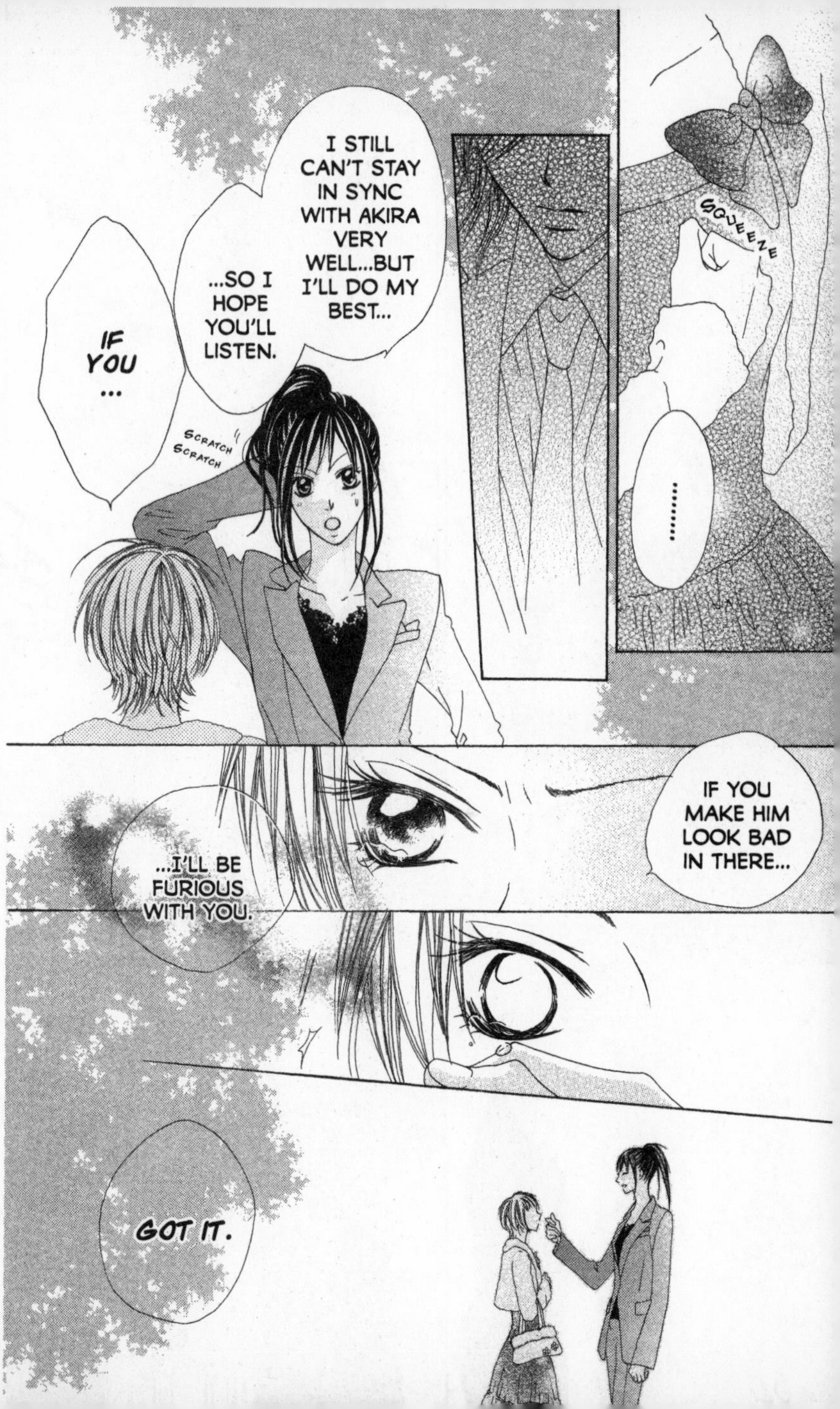
SQUEEZE
......
I STILL CAN'T STAY IN SYNC WITH AKIRA VERY WELL...BUT I'LL DO MY BEST...
...SO I HOPE YOU'LL LISTEN.
SCRATCH SCRATCH
IF YOU ...
IF YOU MAKE HIM LOOK BAD IN THERE...
...I'LL BE FURIOUS WITH YOU.
GOT IT.

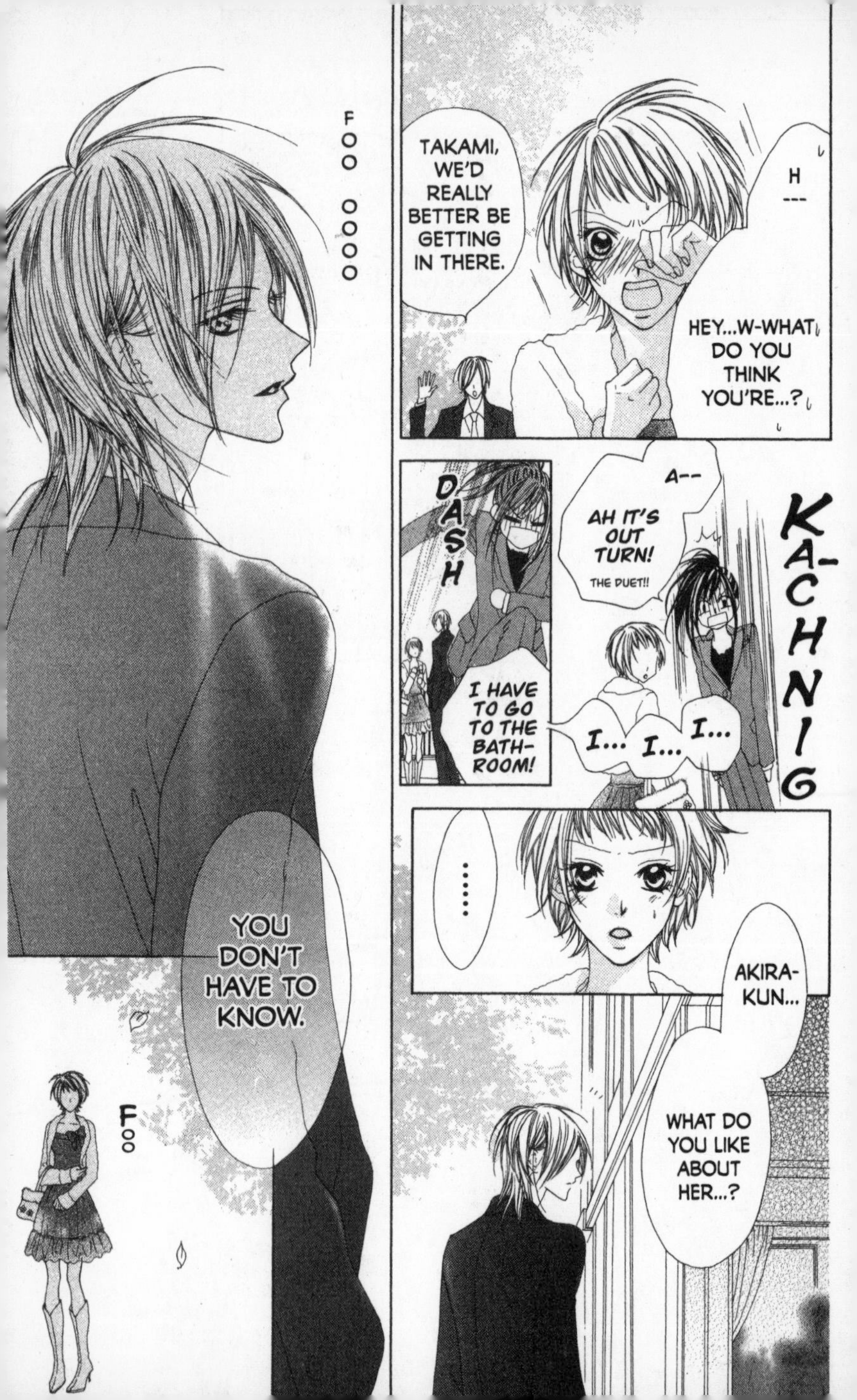
H---
HEY...W-WHAT DO YOU THINK YOU'RE...?
TAKAMI, WE'D REALLY BETTER BE GETTING IN THERE.
KACHNIG
A--
AH IT'S OUT TURN!
THE DUET!!
I... I... I...
DASH
I HAVE TO GO TO THE BATHROOM!
AKIRA-KUN...
......
WHAT DO YOU LIKE ABOUT HER...?
FOO OOOO
YOU DON'T HAVE TO KNOW.
FOO

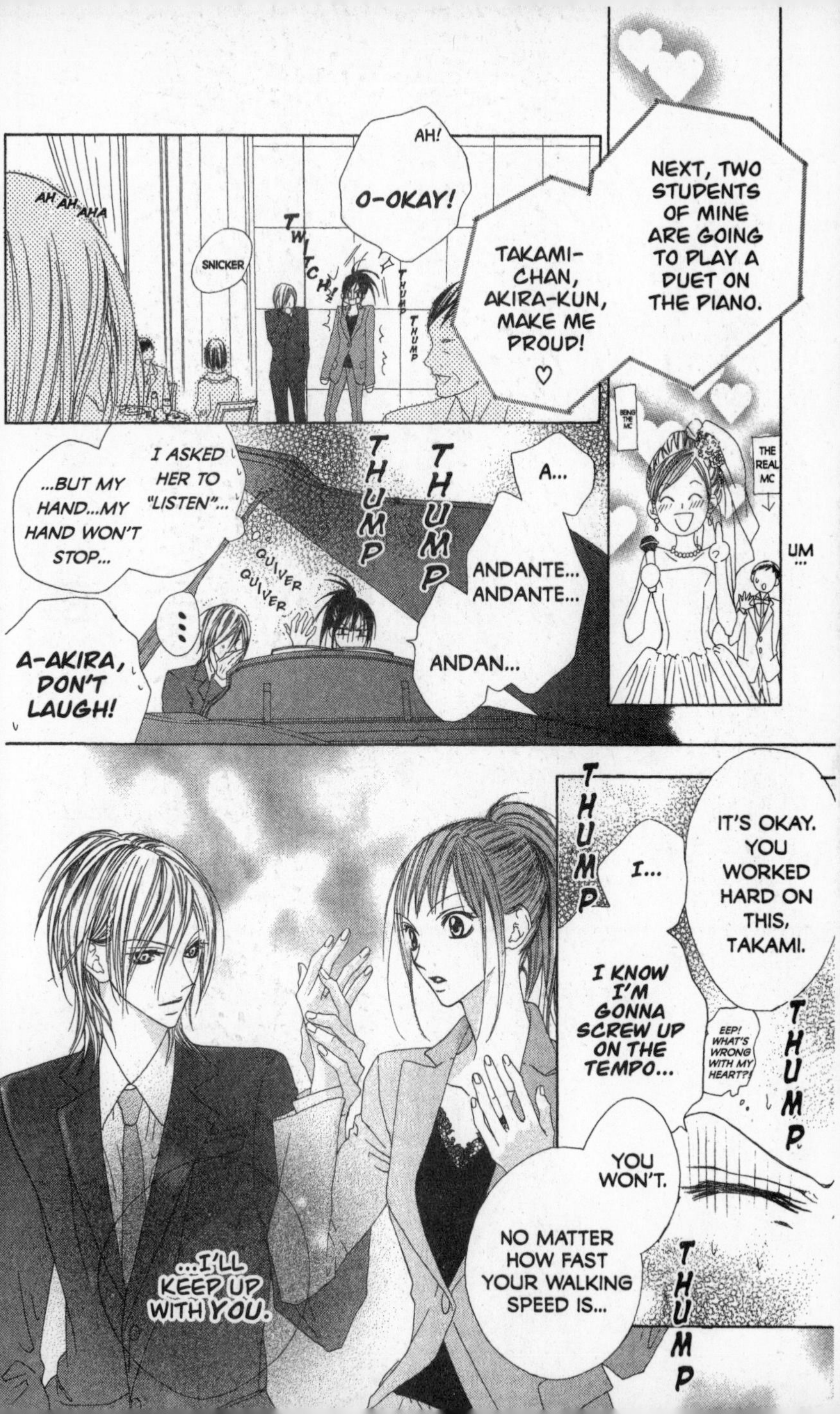
NEXT, TWO STUDENTS OF MINE ARE GOING TO PLAY A DUET ON THE PIANO.
TAKAMI-CHAN, AKIRA-KUN, MAKE ME PROUD! ♡
BEING THE MC
THE REAL MC
UM...
AH!
O-OKAY!
THUMP
THUMP
TWITCH
SNICKER
AH AH AHA
THUMP
THUMP
A...
ANDANTE... ANDANTE...
ANDAN...
I ASKED HER TO "LISTEN"...
...BUT MY HAND...MY HAND WON'T STOP...
QUIVER QUIVER
...
A-AKIRA, DON'T LAUGH!
IT'S OKAY. YOU WORKED HARD ON THIS, TAKAMI.
THUMP
I...
THUMP
EEP! WHAT'S WRONG WITH MY HEART?!
I KNOW I'M GONNA SCREW UP ON THE TEMPO...
YOU WON'T.
NO MATTER HOW FAST YOUR WALKING SPEED IS...
THUMP
...I'LL KEEP UP WITH YOU.

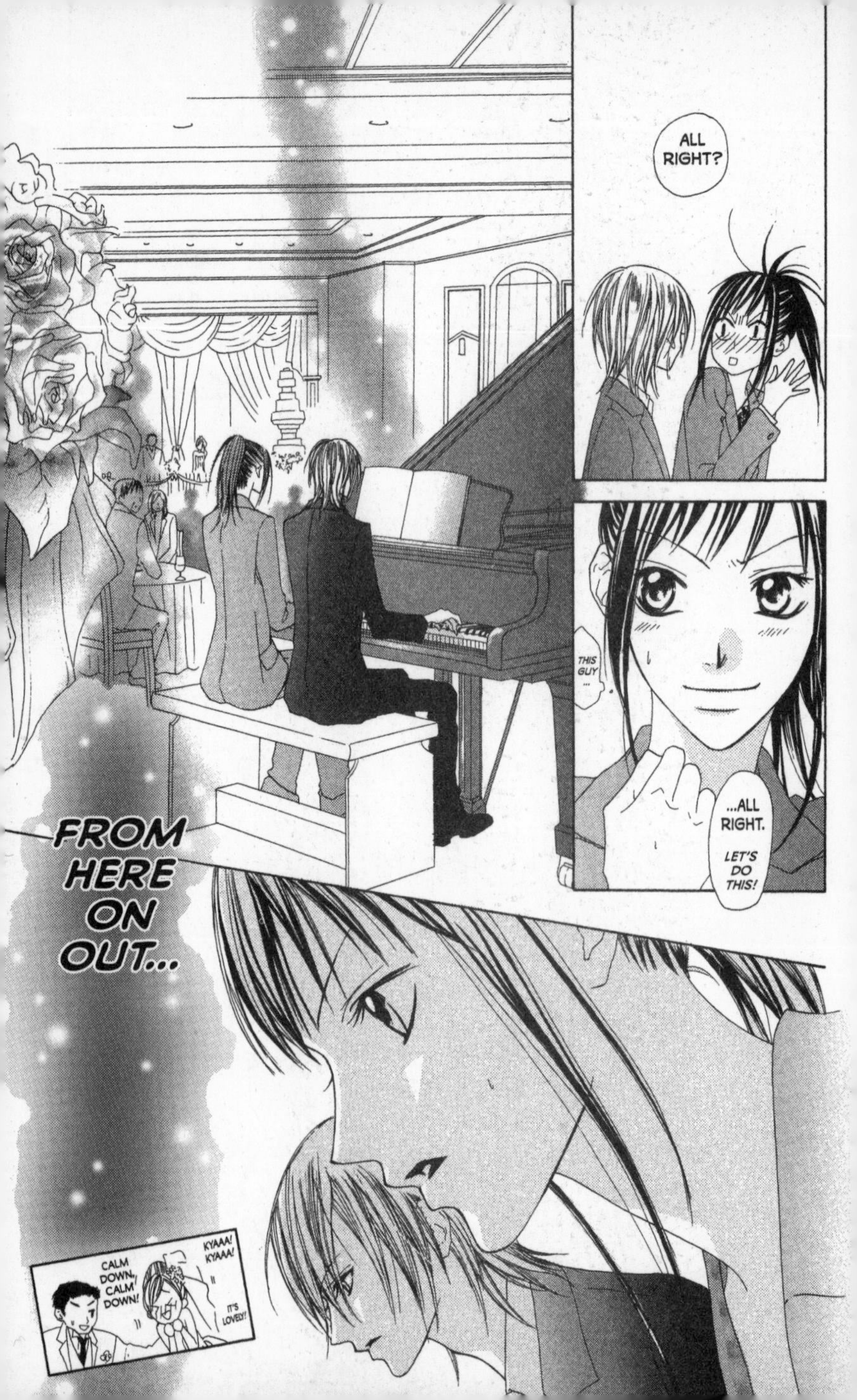
ALL RIGHT?
THIS GUY...
...ALL RIGHT.
LET'S DO THIS!
FROM HERE ON OUT...
KYAAA! KYAAA!
CALM DOWN, CALM DOWN!
IT'S LOVELY!

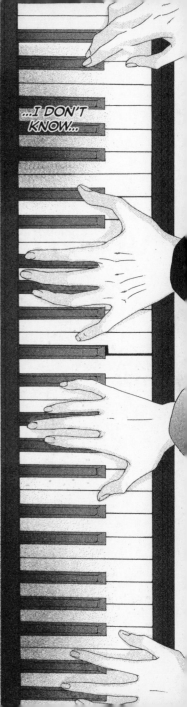

...I DON'T KNOW...

...WHAT KIND OF PLACE I'M GOING TO END UP...

...BUT IT SEEMS LIKE...

...I CAN ONLY WALK AT MY OWN SPEED.

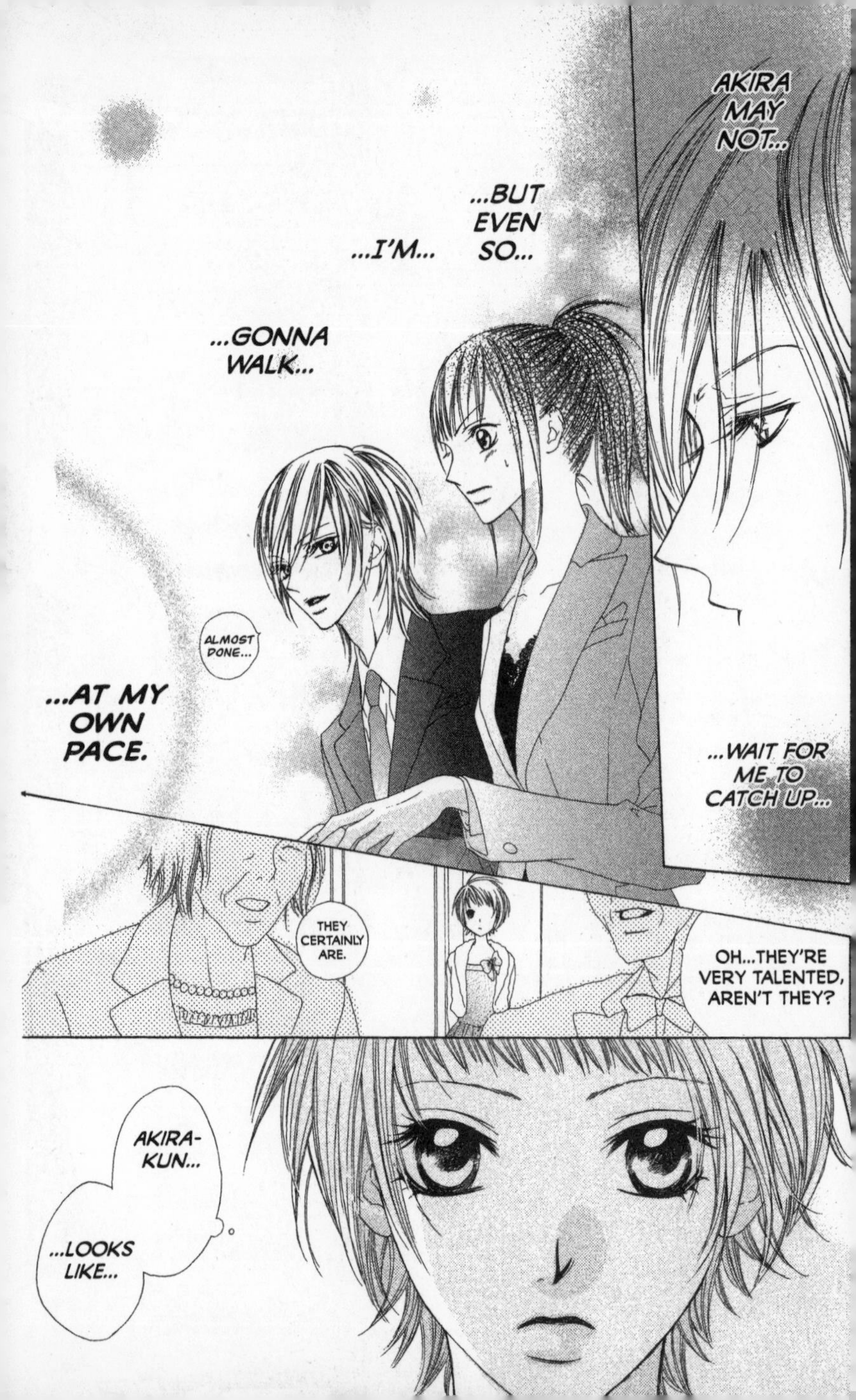
AKIRA MAY NOT...
...WAIT FOR ME TO CATCH UP...
...BUT EVEN SO...
...I'M...
...GONNA WALK...
ALMOST DONE...
...AT MY OWN PACE.
OH...THEY'RE VERY TALENTED, AREN'T THEY?
THEY CERTAINLY ARE.
AKIRA-KUN...
...LOOKS LIKE...

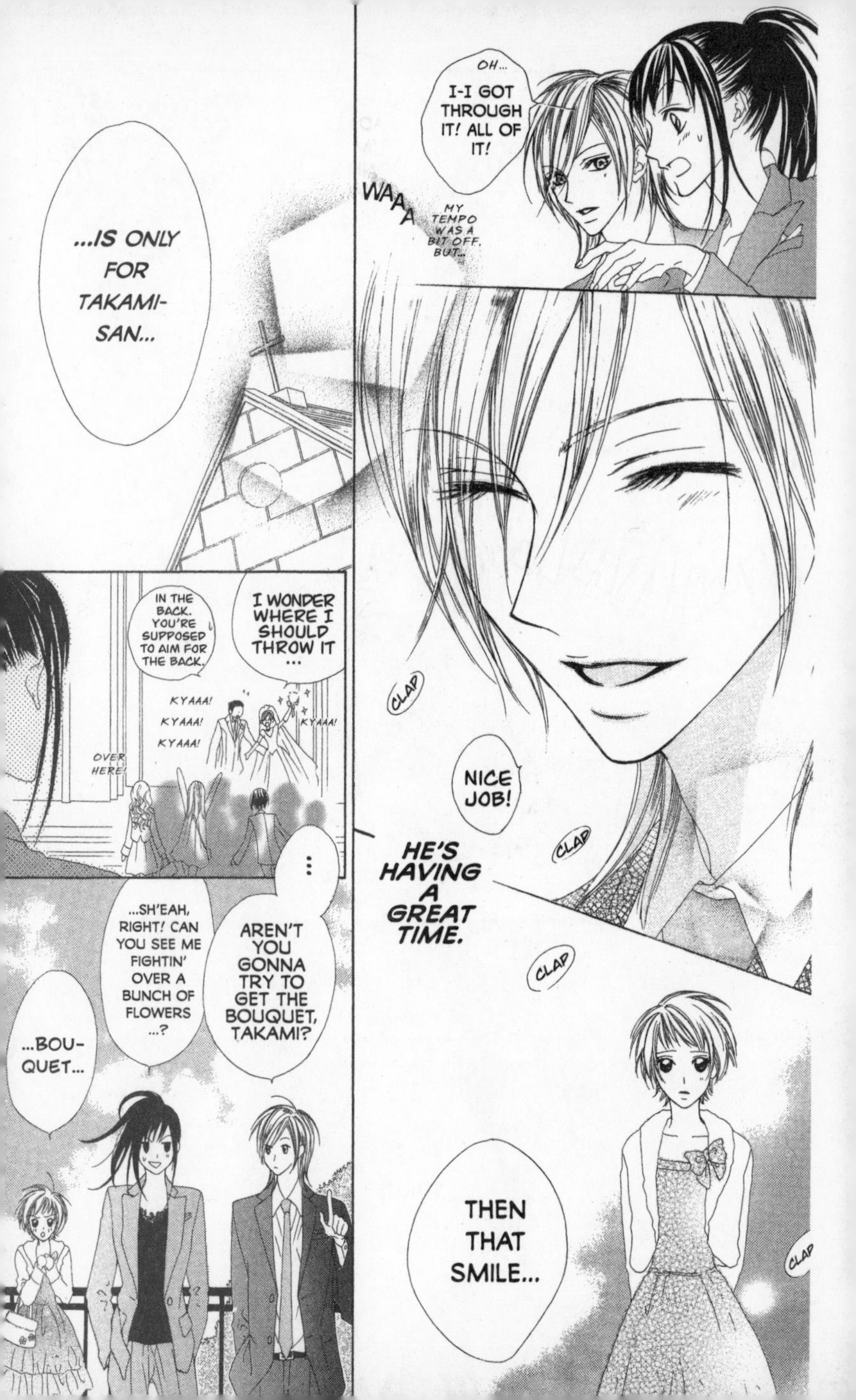
OH...
I-I GOT THROUGH IT! ALL OF IT!
WAAA
MY TEMPO WAS A BIT OFF, BUT...
CLAP
NICE JOB!
CLAP
HE'S HAVING A GREAT TIME.
CLAP
THEN THAT SMILE...
CLAP
...IS ONLY FOR TAKAMI-SAN...
I WONDER WHERE I SHOULD THROW IT ...
IN THE BACK. YOU'RE SUPPOSED TO AIM FOR THE BACK.
KYAAA!
KYAAA!
KYAAA!
KYAAA!
OVER HERE!
...
AREN'T YOU GONNA TRY TO GET THE BOUQUET, TAKAMI?
...SH'EAH, RIGHT! CAN YOU SEE ME FIGHTIN' OVER A BUNCH OF FLOWERS ...?
...BOU-QUET...

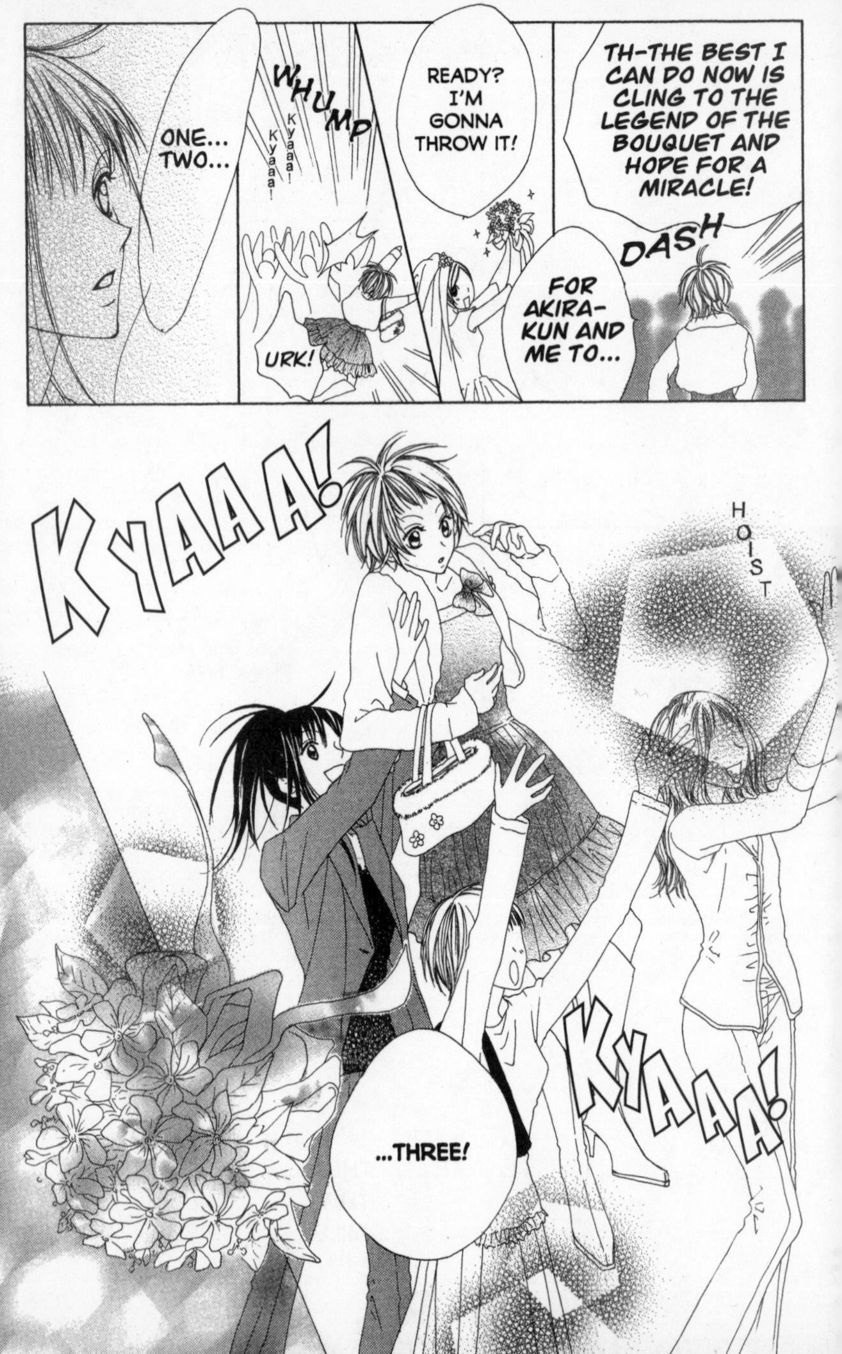

TH-THE BEST I CAN DO NOW IS CLING TO THE LEGEND OF THE BOUQUET AND HOPE FOR A MIRACLE!
DASH
FOR AKIRA-KUN AND ME TO...
READY? I'M GONNA THROW IT!
WHUMP
Kyaaa!
Kyaaa!
URK!
ONE... TWO...
HOIST
KYAAA!
KYAAA!
...THREE!

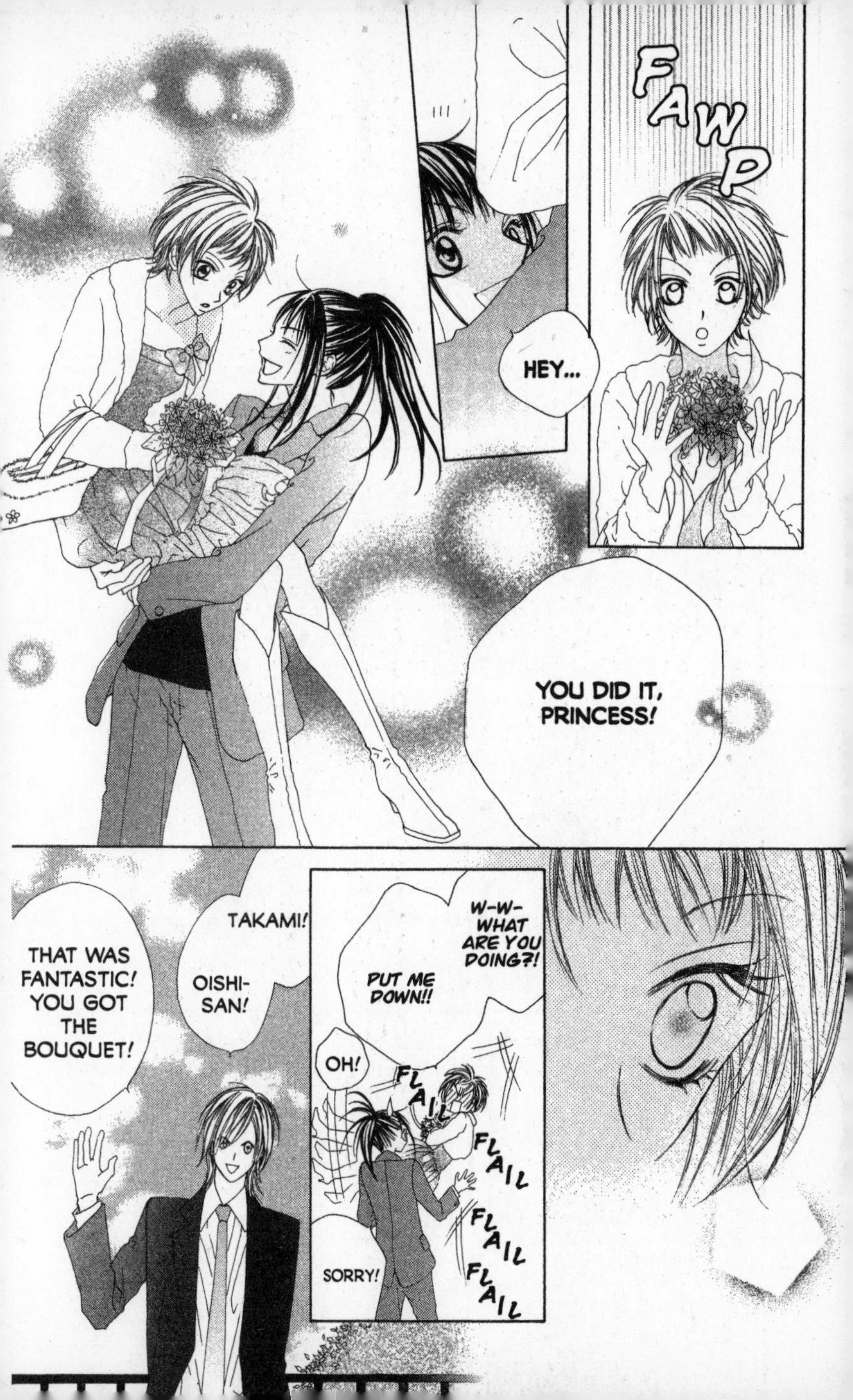
FAWP
HEY...
YOU DID IT, PRINCESS!
W-W-WHAT ARE YOU DOING?!
PUT ME DOWN!!
OH!
FLAIL
FLAIL
FLAIL
FLAIL
SORRY!
TAKAMI!
OISHI-SAN!
THAT WAS FANTASTIC! YOU GOT THE BOUQUET!

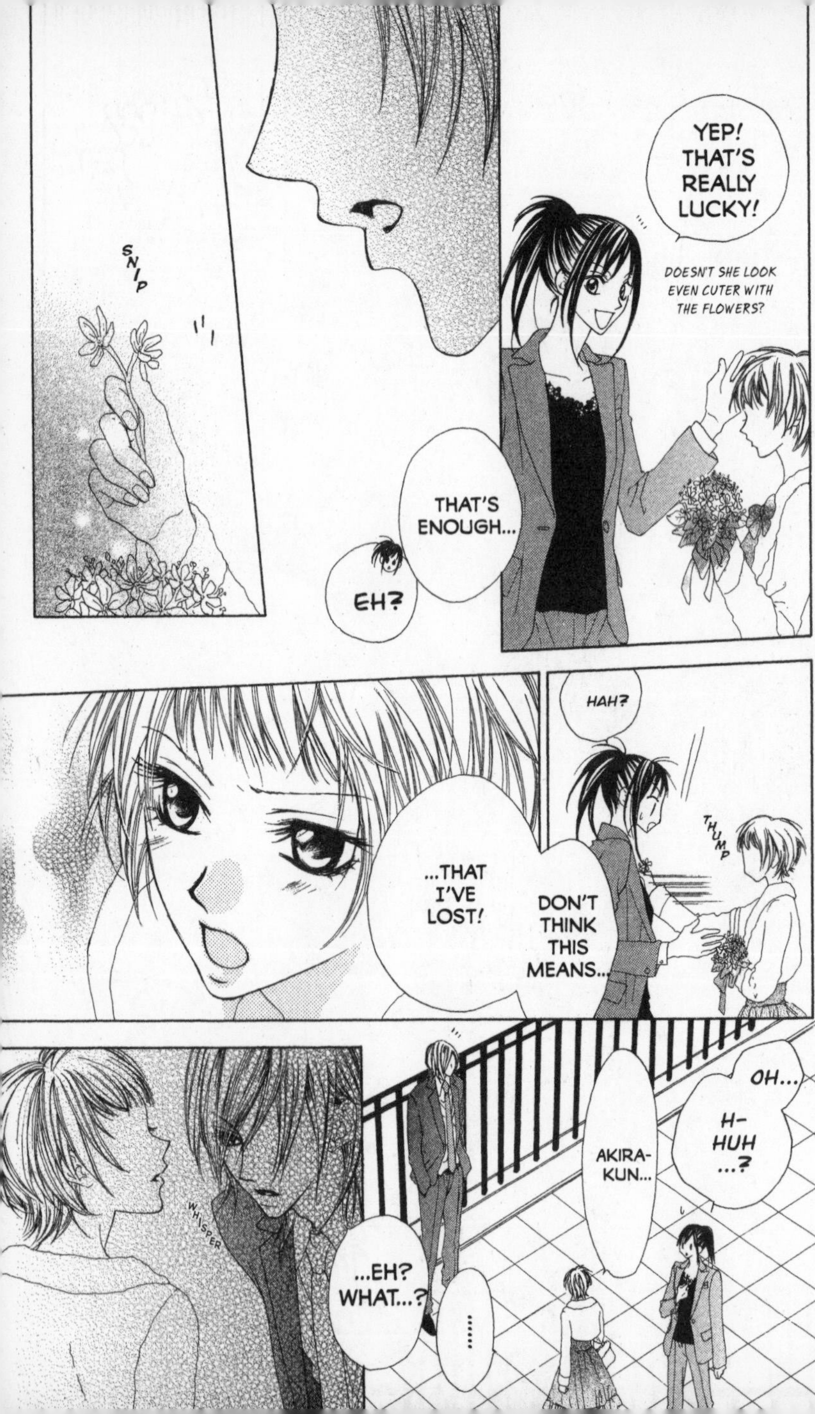

YEP! THAT'S REALLY LUCKY!
DOESN'T SHE LOOK EVEN CUTER WITH THE FLOWERS?
THAT'S ENOUGH...
EH?
SNIP
HAH?
THUMP
DON'T THINK THIS MEANS...
...THAT I'VE LOST!
OH...
H-HUH...?
AKIRA-KUN...
...EH? WHAT...?
......
WHISPER

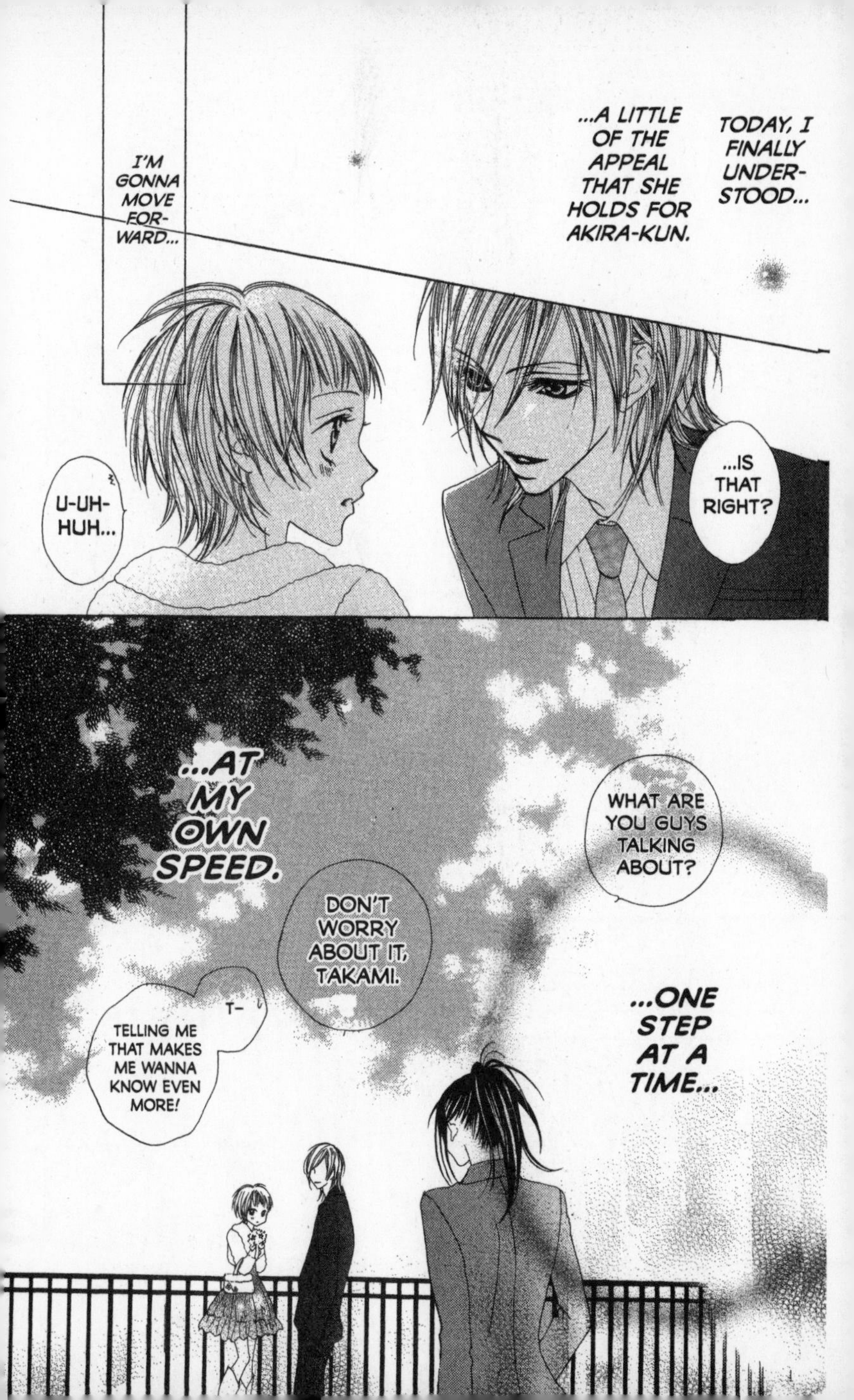
TODAY, I FINALLY UNDERSTOOD...
...A LITTLE OF THE APPEAL THAT SHE HOLDS FOR AKIRA-KUN.
I'M GONNA MOVE FORWARD...
...IS THAT RIGHT?
U-UH-HUH...
WHAT ARE YOU GUYS TALKING ABOUT?
...ONE STEP AT A TIME...
DON'T WORRY ABOUT IT, TAKAMI.
...AT MY OWN SPEED.
T-
TELLING ME THAT MAKES ME WANNA KNOW EVEN MORE!

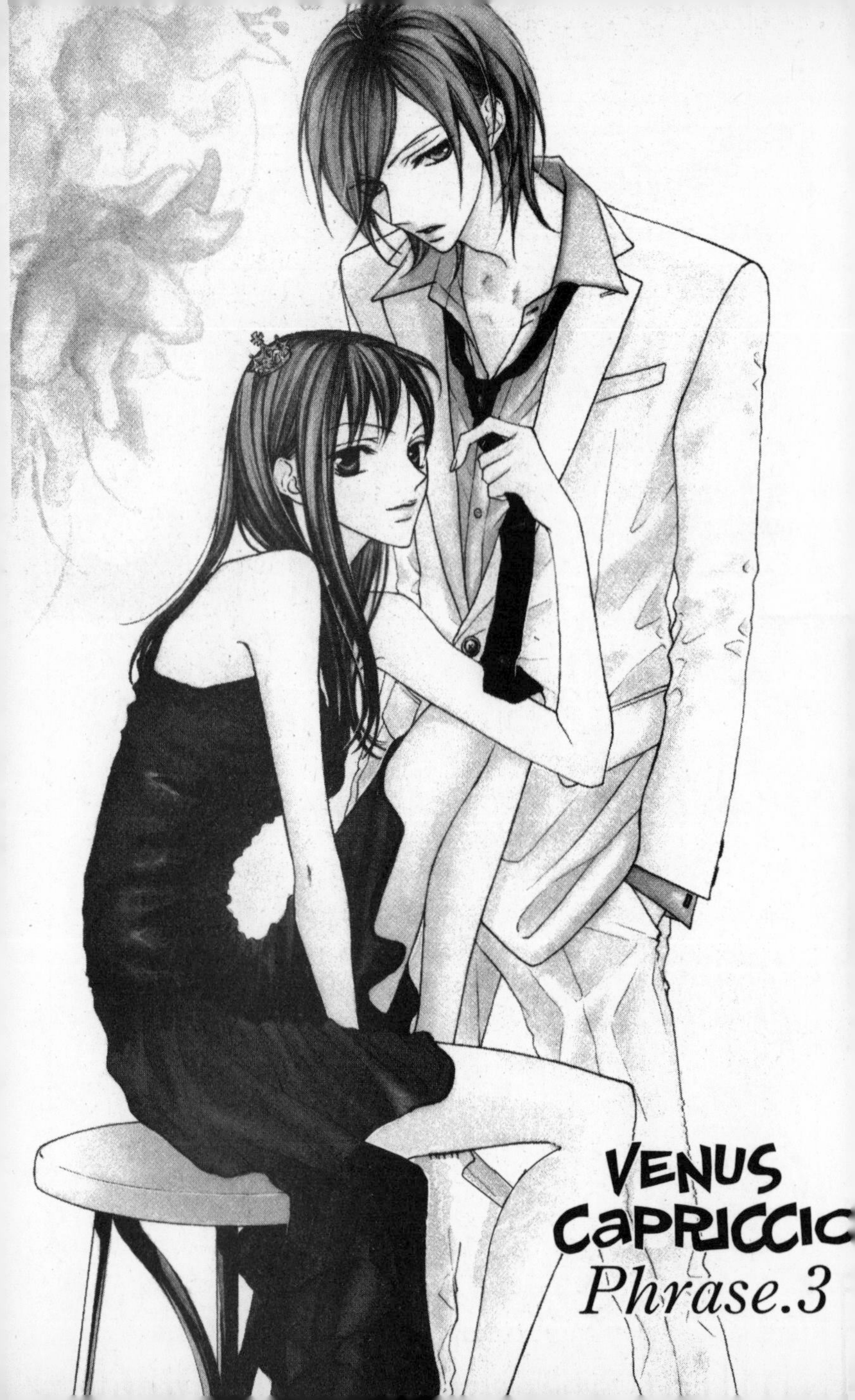
VENUS CAPRICCIO
Phrase.3

CHARACTER INTRODUCTION

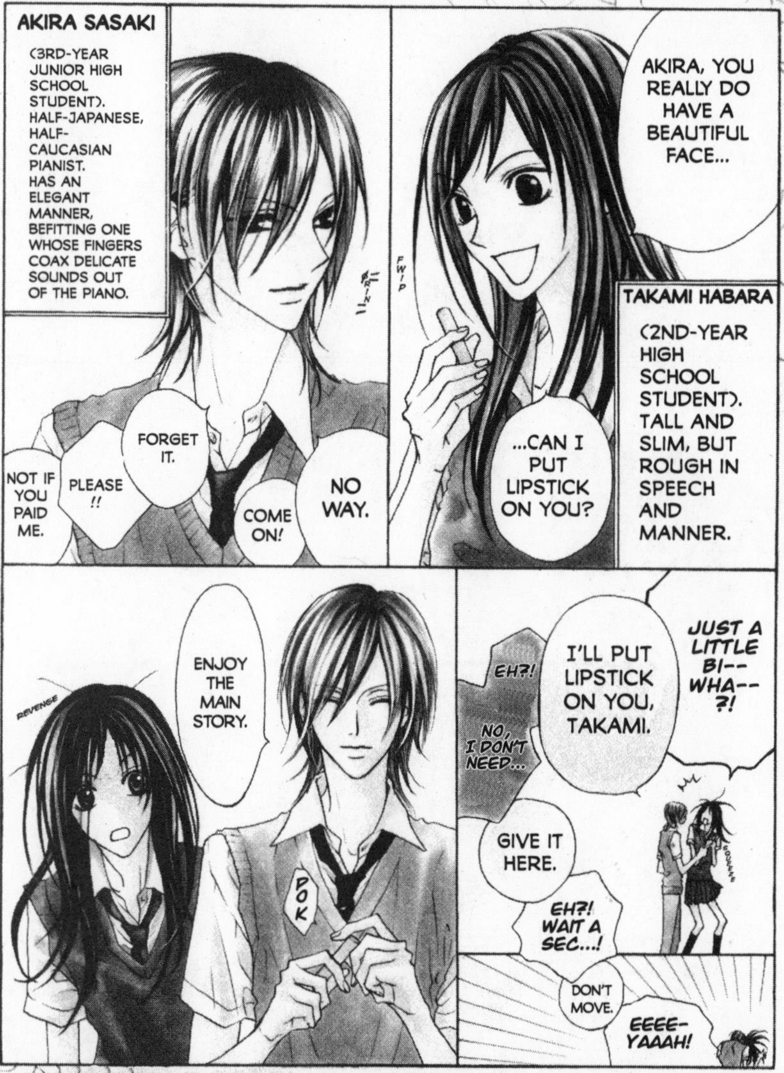
AKIRA, YOU REALLY DO HAVE A BEAUTIFUL FACE...
FWIP
TAKAMI HABARA
(2ND-YEAR HIGH SCHOOL STUDENT). TALL AND SLIM, BUT ROUGH IN SPEECH AND MANNER.
...CAN I PUT LIPSTICK ON YOU?
AKIRA SASAKI
(3RD-YEAR JUNIOR HIGH SCHOOL STUDENT). HALF-JAPANESE, HALF-CAUCASIAN PIANIST. HAS AN ELEGANT MANNER, BEFITTING ONE WHOSE FINGERS COAX DELICATE SOUNDS OUT OF THE PIANO.
NO WAY.
COME ON!
FORGET IT.
PLEASE!!
NOT IF YOU PAID ME.
JUST A LITTLE BI-- WHA--?!
I'LL PUT LIPSTICK ON YOU, TAKAMI.
EH?!
NO, I DON'T NEED...
GIVE IT HERE.
EH?! WAIT A SEC...!
DON'T MOVE.
EEEE-YAAAH!
ENJOY THE MAIN STORY.
REVENGE
POK

LET'S GO! THIS CHARACTER INTRODUCTION WAS PUBLISHED IN ISSUE #15 OF JAPANESE MAGAZINE "HANA TO YUME".

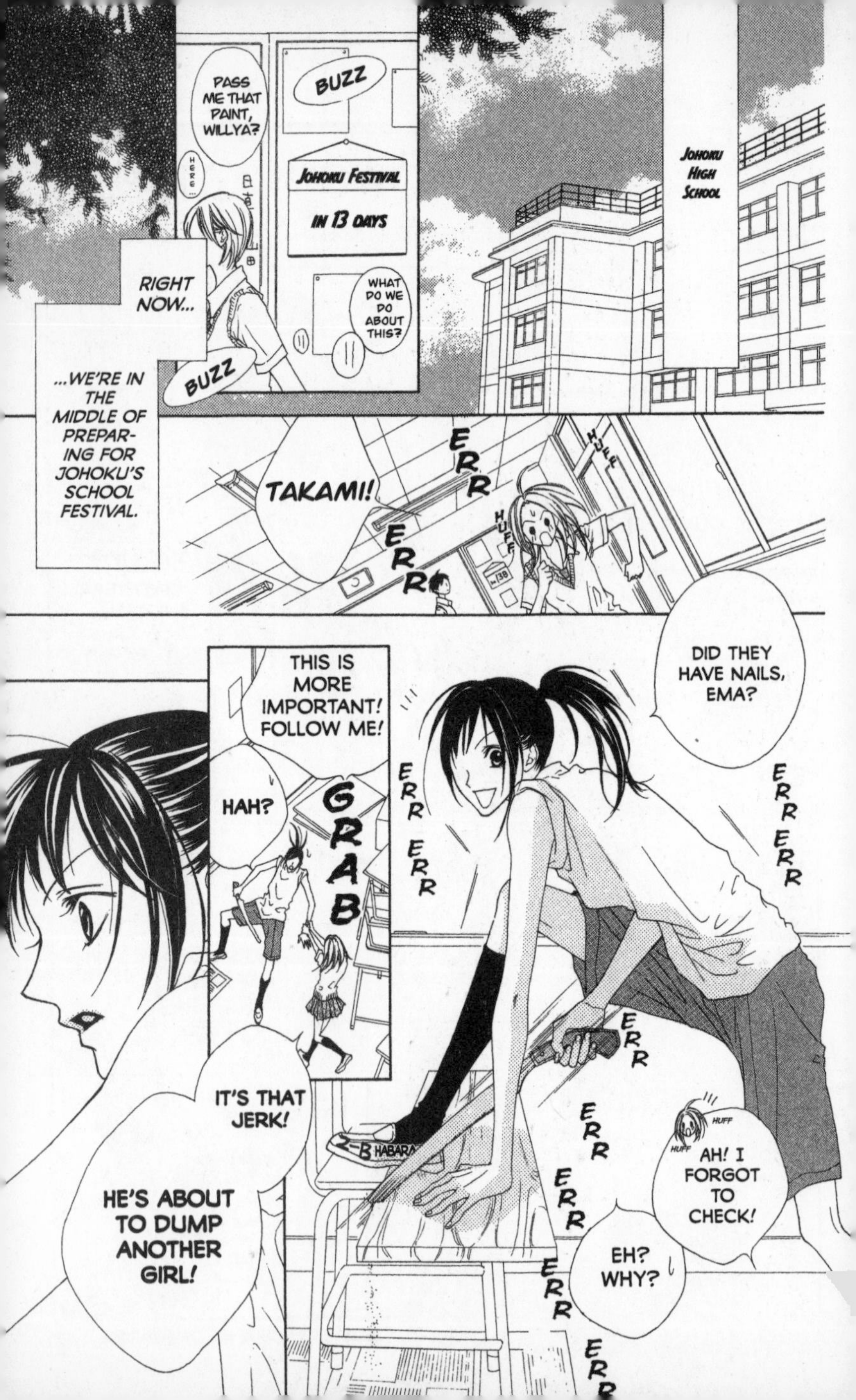
JOHOKU HIGH SCHOOL
PASS ME THAT PAINT, WILLYA?
BUZZ
HERE...
JOHOKU FESTIVAL IN 13 DAYS
WHAT DO WE DO ABOUT THIS?
BUZZ
RIGHT NOW...
...WE'RE IN THE MIDDLE OF PREPARING FOR JOHOKU'S SCHOOL FESTIVAL.
HUFF
ERR
ERR
HUFF
TAKAMI!
ERR ERR
DID THEY HAVE NAILS, EMA?
ERR ERR ERR
ERR ERR
ERR ERR
ERR ERR
HUFF HUFF
AH! I FORGOT TO CHECK!
ERR
ERR
ERR
EH? WHY?
THIS IS MORE IMPORTANT! FOLLOW ME!
HAH?
GRAB
IT'S THAT JERK!
HE'S ABOUT TO DUMP ANOTHER GIRL!

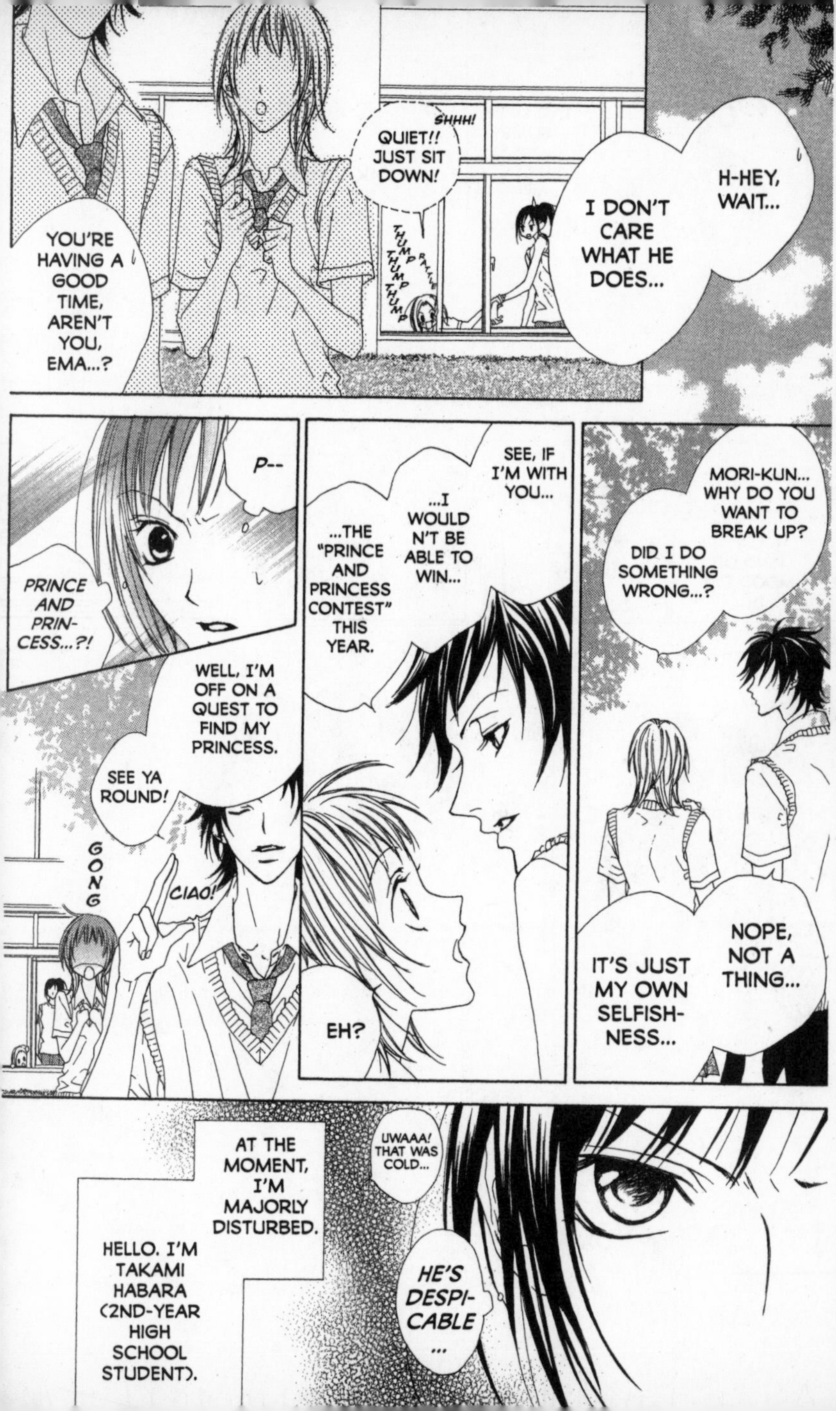
H-HEY, WAIT...
I DON'T CARE WHAT HE DOES...
SHHH!
QUIET!! JUST SIT DOWN!
THUMP THUMP THUMP THUMP
RATTLE
YOU'RE HAVING A GOOD TIME, AREN'T YOU, EMA...?
MORI-KUN... WHY DO YOU WANT TO BREAK UP?
DID I DO SOMETHING WRONG...?
NOPE, NOT A THING...
IT'S JUST MY OWN SELFISHNESS...
SEE, IF I'M WITH YOU...
...I WOULDN'T BE ABLE TO WIN...
...THE "PRINCE AND PRINCESS CONTEST" THIS YEAR.
EH?
P--
PRINCE AND PRINCESS...?!
WELL, I'M OFF ON A QUEST TO FIND MY PRINCESS.
SEE YA ROUND!
CIAO!
GONG
UWAAA! THAT WAS COLD...
HE'S DESPICABLE...
AT THE MOMENT, I'M MAJORLY DISTURBED.
HELLO. I'M TAKAMI HABARA (2ND-YEAR HIGH SCHOOL STUDENT).

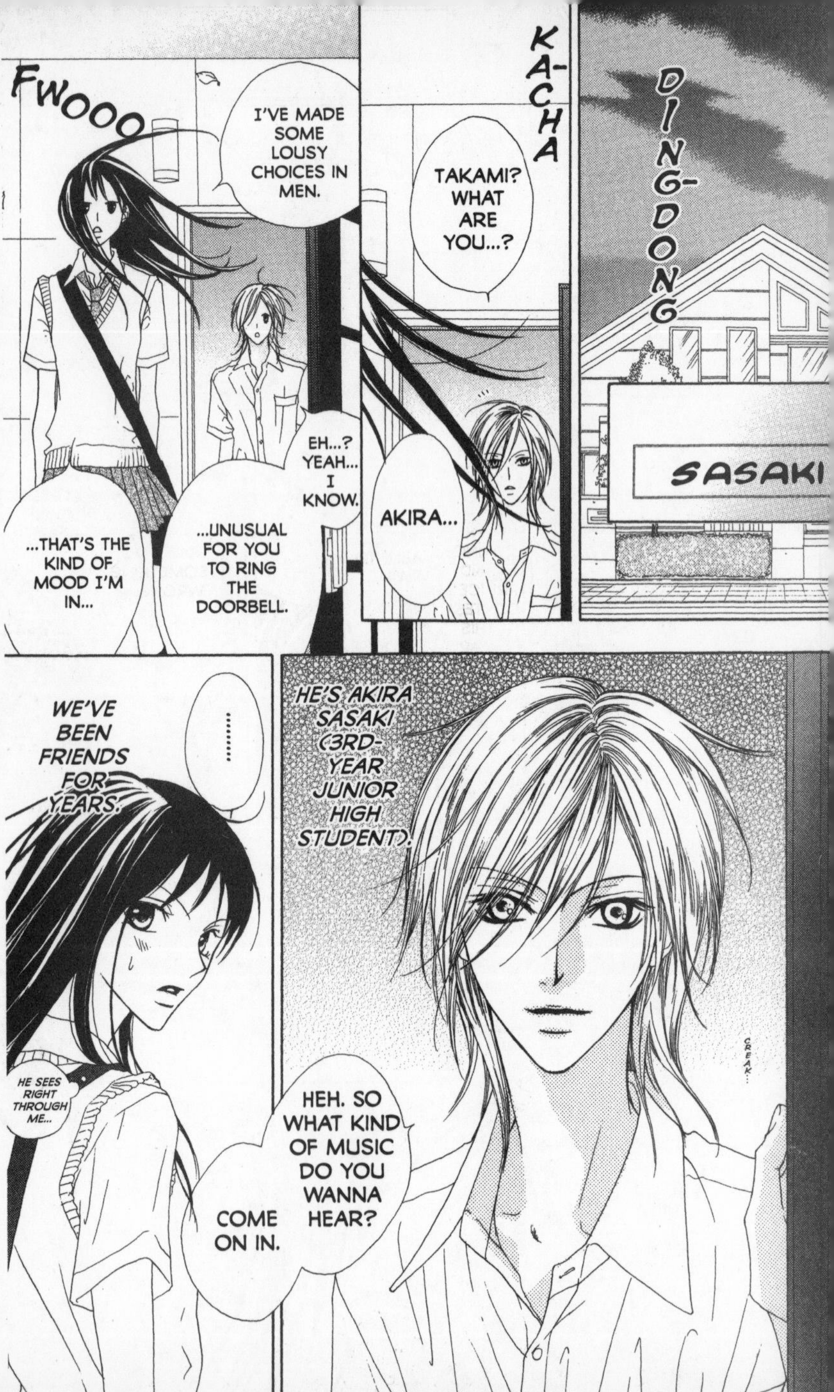
DINGDONG
SASAKI
KACHA
TAKAMI? WHAT ARE YOU...?
AKIRA...
I'VE MADE SOME LOUSY CHOICES IN MEN.
FWOOOO
EH...? YEAH... I KNOW.
...UNUSUAL FOR YOU TO RING THE DOORBELL.
...THAT'S THE KIND OF MOOD I'M IN...
HE'S AKIRA SASAKI (3RD-YEAR JUNIOR HIGH STUDENT).
CREAK...
HEH. SO WHAT KIND OF MUSIC DO YOU WANNA HEAR?
COME ON IN.
......
WE'VE BEEN FRIENDS FOR YEARS.
HE SEES RIGHT THROUGH ME...

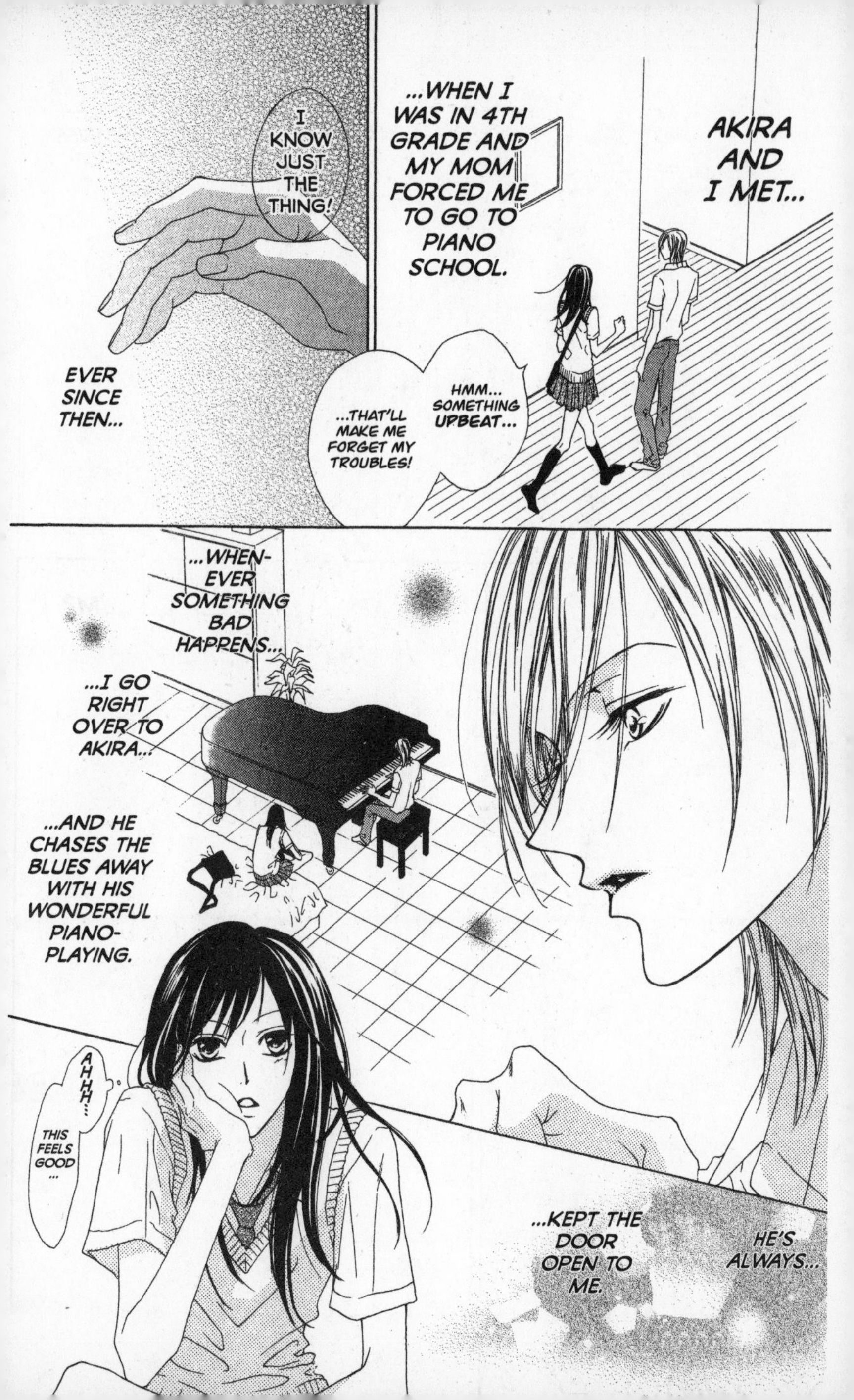
AKIRA AND I MET...
...WHEN I WAS IN 4TH GRADE AND MY MOM FORCED ME TO GO TO PIANO SCHOOL.
HMM... SOMETHING UPBEAT...
...THAT'LL MAKE ME FORGET MY TROUBLES!
I KNOW JUST THE THING!
EVER SINCE THEN...
...WHENEVER SOMETHING BAD HAPPENS...
...I GO RIGHT OVER TO AKIRA...
...AND HE CHASES THE BLUES AWAY WITH HIS WONDERFUL PIANO-PLAYING.
HE'S ALWAYS...
...KEPT THE DOOR OPEN TO ME.
AHHH...
THIS FEELS GOOD...

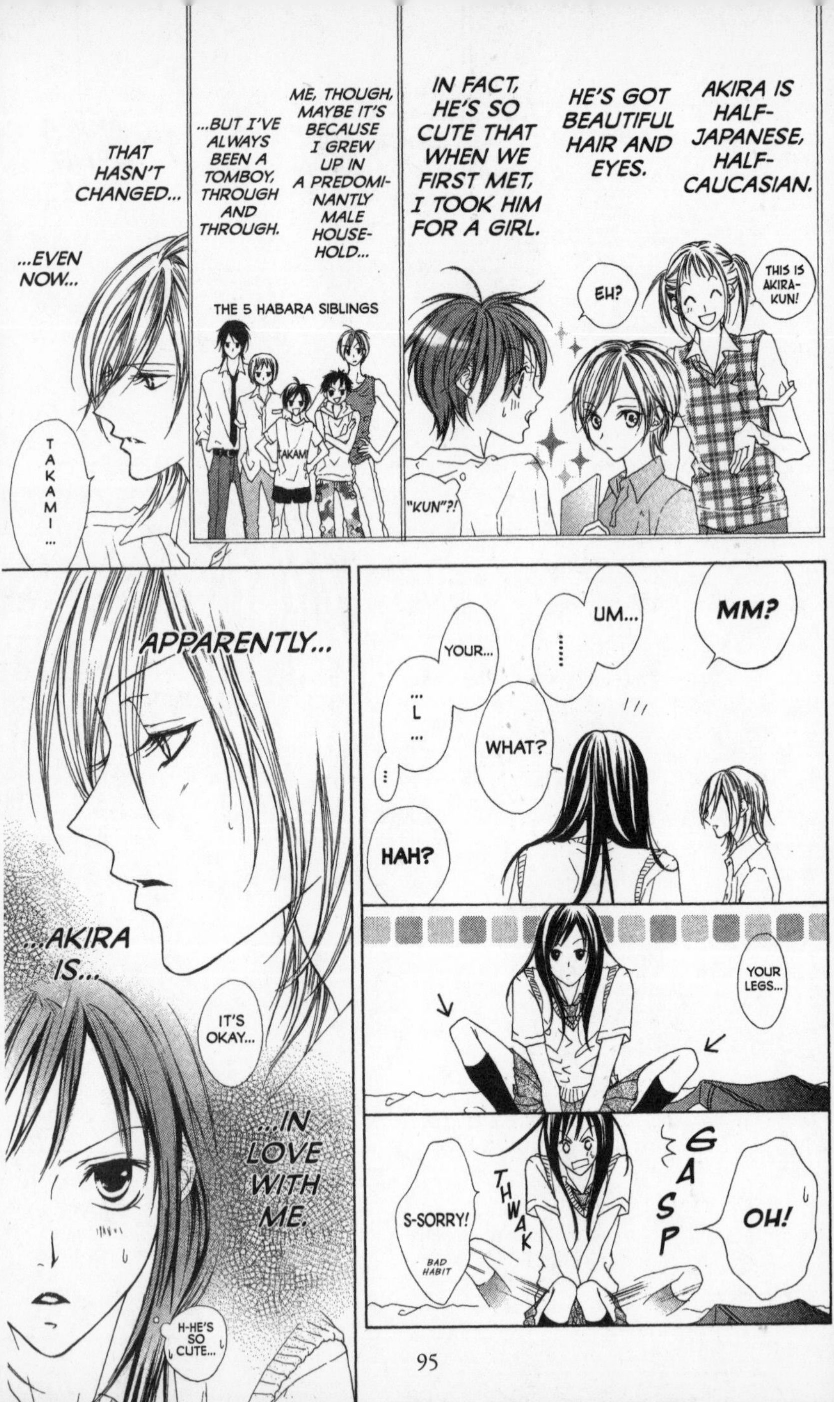
AKIRA IS HALF-JAPANESE, HALF-CAUCASIAN.
HE'S GOT BEAUTIFUL HAIR AND EYES.
IN FACT, HE'S SO CUTE THAT WHEN WE FIRST MET, I TOOK HIM FOR A GIRL.
THIS IS AKIRA-KUN!
EH?
"KUN"?!
ME, THOUGH, MAYBE IT'S BECAUSE I GREW UP IN A PREDOMI-NANTLY MALE HOUSE-HOLD...
...BUT I'VE ALWAYS BEEN A TOMBOY, THROUGH AND THROUGH.
THE 5 HABARA SIBLINGS
TAKAMI
THAT HASN'T CHANGED...
...EVEN NOW...
TAKAMI...
MM?
UM...
......
YOUR...
...L...
WHAT?
...
HAH?
YOUR LEGS...
OH!
GASP
THWAK
S-SORRY!
BAD HABIT
APPARENTLY...
...AKIRA IS...
IT'S OKAY...
...IN LOVE WITH ME.
H-HE'S SO CUTE...

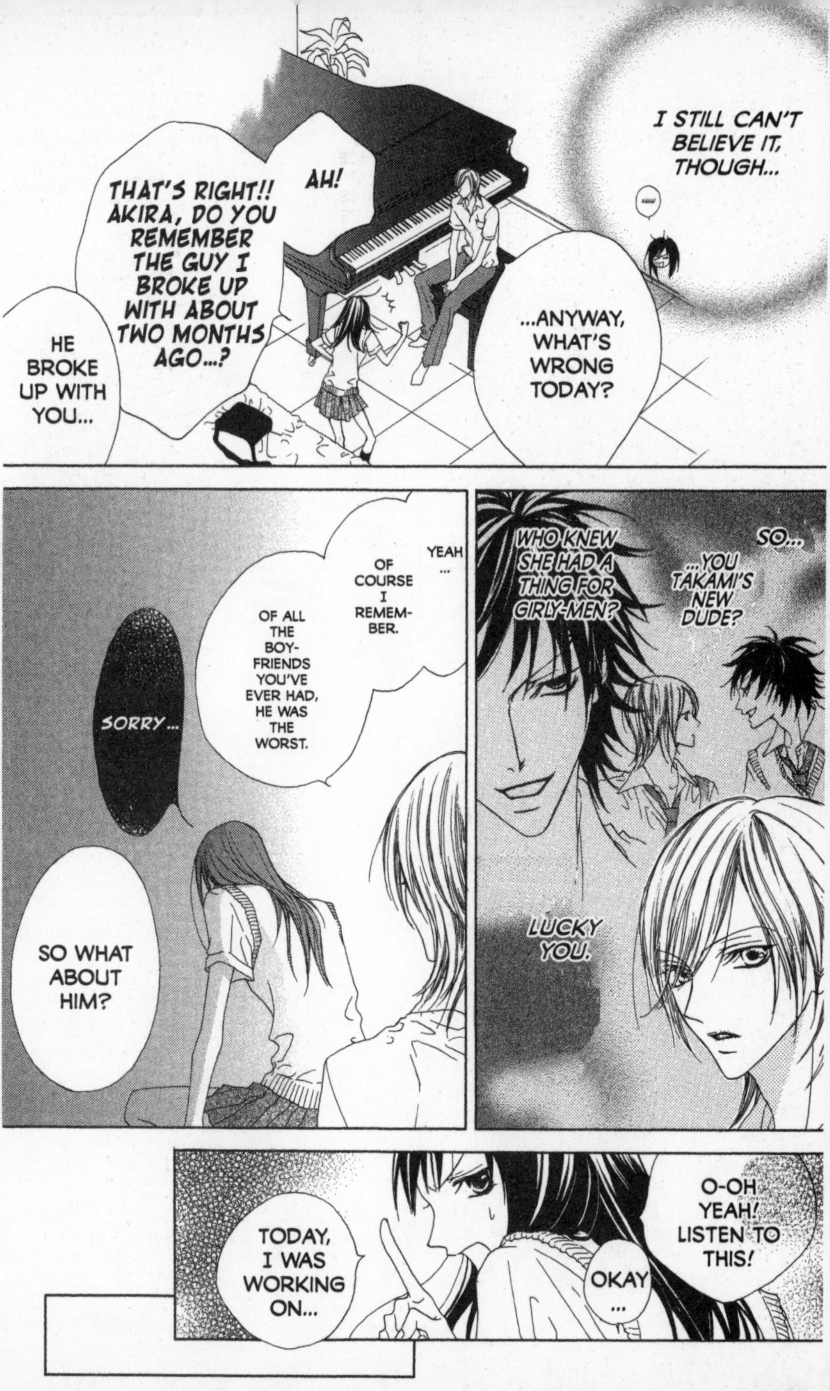
I STILL CAN'T BELIEVE IT, THOUGH...
...ANYWAY, WHAT'S WRONG TODAY?
AH!
THAT'S RIGHT!! AKIRA, DO YOU REMEMBER THE GUY I BROKE UP WITH ABOUT TWO MONTHS AGO...?
HE BROKE UP WITH YOU...
SO...
...YOU TAKAMI'S NEW DUDE?
WHO KNEW SHE HAD A THING FOR GIRLY-MEN?
LUCKY YOU.
YEAH...
OF COURSE I REMEMBER.
OF ALL THE BOY-FRIENDS YOU'VE EVER HAD, HE WAS THE WORST.
SORRY...
SO WHAT ABOUT HIM?
O-OH YEAH! LISTEN TO THIS!
OKAY...
TODAY, I WAS WORKING ON...

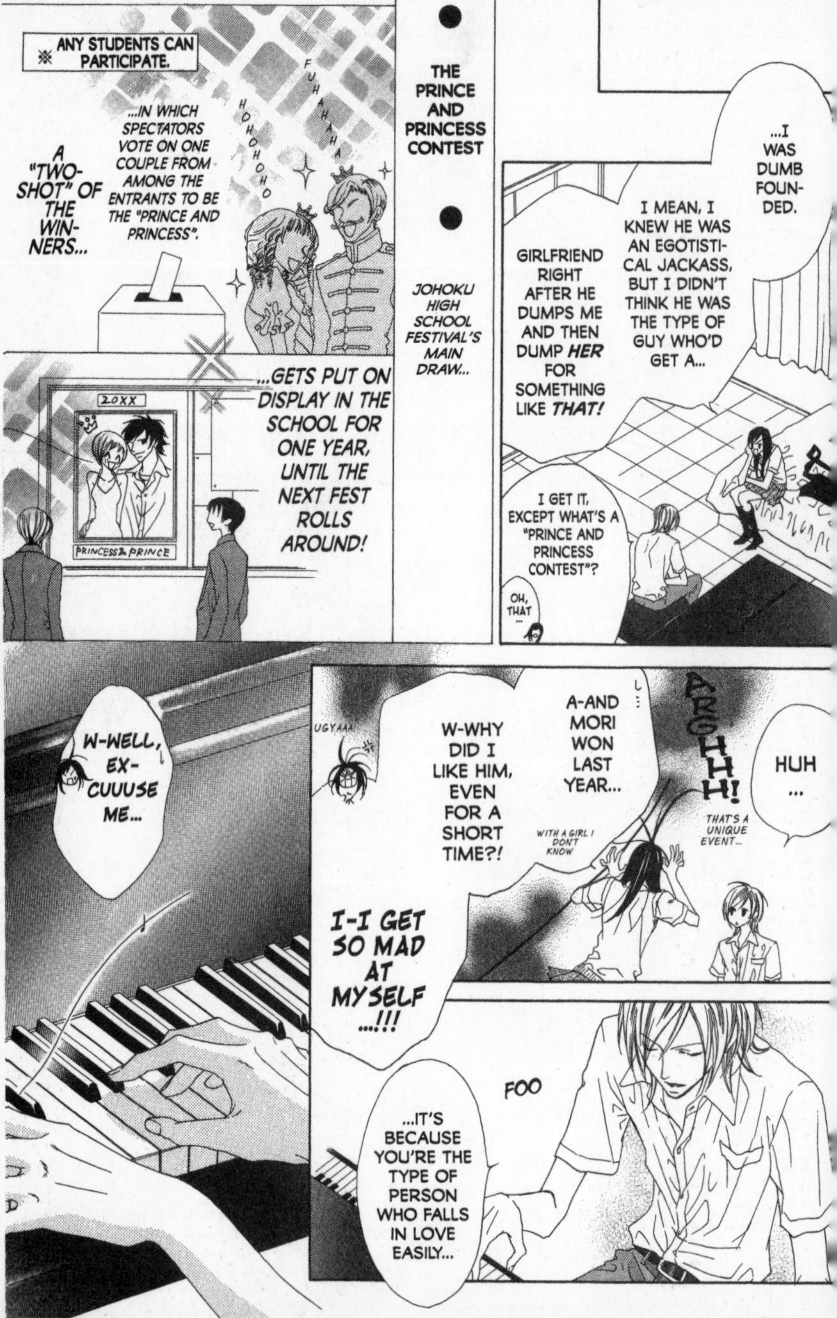
...I WAS DUMBFOUNDED.
I MEAN, I KNEW HE WAS AN EGOTISTICAL JACKASS, BUT I DIDN'T THINK HE WAS THE TYPE OF GUY WHO'D GET A...
GIRLFRIEND RIGHT AFTER HE DUMPS ME AND THEN DUMP HER FOR SOMETHING LIKE THAT!
I GET IT, EXCEPT WHAT'S A "PRINCE AND PRINCESS CONTEST"?
OH, THAT ...
THE PRINCE AND PRINCESS CONTEST
JOHOKU HIGH SCHOOL FESTIVAL'S MAIN DRAW...
※ ANY STUDENTS CAN PARTICIPATE.
FUHAHAHA
HOHOHOHO
...IN WHICH SPECTATORS VOTE ON ONE COUPLE FROM AMONG THE ENTRANTS TO BE THE "PRINCE AND PRINCESS".
A "TWO-SHOT" OF THE WINNERS...
...GETS PUT ON DISPLAY IN THE SCHOOL FOR ONE YEAR, UNTIL THE NEXT FEST ROLLS AROUND!
20XX
PRINCESS & PRINCE
HUH ...
THAT'S A UNIQUE EVENT...
ARGHHH!
A-AND MORI WON LAST YEAR...
WITH A GIRL I DON'T KNOW
W-WHY DID I LIKE HIM, EVEN FOR A SHORT TIME?!
UGYAAA
I-I GET SO MAD AT MYSELF ...!!!
FOO
...IT'S BECAUSE YOU'RE THE TYPE OF PERSON WHO FALLS IN LOVE EASILY...
W-WELL, EXCUUUSE ME...

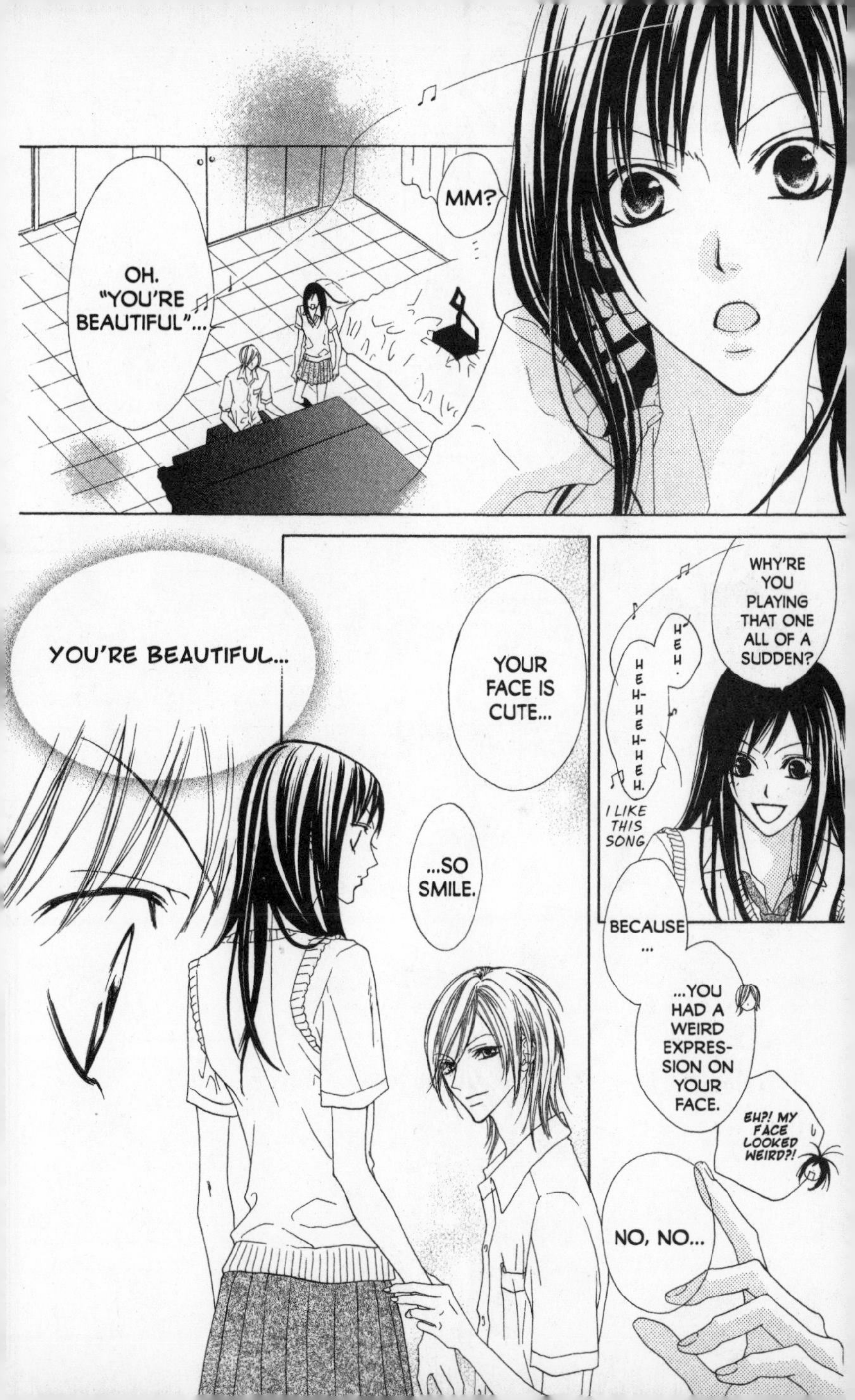
MM?
OH. "YOU'RE BEAUTIFUL"...
WHY'RE YOU PLAYING THAT ONE ALL OF A SUDDEN?
HEH. HEH-HEH-HEH-HEH.
I LIKE THIS SONG
BECAUSE...
...YOU HAD A WEIRD EXPRESSION ON YOUR FACE.
EH?! MY FACE LOOKED WEIRD?!
NO, NO...
YOUR FACE IS CUTE...
...SO SMILE.
YOU'RE BEAUTIFUL...

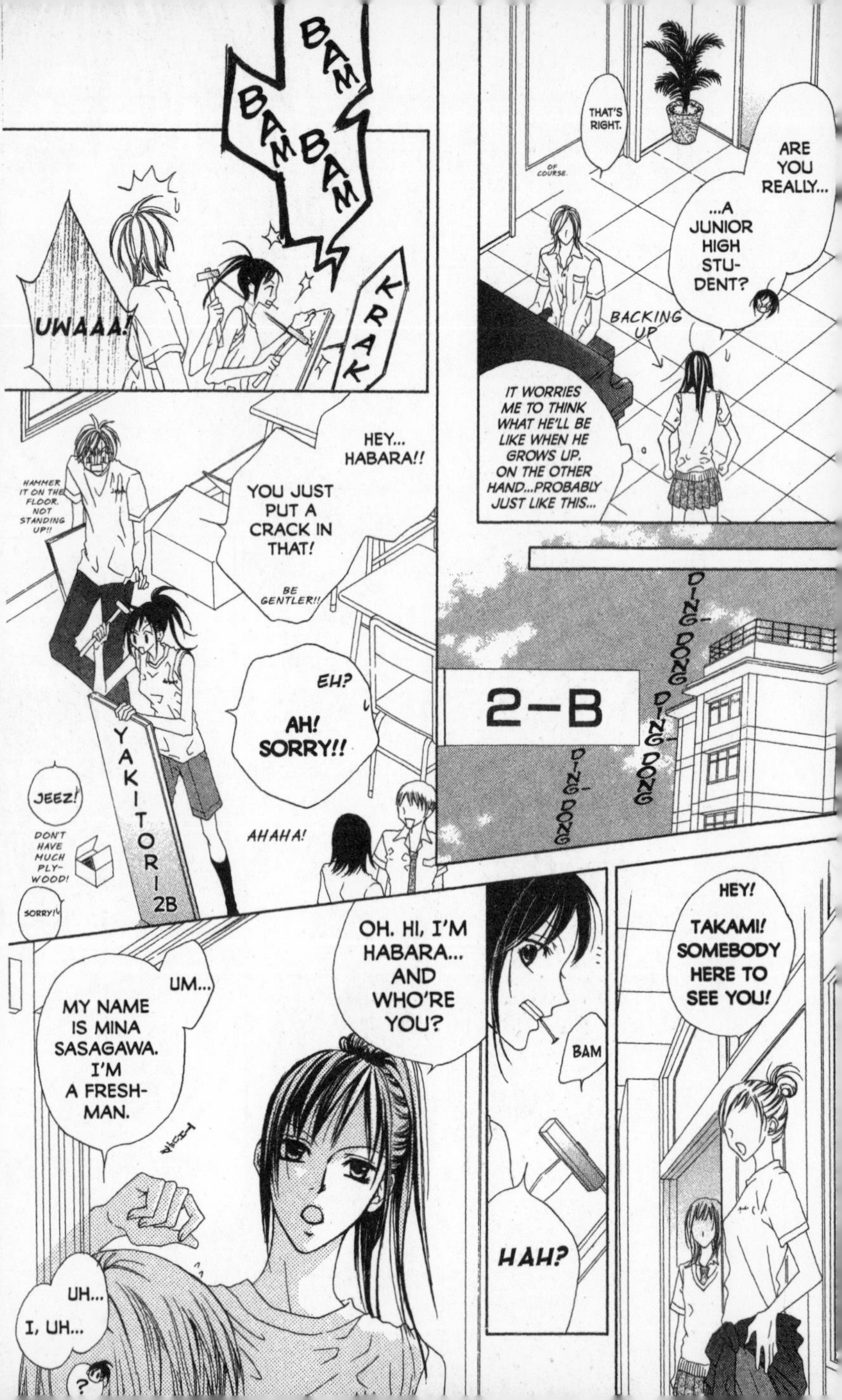

ARE YOU REALLY...
...A JUNIOR HIGH STUDENT?
THAT'S RIGHT.
OF COURSE.
BACKING UP
IT WORRIES ME TO THINK WHAT HE'LL BE LIKE WHEN HE GROWS UP. ON THE OTHER HAND...PROBABLY JUST LIKE THIS...
DING-DONG DING-DONG
2-B
DING-DONG DING-DONG
BAM BAM BAM BAM
KRAK
UWAAA!
HEY... HABARA!!
YOU JUST PUT A CRACK IN THAT!
BE GENTLER!!
HAMMER IT ON THE FLOOR, NOT STANDING UP!!
EH?
AH! SORRY!!
AHAHA!
YAKITORI 2B
JEEZ!
DON'T HAVE MUCH PLYWOOD!
SORRY!!
HEY!
TAKAMI! SOMEBODY HERE TO SEE YOU!
BAM
HAH?
OH. HI, I'M HABARA... AND WHO'RE YOU?
UM...
MY NAME IS MINA SASAGAWA. I'M A FRESHMAN.
UH...
I, UH...
?

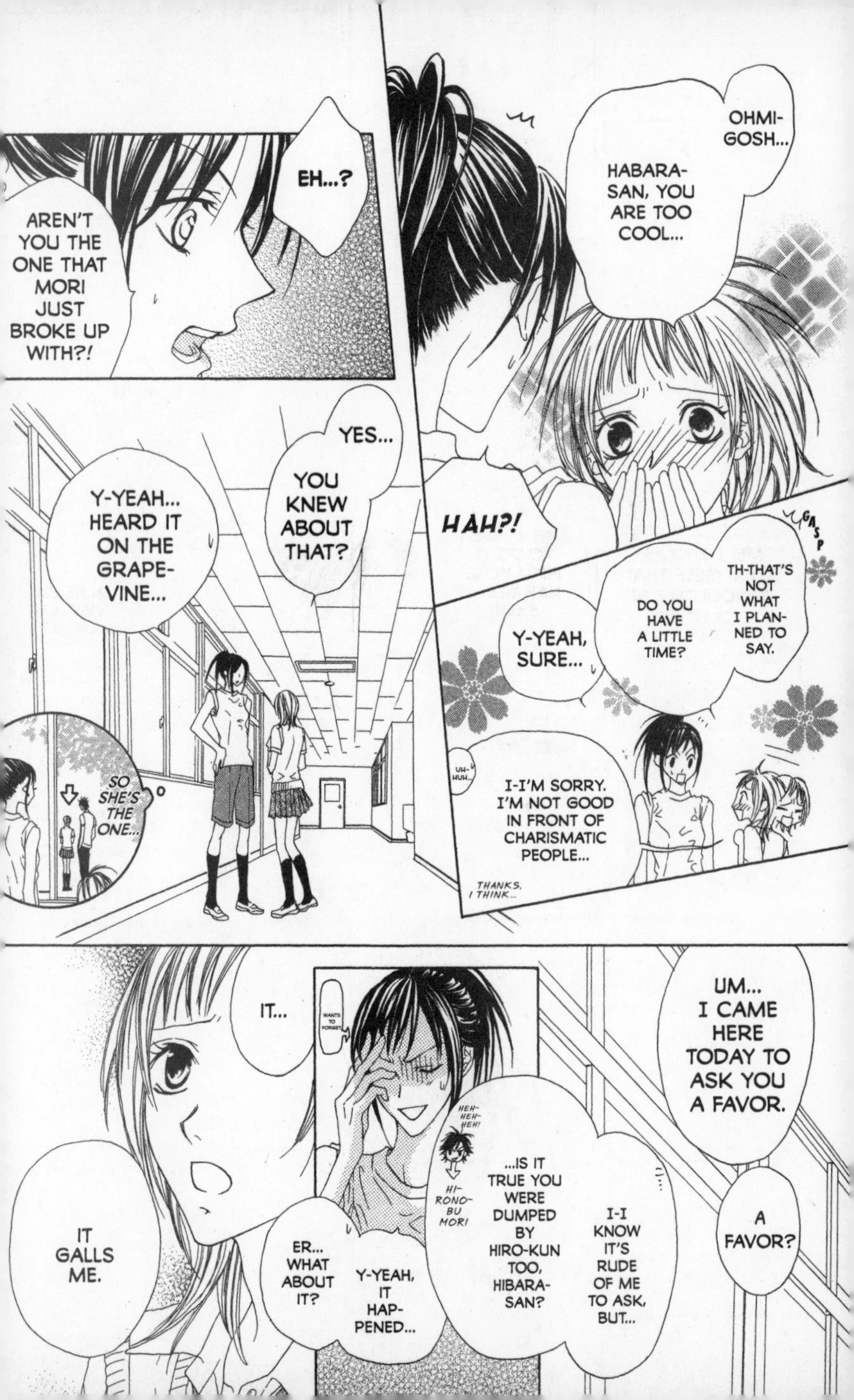
OHMI-GOSH...
HABARA-SAN, YOU ARE TOO COOL...
HAH?!
GASP
TH-THAT'S NOT WHAT I PLANNED TO SAY.
DO YOU HAVE A LITTLE TIME?
Y-YEAH, SURE...
I-I'M SORRY. I'M NOT GOOD IN FRONT OF CHARISMATIC PEOPLE...
UH-HUH...
THANKS, I THINK...
EH...?
AREN'T YOU THE ONE THAT MORI JUST BROKE UP WITH?!
YES...
YOU KNEW ABOUT THAT?
Y-YEAH... HEARD IT ON THE GRAPE-VINE...
SO SHE'S THE ONE...
UM... I CAME HERE TODAY TO ASK YOU A FAVOR.
A FAVOR?
I-I KNOW IT'S RUDE OF ME TO ASK, BUT...
...IS IT TRUE YOU WERE DUMPED BY HIRO-KUN TOO, HIBARA-SAN?
HEH-HEH-HEH!
HIRO-NOBU MORI
WANTS TO FORGET
Y-YEAH, IT HAP-PENED...
ER... WHAT ABOUT IT?
IT...
IT GALLS ME.

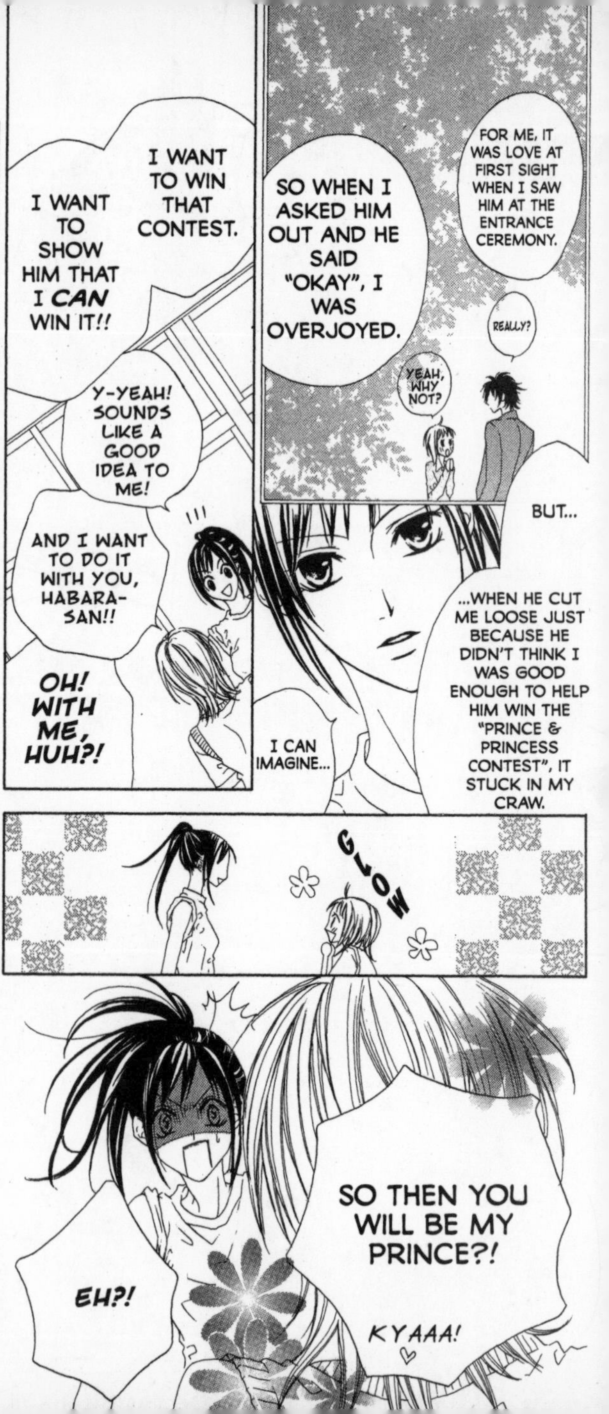
FOR ME, IT WAS LOVE AT FIRST SIGHT WHEN I SAW HIM AT THE ENTRANCE CEREMONY.
SO WHEN I ASKED HIM OUT AND HE SAID "OKAY", I WAS OVERJOYED.
REALLY?
YEAH, WHY NOT?
BUT...
...WHEN HE CUT ME LOOSE JUST BECAUSE HE DIDN'T THINK I WAS GOOD ENOUGH TO HELP HIM WIN THE "PRINCE & PRINCESS CONTEST", IT STUCK IN MY CRAW.
I CAN IMAGINE...
I WANT TO WIN THAT CONTEST.
I WANT TO SHOW HIM THAT I *CAN* WIN IT!!
Y-YEAH! SOUNDS LIKE A GOOD IDEA TO ME!
AND I WANT TO DO IT WITH YOU, HABARA-SAN!!
OH! WITH ME, HUH?!
GLOW
SO THEN YOU WILL BE MY PRINCE?!
EH?!
KYAAA!

3

FROM THIS EPISODE, I GOT MY FIRST SHORT-TERM SERIALIZED RUN.

BEFORE THE DECISION TO DO IT OR NOT CAME DOWN, I SHOWED THE PLOT TO AN EDITOR, WHO REGARDED IT WITH SOME DOUBTS. AT THE TIME, I THOUGHT TO MYSELF THAT IT WOULDN'T BE PICKED UP.

A LITTLE TIME PASSED AND AROUND THE TIME I FINISHED THE PLOT FOR THESE THREE EPISODES, I GOT A CALL SAYING THE MAGAZINE WAS GOING TO GO WITH IT.

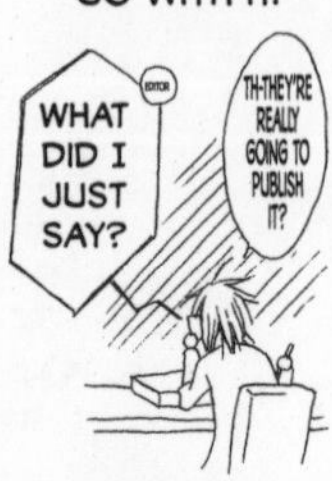
EDITOR
WHAT DID I JUST SAY?
TH-THEY'RE REALLY GOING TO PUBLISH IT?

I DOUBTED IT UNTIL THEN.

AND IT'S ALL BECAUSE OF YOU READERS. THANK YOU SO MUCH!!

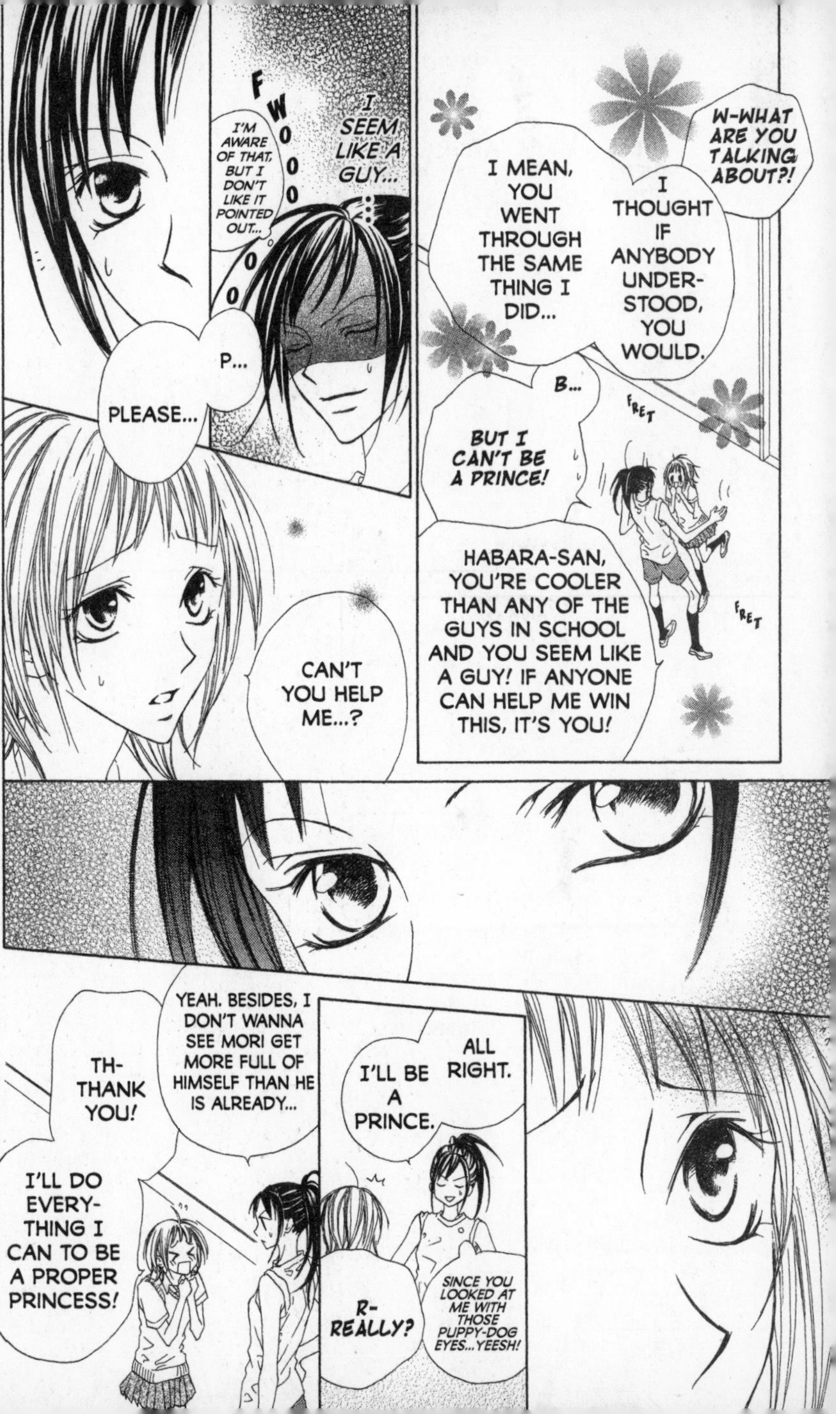
W-WHAT ARE YOU TALKING ABOUT?!
I THOUGHT IF ANYBODY UNDERSTOOD, YOU WOULD.
I MEAN, YOU WENT THROUGH THE SAME THING I DID...
B...
BUT I CAN'T BE A PRINCE!
FRET
FRET
HABARA-SAN, YOU'RE COOLER THAN ANY OF THE GUYS IN SCHOOL AND YOU SEEM LIKE A GUY! IF ANYONE CAN HELP ME WIN THIS, IT'S YOU!
I SEEM LIKE A GUY...
FWOOOOOO
I'M AWARE OF THAT, BUT I DON'T LIKE IT POINTED OUT...
P...
PLEASE...
CAN'T YOU HELP ME...?
ALL RIGHT.
I'LL BE A PRINCE.
SINCE YOU LOOKED AT ME WITH THOSE PUPPY-DOG EYES...YEESH!
R-REALLY?
YEAH. BESIDES, I DON'T WANNA SEE MORI GET MORE FULL OF HIMSELF THAN HE IS ALREADY...
TH-THANK YOU!
I'LL DO EVERYTHING I CAN TO BE A PROPER PRINCESS!

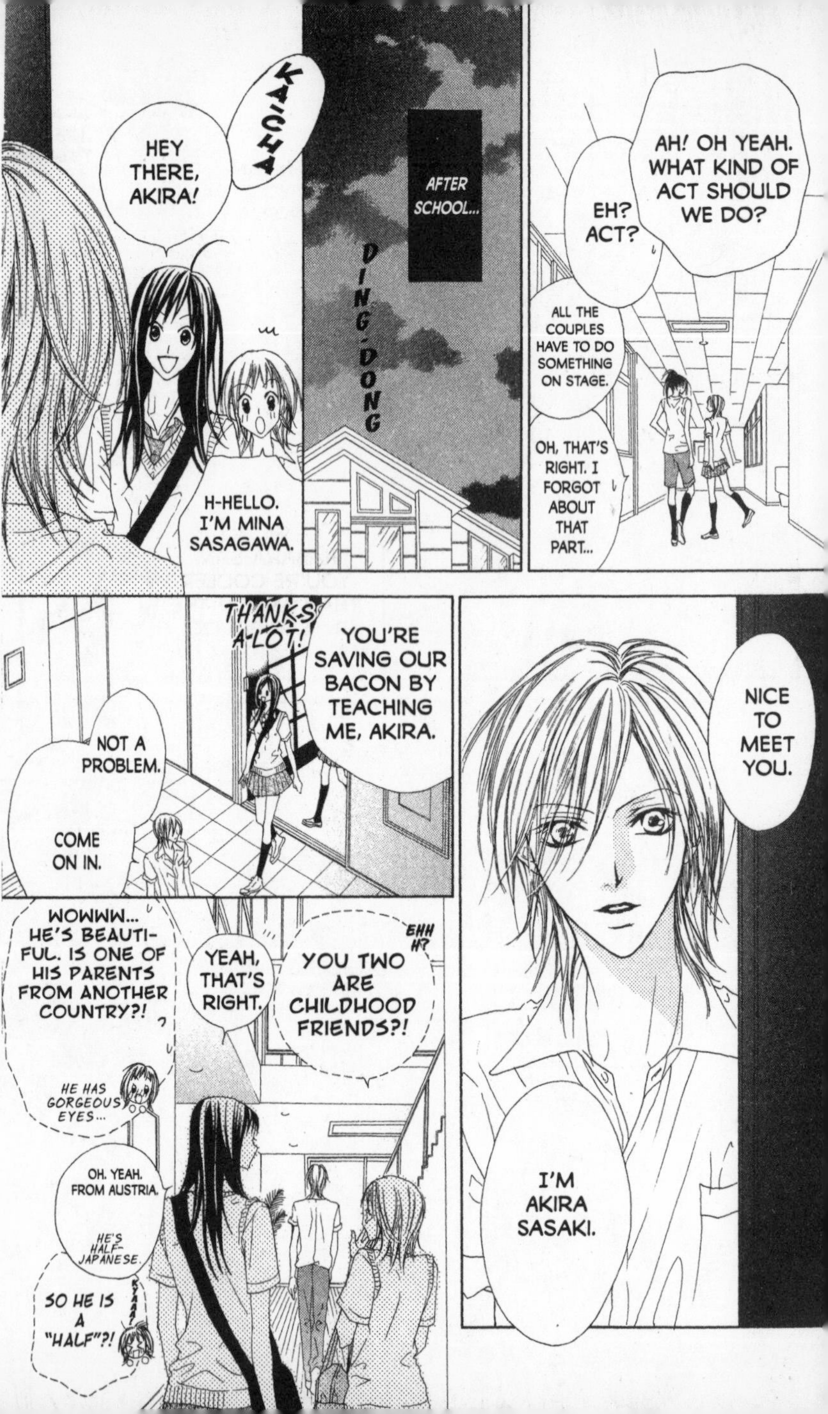
AH! OH YEAH. WHAT KIND OF ACT SHOULD WE DO?
EH? ACT?
ALL THE COUPLES HAVE TO DO SOMETHING ON STAGE.
OH, THAT'S RIGHT. I FORGOT ABOUT THAT PART...
AFTER SCHOOL...
DING-DONG
KA-CHA
HEY THERE, AKIRA!
H-HELLO. I'M MINA SASAGAWA.
NICE TO MEET YOU.
I'M AKIRA SASAKI.
THANKS-A-LOT!
YOU'RE SAVING OUR BACON BY TEACHING ME, AKIRA.
NOT A PROBLEM.
COME ON IN.
EHHH?
YOU TWO ARE CHILDHOOD FRIENDS?!
YEAH, THAT'S RIGHT.
WOWWW... HE'S BEAUTIFUL. IS ONE OF HIS PARENTS FROM ANOTHER COUNTRY?!
HE HAS GORGEOUS EYES...
OH. YEAH. FROM AUSTRIA.
HE'S HALF-JAPANESE.
SO HE IS A "HALF"?!

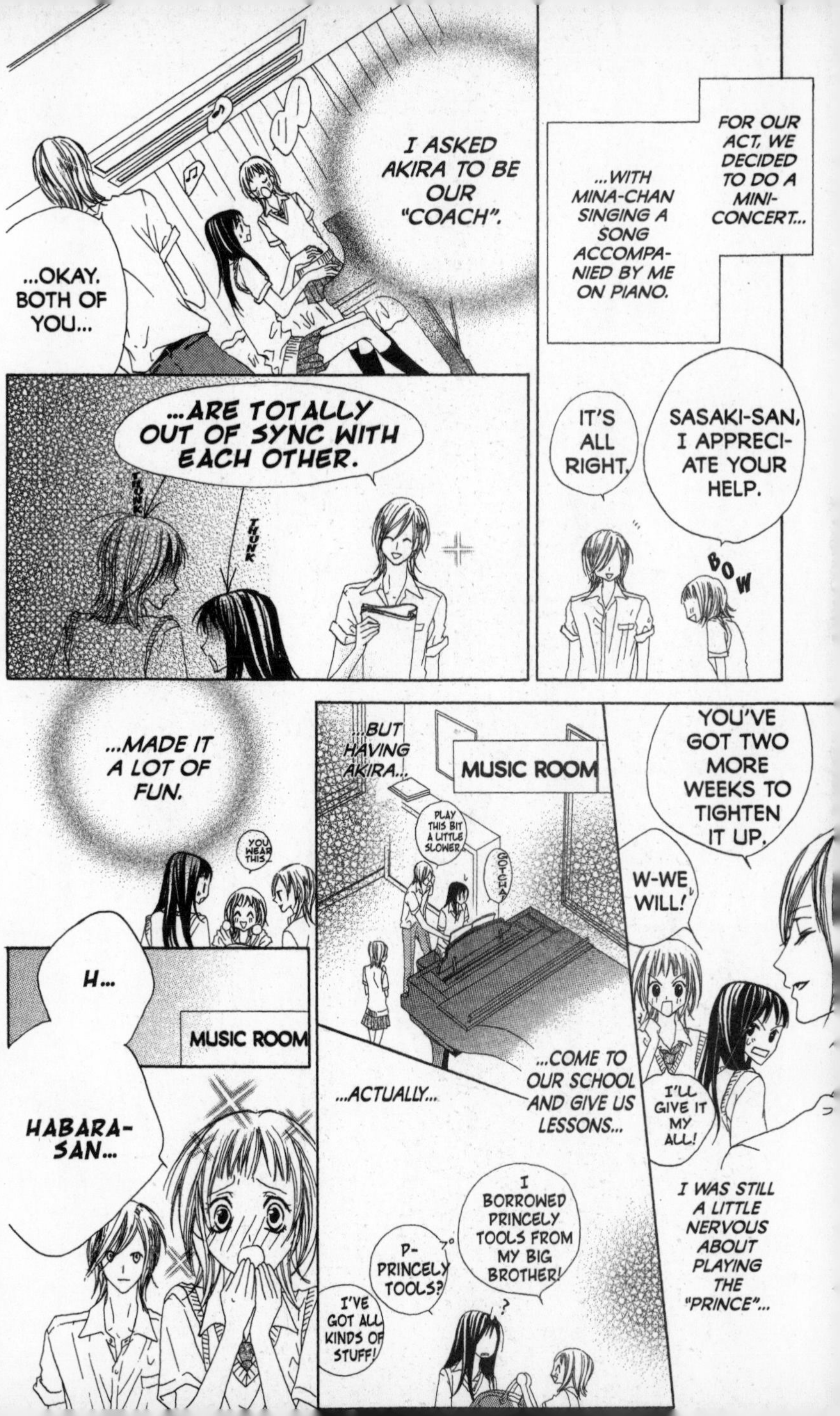
FOR OUR ACT, WE DECIDED TO DO A MINI-CONCERT...
...WITH MINA-CHAN SINGING A SONG ACCOMPANIED BY ME ON PIANO.
I ASKED AKIRA TO BE OUR "COACH".
...OKAY. BOTH OF YOU...
SASAKI-SAN, I APPRECIATE YOUR HELP.
BOW
IT'S ALL RIGHT.
...ARE TOTALLY OUT OF SYNC WITH EACH OTHER.
THUNK
THUNK
YOU'VE GOT TWO MORE WEEKS TO TIGHTEN IT UP.
W-WE WILL!
I'LL GIVE IT MY ALL!
I WAS STILL A LITTLE NERVOUS ABOUT PLAYING THE "PRINCE"...
...BUT HAVING AKIRA...
MUSIC ROOM
PLAY THIS BIT A LITTLE SLOWER.
GOTCHA!
...COME TO OUR SCHOOL AND GIVE US LESSONS...
...ACTUALLY...
I BORROWED PRINCELY TOOLS FROM MY BIG BROTHER!
P-PRINCELY TOOLS?
I'VE GOT ALL KINDS OF STUFF!
...MADE IT A LOT OF FUN.
YOU WEAR THIS...
H...
MUSIC ROOM
HABARA-SAN...

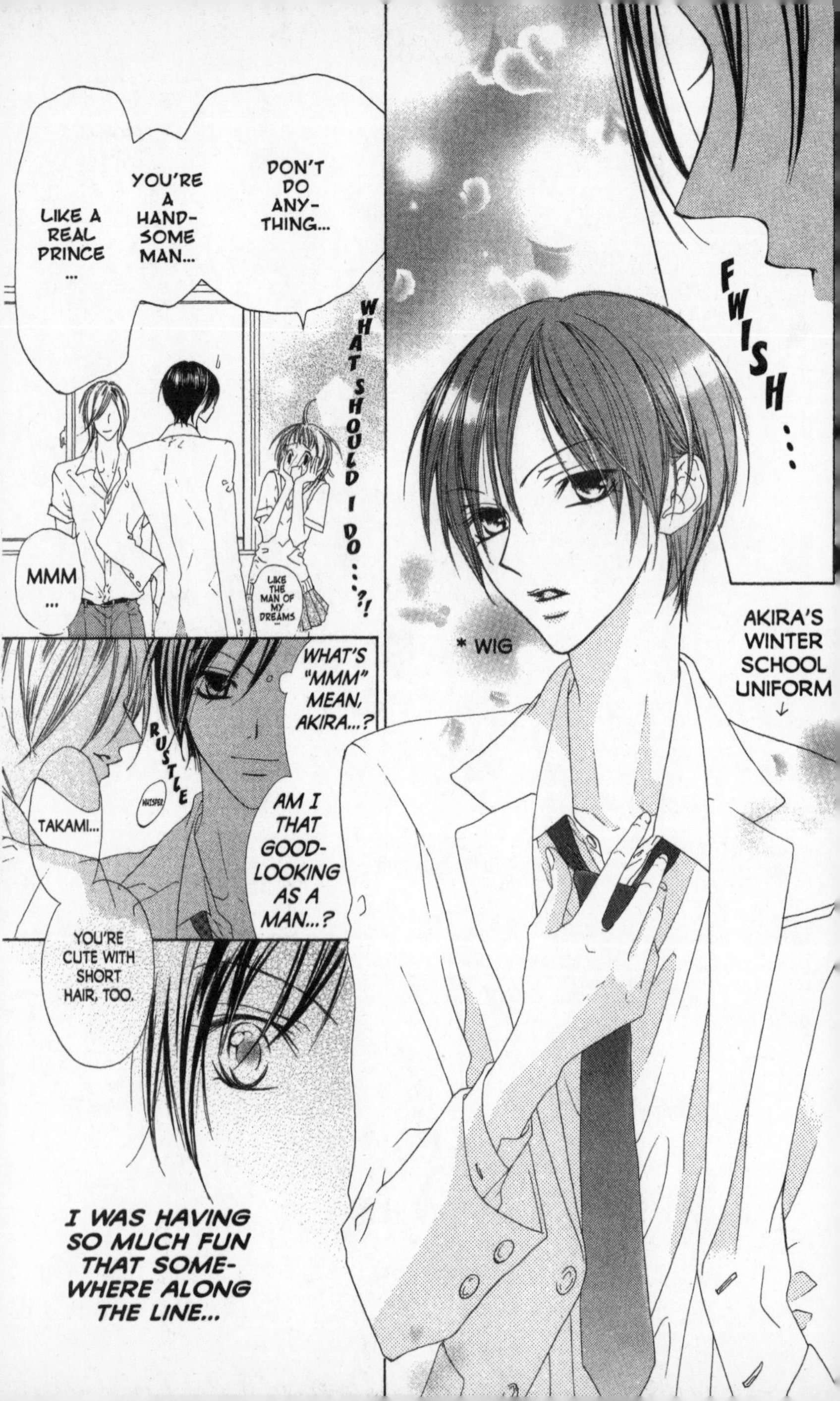
FWISH...
* WIG
AKIRA'S WINTER SCHOOL UNIFORM ↓
DON'T DO ANYTHING...
YOU'RE A HANDSOME MAN...
LIKE A REAL PRINCE...
WHAT SHOULD I DO...?!
LIKE THE MAN OF MY DREAMS...
MMM...
WHAT'S "MMM" MEAN, AKIRA...?
RUSTLE
AM I THAT GOOD-LOOKING AS A MAN...?
WHISPER
TAKAMI...
YOU'RE CUTE WITH SHORT HAIR, TOO.
I WAS HAVING SO MUCH FUN THAT SOME-WHERE ALONG THE LINE...

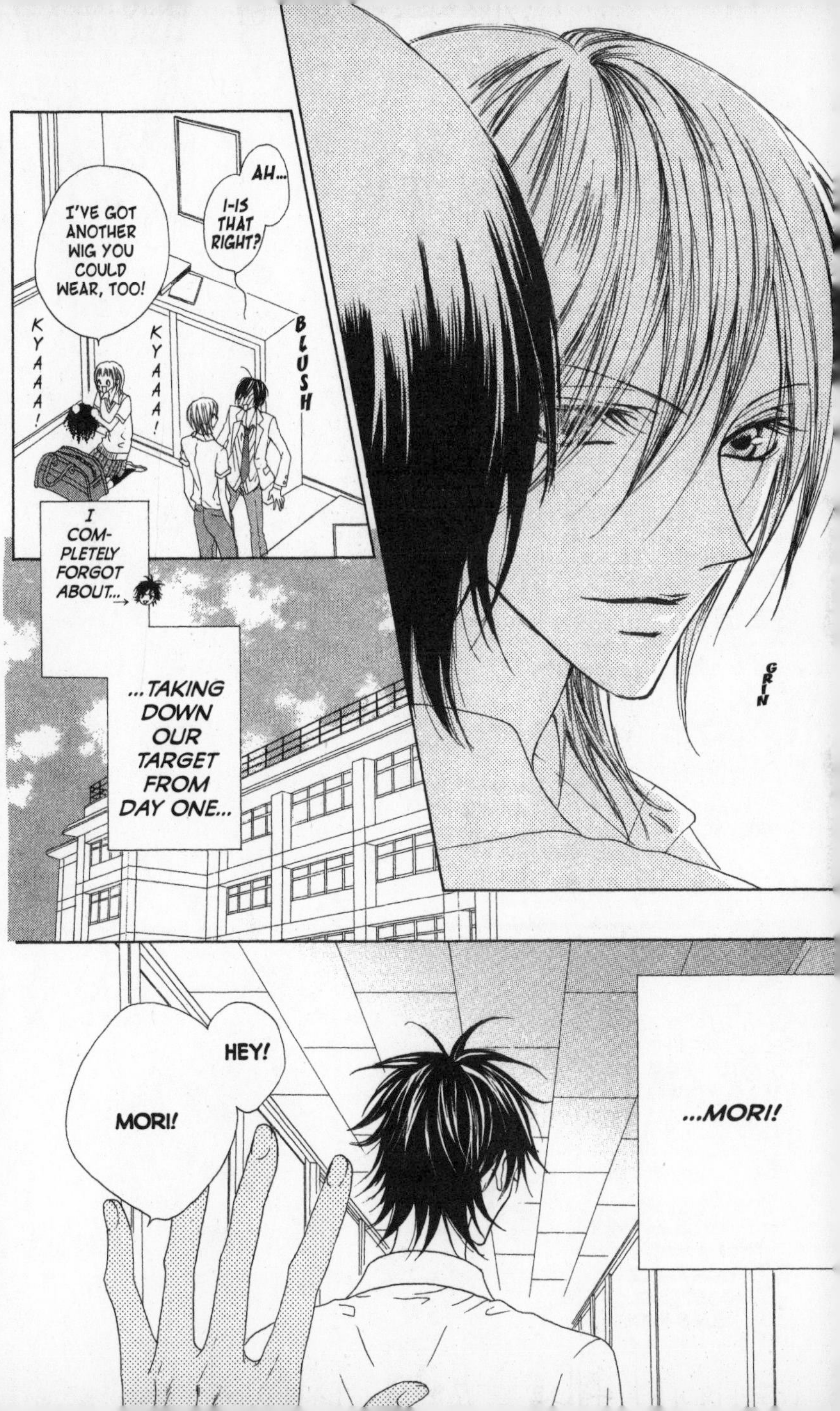
GRIN
AH... I-IS THAT RIGHT?
BLUSH
I'VE GOT ANOTHER WIG YOU COULD WEAR, TOO!
KYAAAA!
KYAAAA!
I COM-PLETELY FORGOT ABOUT...
...TAKING DOWN OUR TARGET FROM DAY ONE...
...MORI!
HEY! MORI!

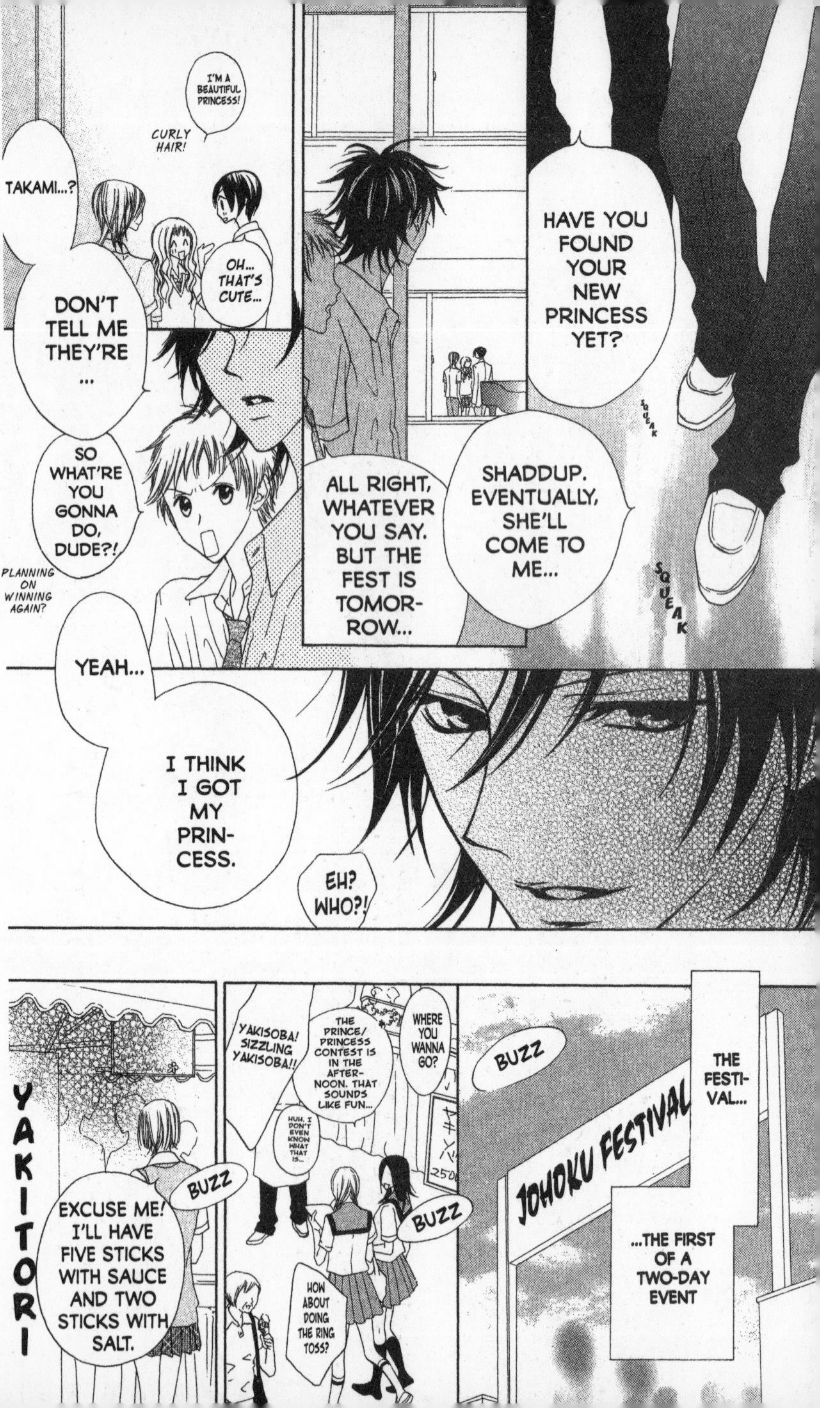
HAVE YOU FOUND YOUR NEW PRINCESS YET?
SQUEAK
SQUEAK
SHADDUP. EVENTUALLY, SHE'LL COME TO ME...
ALL RIGHT, WHATEVER YOU SAY. BUT THE FEST IS TOMORROW...
I'M A BEAUTIFUL PRINCESS!
CURLY HAIR!
TAKAMI...?
OH... THAT'S CUTE...
DON'T TELL ME THEY'RE ...
SO WHAT'RE YOU GONNA DO, DUDE?!
PLANNING ON WINNING AGAIN?
YEAH...
I THINK I GOT MY PRINCESS.
EH? WHO?!
THE FESTIVAL...
JOHOKU FESTIVAL
BUZZ
...THE FIRST OF A TWO-DAY EVENT
WHERE YOU WANNA GO?
THE PRINCE/PRINCESS CONTEST IS IN THE AFTERNOON. THAT SOUNDS LIKE FUN...
YAKISOBA! SIZZLING YAKISOBA!!
HUH, I DON'T EVEN KNOW WHAT THAT IS...
BUZZ
HOW ABOUT DOING THE RING TOSS?
YAKITORI
BUZZ
EXCUSE ME! I'LL HAVE FIVE STICKS WITH SAUCE AND TWO STICKS WITH SALT.

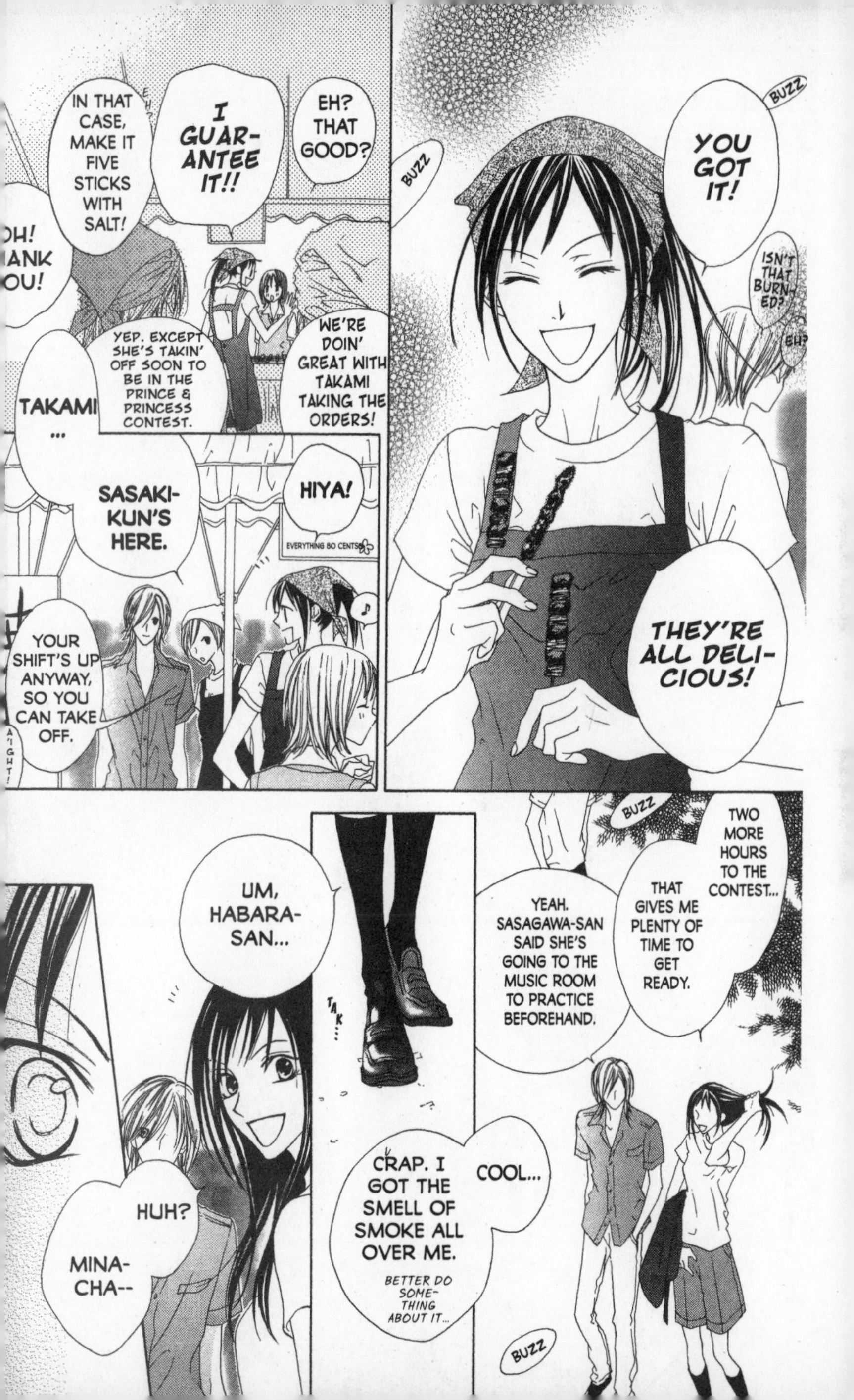
YOU GOT IT!
BUZZ
ISN'T THAT BURNED?
EH?
BUZZ
THEY'RE ALL DELICIOUS!
EH? THAT GOOD?
I GUARANTEE IT!!
EH?
IN THAT CASE, MAKE IT FIVE STICKS WITH SALT!
OH! ANK OU!
WE'RE DOIN' GREAT WITH TAKAMI TAKING THE ORDERS!
YEP. EXCEPT SHE'S TAKIN' OFF SOON TO BE IN THE PRINCE & PRINCESS CONTEST.
TAKAMI ...
HIYA!
SASAKI-KUN'S HERE.
EVERYTHING 80 CENTS
YOUR SHIFT'S UP ANYWAY, SO YOU CAN TAKE OFF.
A'IGHT!
BUZZ
TWO MORE HOURS TO THE CONTEST...
THAT GIVES ME PLENTY OF TIME TO GET READY.
YEAH. SASAGAWA-SAN SAID SHE'S GOING TO THE MUSIC ROOM TO PRACTICE BEFOREHAND.
COOL...
CRAP. I GOT THE SMELL OF SMOKE ALL OVER ME.
BETTER DO SOMETHING ABOUT IT...
BUZZ
TAK...
UM, HABARA-SAN...
HUH?
MINA-CHA--

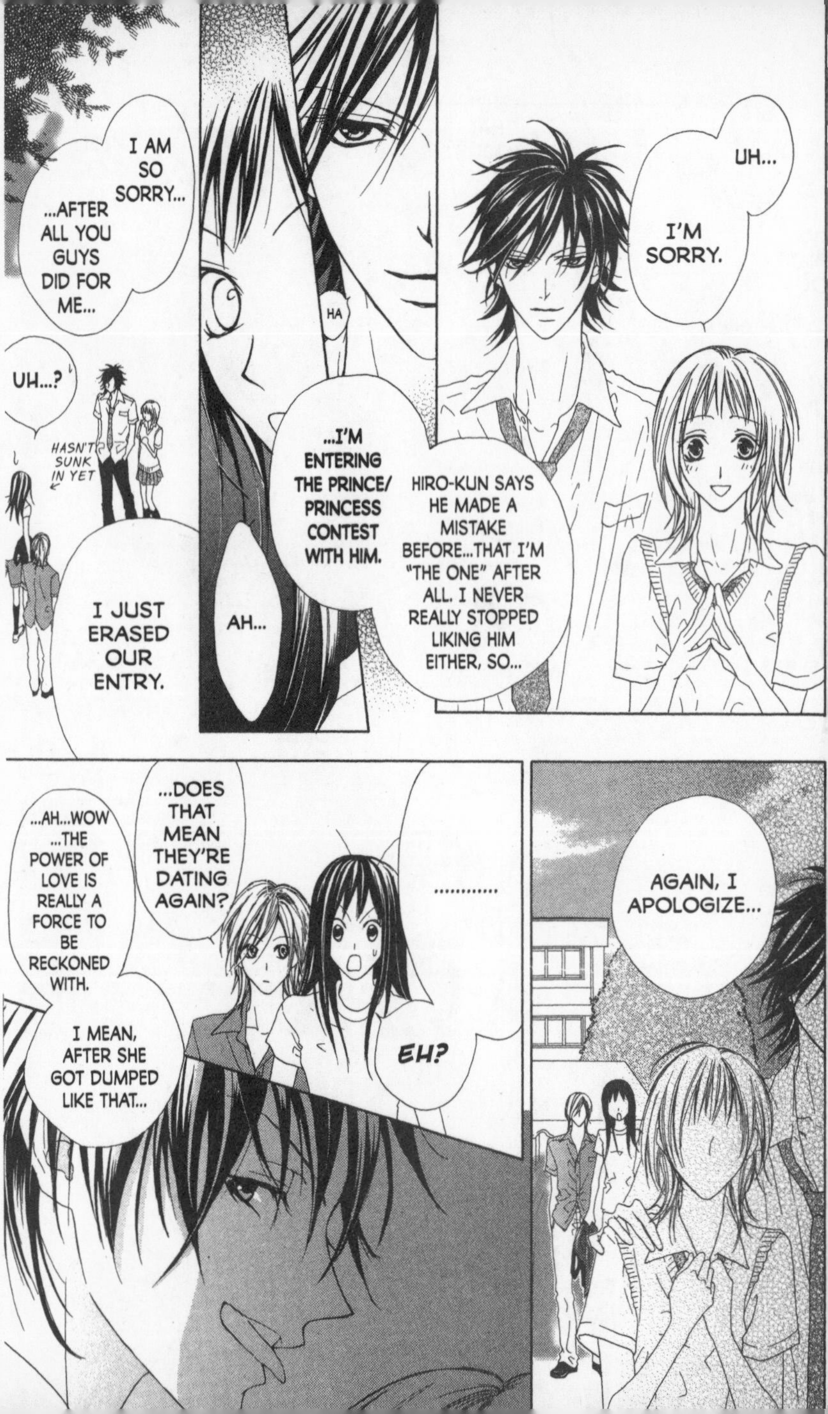
UH...
I'M SORRY.
HIRO-KUN SAYS HE MADE A MISTAKE BEFORE...THAT I'M "THE ONE" AFTER ALL. I NEVER REALLY STOPPED LIKING HIM EITHER, SO...
HA
...I'M ENTERING THE PRINCE/PRINCESS CONTEST WITH HIM.
AH...
I AM SO SORRY...
...AFTER ALL YOU GUYS DID FOR ME...
I JUST ERASED OUR ENTRY.
UH...?
HASN'T SUNK IN YET
AGAIN, I APOLOGIZE...
....
EH?
...DOES THAT MEAN THEY'RE DATING AGAIN?
...AH...WOW ...THE POWER OF LOVE IS REALLY A FORCE TO BE RECKONED WITH.
I MEAN, AFTER SHE GOT DUMPED LIKE THAT...

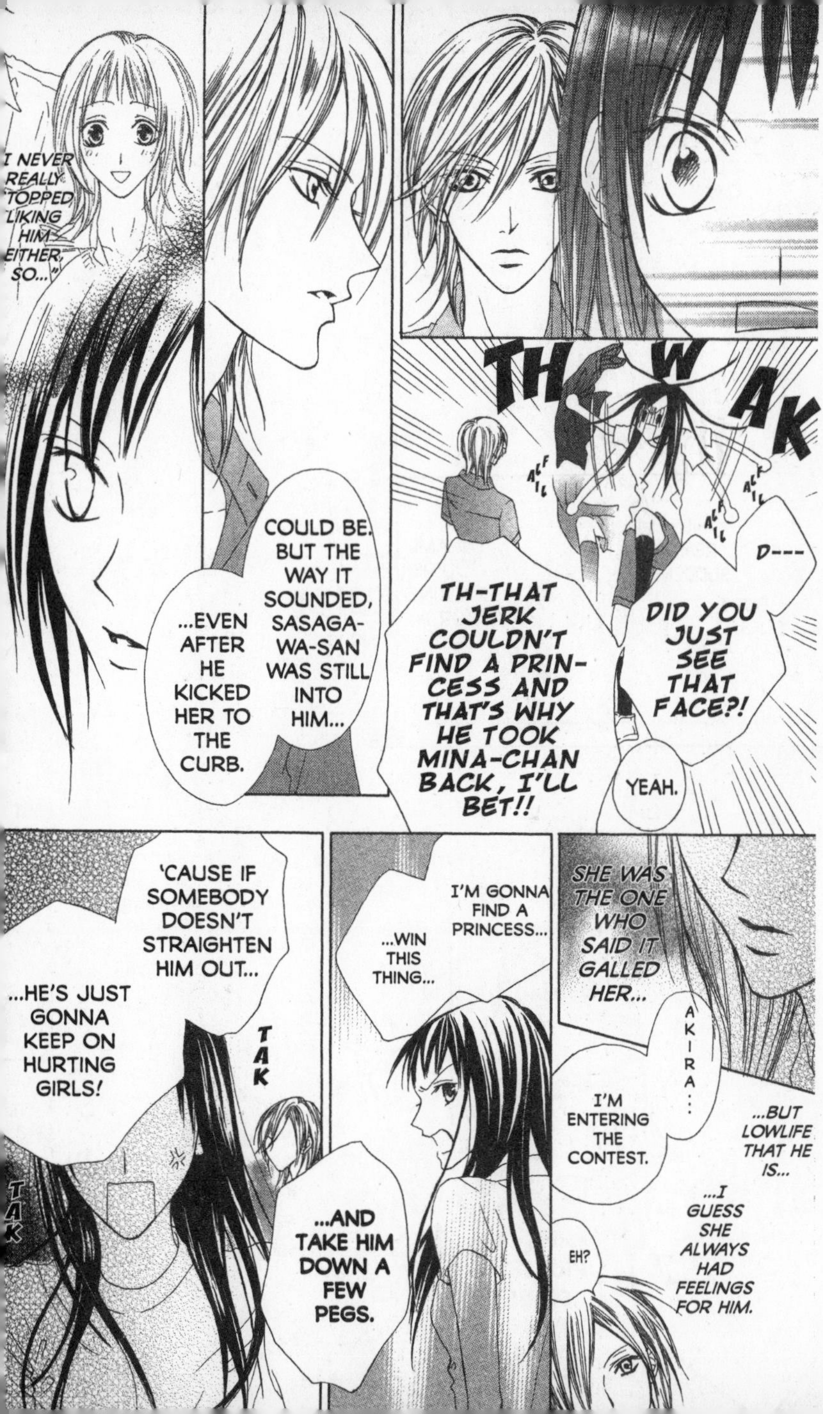
THWAK
D---
DID YOU JUST SEE THAT FACE?!
YEAH.
TH-THAT JERK COULDN'T FIND A PRINCESS AND THAT'S WHY HE TOOK MINA-CHAN BACK, I'LL BET!!
COULD BE. BUT THE WAY IT SOUNDED, SASAGAWA-SAN WAS STILL INTO HIM...
...EVEN AFTER HE KICKED HER TO THE CURB.
I NEVER REALLY 'TOPPED LIKING HIM EITHER, SO..."
SHE WAS THE ONE WHO SAID IT GALLED HER...
...BUT LOWLIFE THAT HE IS...
...I GUESS SHE ALWAYS HAD FEELINGS FOR HIM.
AKIRA...
I'M ENTERING THE CONTEST.
EH?
I'M GONNA FIND A PRINCESS...
...WIN THIS THING...
...AND TAKE HIM DOWN A FEW PEGS.
'CAUSE IF SOMEBODY DOESN'T STRAIGHTEN HIM OUT...
...HE'S JUST GONNA KEEP ON HURTING GIRLS!
TAK
TAK

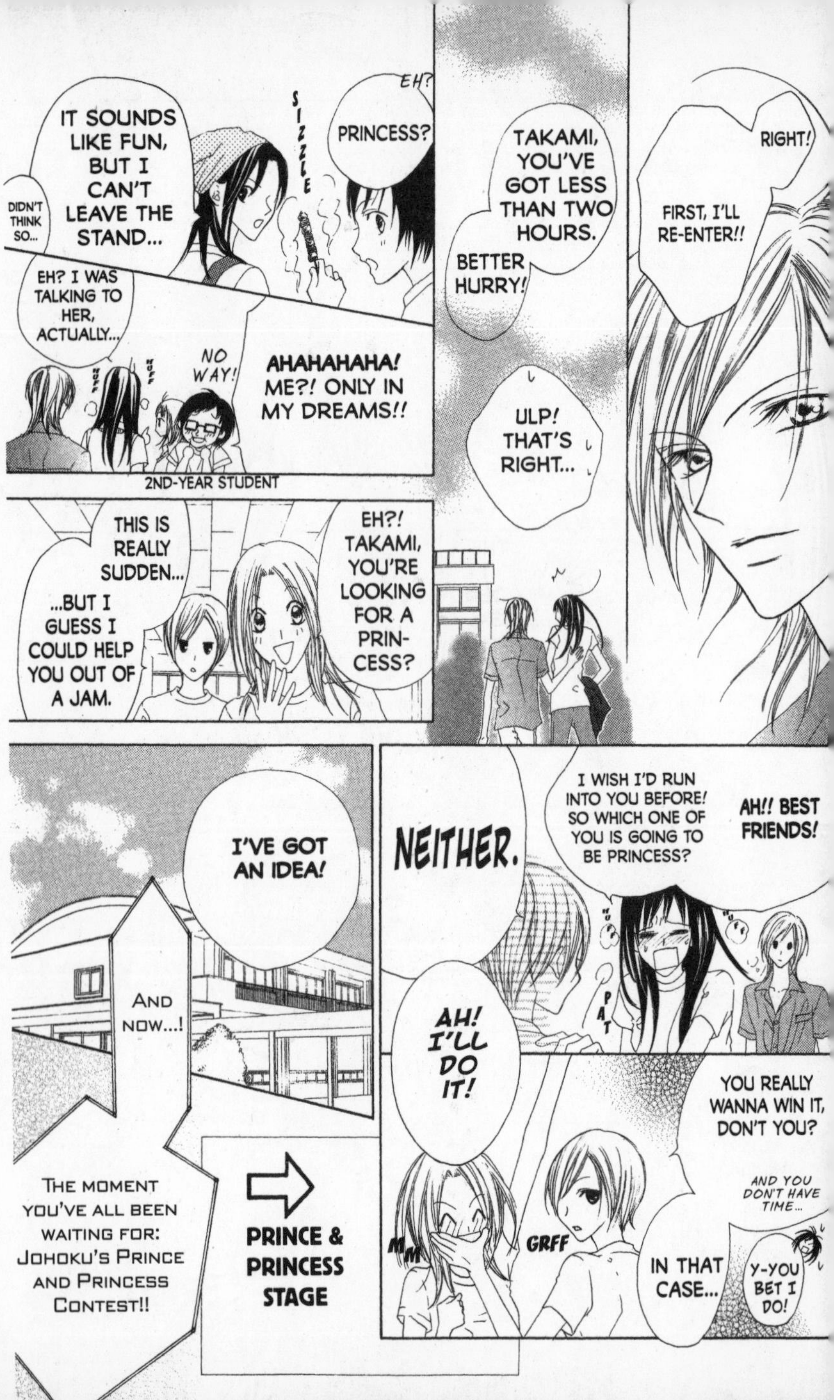
RIGHT!
FIRST, I'LL RE-ENTER!!
TAKAMI, YOU'VE GOT LESS THAN TWO HOURS.
BETTER HURRY!
ULP! THAT'S RIGHT...
EH?
PRINCESS?
SIZZLE
IT SOUNDS LIKE FUN, BUT I CAN'T LEAVE THE STAND...
DIDN'T THINK SO...
AHAHAHAHA! ME?! ONLY IN MY DREAMS!!
NO WAY!
EH? I WAS TALKING TO HER, ACTUALLY...
HUFF
HUFF
2ND-YEAR STUDENT
EH?! TAKAMI, YOU'RE LOOKING FOR A PRIN-CESS?
THIS IS REALLY SUDDEN...
...BUT I GUESS I COULD HELP YOU OUT OF A JAM.
AH!! BEST FRIENDS!
I WISH I'D RUN INTO YOU BEFORE! SO WHICH ONE OF YOU IS GOING TO BE PRINCESS?
NEITHER.
HUFF
HUFF
PAT
AH! I'LL DO IT!
YOU REALLY WANNA WIN IT, DON'T YOU?
AND YOU DON'T HAVE TIME...
Y-YOU BET I DO!
IN THAT CASE...
GRFF
MM
I'VE GOT AN IDEA!
AND NOW...!
THE MOMENT YOU'VE ALL BEEN WAITING FOR: JOHOKU'S PRINCE AND PRINCESS CONTEST!!
PRINCE & PRINCESS STAGE

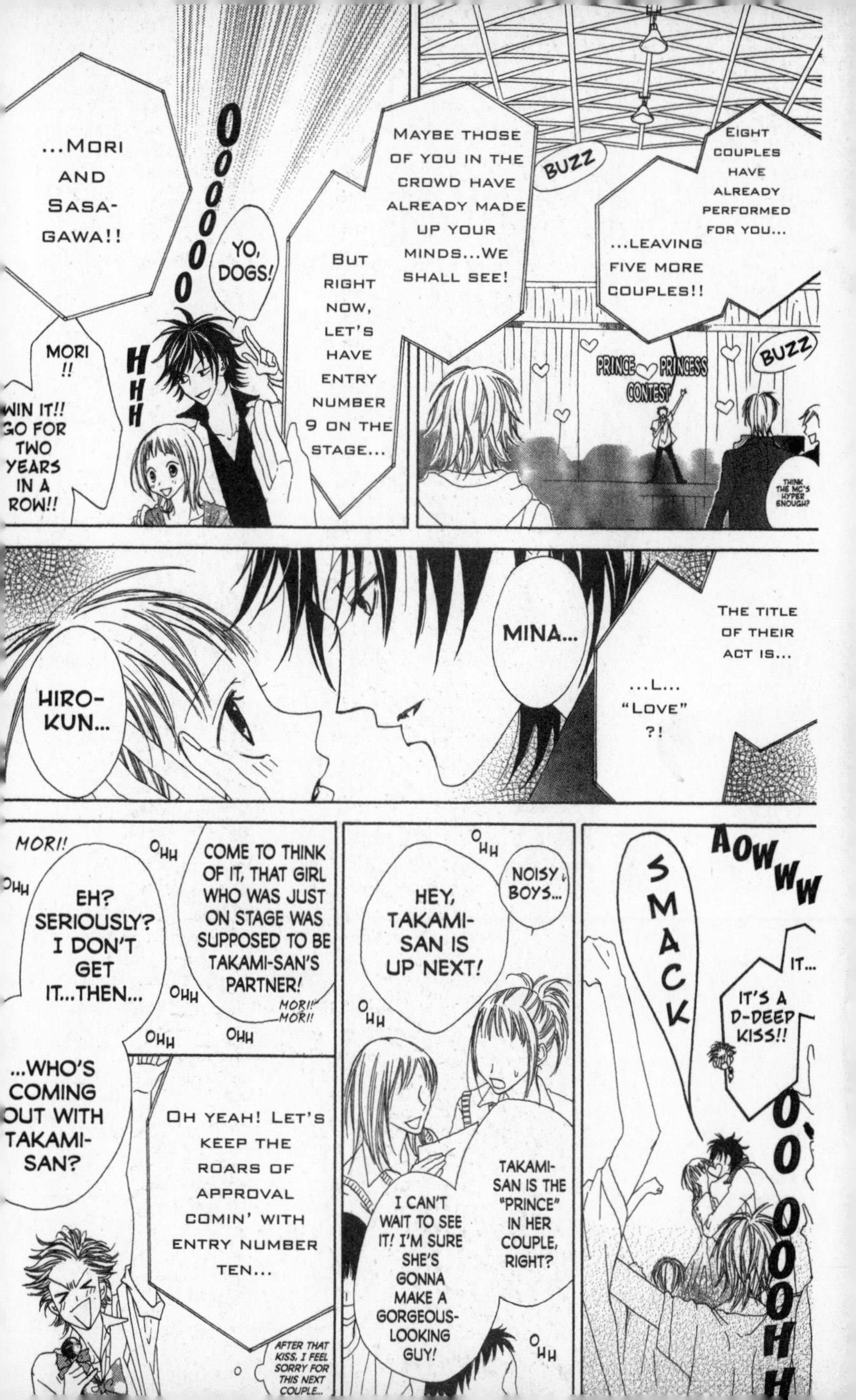

Eight couples have already performed for you...
...leaving five more couples!!
BUZZ
Maybe those of you in the crowd have already made up your minds...we shall see!
BUZZ
PRINCE PRINCESS CONTEST
Think the MC's hyper enough?
But right now, let's have entry number 9 on the stage...
...Mori and Sasa-gawa!!
OOOOOOO
HHH
Yo, dogs!
Mori!!
Win it!! Go for two years in a row!!
The title of their act is...
...L... "Love" ?!
Mina...
Hiro-kun...
AOWWW
SMACK
It...
It's a d-deep kiss!!
OOOOOOH
Noisy boys...
Hey, Takami-san is up next!
Ohh
Ohh
Takami-san is the "prince" in her couple, right?
I can't wait to see it! I'm sure she's gonna make a gorgeous-looking guy!
Ohh
Mori!
Ohh
Come to think of it, that girl who was just on stage was supposed to be Takami-san's partner!
Ohh
Eh? Seriously? I don't get it...then...
Ohh
Mori!! Mori!!
Ohh
Ohh
...who's coming out with Takami-san?
Oh yeah! Let's keep the roars of approval comin' with entry number ten...
After that kiss, I feel sorry for this next couple...

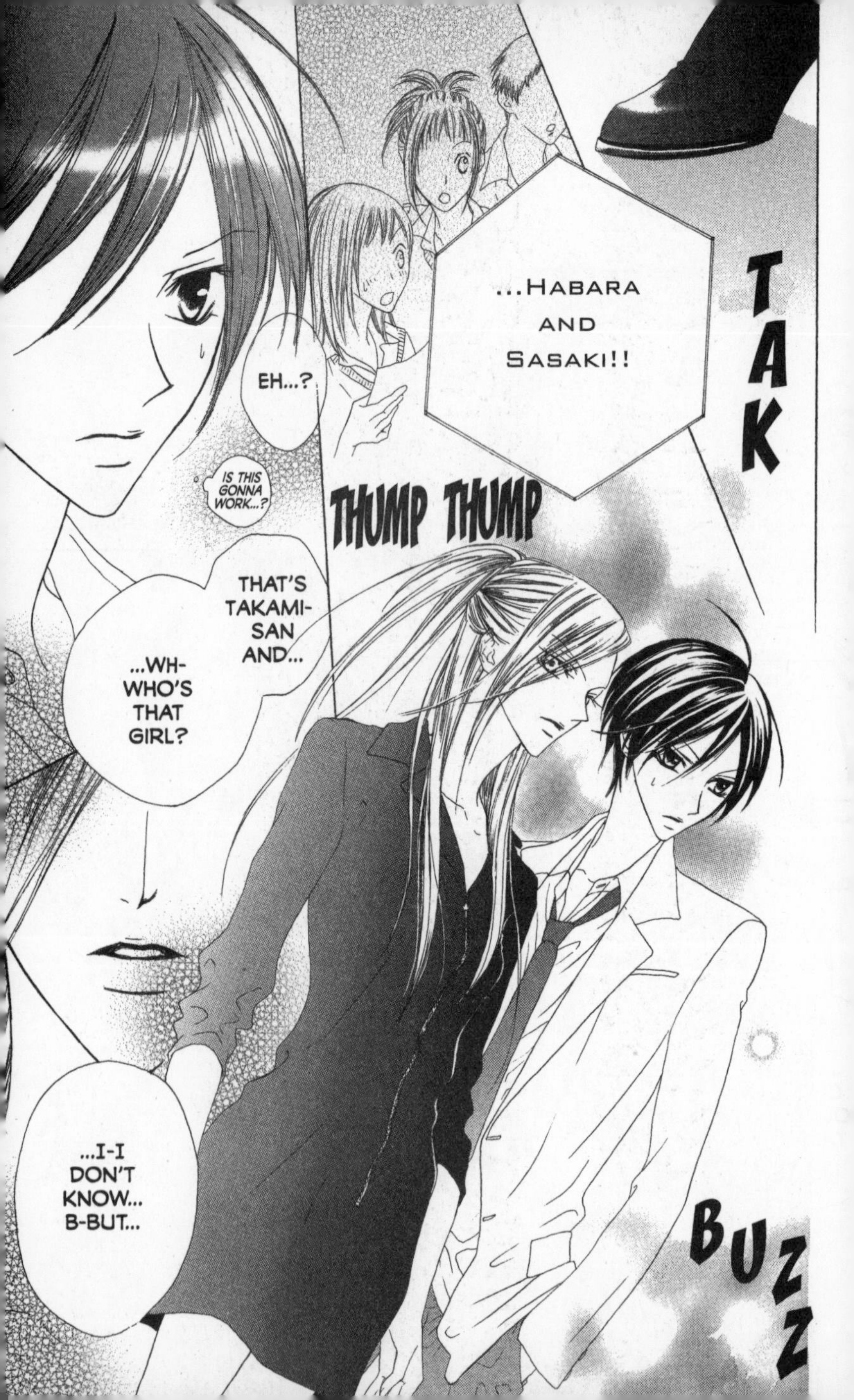
TAK
...HABARA AND SASAKI!!
EH...?
IS THIS GONNA WORK...?
THUMP THUMP
BUZZ
THAT'S TAKAMI-SAN AND...
...WH-WHO'S THAT GIRL?
...I-I DON'T KNOW... B-BUT...

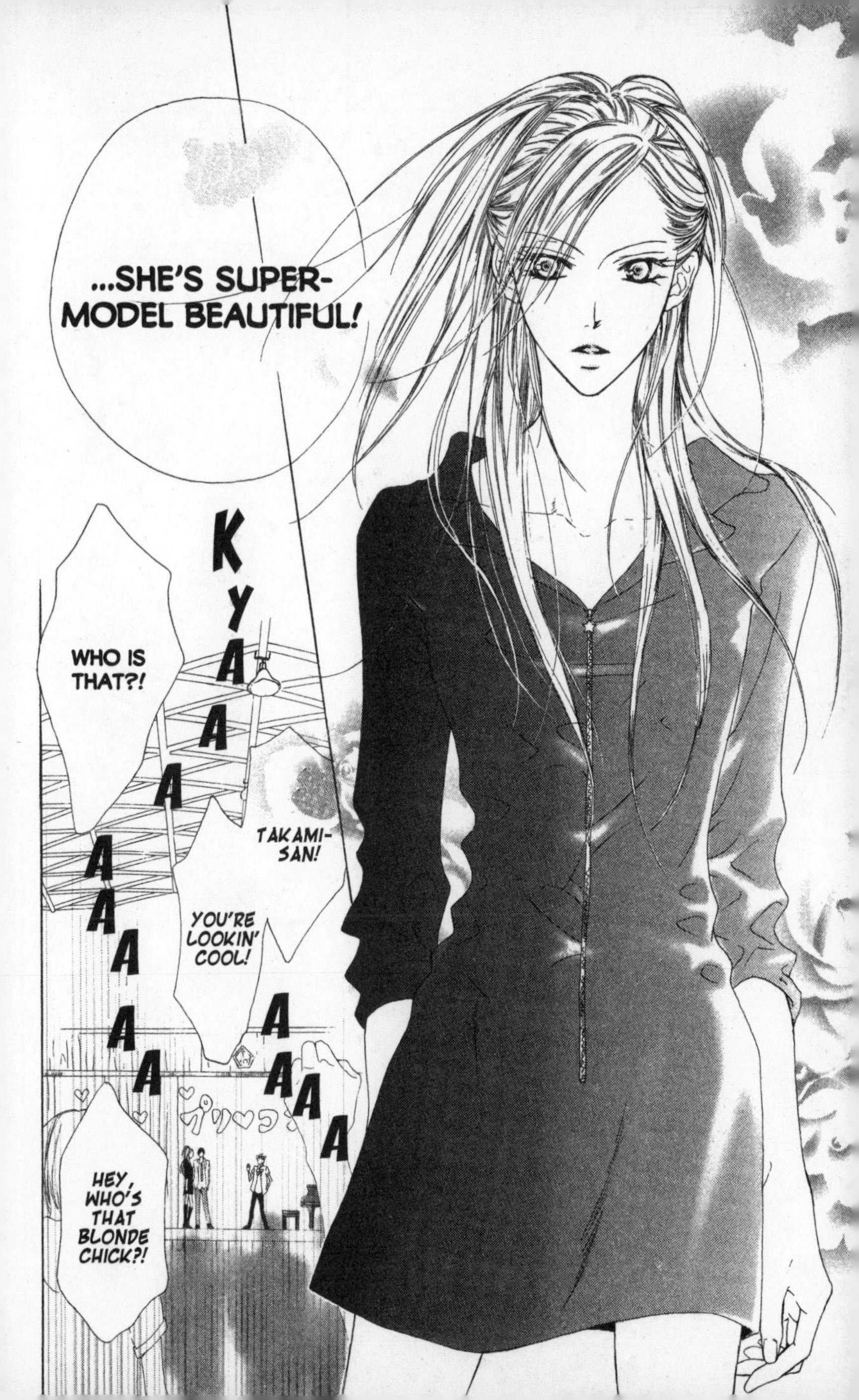
...SHE'S SUPER-MODEL BEAUTIFUL!
KYAAAAAAAAAAAAAA
TAKAMI-SAN!
WHO IS THAT?!
YOU'RE LOOKIN' COOL!
HEY, WHO'S THAT BLONDE CHICK?!

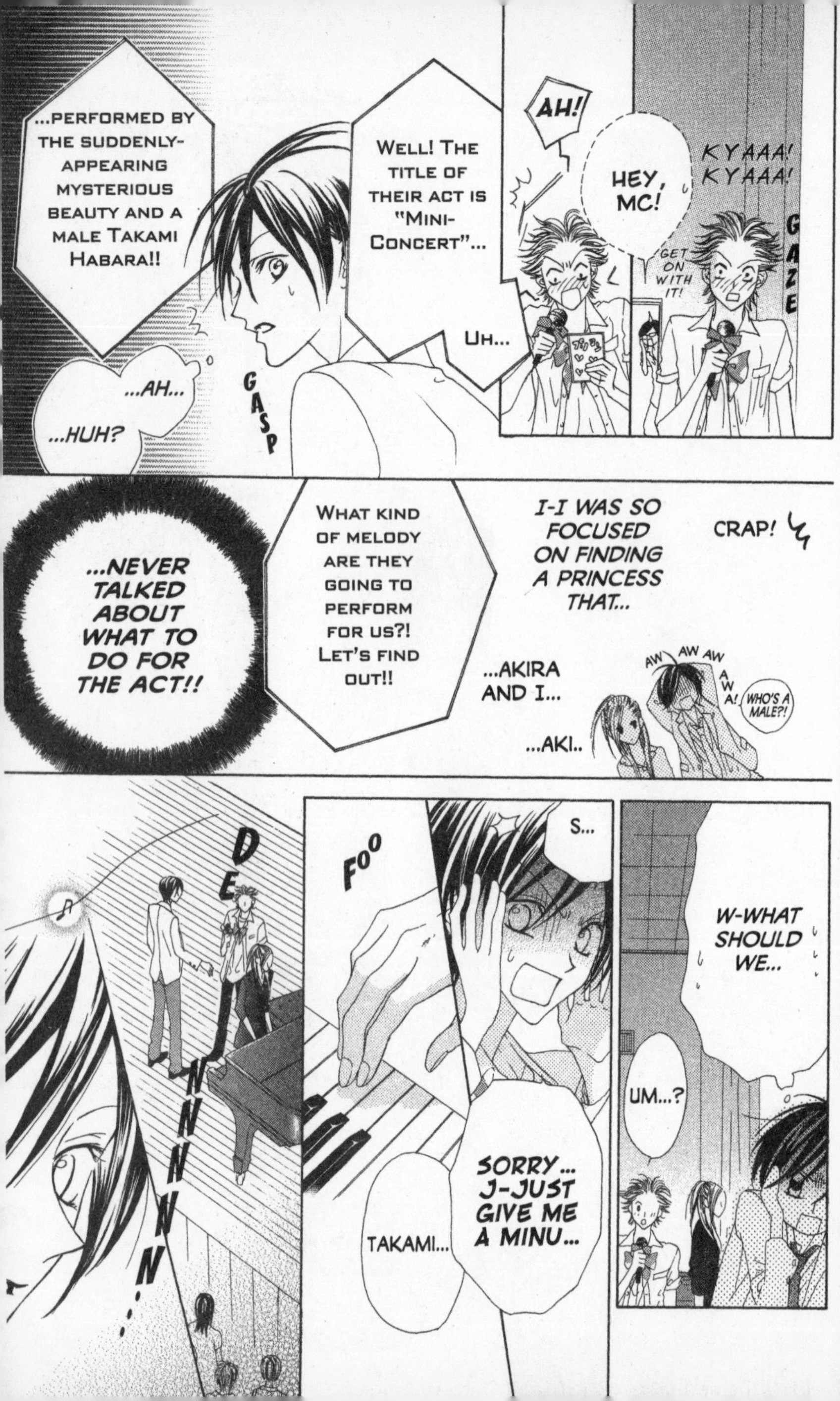
KYAAA! KYAAA!
GAZE
HEY, MC!
GET ON WITH IT!
AH!
WELL! THE TITLE OF THEIR ACT IS "MINI-CONCERT"...
UH...
...PERFORMED BY THE SUDDENLY-APPEARING MYSTERIOUS BEAUTY AND A MALE TAKAMI HABARA!!
GASP
...AH...
...HUH?
CRAP!
I-I WAS SO FOCUSED ON FINDING A PRINCESS THAT...
...AKIRA AND I...
AW AW AW AWA!
WHO'S A MALE?!
...AKI..
WHAT KIND OF MELODY ARE THEY GOING TO PERFORM FOR US?! LET'S FIND OUT!!
...NEVER TALKED ABOUT WHAT TO DO FOR THE ACT!!
W-WHAT SHOULD WE...
UM...?
S...
FOO
SORRY... J-JUST GIVE ME A MINU...
TAKAMI...
DENNNNNNNN...

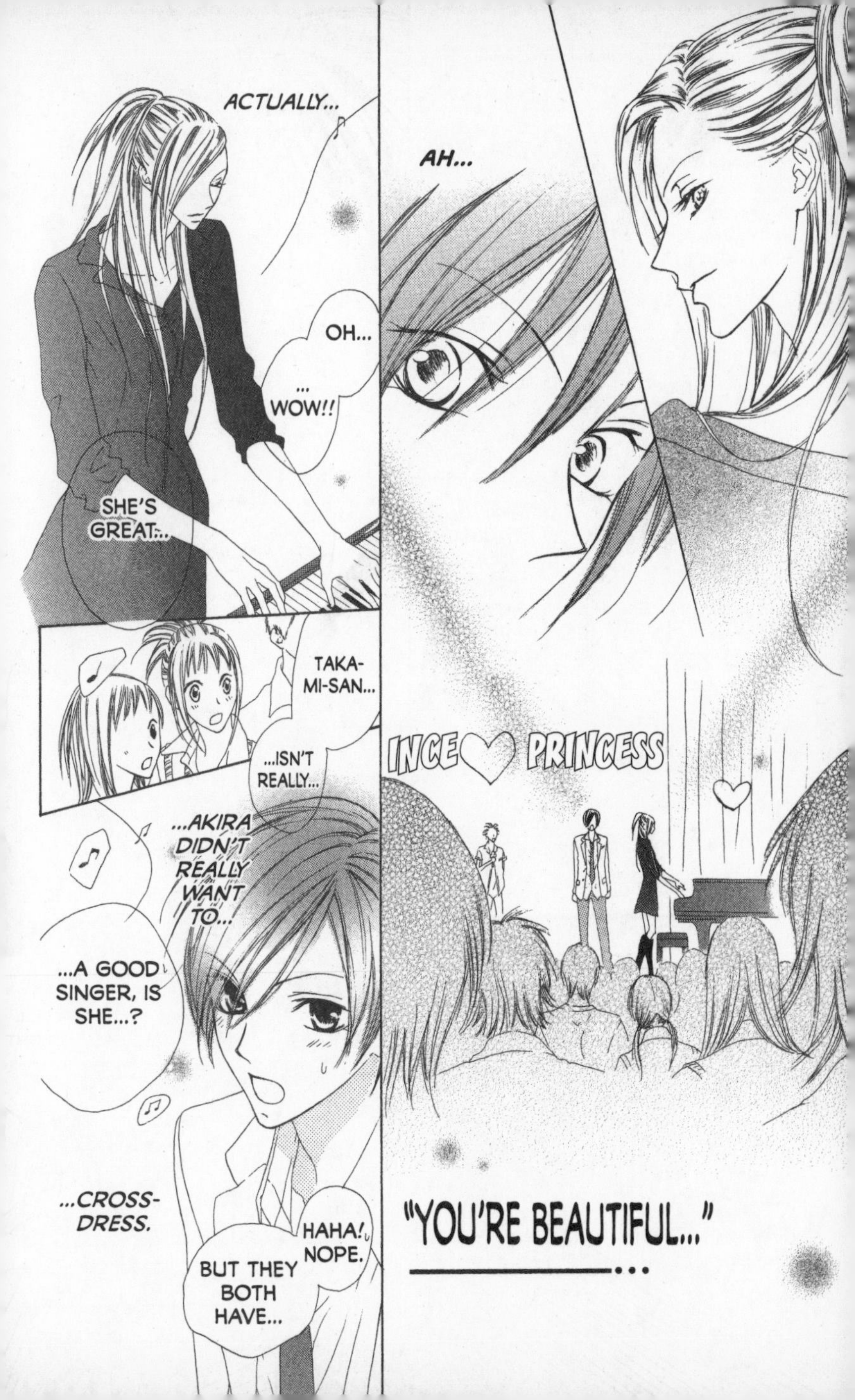
AH...
INCE♥ PRINCESS
"YOU'RE BEAUTIFUL..."
ACTUALLY...
OH...
...WOW!!
SHE'S GREAT...
TAKA-MI-SAN...
...ISN'T REALLY...
...A GOOD SINGER, IS SHE...?
HAHA! NOPE.
BUT THEY BOTH HAVE...
...AKIRA DIDN'T REALLY WANT TO...
...CROSS-DRESS.

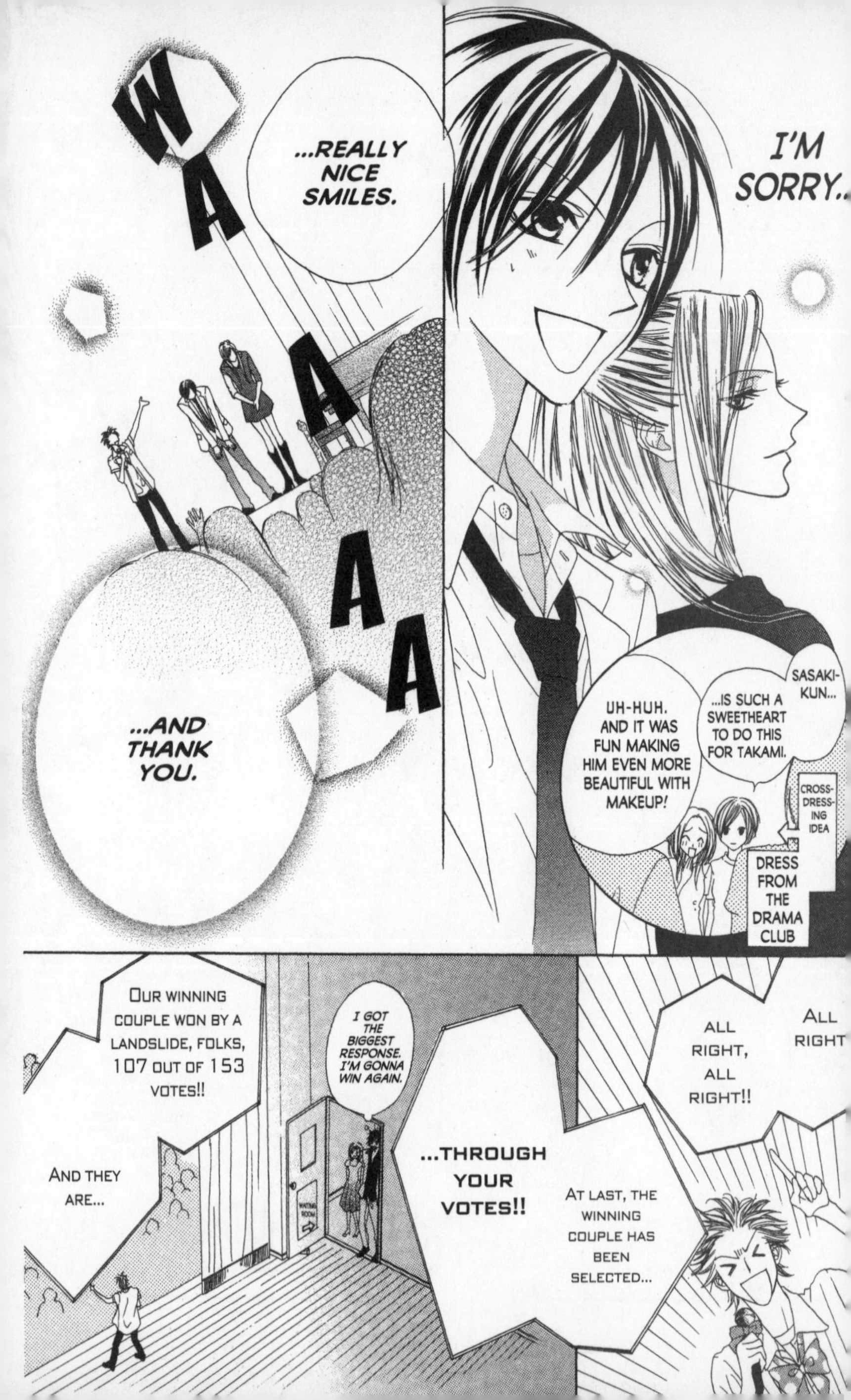
I'M SORRY...
SASAKI-KUN...
...IS SUCH A SWEETHEART TO DO THIS FOR TAKAMI.
UH-HUH. AND IT WAS FUN MAKING HIM EVEN MORE BEAUTIFUL WITH MAKEUP!
CROSS-DRESSING IDEA
DRESS FROM THE DRAMA CLUB
...REALLY NICE SMILES.
WAAAA
...AND THANK YOU.
ALL RIGHT
ALL RIGHT, ALL RIGHT!!
AT LAST, THE WINNING COUPLE HAS BEEN SELECTED...
...THROUGH YOUR VOTES!!
I GOT THE BIGGEST RESPONSE. I'M GONNA WIN AGAIN.
OUR WINNING COUPLE WON BY A LANDSLIDE, FOLKS, 107 OUT OF 153 VOTES!!
AND THEY ARE...

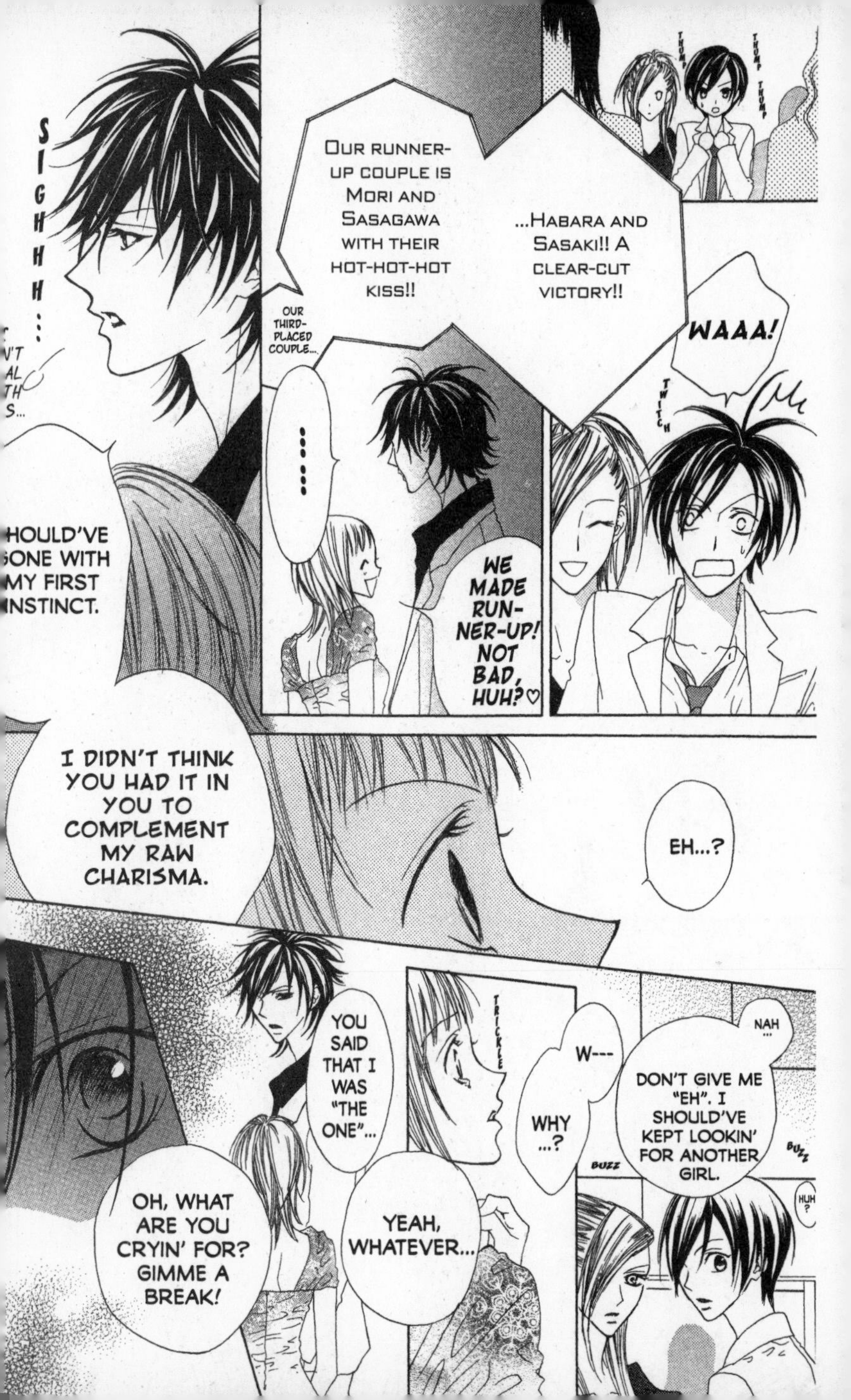
THUMP THUMP THUMP
OUR THIRD-PLACED COUPLE...
OUR RUNNER-UP COUPLE IS MORI AND SASAGAWA WITH THEIR HOT-HOT-HOT KISS!!
......
WE MADE RUNNER-UP! NOT BAD, HUH?♡
...HABARA AND SASAKI!! A CLEAR-CUT VICTORY!!
WAAA!
TWITCH
SIGHHH...
HOULD'VE GONE WITH MY FIRST INSTINCT.
EH...?
I DIDN'T THINK YOU HAD IT IN YOU TO COMPLEMENT MY RAW CHARISMA.
NAH...
DON'T GIVE ME "EH". I SHOULD'VE KEPT LOOKIN' FOR ANOTHER GIRL.
BUZZ
BUZZ
HUH?
W--- WHY...?
TRICKLE
YOU SAID THAT I WAS "THE ONE"...
YEAH, WHATEVER...
OH, WHAT ARE YOU CRYIN' FOR? GIMME A BREAK!

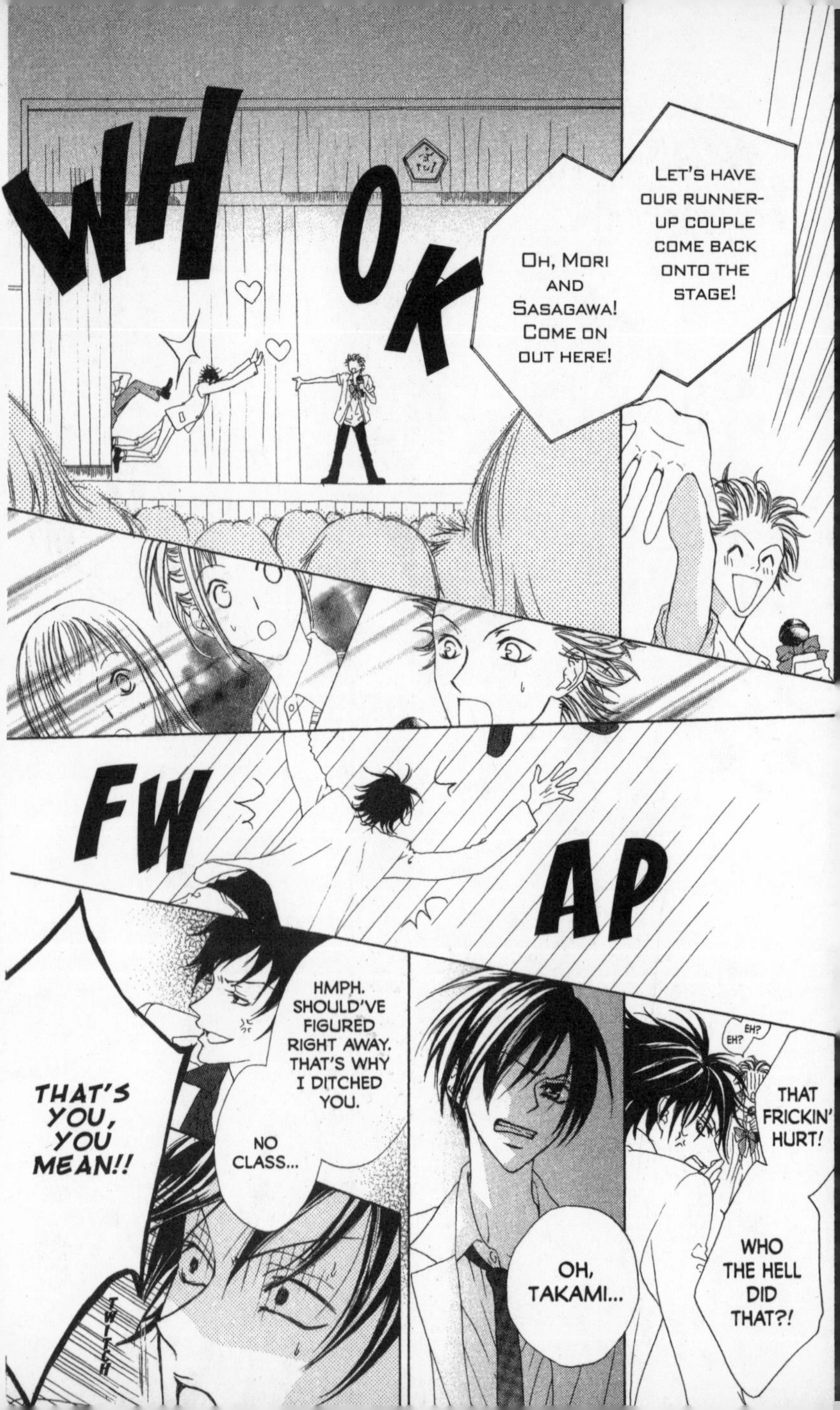
LET'S HAVE OUR RUNNER-UP COUPLE COME BACK ONTO THE STAGE!
OH, MORI AND SASAGAWA! COME ON OUT HERE!
WHOK
FWAP
EH? EH?
THAT FRICKIN' HURT!
WHO THE HELL DID THAT?!
OH, TAKAMI...
HMPH. SHOULD'VE FIGURED RIGHT AWAY. THAT'S WHY I DITCHED YOU.
NO CLASS...
THAT'S YOU, YOU MEAN!!
TWITCH

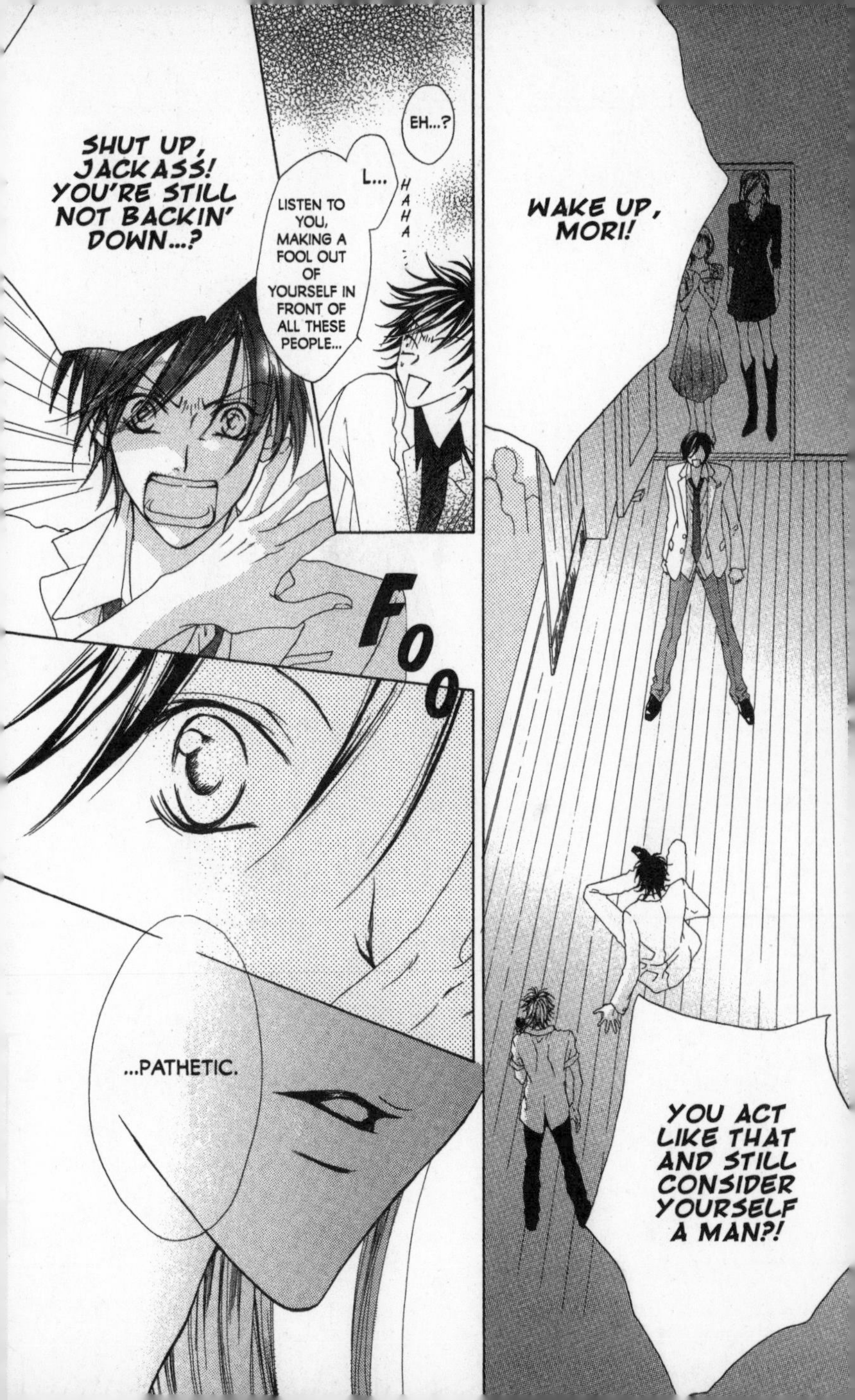
WAKE UP, MORI!
YOU ACT LIKE THAT AND STILL CONSIDER YOURSELF A MAN?!
EH...?
HAHA...
L...
LISTEN TO YOU, MAKING A FOOL OUT OF YOURSELF IN FRONT OF ALL THESE PEOPLE...
SHUT UP, JACKASS! YOU'RE STILL NOT BACKIN' DOWN...?
FOO
...PATHETIC.

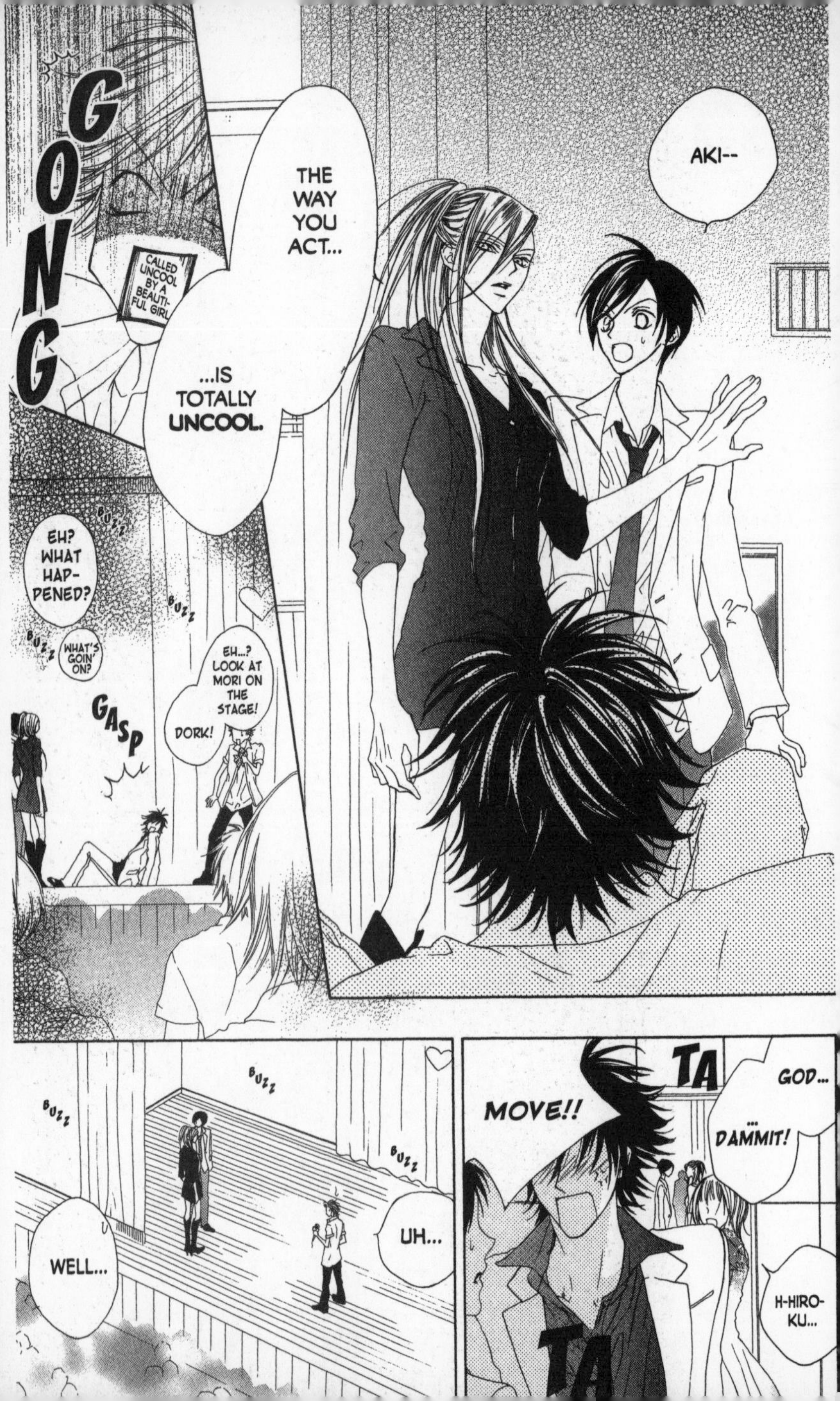
AKI--
THE WAY YOU ACT...
...IS TOTALLY UNCOOL.
GONG
CALLED UNCOOL BY A BEAUTI-FUL GIRL
BUZZ
EH...? LOOK AT MORI ON THE STAGE!
DORK!
BUZZ
EH? WHAT HAP-PENED?
BUZZ
WHAT'S GOIN' ON?
GASP
GOD... ...DAMMIT!
TA
MOVE!!
H-HIRO-KU...
TA
BUZZ
BUZZ
UH...
BUZZ
WELL...

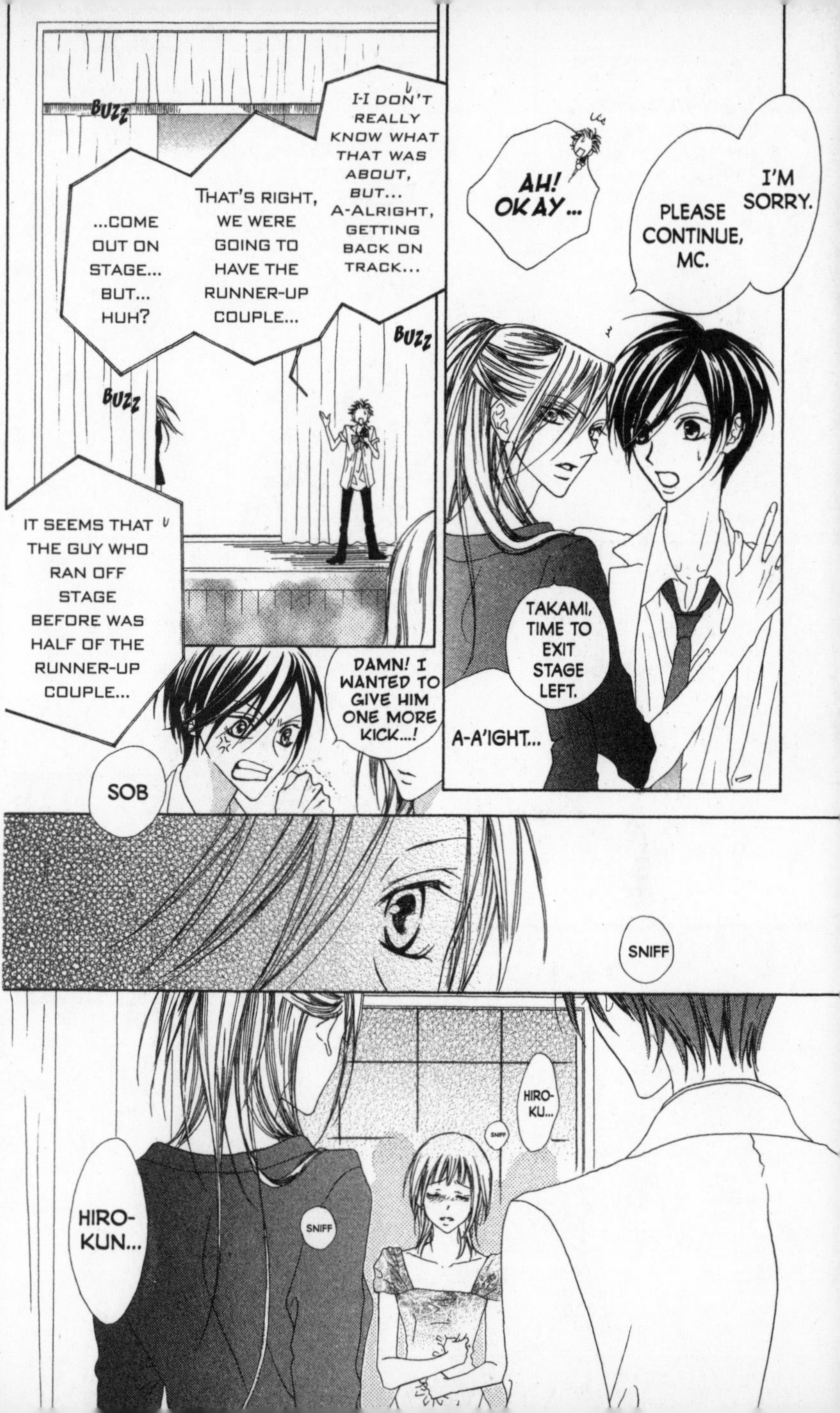
I'M SORRY.
PLEASE CONTINUE, MC.
AH! OKAY...
TAKAMI, TIME TO EXIT STAGE LEFT.
A-A'IGHT...
BUZZ
I-I DON'T REALLY KNOW WHAT THAT WAS ABOUT, BUT... A-ALRIGHT, GETTING BACK ON TRACK...
THAT'S RIGHT, WE WERE GOING TO HAVE THE RUNNER-UP COUPLE...
...COME OUT ON STAGE... BUT... HUH?
BUZZ
BUZZ
IT SEEMS THAT THE GUY WHO RAN OFF STAGE BEFORE WAS HALF OF THE RUNNER-UP COUPLE...
DAMN! I WANTED TO GIVE HIM ONE MORE KICK...!
SOB
SNIFF
HIRO-KU...
SNIFF
HIRO-KUN...
SNIFF

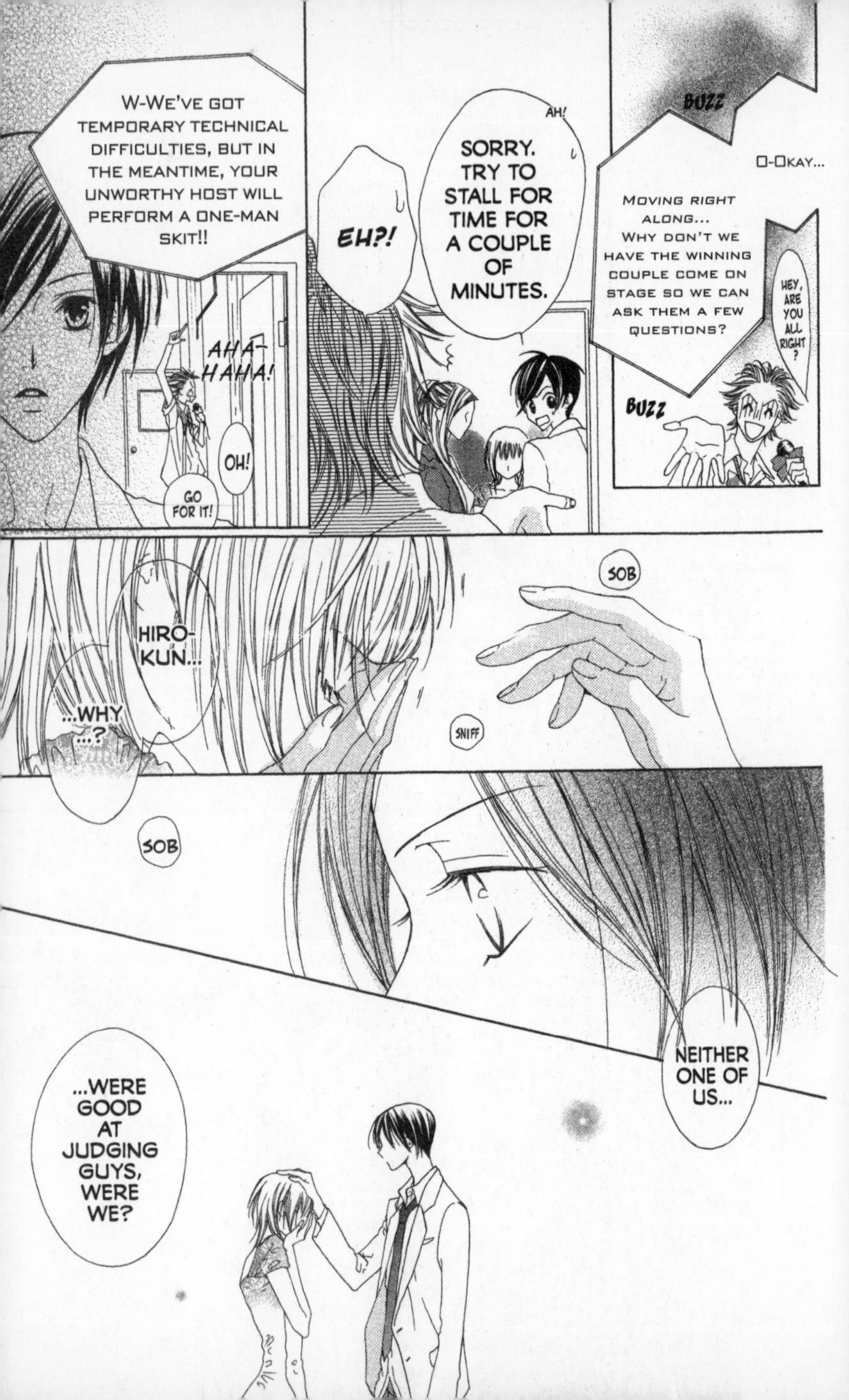
BUZZ
O-OKAY...
MOVING RIGHT ALONG... WHY DON'T WE HAVE THE WINNING COUPLE COME ON STAGE SO WE CAN ASK THEM A FEW QUESTIONS?
HEY, ARE YOU ALL RIGHT?
BUZZ
AH!
SORRY. TRY TO STALL FOR TIME FOR A COUPLE OF MINUTES.
EH?!
W-WE'VE GOT TEMPORARY TECHNICAL DIFFICULTIES, BUT IN THE MEANTIME, YOUR UNWORTHY HOST WILL PERFORM A ONE-MAN SKIT!!
AHAHAHA!
OH!
GO FOR IT!
SOB
SNIFF
HIRO-KUN...
...WHY...?
SOB
NEITHER ONE OF US...
...WERE GOOD AT JUDGING GUYS, WERE WE?

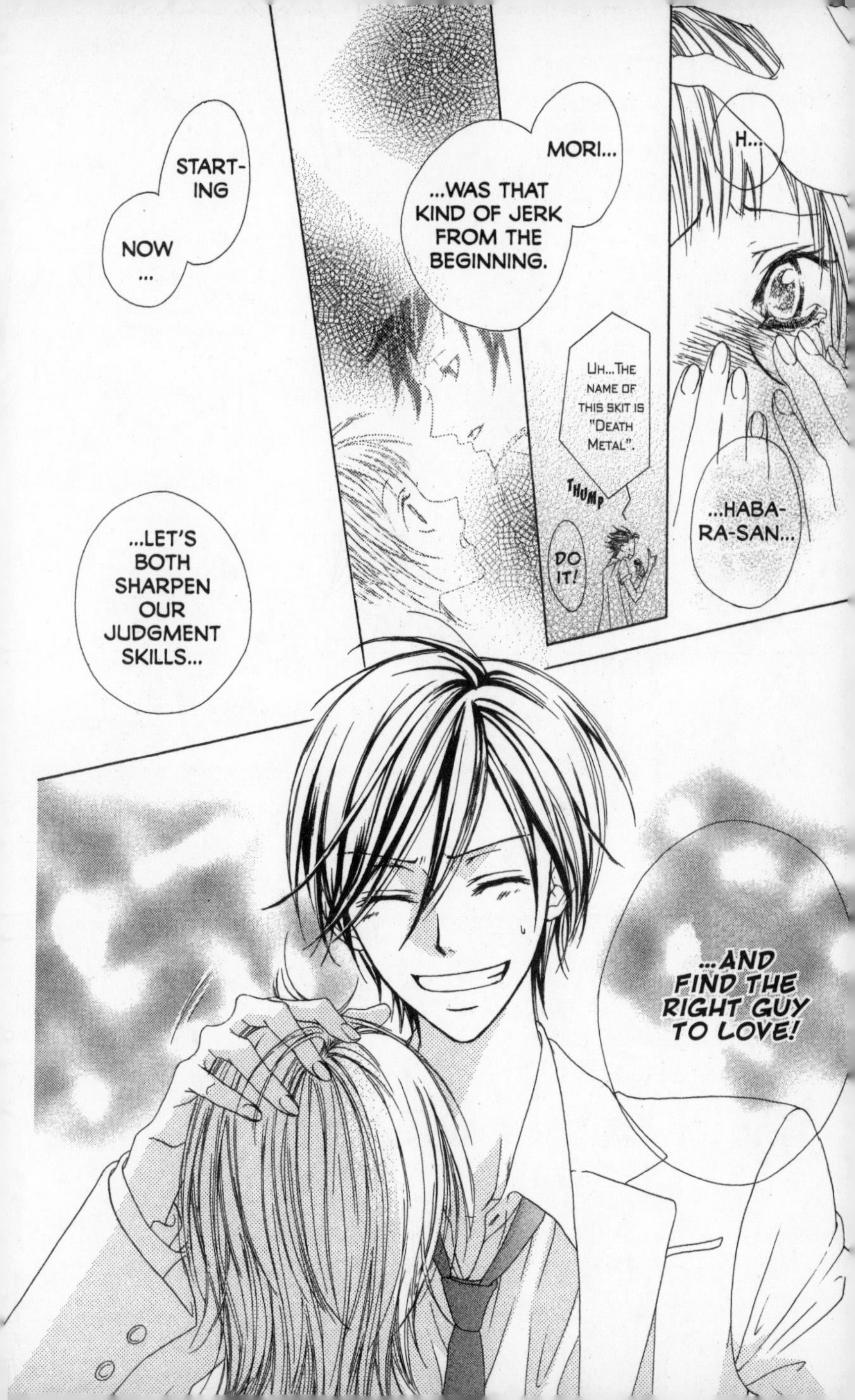
H...
...HABARA-SAN...
MORI...
...WAS THAT KIND OF JERK FROM THE BEGINNING.
UH...THE NAME OF THIS SKIT IS "DEATH METAL".
THUMP
DO IT!
STARTING NOW...
...LET'S BOTH SHARPEN OUR JUDGMENT SKILLS...
...AND FIND THE RIGHT GUY TO LOVE!

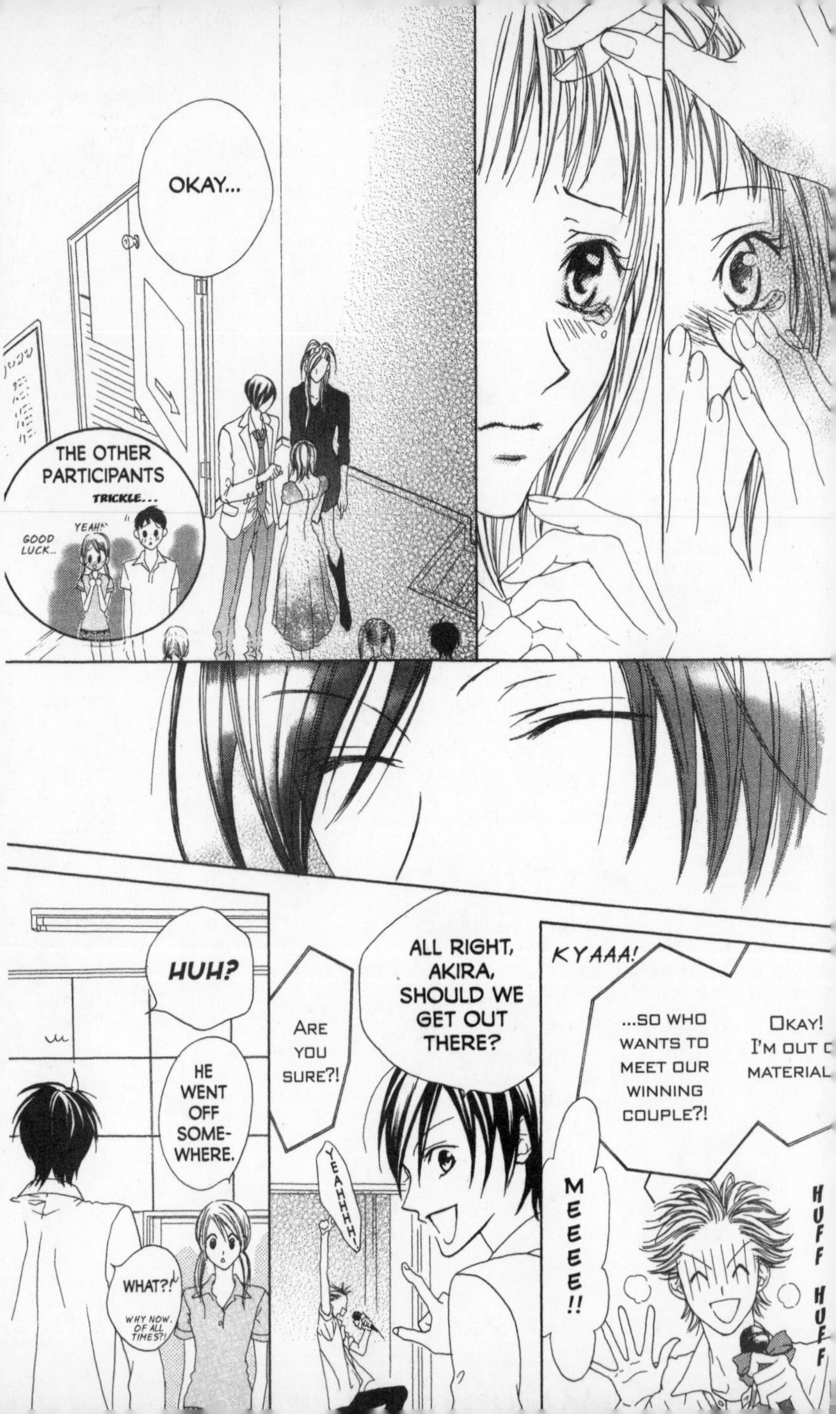
OKAY...
THE OTHER PARTICIPANTS
TRICKLE...
YEAH
GOOD LUCK...
KYAAA!
OKAY! I'M OUT MATERIAL
...SO WHO WANTS TO MEET OUR WINNING COUPLE?!
MEEEE!!
HUFF HUFF
ALL RIGHT, AKIRA, SHOULD WE GET OUT THERE?
ARE YOU SURE?!
YEAHHHH!
HUH?
HE WENT OFF SOME-WHERE.
WHAT?!
WHY NOW, OF ALL TIMES?!

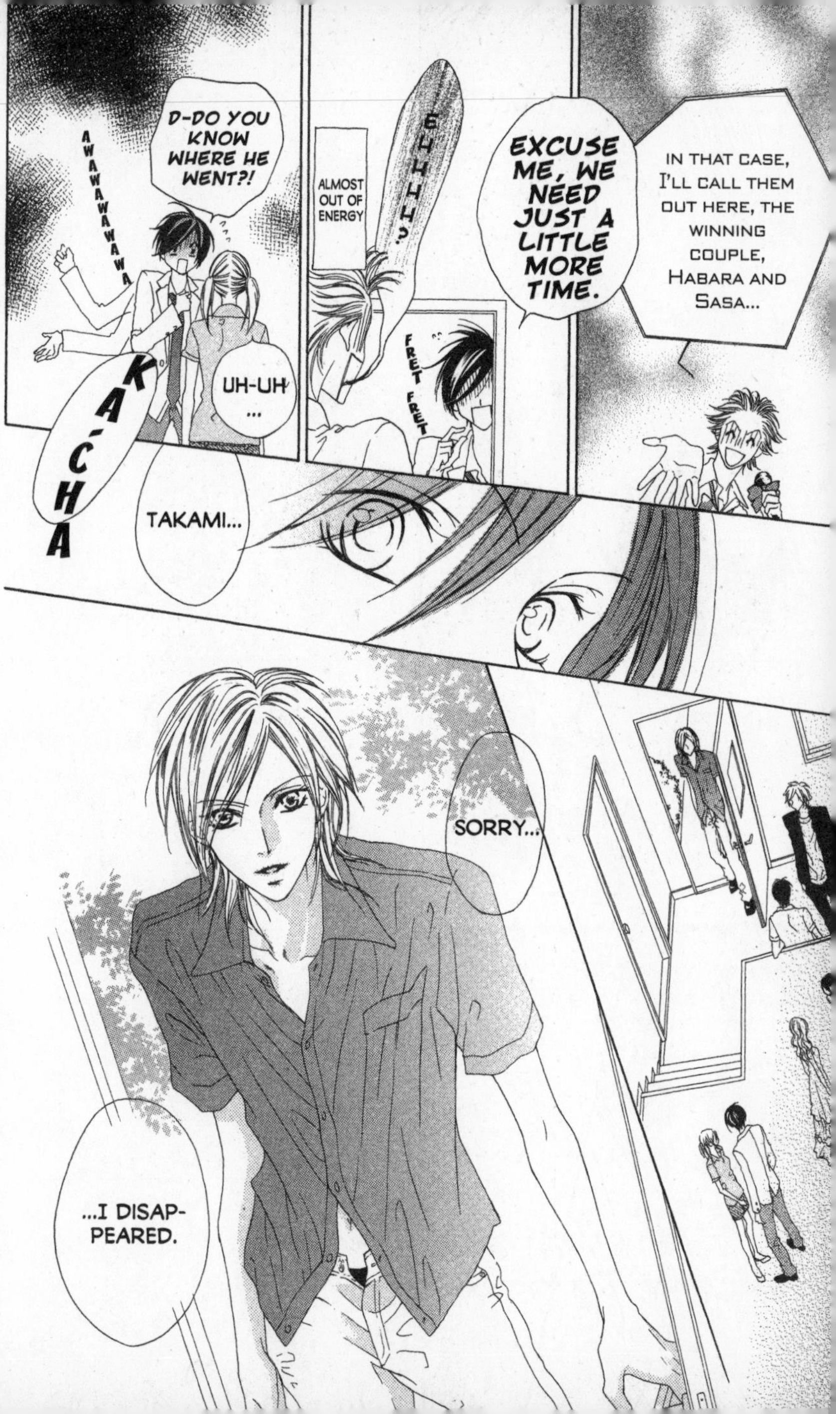

IN THAT CASE, I'LL CALL THEM OUT HERE, THE WINNING COUPLE, HABARA AND SASA...
EXCUSE ME, WE NEED JUST A LITTLE MORE TIME.
EHHHH?
FRET FRET
ALMOST OUT OF ENERGY
D-DO YOU KNOW WHERE HE WENT?!
AWAWAWAWAWAWAWA
UH-UH ...
KA-CHA
TAKAMI...
SORRY...
...I DISAPPEARED.

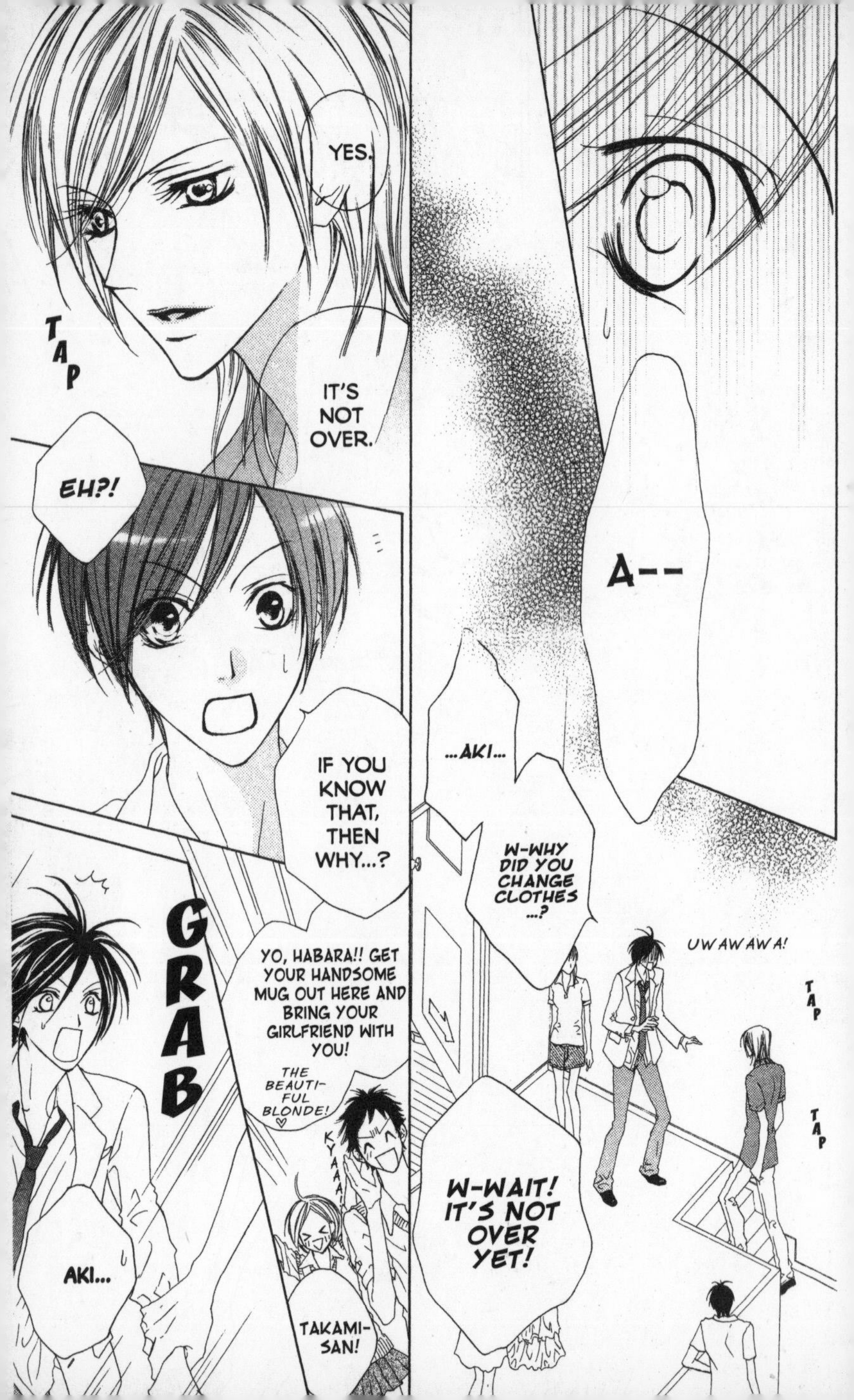
A--
UWAWAWA!
TAP
TAP
...AKI...
W-WHY DID YOU CHANGE CLOTHES ...?
W-WAIT! IT'S NOT OVER YET!
YES.
IT'S NOT OVER.
TAP
EH?!
IF YOU KNOW THAT, THEN WHY...?
YO, HABARA!! GET YOUR HANDSOME MUG OUT HERE AND BRING YOUR GIRLFRIEND WITH YOU!
GRAB
THE BEAUTIFUL BLONDE! ♡
KYAAA!
TAKAMI-SAN!
AKI...

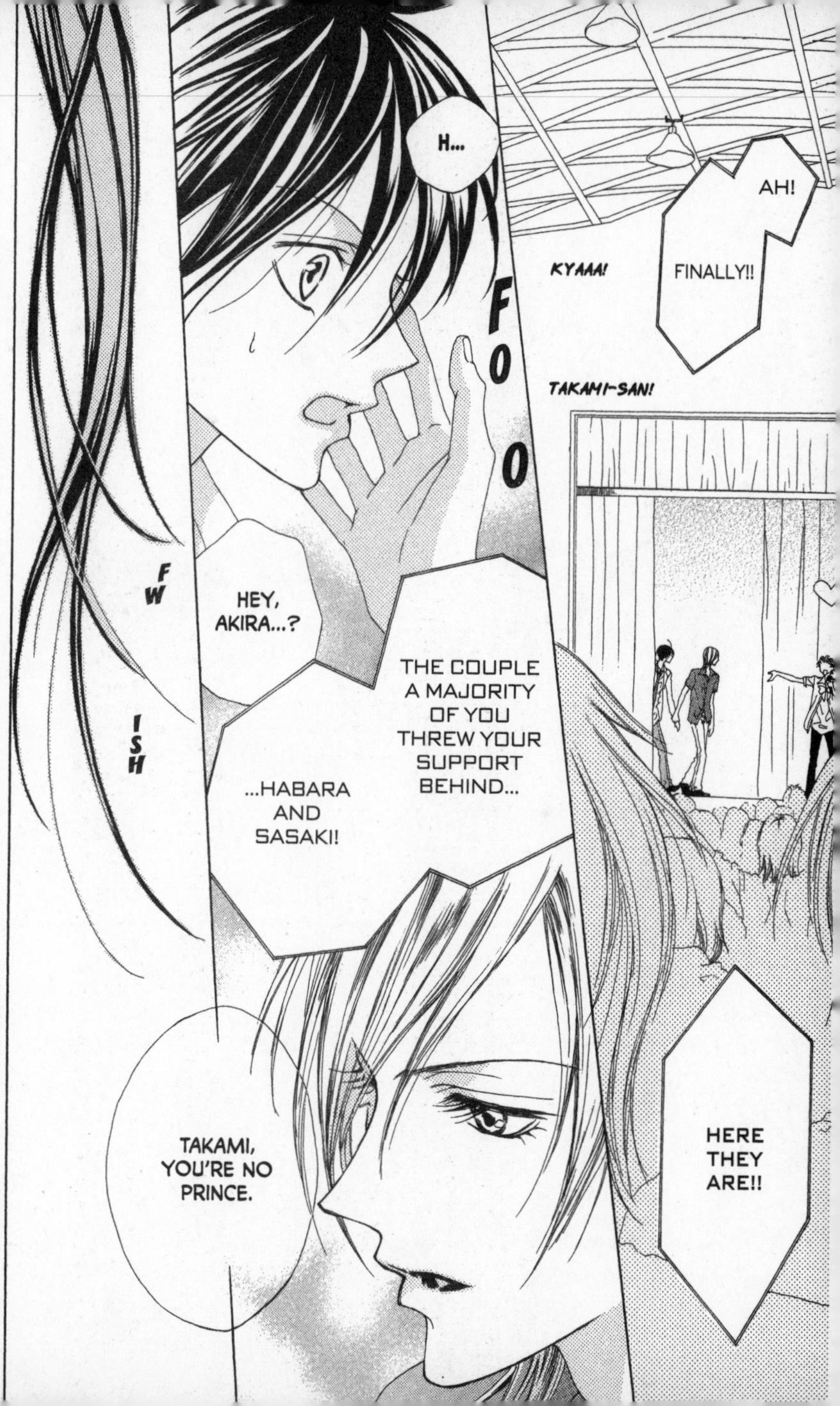
AH!
FINALLY!!
KYAAA!
TAKAMI-SAN!
HERE THEY ARE!!
THE COUPLE A MAJORITY OF YOU THREW YOUR SUPPORT BEHIND...
...HABARA AND SASAKI!
H...
FOOO
HEY, AKIRA...?
TAKAMI, YOU'RE NO PRINCE.
FWISH

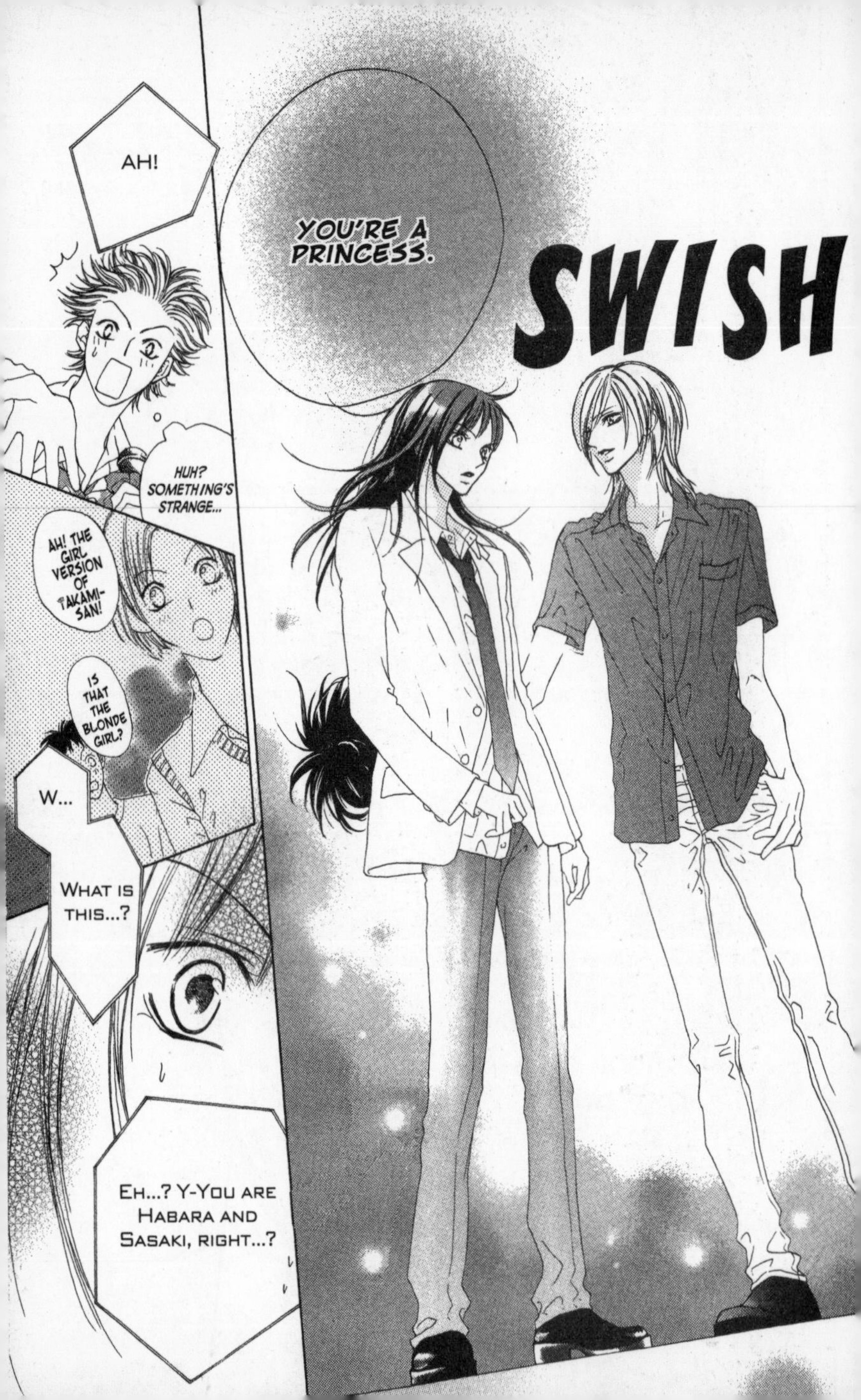
YOU'RE A PRINCESS.
SWISH
AH!
HUH? SOMETHING'S STRANGE...
AH! THE GIRL VERSION OF TAKAMI-SAN!
IS THAT THE BLONDE GIRL?
W...
WHAT IS THIS...?
EH...? Y-YOU ARE HABARA AND SASAKI, RIGHT...?

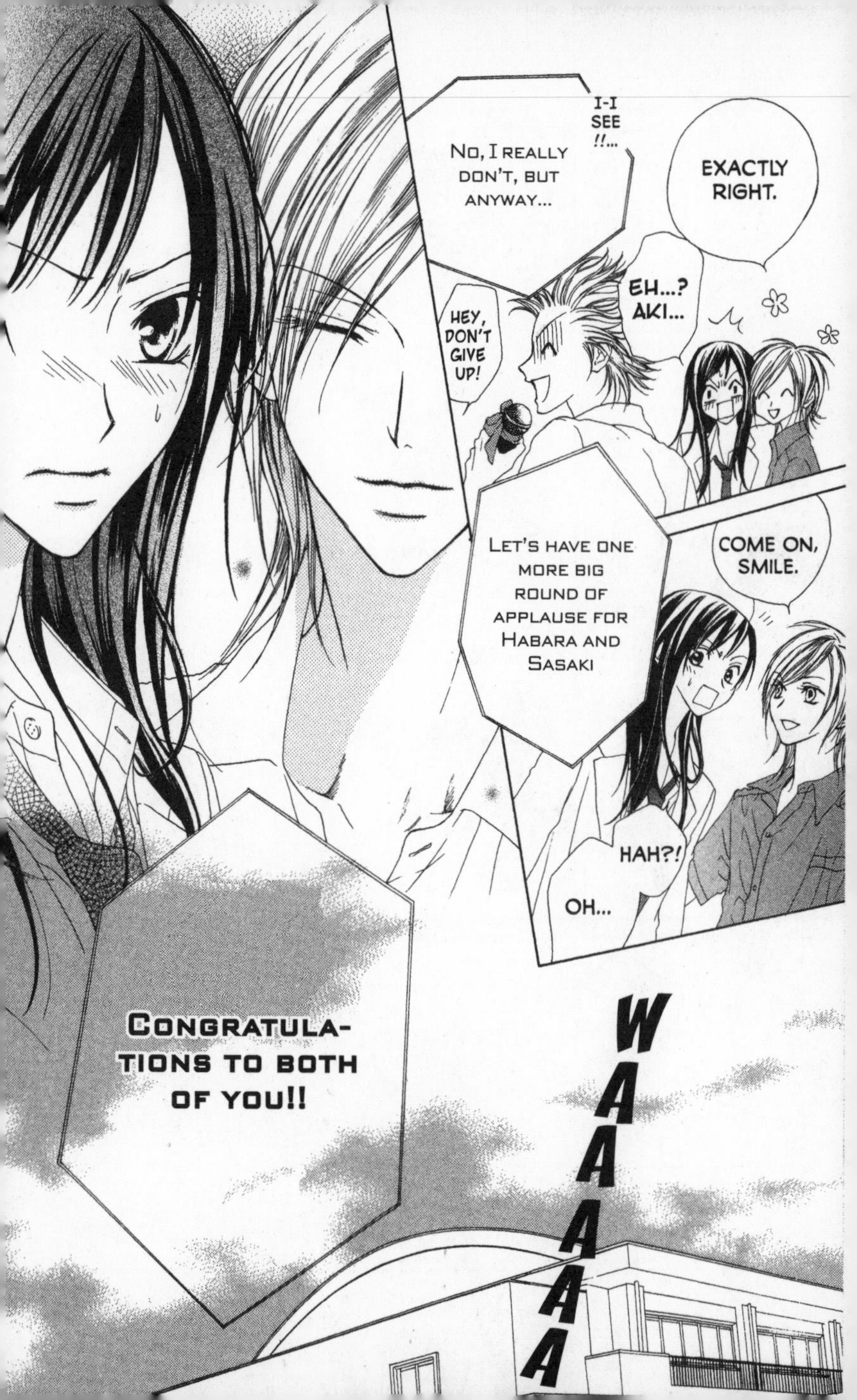
EXACTLY RIGHT.
EH...? AKI...
I-I SEE !!...
NO, I REALLY DON'T, BUT ANYWAY...
HEY, DON'T GIVE UP!
COME ON, SMILE.
LET'S HAVE ONE MORE BIG ROUND OF APPLAUSE FOR HABARA AND SASAKI
HAH?!
OH...
CONGRATULA-TIONS TO BOTH OF YOU!!
WAAAAAA

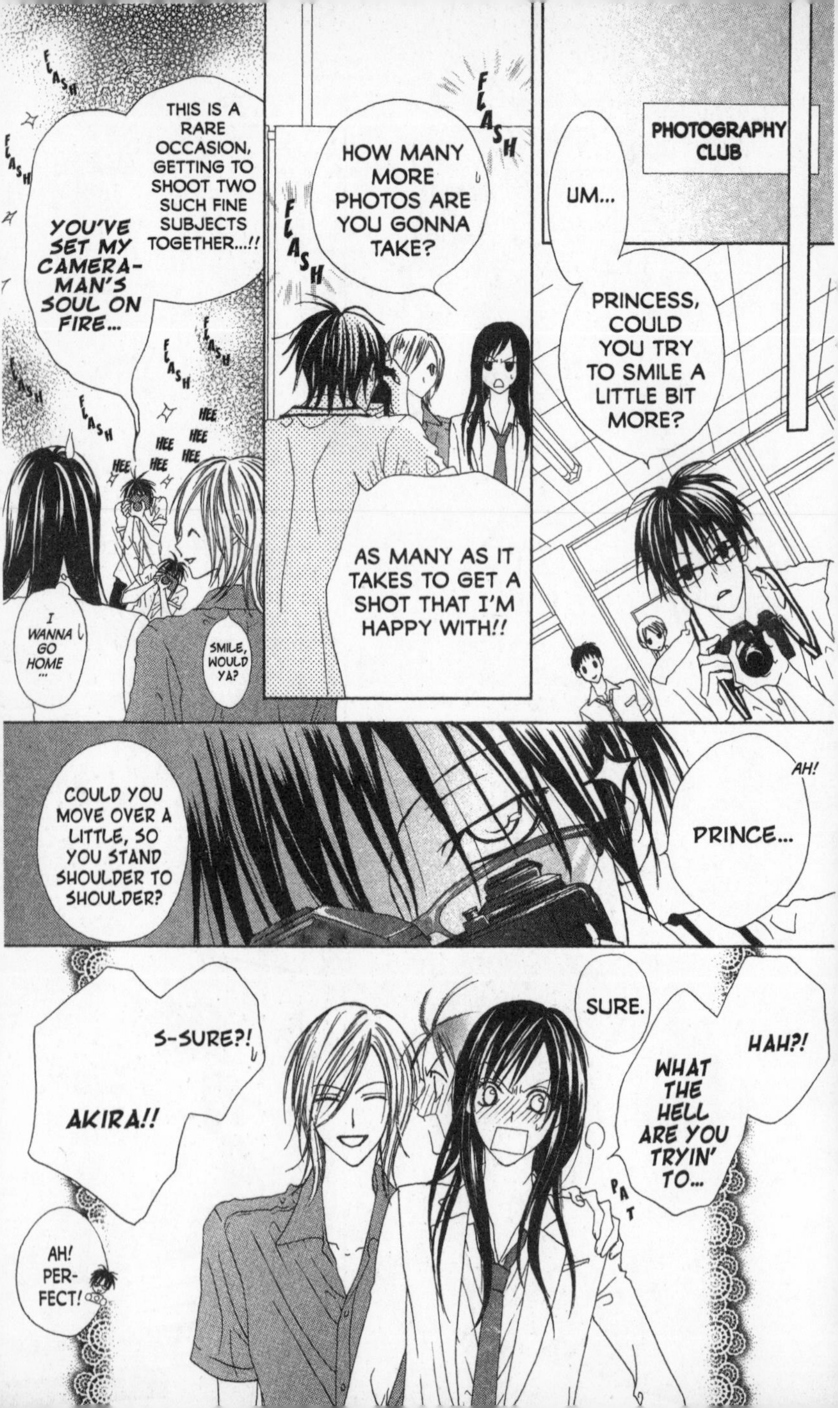
PHOTOGRAPHY CLUB
UM...
PRINCESS, COULD YOU TRY TO SMILE A LITTLE BIT MORE?
FLASH
HOW MANY MORE PHOTOS ARE YOU GONNA TAKE?
FLASH
AS MANY AS IT TAKES TO GET A SHOT THAT I'M HAPPY WITH!!
FLASH
THIS IS A RARE OCCASION, GETTING TO SHOOT TWO SUCH FINE SUBJECTS TOGETHER...!!
YOU'VE SET MY CAMERA-MAN'S SOUL ON FIRE...
FLASH
FLASH
FLASH
FLASH
FLASH
HEE HEE HEE HEE HEE HEE HEE
SMILE, WOULD YA?
I WANNA GO HOME...
AH!
PRINCE...
COULD YOU MOVE OVER A LITTLE, SO YOU STAND SHOULDER TO SHOULDER?
SURE.
HAH?!
WHAT THE HELL ARE YOU TRYIN' TO...
PAT
S-SURE?!
AKIRA!!
AH! PER-FECT!

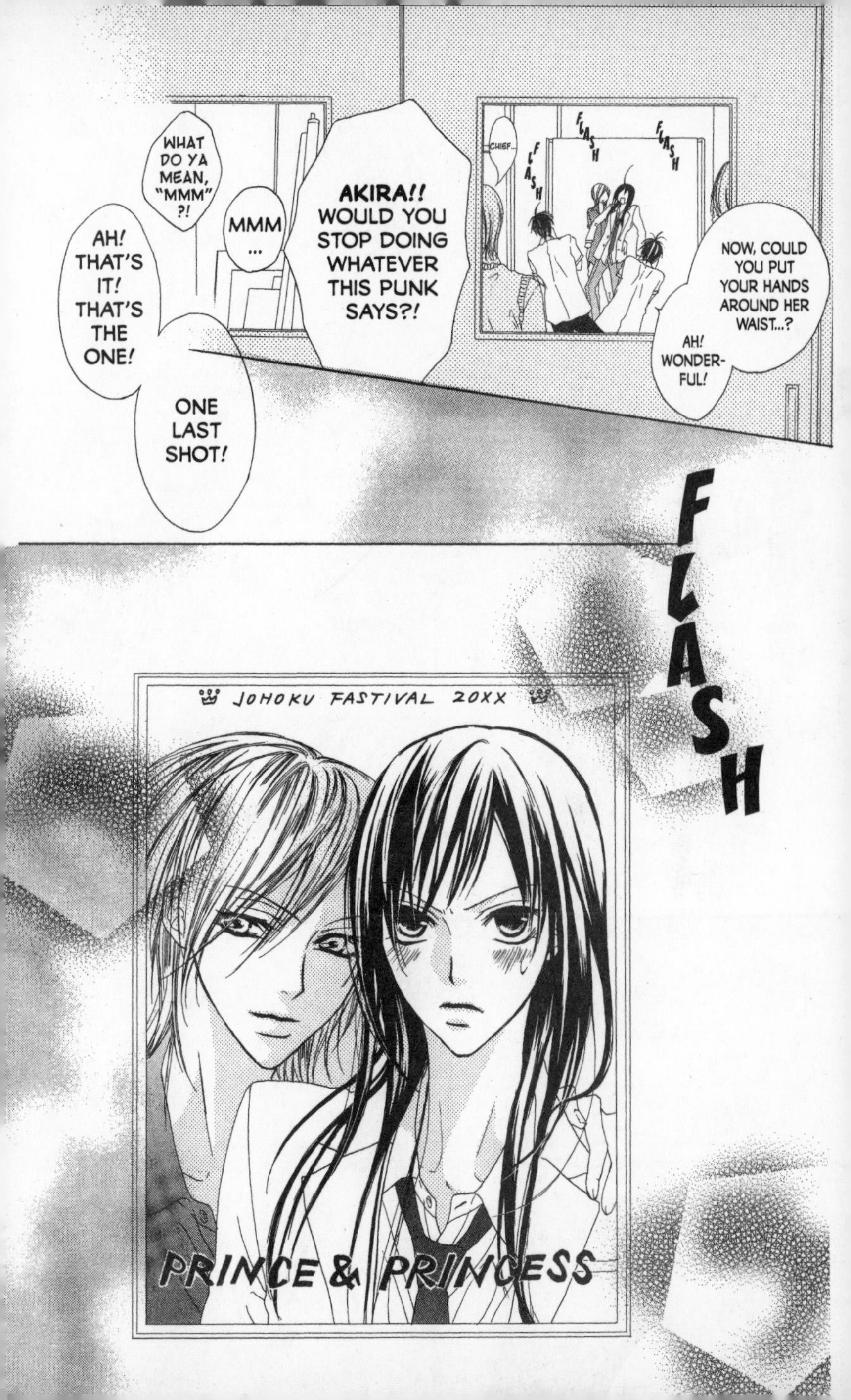
CHIEF...
FLASH
FLASH
FLASH
NOW, COULD YOU PUT YOUR HANDS AROUND HER WAIST...?
AH! WONDERFUL!
AKIRA!! WOULD YOU STOP DOING WHATEVER THIS PUNK SAYS?!
MMM...
WHAT DO YA MEAN, "MMM" ?!
AH! THAT'S IT! THAT'S THE ONE!
ONE LAST SHOT!
FLASH
JOHOKU FASTIVAL 20XX
PRINCE & PRINCESS

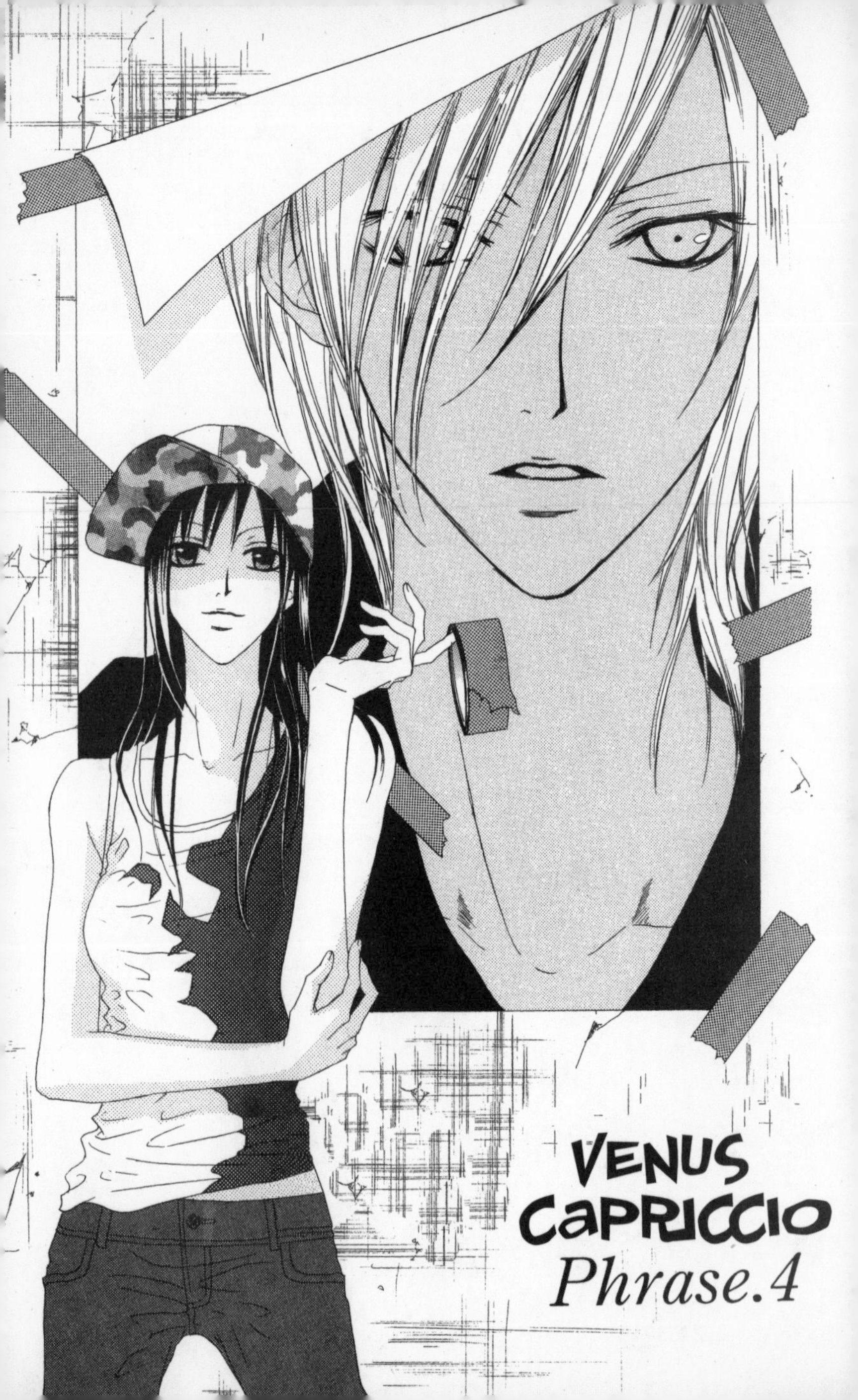
VENUS
CAPRICCIO
Phrase.4

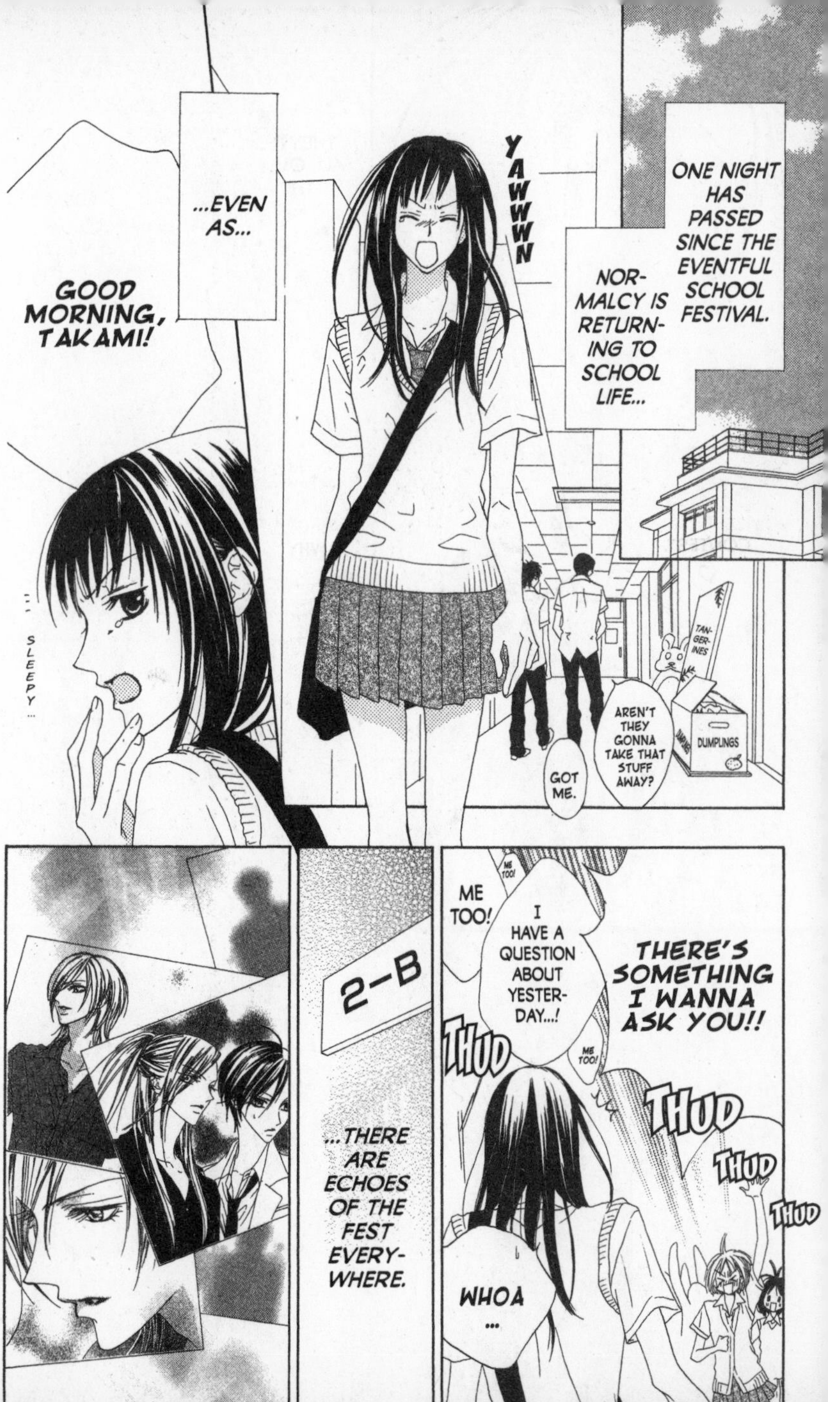
ONE NIGHT HAS PASSED SINCE THE EVENTFUL SCHOOL FESTIVAL.
NOR-MALCY IS RETURN-ING TO SCHOOL LIFE...
YAWWWN
TAN-GER-INES
DUMPLINGS
DUMPLINGS
AREN'T THEY GONNA TAKE THAT STUFF AWAY?
GOT ME.
...EVEN AS...
GOOD MORNING, TAKAMI!
SLEEPY...
THERE'S SOMETHING I WANNA ASK YOU!!
I HAVE A QUESTION ABOUT YESTER-DAY...!
ME TOO!
ME TOO!
ME TOO!
THUD
THUD
THUD
THUD
WHOA...
2-B
...THERE ARE ECHOES OF THE FEST EVERY-WHERE.

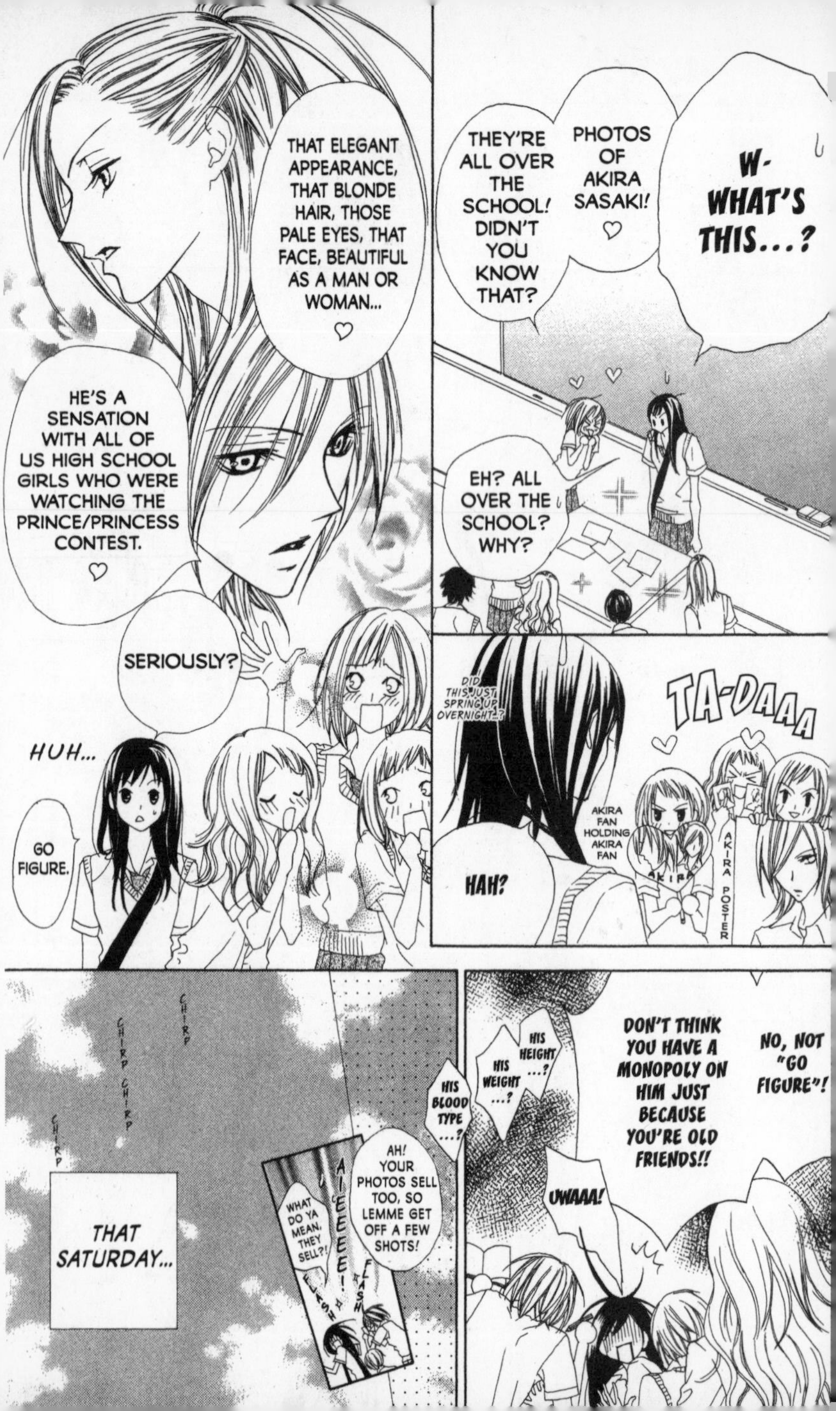
W-WHAT'S THIS...?
PHOTOS OF AKIRA SASAKI! ♡
THEY'RE ALL OVER THE SCHOOL! DIDN'T YOU KNOW THAT?
EH? ALL OVER THE SCHOOL? WHY?
TA-DAAAA
DID THIS JUST SPRING UP OVERNIGHT...?
AKIRA POSTER
AKIRA FAN HOLDING AKIRA FAN
AKIRA
HAH?
THAT ELEGANT APPEARANCE, THAT BLONDE HAIR, THOSE PALE EYES, THAT FACE, BEAUTIFUL AS A MAN OR WOMAN... ♡
HE'S A SENSATION WITH ALL OF US HIGH SCHOOL GIRLS WHO WERE WATCHING THE PRINCE/PRINCESS CONTEST. ♡
SERIOUSLY?
HUH...
GO FIGURE.
NO, NOT "GO FIGURE"!
DON'T THINK YOU HAVE A MONOPOLY ON HIM JUST BECAUSE YOU'RE OLD FRIENDS!!
HIS HEIGHT...?
HIS WEIGHT...?
HIS BLOOD TYPE...?
UWAAA!
CHIRP
CHIRP CHIRP
CHIRP
THAT SATURDAY...
AH! YOUR PHOTOS SELL TOO, SO LEMME GET OFF A FEW SHOTS!
AIEEEEE!
WHAT DO YA MEAN, THEY SELL?!
FLASH
FLASH

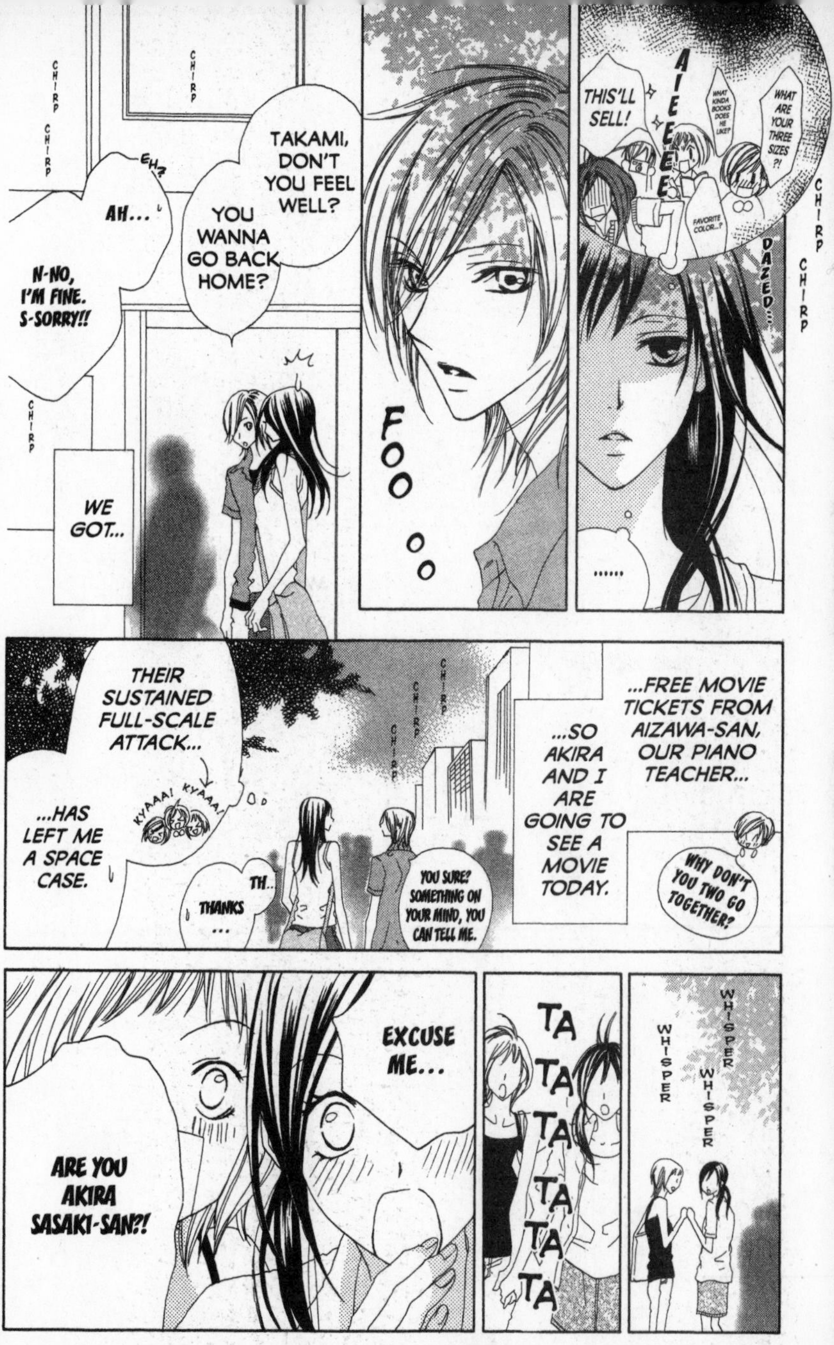
WHAT ARE YOUR THREE SIZES?!
WHAT KINDA BOOKS DOES HE LIKE?
AIEEEEE
THIS'LL SELL!
FAVORITE COLOR...?
CHIRP
CHIRP
DAZED...
......
FOO
OO
TAKAMI, DON'T YOU FEEL WELL?
YOU WANNA GO BACK HOME?
CHIRP
CHIRP CHIRP
EH?
AH...
N-NO, I'M FINE. S-SORRY!!
CHIRP
WE GOT...
...FREE MOVIE TICKETS FROM AIZAWA-SAN, OUR PIANO TEACHER...
WHY DON'T YOU TWO GO TOGETHER?
...SO AKIRA AND I ARE GOING TO SEE A MOVIE TODAY.
CHIRP
CHIRP
CHIRP
YOU SURE? SOMETHING ON YOUR MIND, YOU CAN TELL ME.
TH... THANKS...
THEIR SUSTAINED FULL-SCALE ATTACK...
KYAAA! KYAAA!
...HAS LEFT ME A SPACE CASE.
WHISPER
WHISPER
WHISPER
WHISPER
TA TA TA TA TA TA TA TA
EXCUSE ME...
ARE YOU AKIRA SASAKI-SAN?!

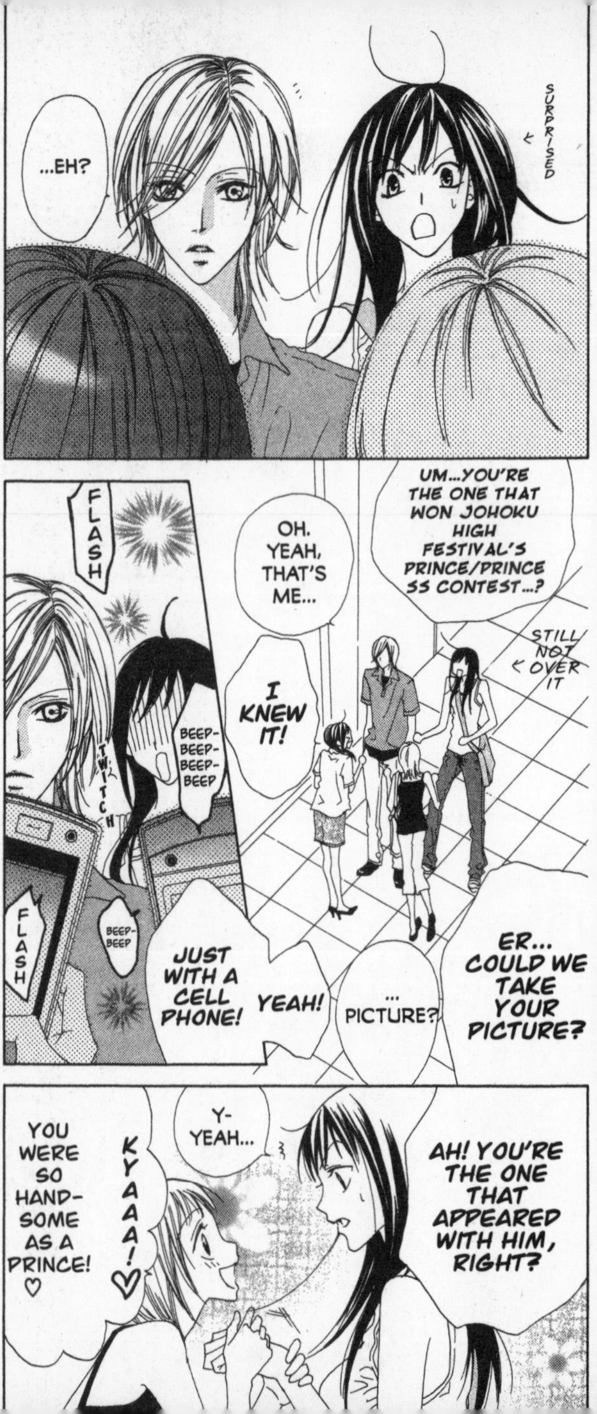
SURPRISED
...EH?
UM...YOU'RE THE ONE THAT WON JOHOKU HIGH FESTIVAL'S PRINCE/PRINCESS CONTEST...?
OH. YEAH, THAT'S ME...
STILL NOT OVER IT
I KNEW IT!
ER... COULD WE TAKE YOUR PICTURE?
... PICTURE?
YEAH!
JUST WITH A CELL PHONE!
FLASH
BEEP-BEEP-BEEP-BEEP
TWITCH
BEEP-BEEP
FLASH
AH! YOU'RE THE ONE THAT APPEARED WITH HIM, RIGHT?
Y-YEAH...
KYAAAA! ♡
YOU WERE SO HANDSOME AS A PRINCE! ♡

4

TITLE.

I DEVELOPED THE CHARACTERS, PLOTTED OUT MOST OF THE STORY AND THEN QUICKLY CAME UP WITH A TITLE. I KNEW I WANTED TO USE "VENUS" AND THEN HAVE SOME MUSIC-RELATED WORD AFTER THAT, SO AFTER DOING SOME INVESTIGATING, I WENT WITH "CAPRICCIO", A FREE-FORM, LIVELY PIECE OF MUSIC, WHICH I THOUGHT WAS A GOOD FIT.

BUT WHEN PEOPLE WHO DON'T KNOW MY MANGA ASK ME WHAT THE TITLE OF MY SERIES IS, I FIND MYSELF TOO EMBARRASSED TO TELL THEM. MAYBE I'D BE TOO EMBARRASSED TO SAY, NO MATTER WHAT THE TITLE.

ON THE OTHER HAND, I HAVE NO TROUBLE SAYING IT IN FRONT OF PEOPLE WHO DO KNOW MY WORK. I WONDER WHY THAT IS...?

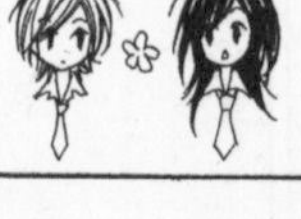

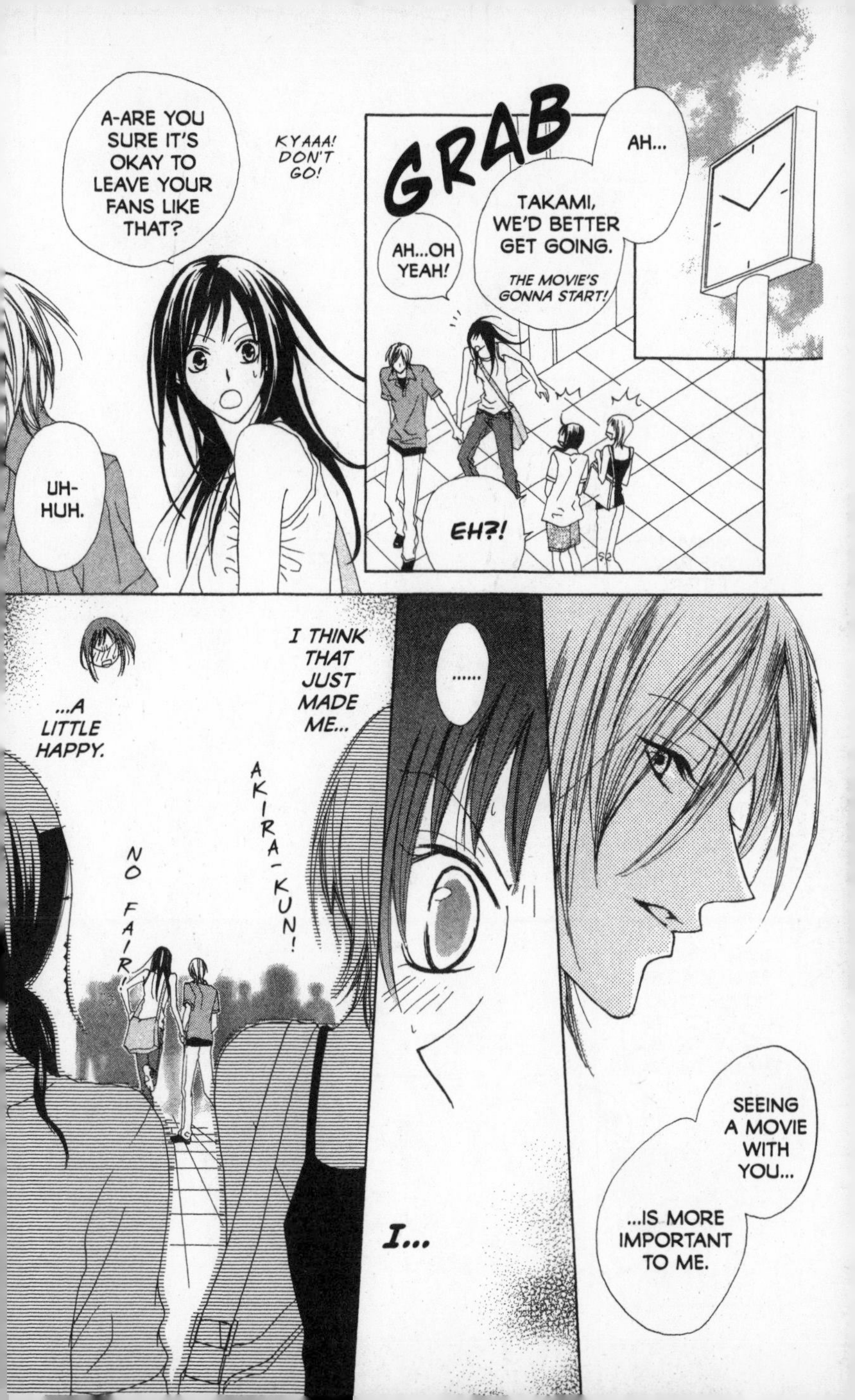
AH...
GRAB
TAKAMI, WE'D BETTER GET GOING.
THE MOVIE'S GONNA START!
AH...OH YEAH!
EH?!
A-ARE YOU SURE IT'S OKAY TO LEAVE YOUR FANS LIKE THAT?
KYAAA! DON'T GO!
UH-HUH.
SEEING A MOVIE WITH YOU...
...IS MORE IMPORTANT TO ME.
......
I...
I THINK THAT JUST MADE ME...
...A LITTLE HAPPY.
AKIRA-KUN!
NO FAIR!

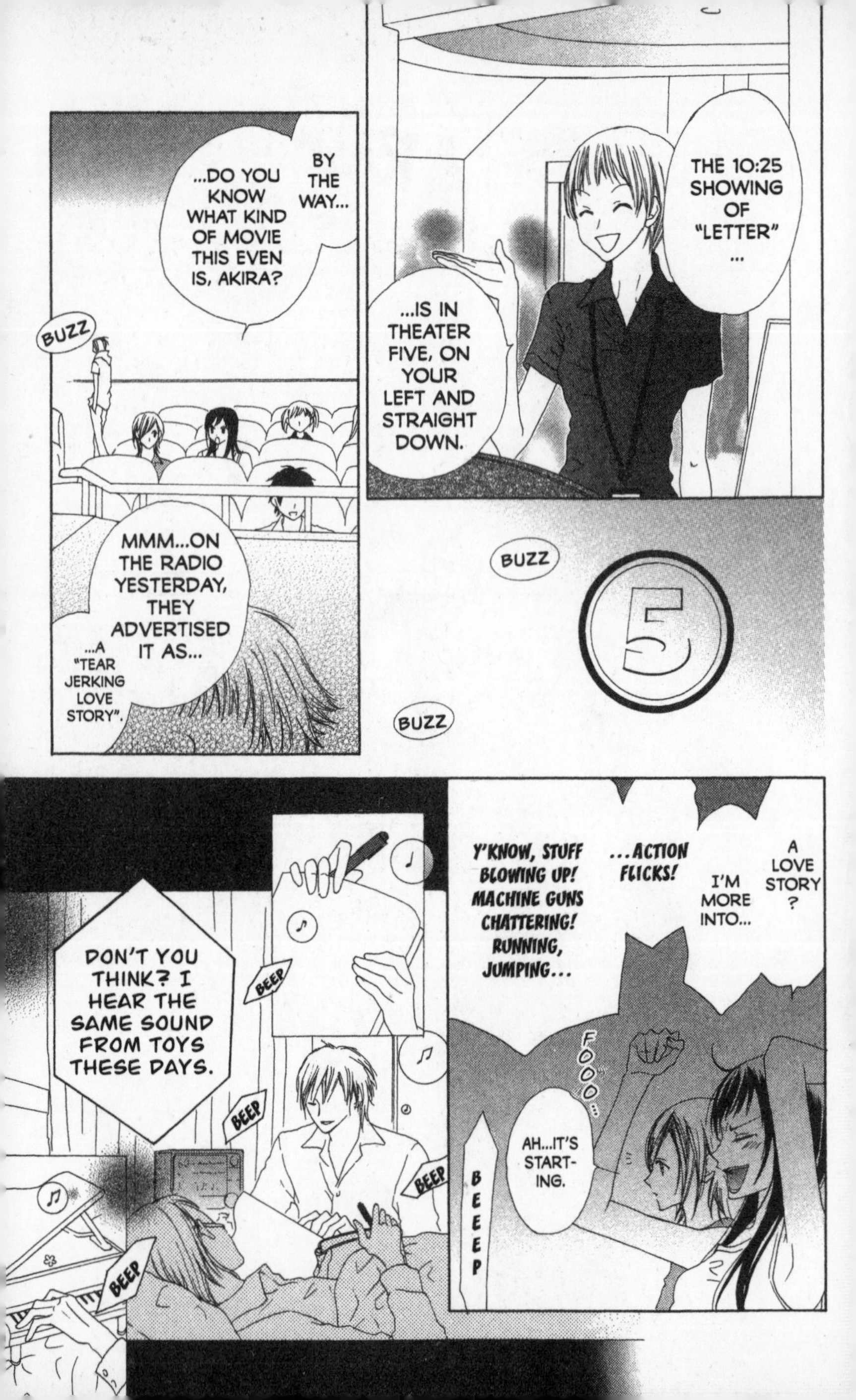
THE 10:25 SHOWING OF "LETTER" ...
...IS IN THEATER FIVE, ON YOUR LEFT AND STRAIGHT DOWN.
BUZZ
BUZZ
BY THE WAY...
...DO YOU KNOW WHAT KIND OF MOVIE THIS EVEN IS, AKIRA?
BUZZ
MMM...ON THE RADIO YESTERDAY, THEY ADVERTISED IT AS...
...A "TEAR JERKING LOVE STORY".
A LOVE STORY?
I'M MORE INTO...
...ACTION FLICKS!
Y'KNOW, STUFF BLOWING UP! MACHINE GUNS CHATTERING! RUNNING, JUMPING...
FOOOO...
AH...IT'S STARTING.
BEEEEP
BEEP
BEEP
BEEP
BEEP
DON'T YOU THINK? I HEAR THE SAME SOUND FROM TOYS THESE DAYS.

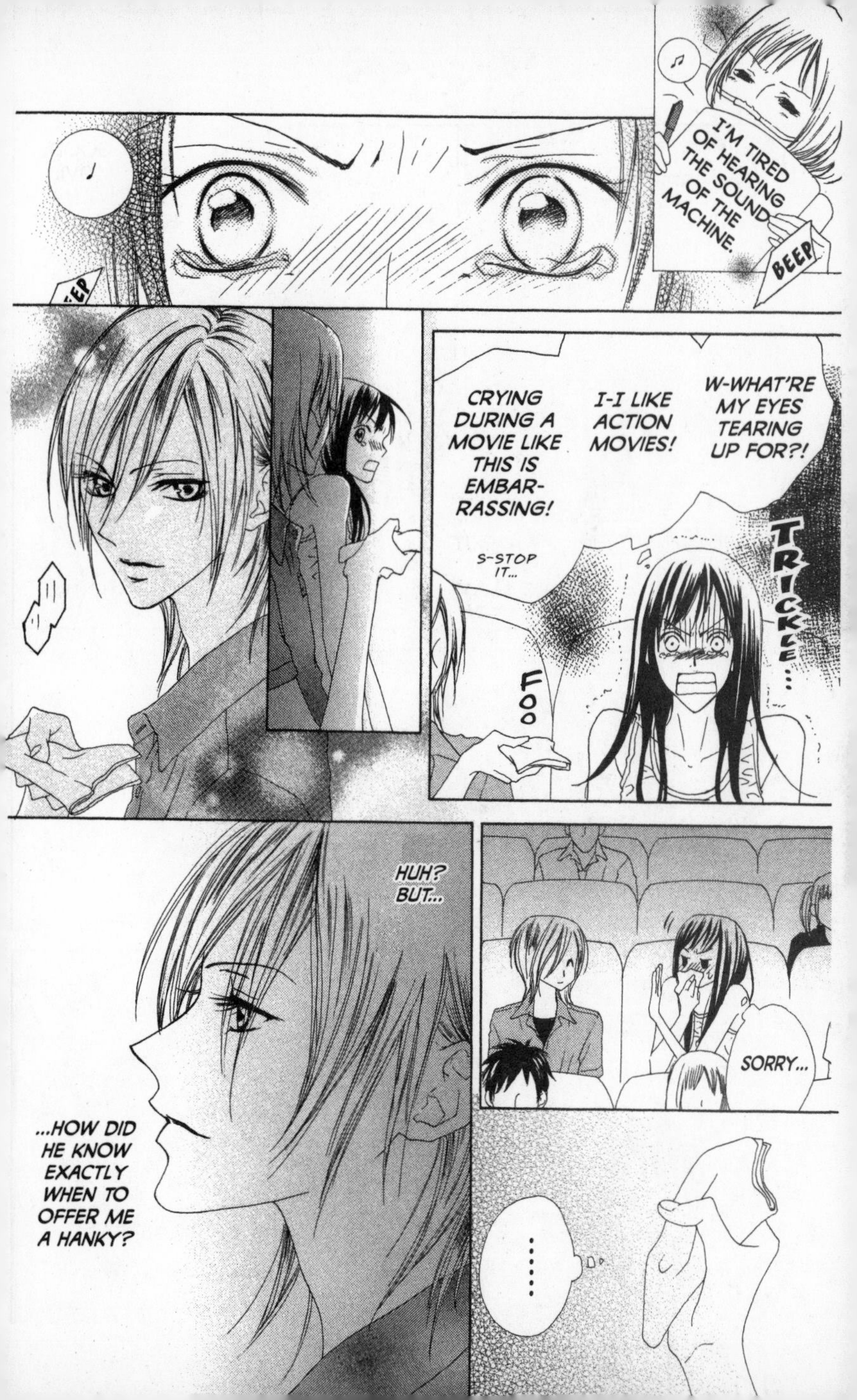
I'M TIRED OF HEARING THE SOUND OF THE MACHINE.
BEEP
EEP
W-WHAT'RE MY EYES TEARING UP FOR?!
I-I LIKE ACTION MOVIES!
CRYING DURING A MOVIE LIKE THIS IS EMBAR-RASSING!
TRICKLE...
S-STOP IT...
FOO
SORRY...
......
HUH? BUT...
...HOW DID HE KNOW EXACTLY WHEN TO OFFER ME A HANKY?

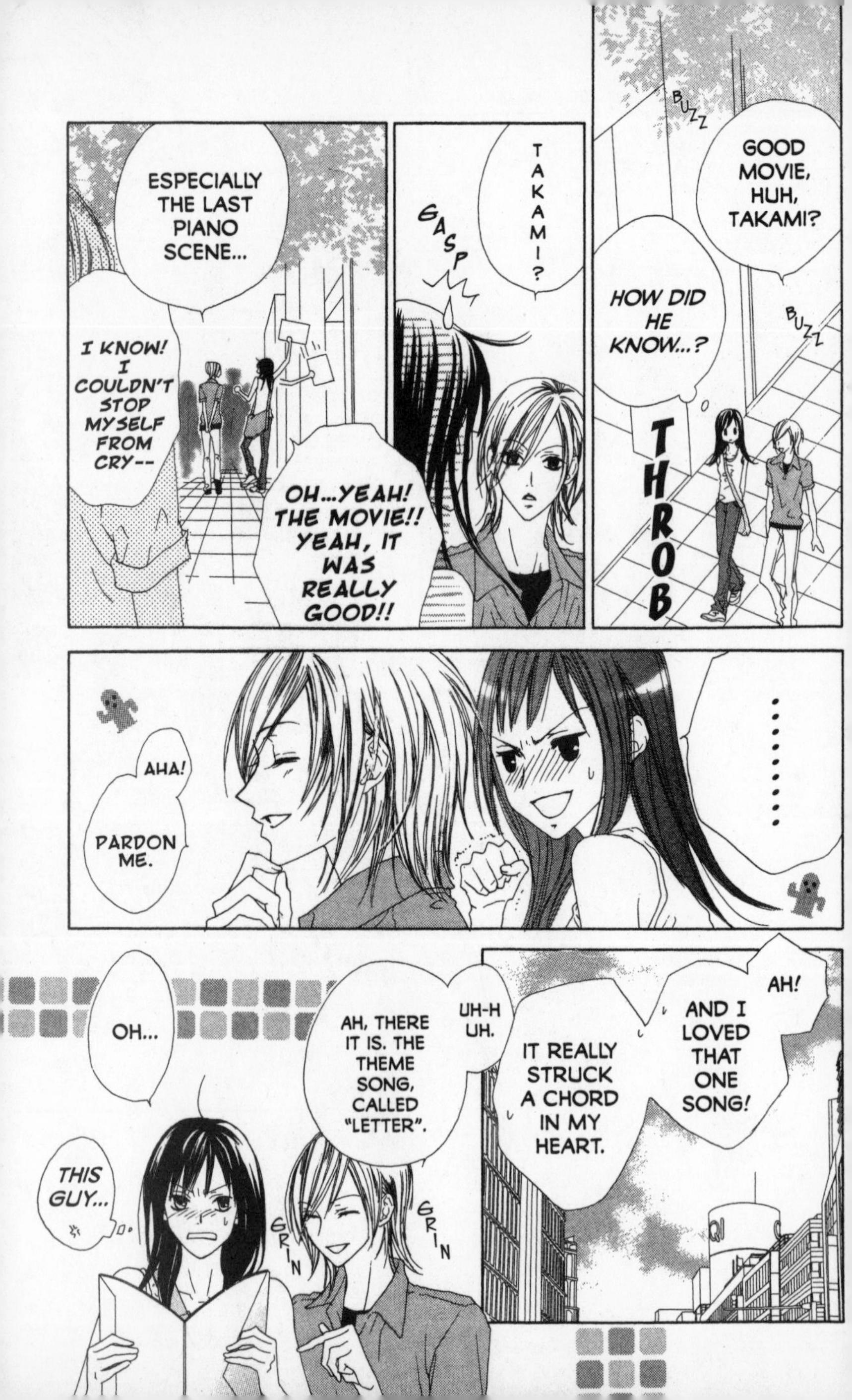
BUZZ
GOOD MOVIE, HUH, TAKAMI?
BUZZ
HOW DID HE KNOW...?
THROB
TAKAMI?
GASP
OH...YEAH! THE MOVIE!! YEAH, IT WAS REALLY GOOD!!
ESPECIALLY THE LAST PIANO SCENE...
I KNOW! I COULDN'T STOP MYSELF FROM CRY--
......
AHA!
PARDON ME.
AH!
AND I LOVED THAT ONE SONG!
IT REALLY STRUCK A CHORD IN MY HEART.
UH-HUH.
AH, THERE IT IS. THE THEME SONG, CALLED "LETTER".
OH...
GRIN
GRIN
THIS GUY...

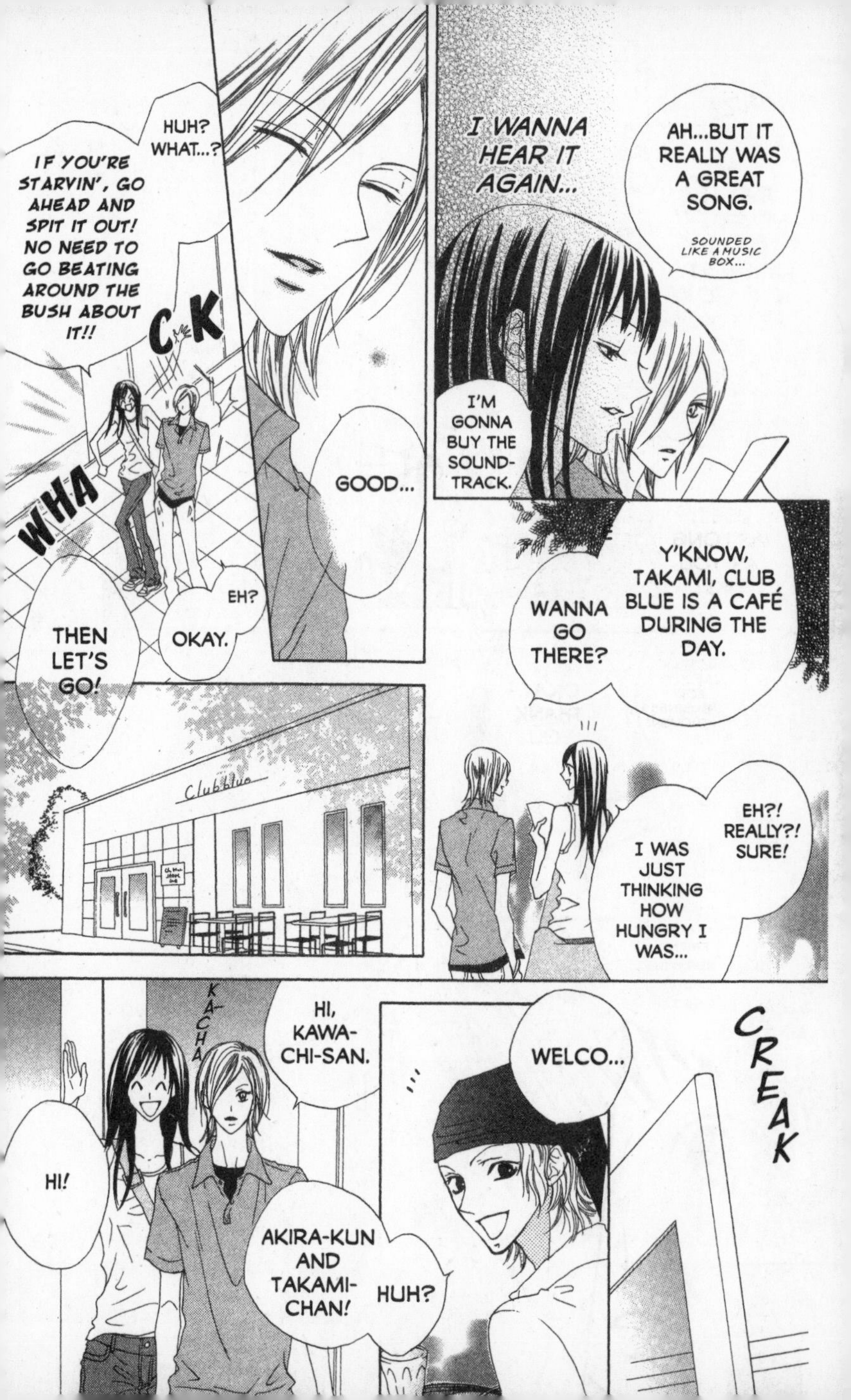
I WANNA HEAR IT AGAIN...
AH...BUT IT REALLY WAS A GREAT SONG.
SOUNDED LIKE A MUSIC BOX...
I'M GONNA BUY THE SOUNDTRACK.
GOOD...
Y'KNOW, TAKAMI, CLUB BLUE IS A CAFÉ DURING THE DAY.
WANNA GO THERE?
EH?! REALLY?! SURE!
I WAS JUST THINKING HOW HUNGRY I WAS...
HUH? WHAT...?
IF YOU'RE STARVIN', GO AHEAD AND SPIT IT OUT! NO NEED TO GO BEATING AROUND THE BUSH ABOUT IT!!
CK
WHA
EH?
OKAY.
THEN LET'S GO!
Clubblue
CREAK
WELCO...
AKIRA-KUN AND TAKAMI-CHAN!
HUH?
KA-CHA
HI, KAWA-CHI-SAN.
HI!

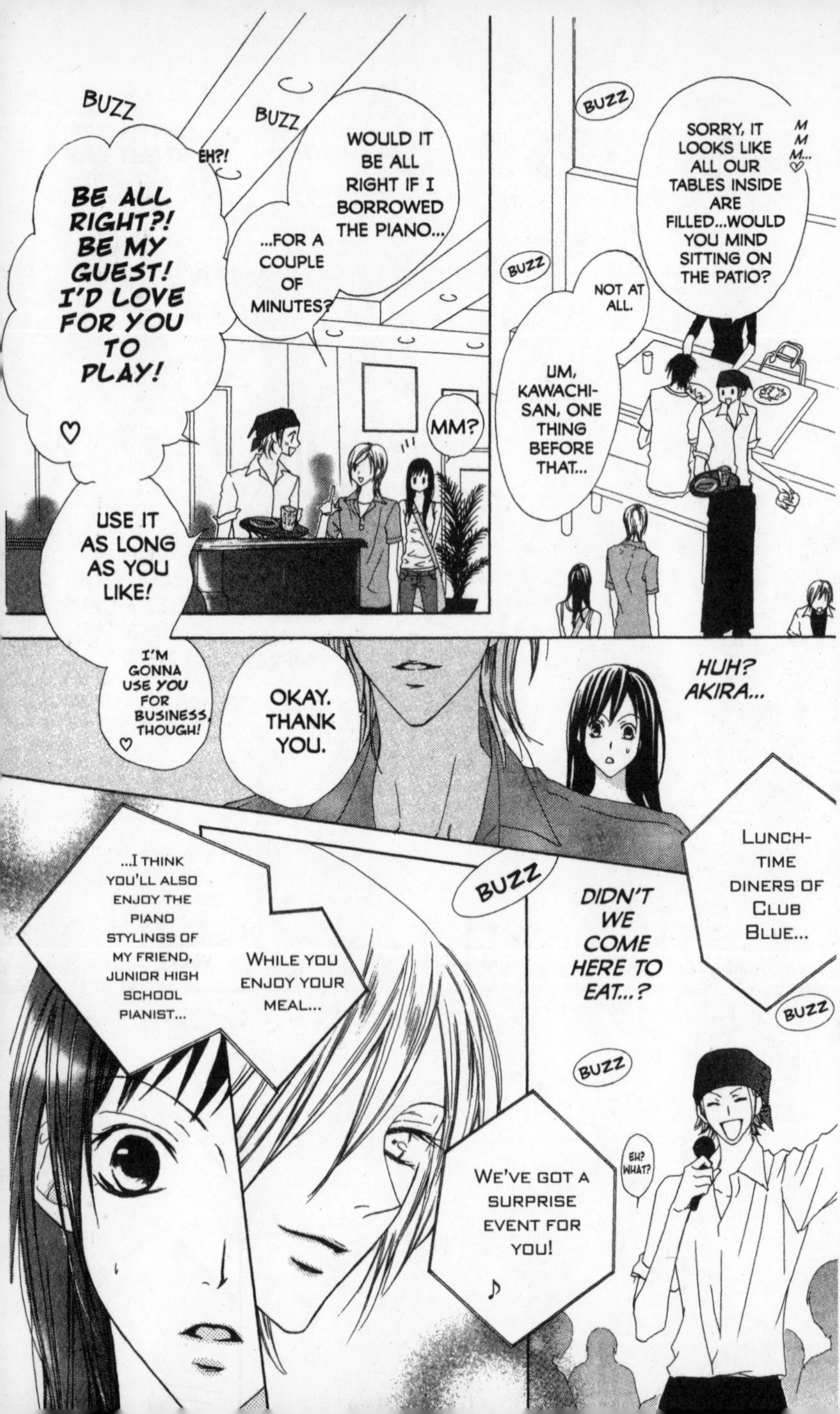
BUZZ
SORRY, IT LOOKS LIKE ALL OUR TABLES INSIDE ARE FILLED...WOULD YOU MIND SITTING ON THE PATIO?
MMM...♡
BUZZ
NOT AT ALL.
UM, KAWACHI-SAN, ONE THING BEFORE THAT...
BUZZ
BUZZ
WOULD IT BE ALL RIGHT IF I BORROWED THE PIANO...
...FOR A COUPLE OF MINUTES?
MM?
EH?!
BE ALL RIGHT?! BE MY GUEST! I'D LOVE FOR YOU TO PLAY! ♡
USE IT AS LONG AS YOU LIKE!
I'M GONNA USE YOU FOR BUSINESS, THOUGH! ♡
HUH? AKIRA...
OKAY. THANK YOU.
LUNCH-TIME DINERS OF CLUB BLUE...
BUZZ
DIDN'T WE COME HERE TO EAT...?
BUZZ
BUZZ
WE'VE GOT A SURPRISE EVENT FOR YOU! ♪
EH? WHAT?
WHILE YOU ENJOY YOUR MEAL...
...I THINK YOU'LL ALSO ENJOY THE PIANO STYLINGS OF MY FRIEND, JUNIOR HIGH SCHOOL PIANIST...

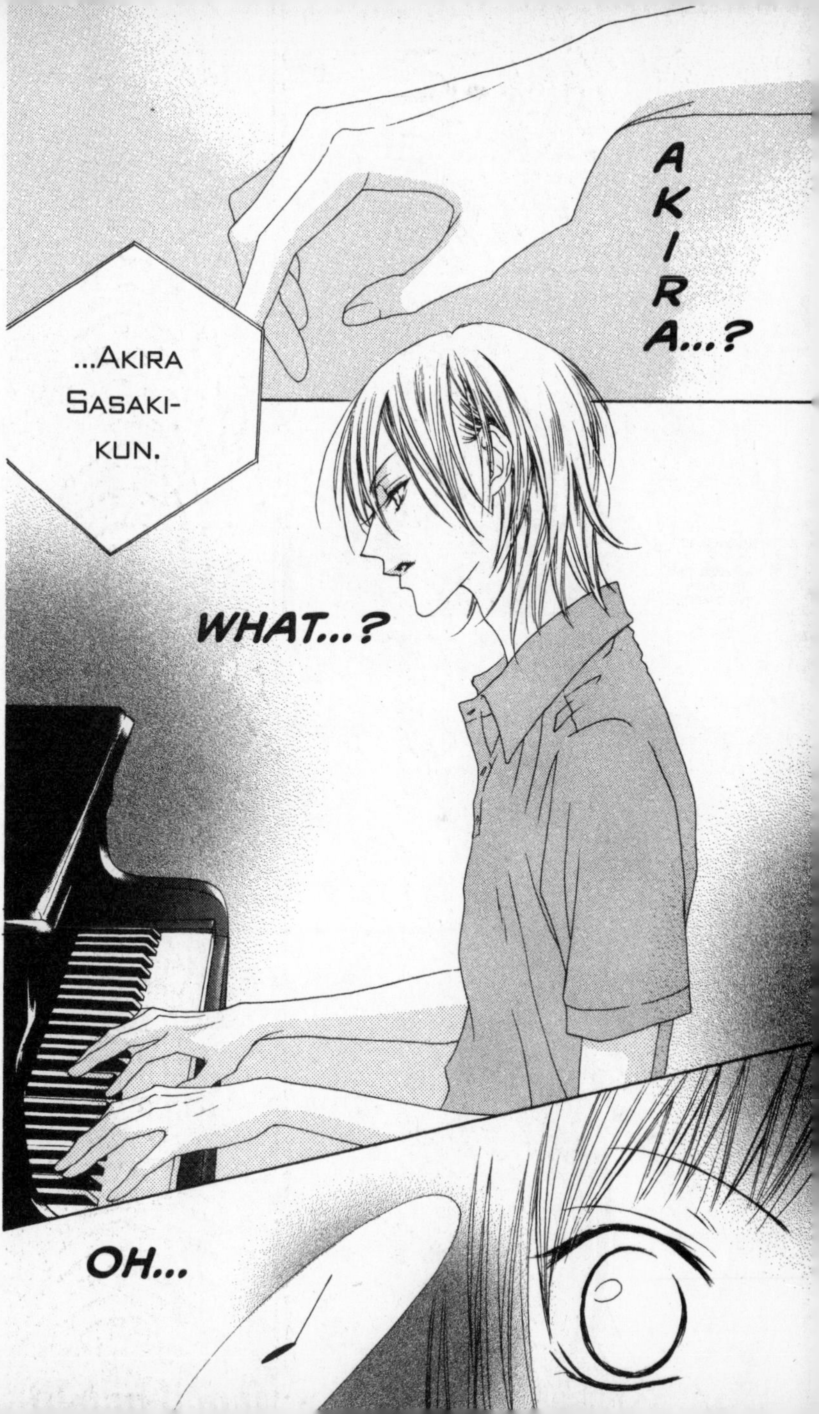
AKIRA...?
...AKIRA SASAKI-KUN.
WHAT...?
OH...

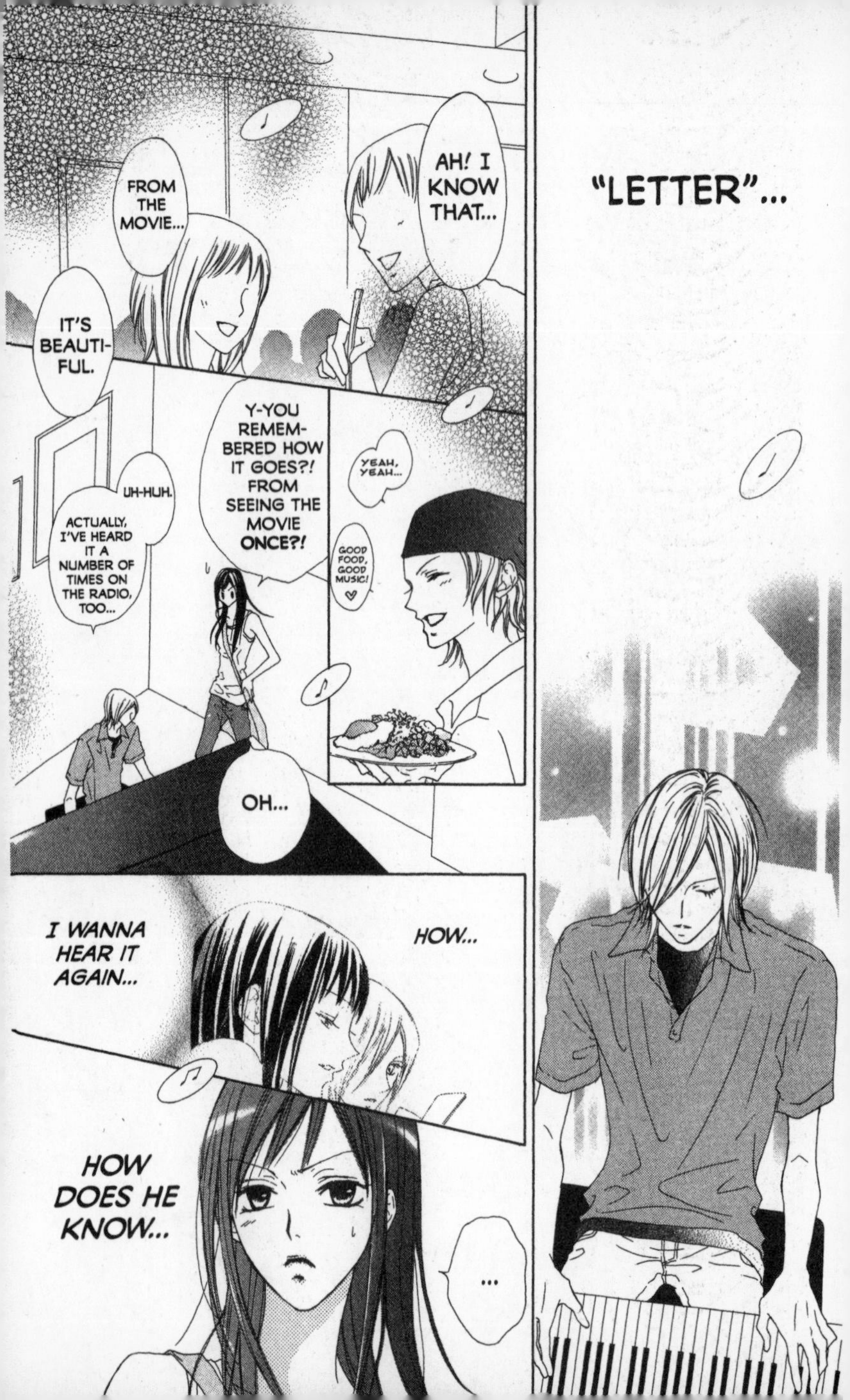
"LETTER"...
AH! I KNOW THAT...
FROM THE MOVIE...
IT'S BEAUTIFUL.
YEAH, YEAH...
GOOD FOOD, GOOD MUSIC! ♥
Y-YOU REMEMBERED HOW IT GOES?! FROM SEEING THE MOVIE ONCE?!
UH-HUH.
ACTUALLY, I'VE HEARD IT A NUMBER OF TIMES ON THE RADIO, TOO...
OH...
HOW...
I WANNA HEAR IT AGAIN...
...
HOW DOES HE KNOW...

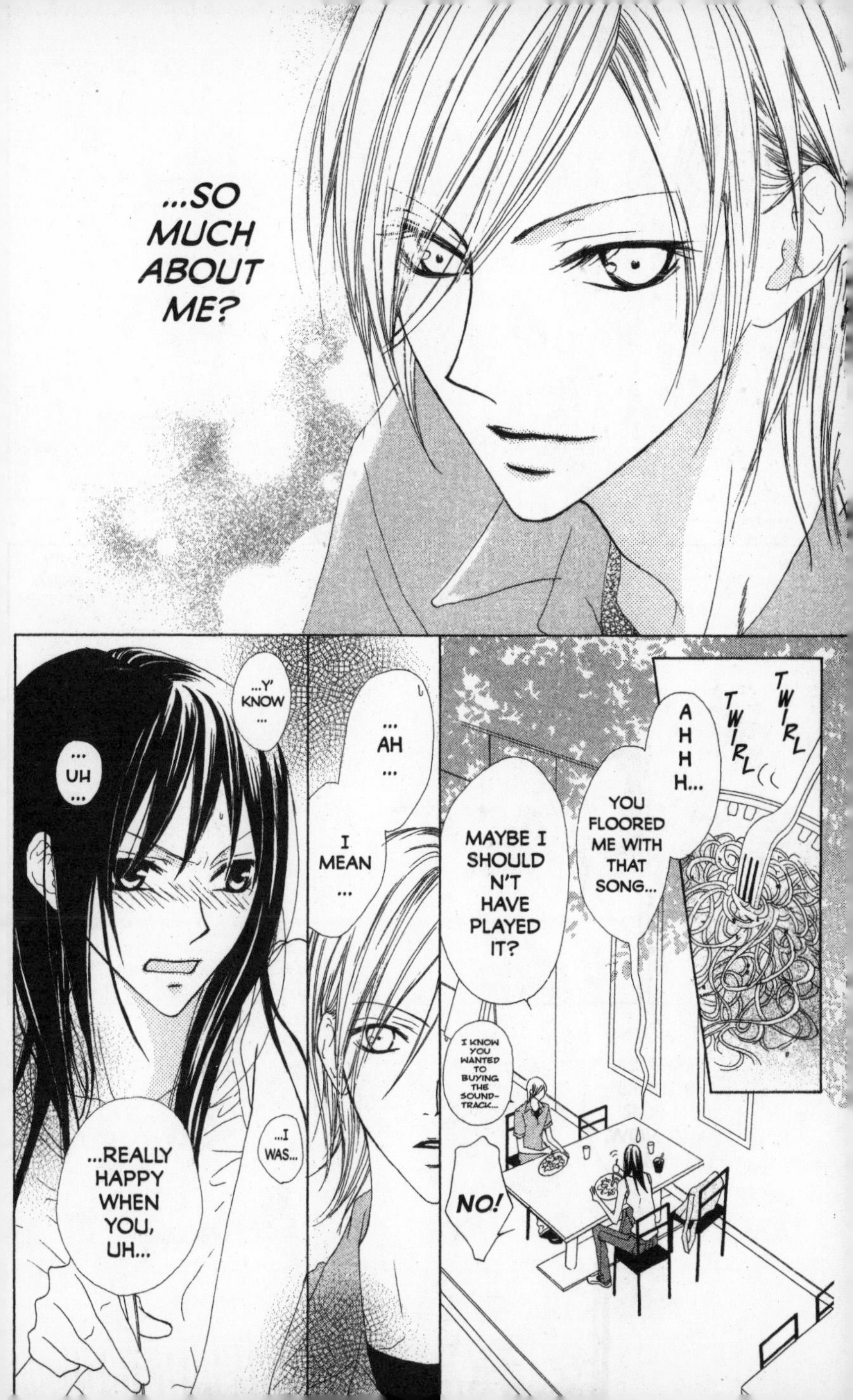

...SO MUCH ABOUT ME?
TWIRL TWIRL
AHHH...
YOU FLOORED ME WITH THAT SONG...
MAYBE I SHOULDN'T HAVE PLAYED IT?
I KNOW YOU WANTED TO BUYING THE SOUND-TRACK...
NO!
...AH...
I MEAN...
...I WAS...
...Y' KNOW...
...UH...
...REALLY HAPPY WHEN YOU, UH...

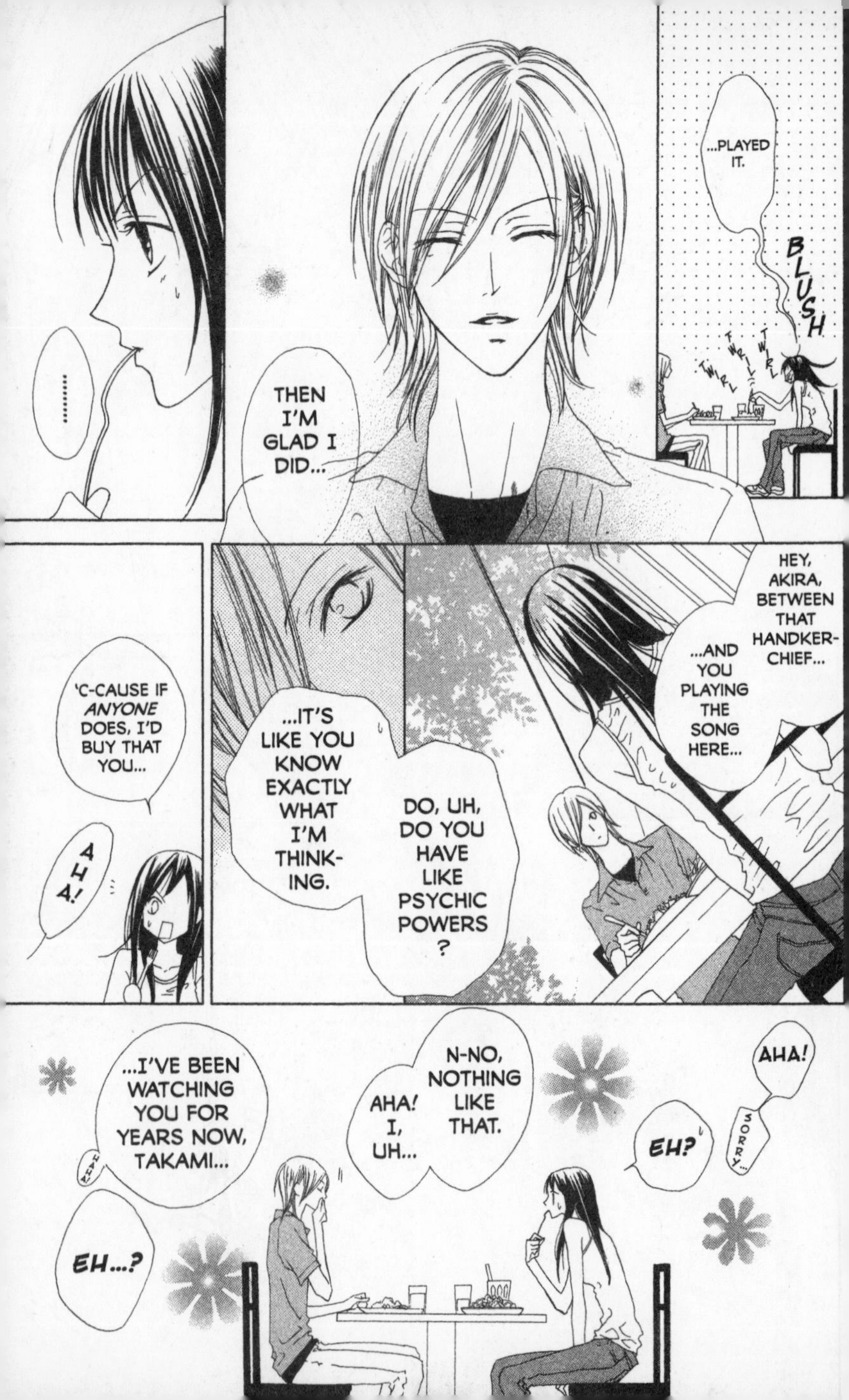
...PLAYED IT.
BLUSH
TWIRL TWIRL TWIRL
THEN I'M GLAD I DID...
....
HEY, AKIRA, BETWEEN THAT HANDKER-CHIEF...
...AND YOU PLAYING THE SONG HERE...
...IT'S LIKE YOU KNOW EXACTLY WHAT I'M THINK-ING.
DO, UH, DO YOU HAVE LIKE PSYCHIC POWERS?
'C-CAUSE IF *ANYONE* DOES, I'D BUY THAT YOU...
AHA!
AHA!
SORRY...
EH?
N-NO, NOTHING LIKE THAT.
AHA! I, UH...
...I'VE BEEN WATCHING YOU FOR YEARS NOW, TAKAMI...
HAHA
EH...?

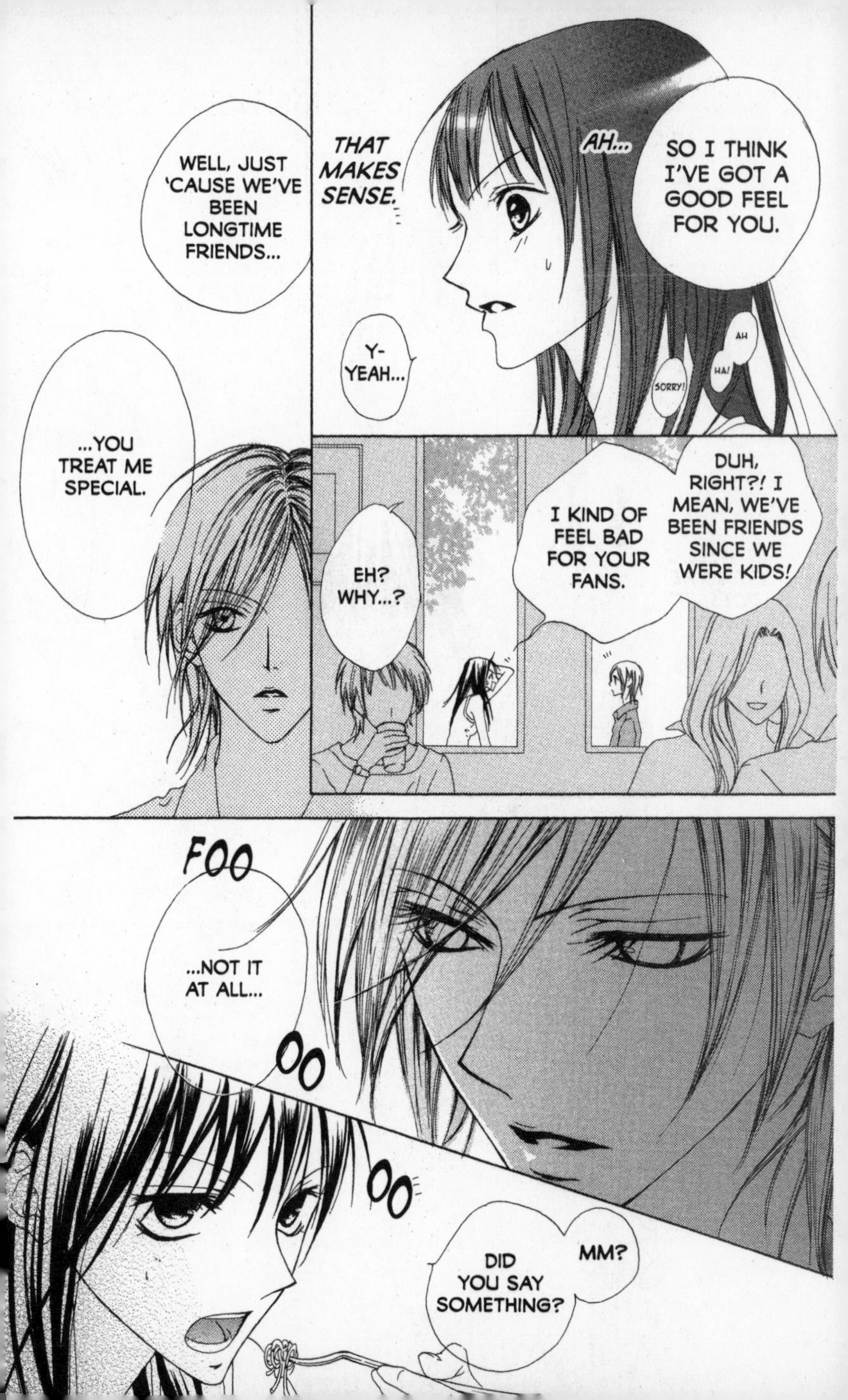
SO I THINK I'VE GOT A GOOD FEEL FOR YOU.
AH...
THAT MAKES SENSE.
Y-YEAH...
AH HA! SORRY!
DUH, RIGHT?! I MEAN, WE'VE BEEN FRIENDS SINCE WE WERE KIDS!
I KIND OF FEEL BAD FOR YOUR FANS.
EH? WHY...?
WELL, JUST 'CAUSE WE'VE BEEN LONGTIME FRIENDS...
...YOU TREAT ME SPECIAL.
...NOT IT AT ALL...
FOO OO OO
MM?
DID YOU SAY SOMETHING?

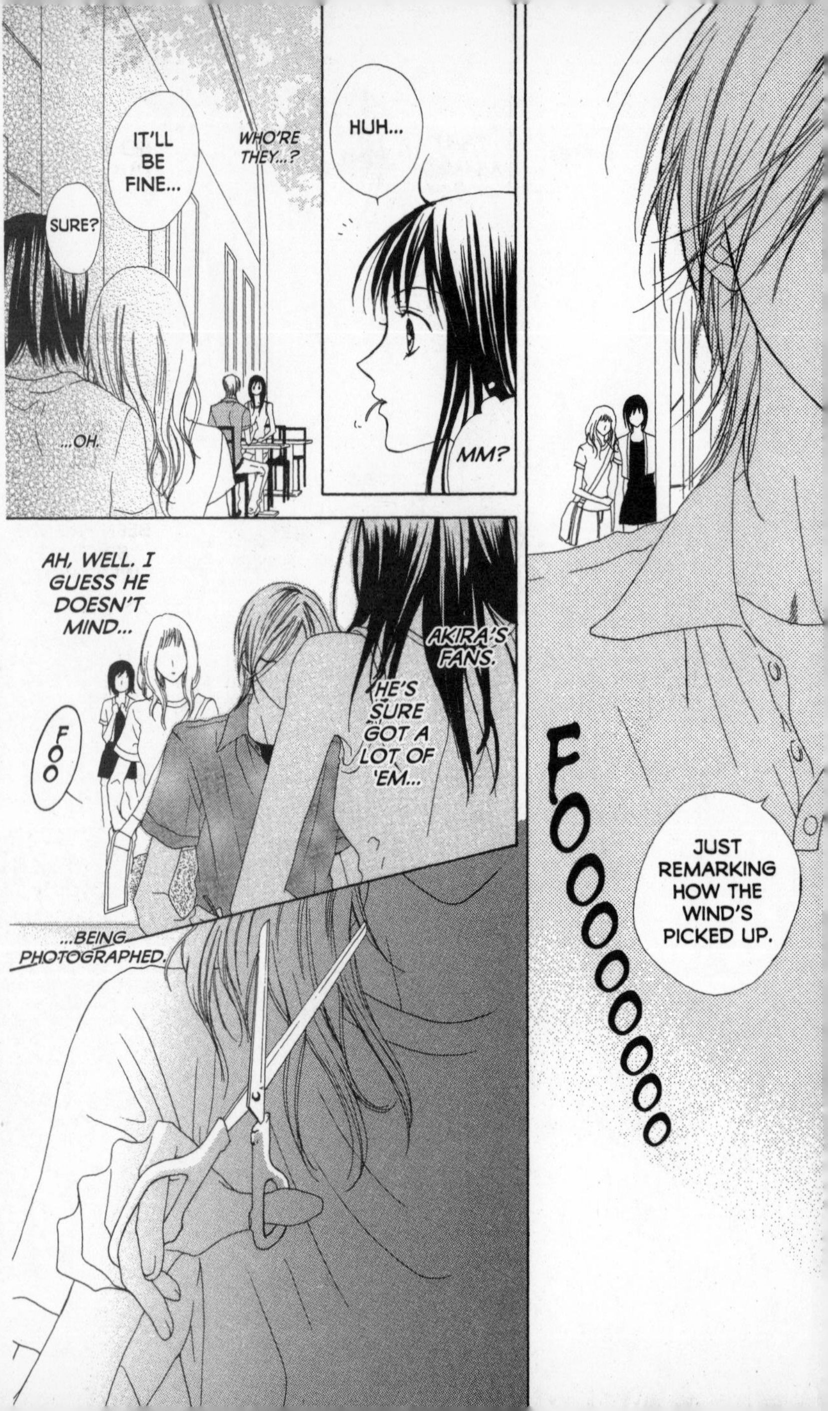
FOOOOOOOO
JUST REMARKING HOW THE WIND'S PICKED UP.
HUH...
MM?
WHO'RE THEY...?
IT'LL BE FINE...
SURE?
...OH.
AKIRA'S FANS.
HE'S SURE GOT A LOT OF 'EM...
AH, WELL. I GUESS HE DOESN'T MIND...
FOO
...BEING PHOTOGRAPHED.

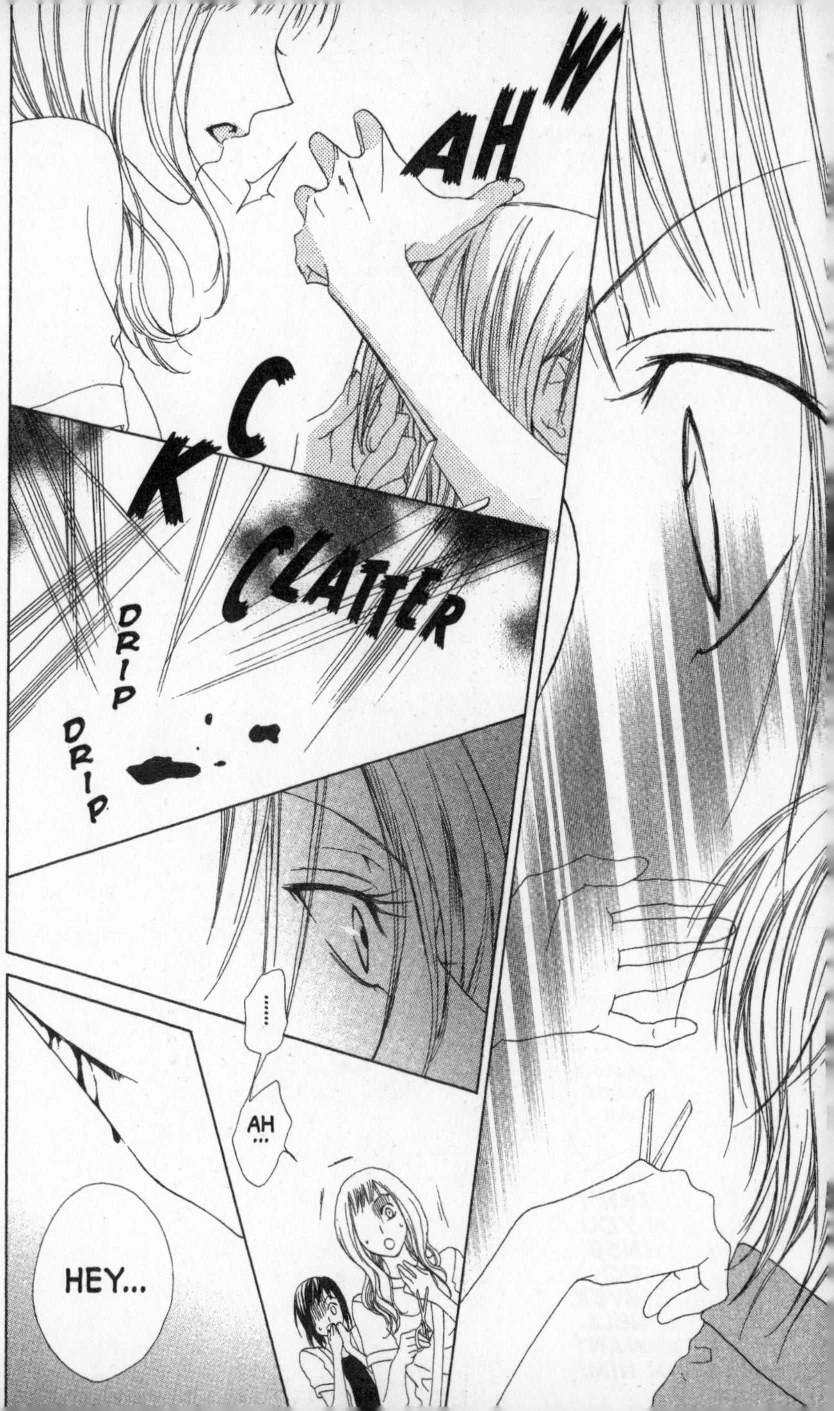
AHW
KC
CLATTER
DRIP
DRIP
......
AH...
HEY...

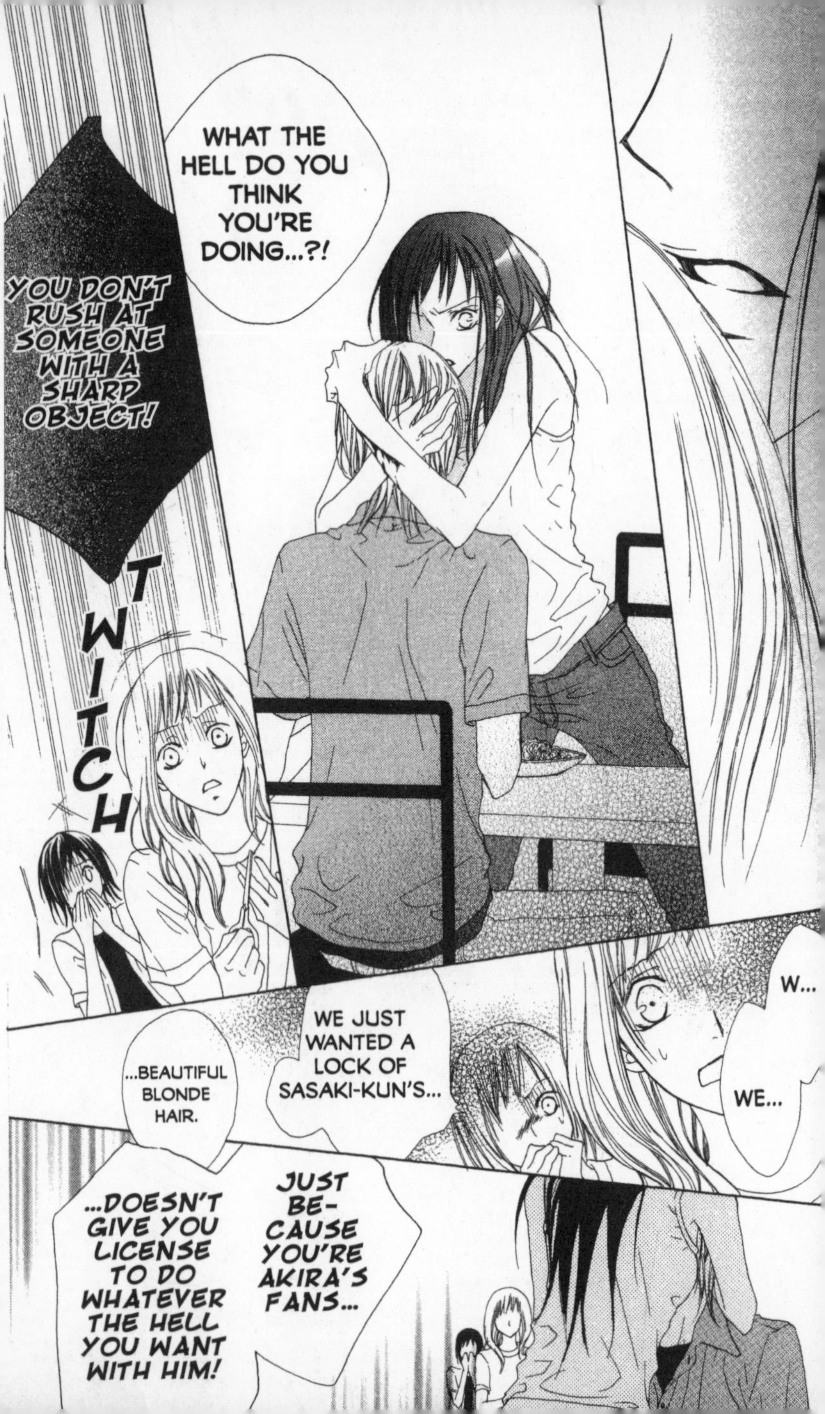
WHAT THE HELL DO YOU THINK YOU'RE DOING...?!
YOU DON'T RUSH AT SOMEONE WITH A SHARP OBJECT!
TWITCH
W...
WE...
WE JUST WANTED A LOCK OF SASAKI-KUN'S...
...BEAUTIFUL BLONDE HAIR.
JUST BE-CAUSE YOU'RE AKIRA'S FANS...
...DOESN'T GIVE YOU LICENSE TO DO WHATEVER THE HELL YOU WANT WITH HIM!

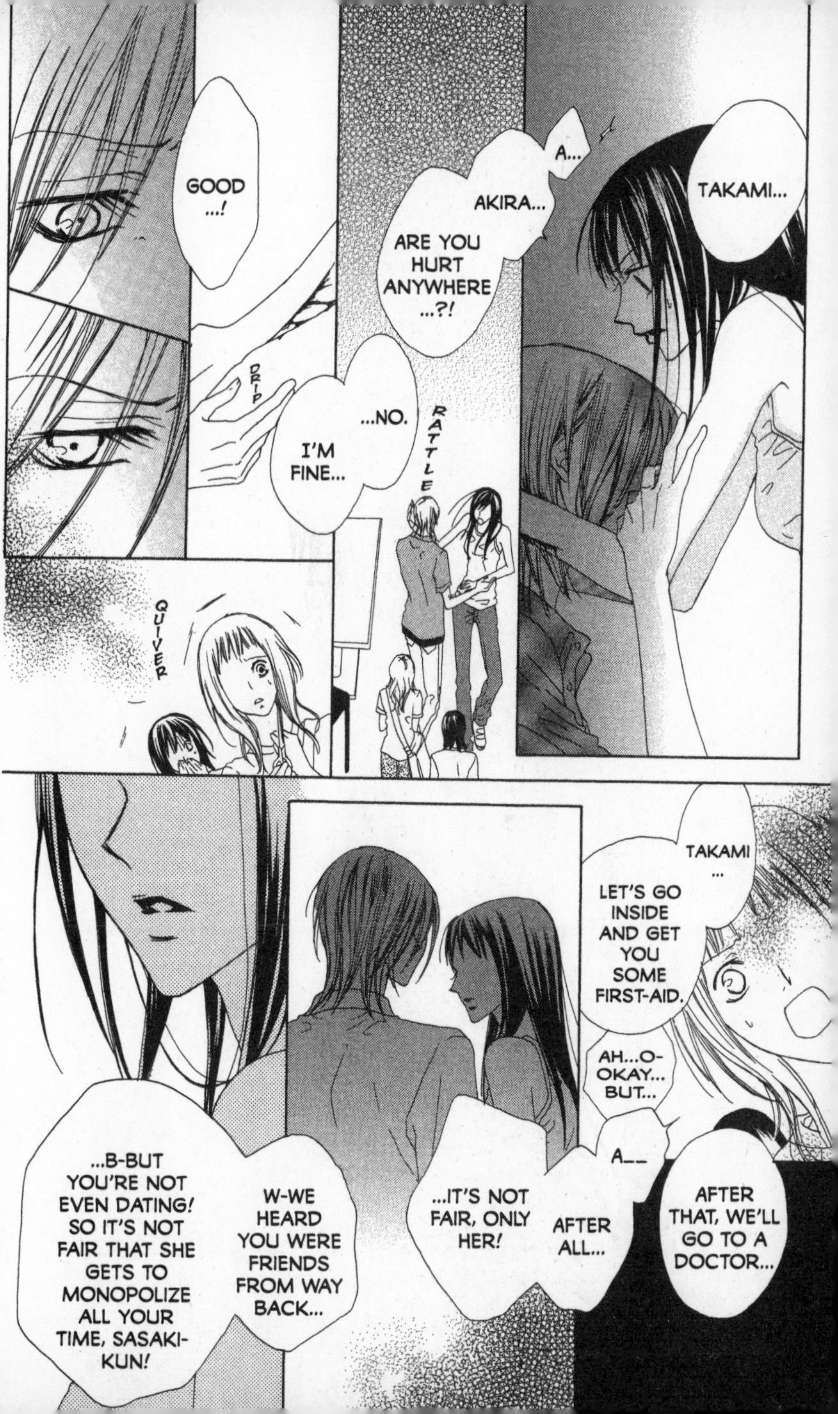
TAKAMI...
A...
AKIRA...
ARE YOU HURT ANYWHERE ...?!
...NO.
I'M FINE...
RATTLE
GOOD ...!
DRIP
QUIVER
TAKAMI ...
LET'S GO INSIDE AND GET YOU SOME FIRST-AID.
AH...O-OKAY... BUT...
AFTER THAT, WE'LL GO TO A DOCTOR...
A__
AFTER ALL...
...IT'S NOT FAIR, ONLY HER!
W-WE HEARD YOU WERE FRIENDS FROM WAY BACK...
...B-BUT YOU'RE NOT EVEN DATING! SO IT'S NOT FAIR THAT SHE GETS TO MONOPOLIZE ALL YOUR TIME, SASAKI-KUN!

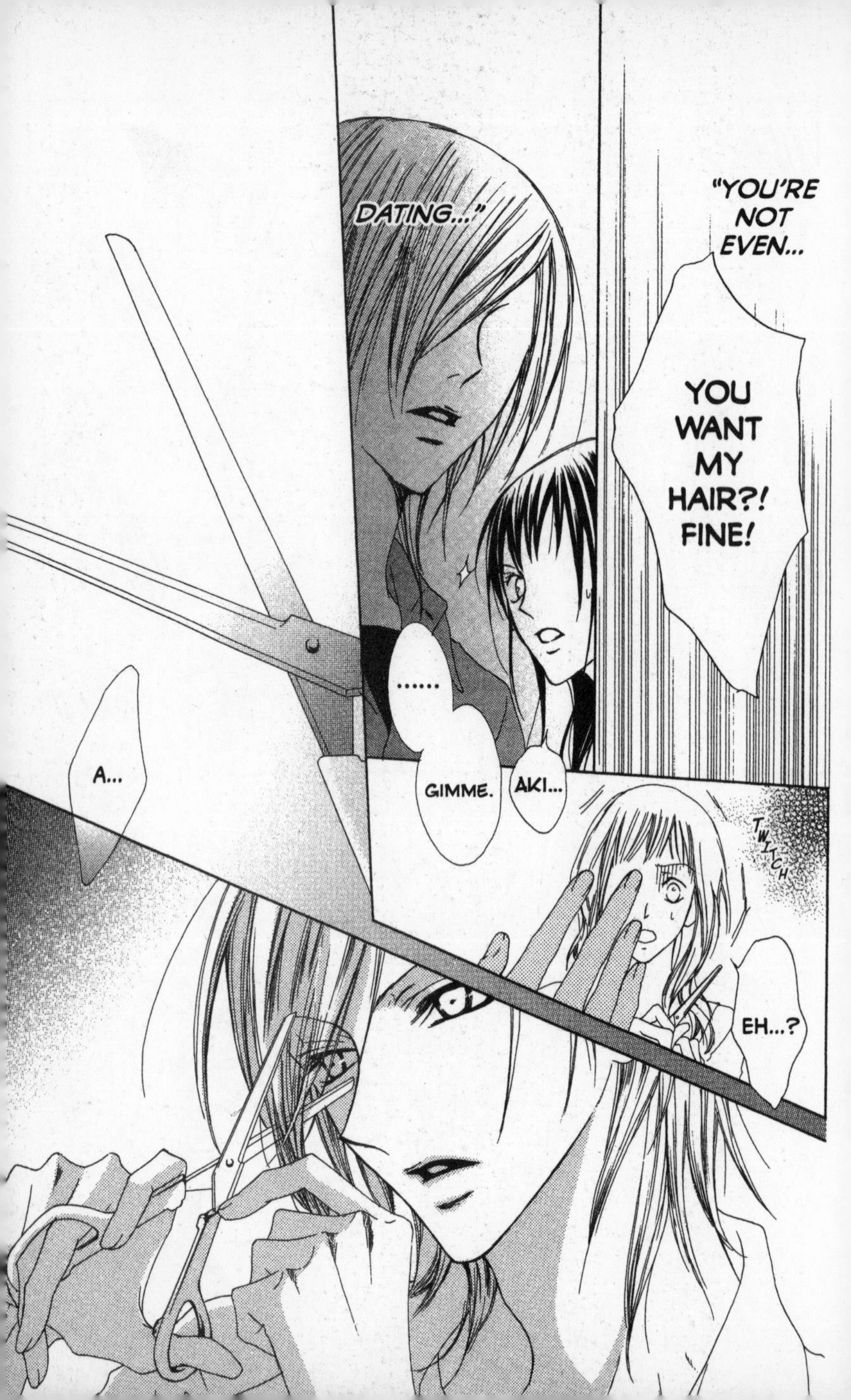
"YOU'RE NOT EVEN...
DATING..."
YOU WANT MY HAIR?! FINE!
......
AKI...
GIMME.
TWITCH
EH...?
A...

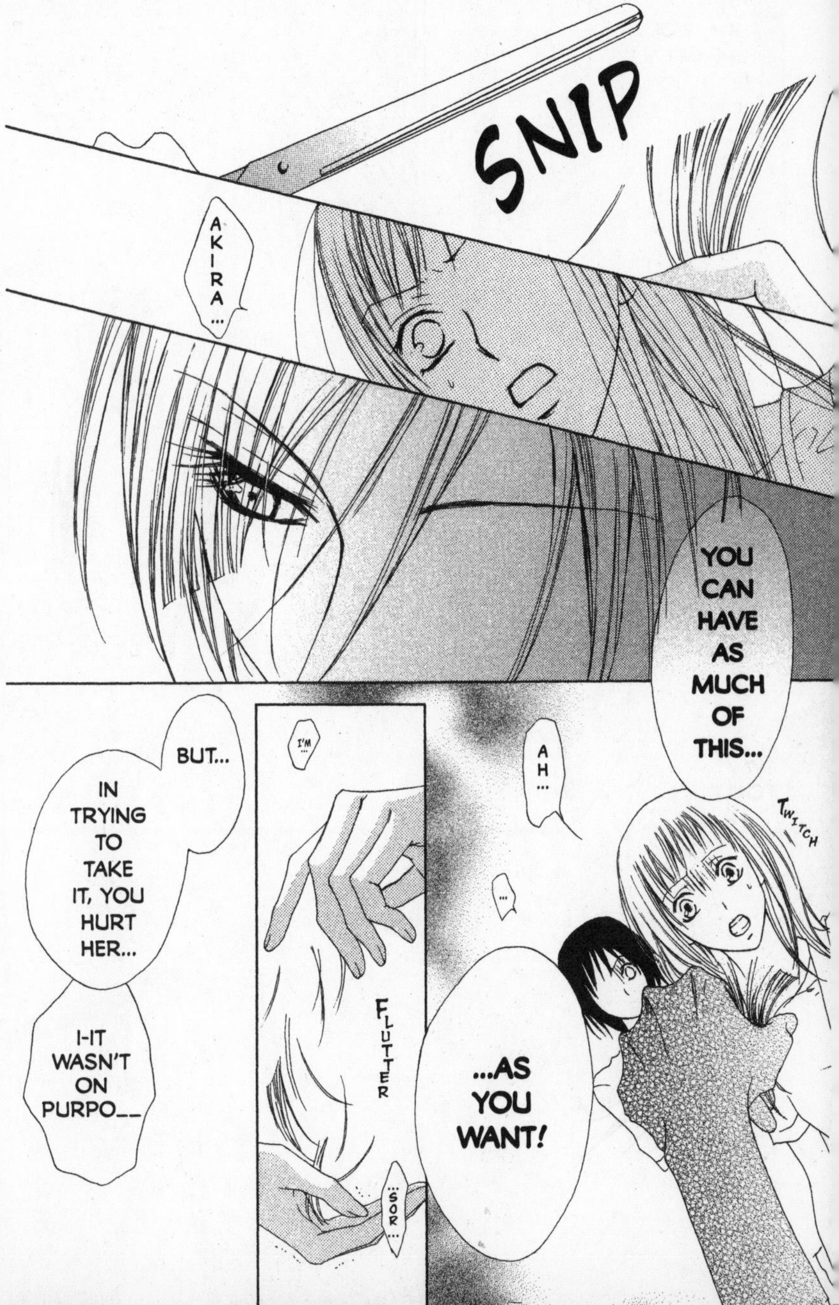
SNIP
AKIRA...
YOU CAN HAVE AS MUCH OF THIS...
TWITCH
AH...
...
...AS YOU WANT!
I'M...
FLUTTER
...SOR...
BUT...
IN TRYING TO TAKE IT, YOU HURT HER...
I-IT WASN'T ON PURPO__

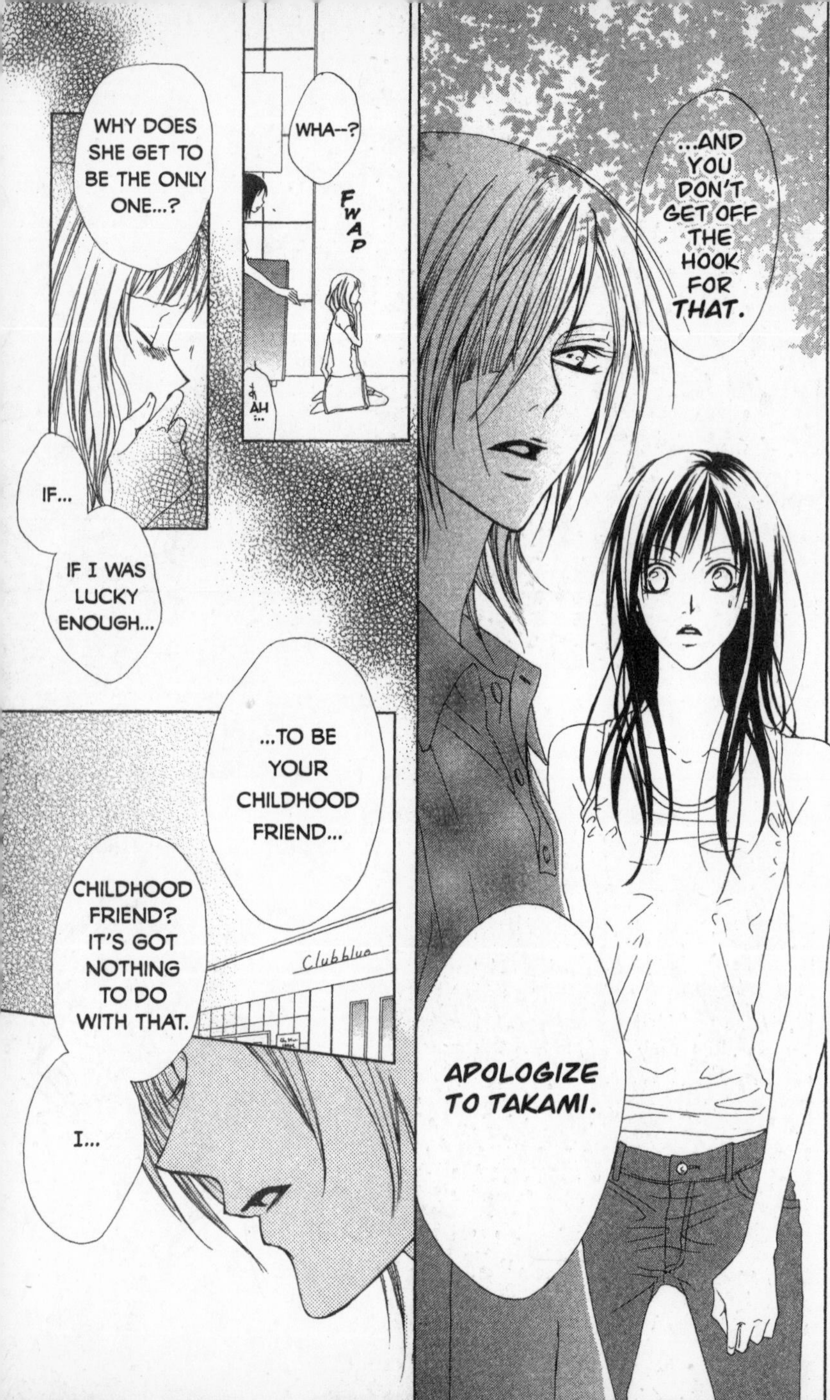
...AND YOU DON'T GET OFF THE HOOK FOR THAT.
APOLOGIZE TO TAKAMI.
WHA--?
FWAP
AH...
WHY DOES SHE GET TO BE THE ONLY ONE...?
IF...
IF I WAS LUCKY ENOUGH...
...TO BE YOUR CHILDHOOD FRIEND...
CHILDHOOD FRIEND? IT'S GOT NOTHING TO DO WITH THAT.
Clubblue
I...

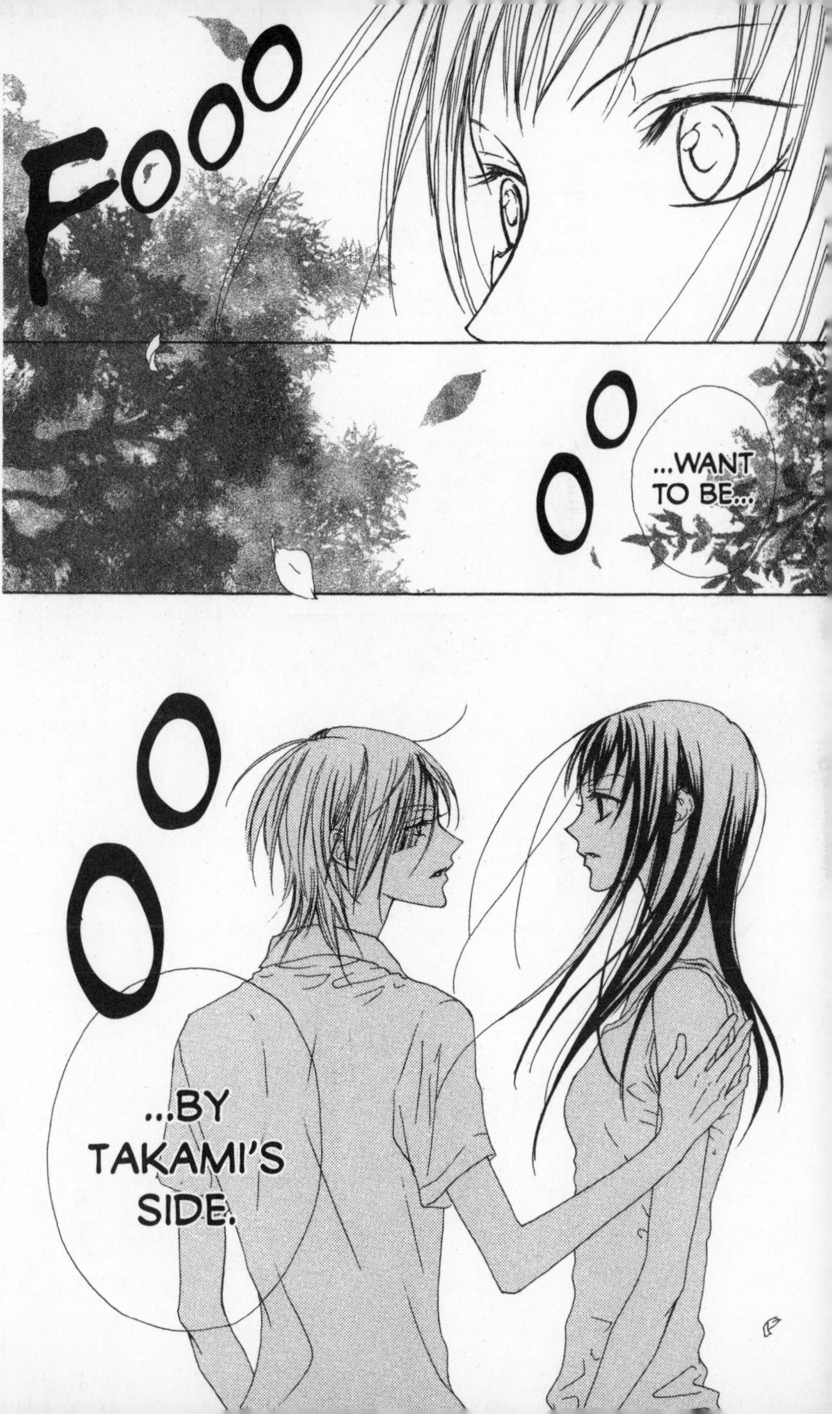
FOOO
...WANT TO BE...
OOO
...BY TAKAMI'S SIDE.

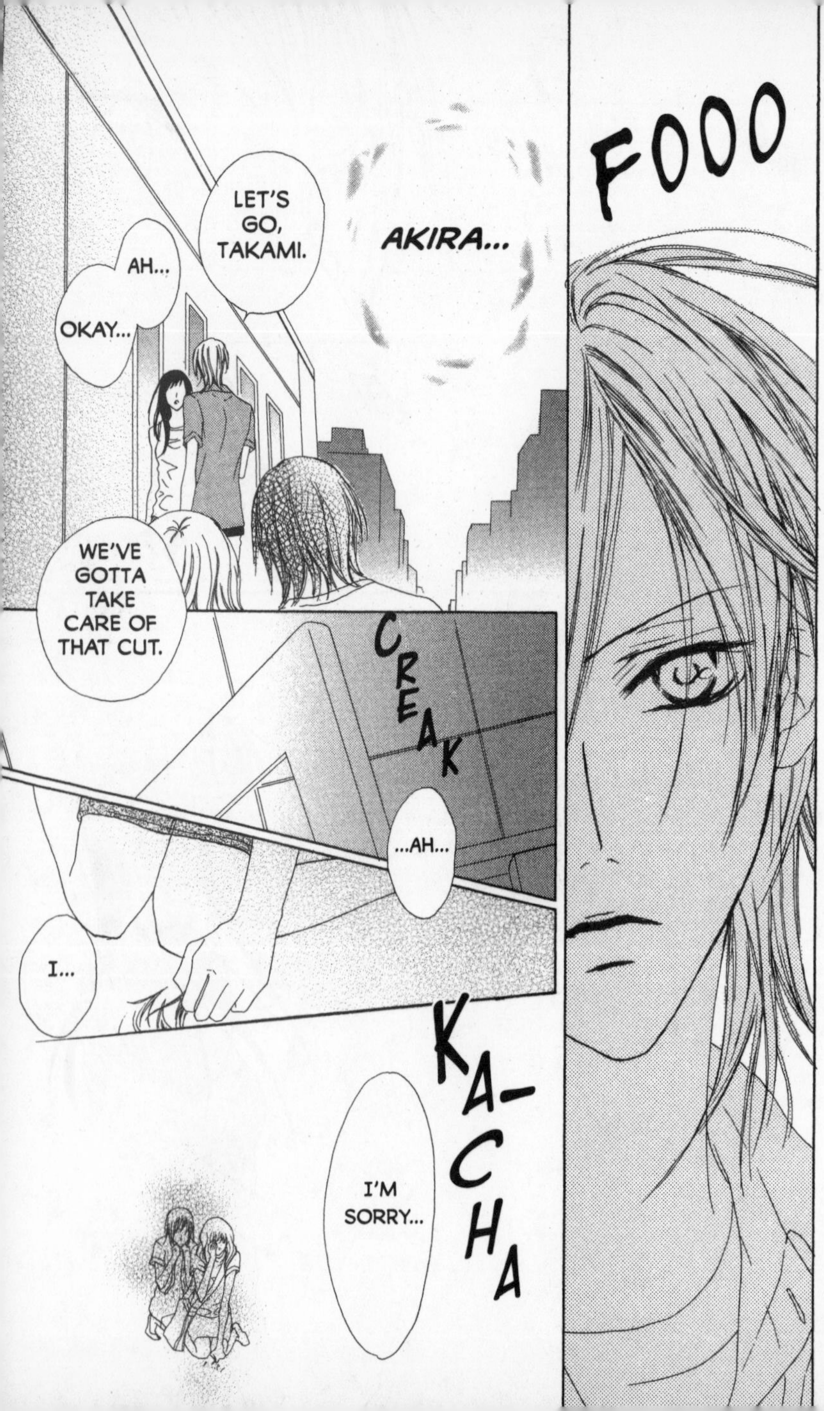
FOOO
AKIRA...
LET'S GO, TAKAMI.
AH...
OKAY...
WE'VE GOTTA TAKE CARE OF THAT CUT.
CREAK
...AH...
I...
KA-CHA
I'M SORRY...

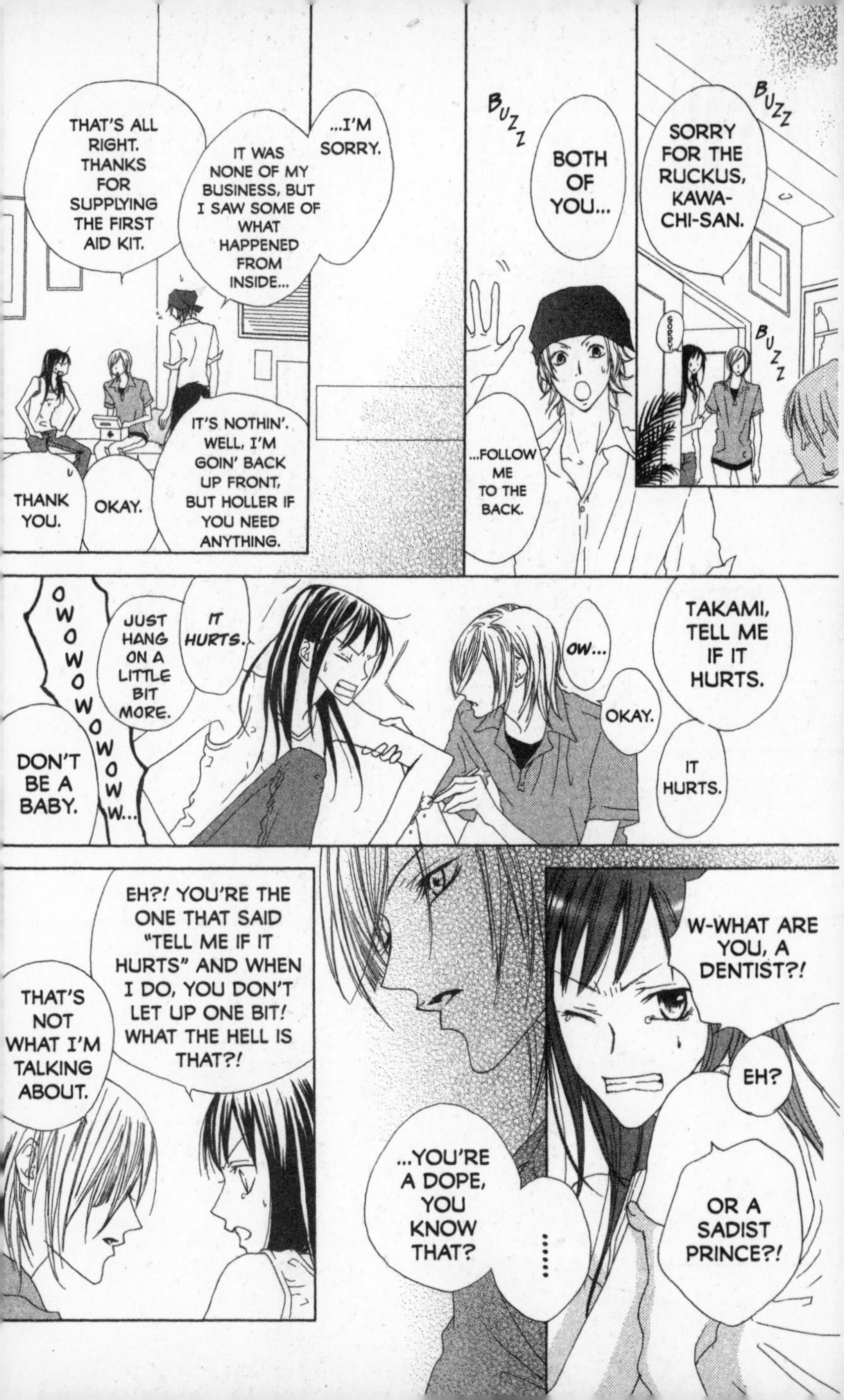
SORRY FOR THE RUCKUS, KAWA-CHI-SAN.
BUZZ
SORRY
BUZZ
BUZZ
BOTH OF YOU...
...FOLLOW ME TO THE BACK.
...I'M SORRY.
IT WAS NONE OF MY BUSINESS, BUT I SAW SOME OF WHAT HAPPENED FROM INSIDE...
THAT'S ALL RIGHT. THANKS FOR SUPPLYING THE FIRST AID KIT.
IT'S NOTHIN'. WELL, I'M GOIN' BACK UP FRONT, BUT HOLLER IF YOU NEED ANYTHING.
OKAY.
THANK YOU.
TAKAMI, TELL ME IF IT HURTS.
OW...
OKAY.
IT HURTS.
IT HURTS.
JUST HANG ON A LITTLE BIT MORE.
OWOWOWOWOWOWOWW...
DON'T BE A BABY.
W-WHAT ARE YOU, A DENTIST?!
EH?
OR A SADIST PRINCE?!
......
...YOU'RE A DOPE, YOU KNOW THAT?
EH?! YOU'RE THE ONE THAT SAID "TELL ME IF IT HURTS" AND WHEN I DO, YOU DON'T LET UP ONE BIT! WHAT THE HELL IS THAT?!
THAT'S NOT WHAT I'M TALKING ABOUT.

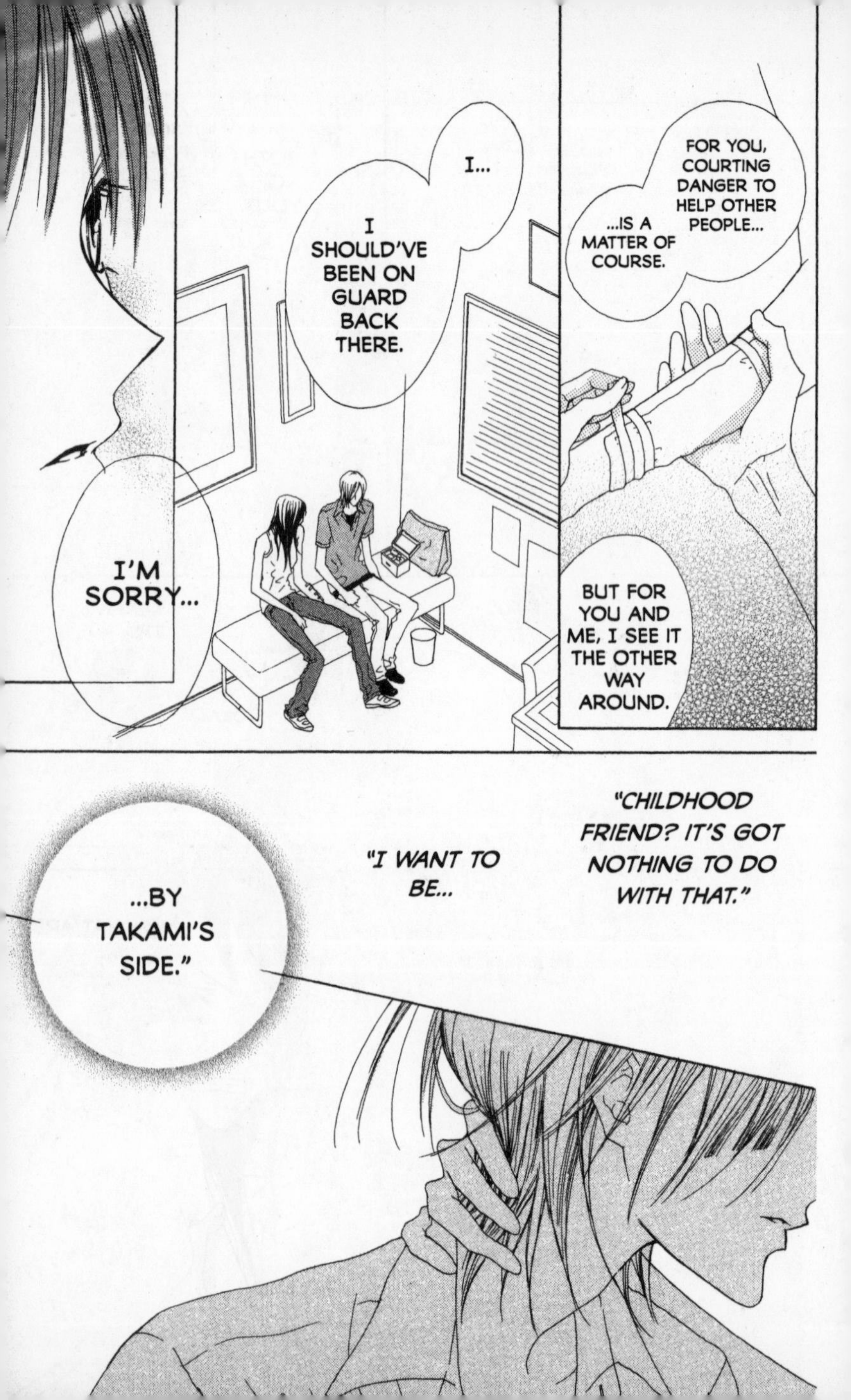
FOR YOU, COURTING DANGER TO HELP OTHER PEOPLE...
...IS A MATTER OF COURSE.
BUT FOR YOU AND ME, I SEE IT THE OTHER WAY AROUND.
I...
I SHOULD'VE BEEN ON GUARD BACK THERE.
I'M SORRY...
"CHILDHOOD FRIEND? IT'S GOT NOTHING TO DO WITH THAT."
"I WANT TO BE...
...BY TAKAMI'S SIDE."

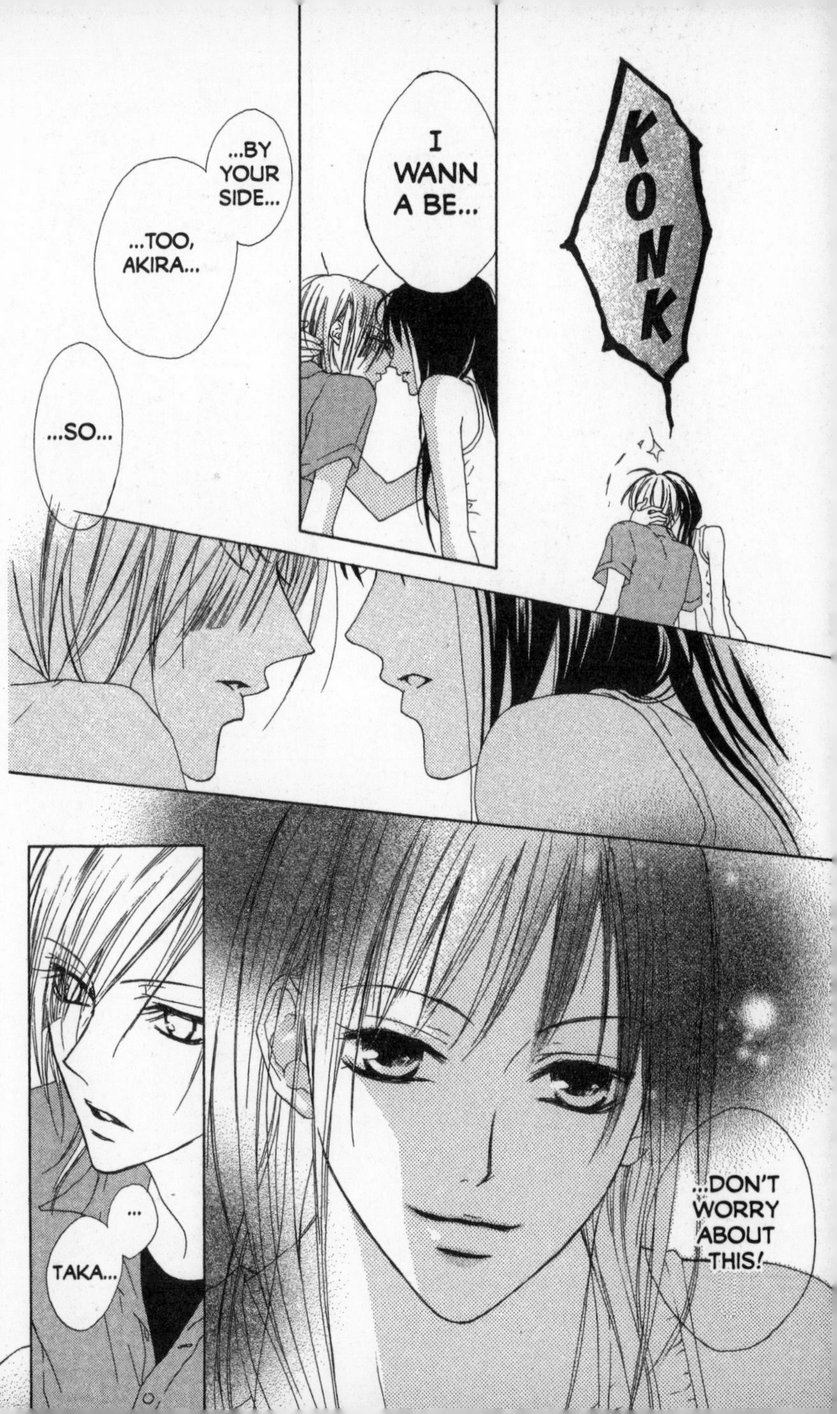
KONK
I WANNA BE...
...BY YOUR SIDE...
...TOO, AKIRA...
...SO...
...DON'T WORRY ABOUT THIS!
... TAKA...

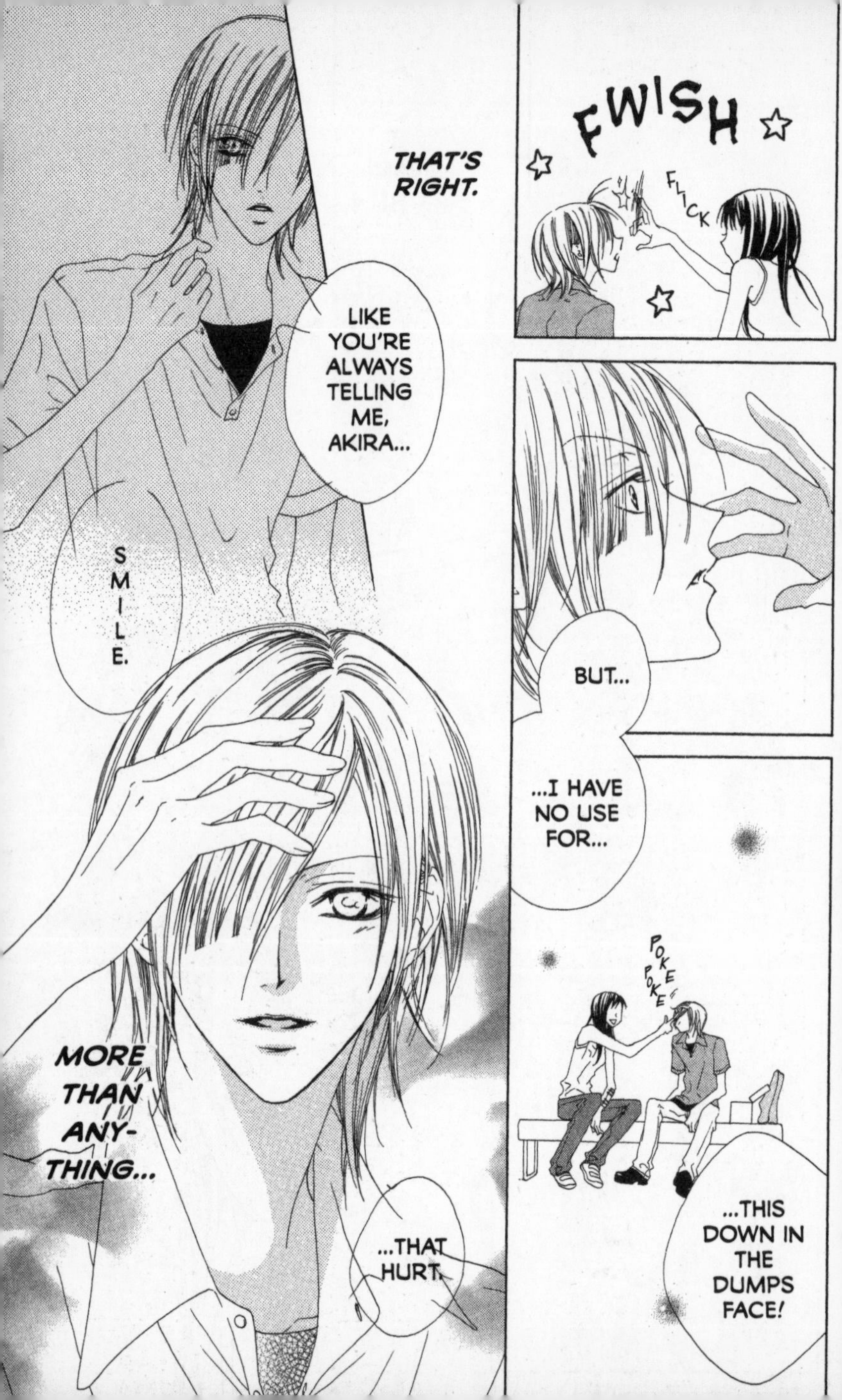
FWISH
FLICK
BUT...
...I HAVE NO USE FOR...
POKE POKE
...THIS DOWN IN THE DUMPS FACE!
THAT'S RIGHT.
LIKE YOU'RE ALWAYS TELLING ME, AKIRA...
SMILE.
MORE THAN ANYTHING...
...THAT HURT.

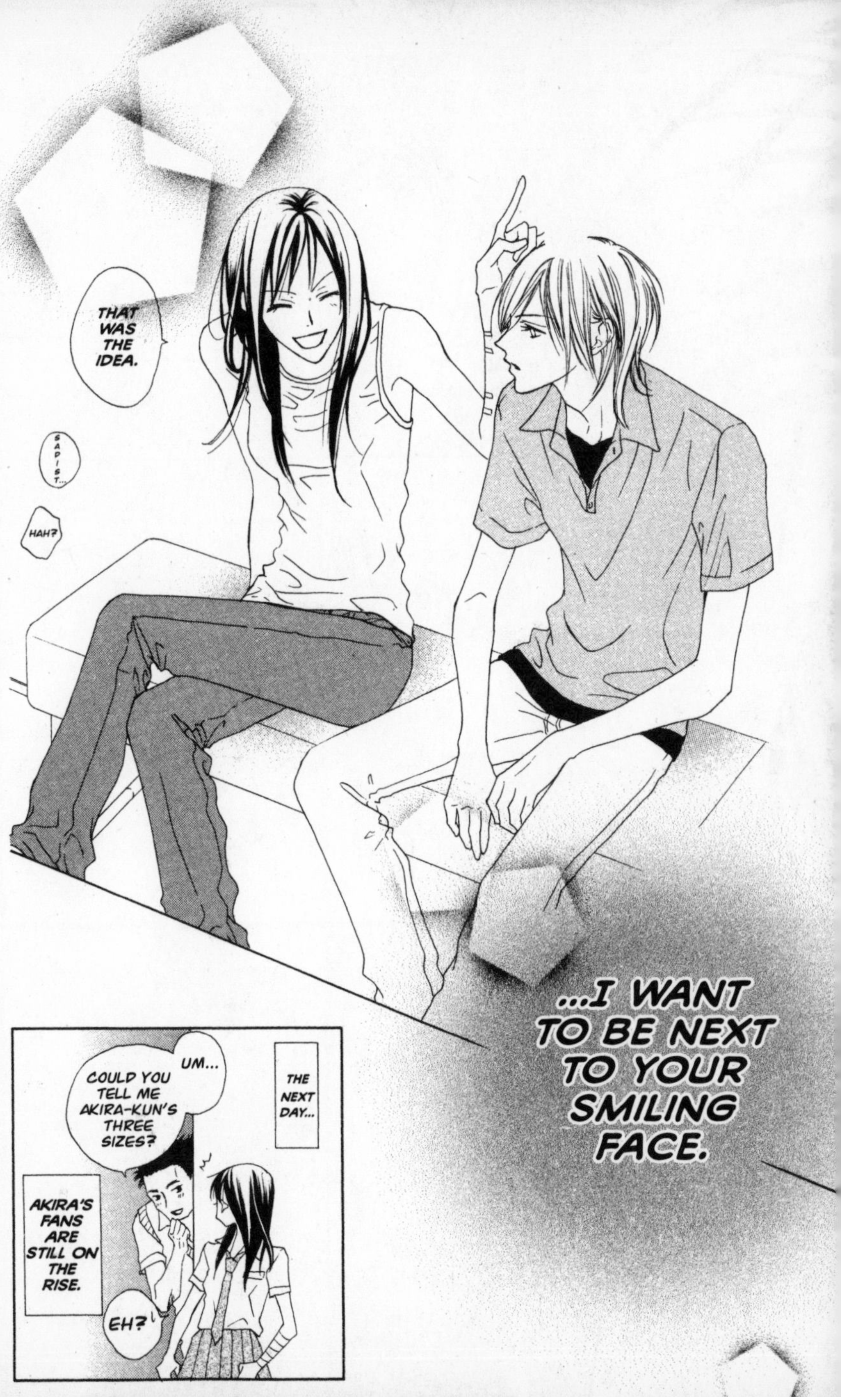
THAT WAS THE IDEA.
SADIST...
HAH?
...I WANT TO BE NEXT TO YOUR SMILING FACE.
THE NEXT DAY...
UM...
COULD YOU TELL ME AKIRA-KUN'S THREE SIZES?
AKIRA'S FANS ARE STILL ON THE RISE.
EH?

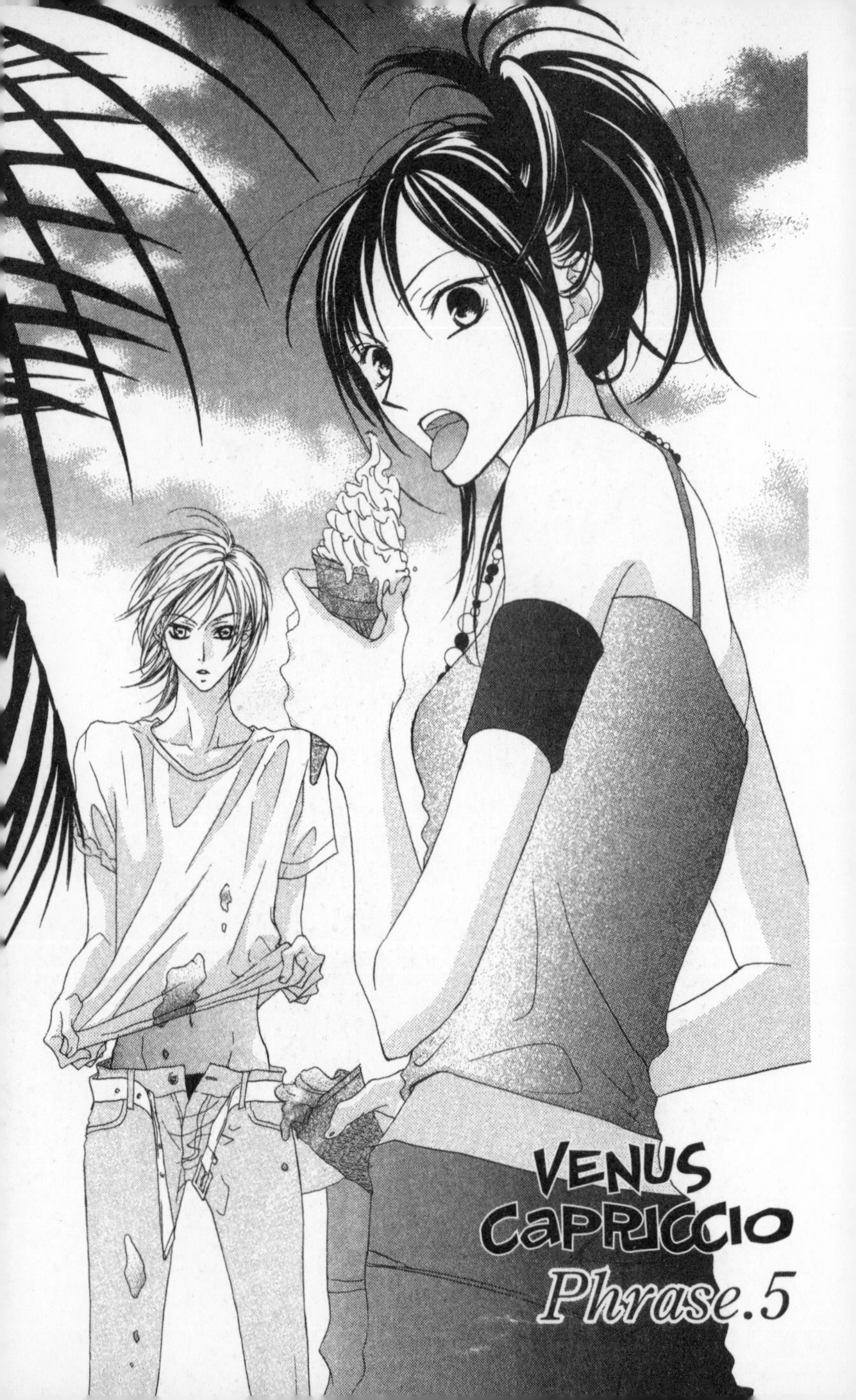
VENUS
CAPRICCIO
Phrase.5

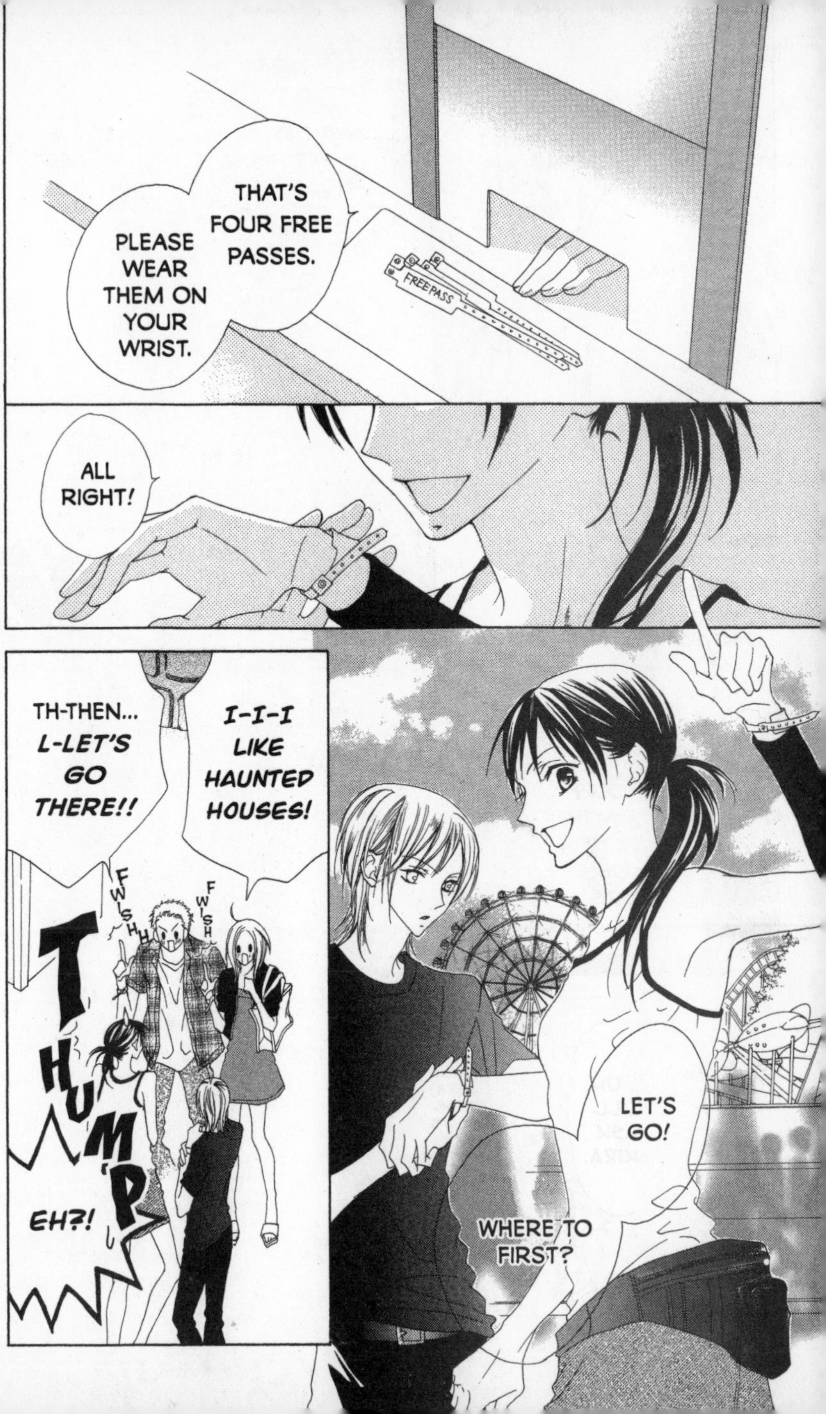
FREEPASS
THAT'S FOUR FREE PASSES.
PLEASE WEAR THEM ON YOUR WRIST.
ALL RIGHT!
LET'S GO!
WHERE TO FIRST?
I-I-I LIKE HAUNTED HOUSES!
TH-THEN... L-LET'S GO THERE!!
FWISH
FWISH
THUMP
EH?!

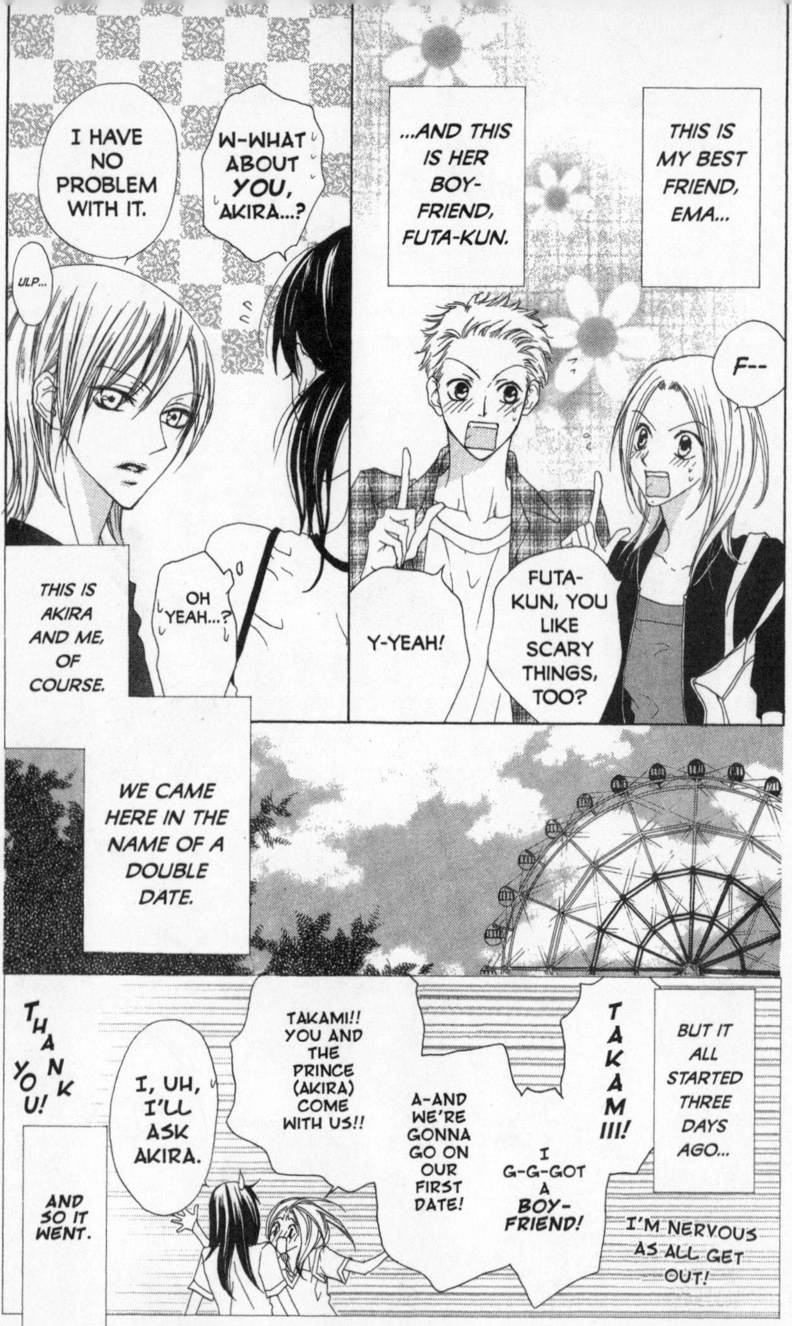
THIS IS MY BEST FRIEND, EMA...
...AND THIS IS HER BOY-FRIEND, FUTA-KUN.
F--
FUTA-KUN, YOU LIKE SCARY THINGS, TOO?
Y-YEAH!
W-WHAT ABOUT YOU, AKIRA...?
I HAVE NO PROBLEM WITH IT.
ULP...
OH YEAH...?
THIS IS AKIRA AND ME, OF COURSE.
WE CAME HERE IN THE NAME OF A DOUBLE DATE.
BUT IT ALL STARTED THREE DAYS AGO...
TAKAMIIII!
I'M NERVOUS AS ALL GET OUT!
I G-G-GOT A BOY-FRIEND!
A-AND WE'RE GONNA GO ON OUR FIRST DATE!
TAKAMI!! YOU AND THE PRINCE (AKIRA) COME WITH US!!
I, UH, I'LL ASK AKIRA.
THANK YOU!
AND SO IT WENT.

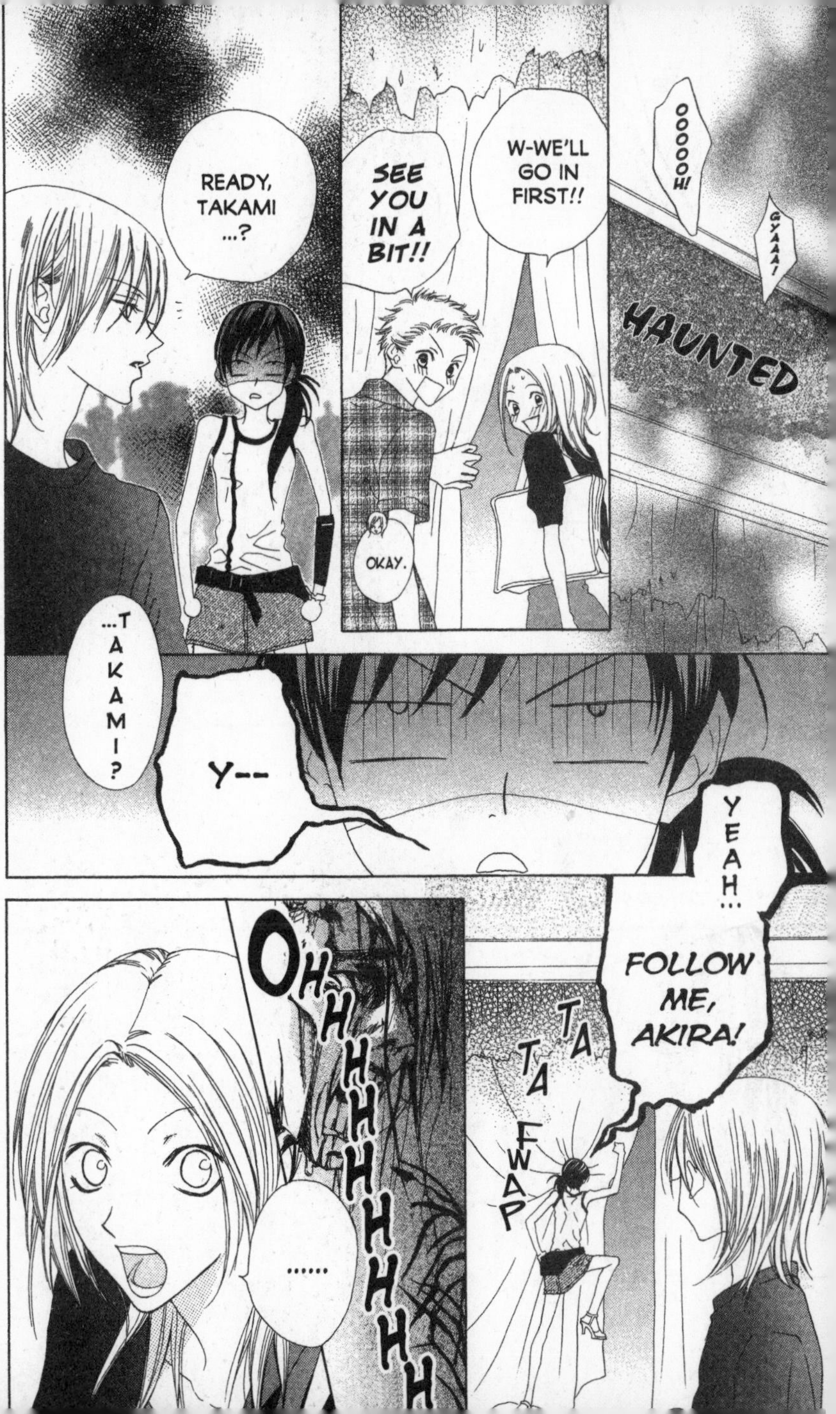
OOOOOOH!
GYAAA!
HAUNTED
W-WE'LL GO IN FIRST!!
SEE YOU IN A BIT!!
OKAY.
READY, TAKAMI ...?
...TAKAMI?
Y--
YEAH...
FOLLOW ME, AKIRA!
TA TA
FWAP
OHHHHHHHHHHH
......

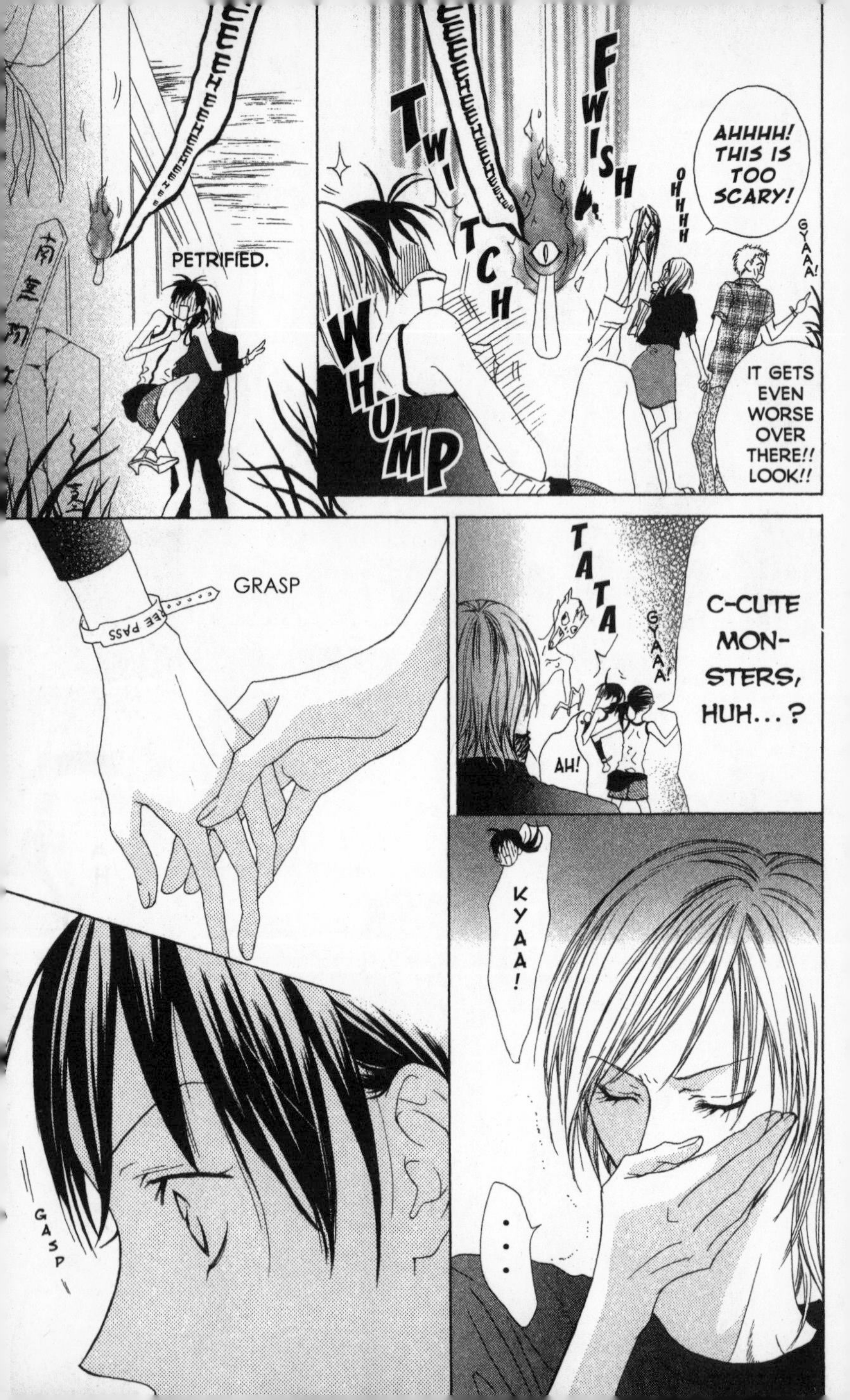
AHHHH! THIS IS TOO SCARY!
OHHHH
GYAAA!
FWISH
TWITCH
WHUMP
IT GETS EVEN WORSE OVER THERE!! LOOK!!
PETRIFIED.
TATA
GYAAA!
C-CUTE MON-STERS, HUH...?
AH!
KYAAA!
...
GRASP
EE PASS
GASP

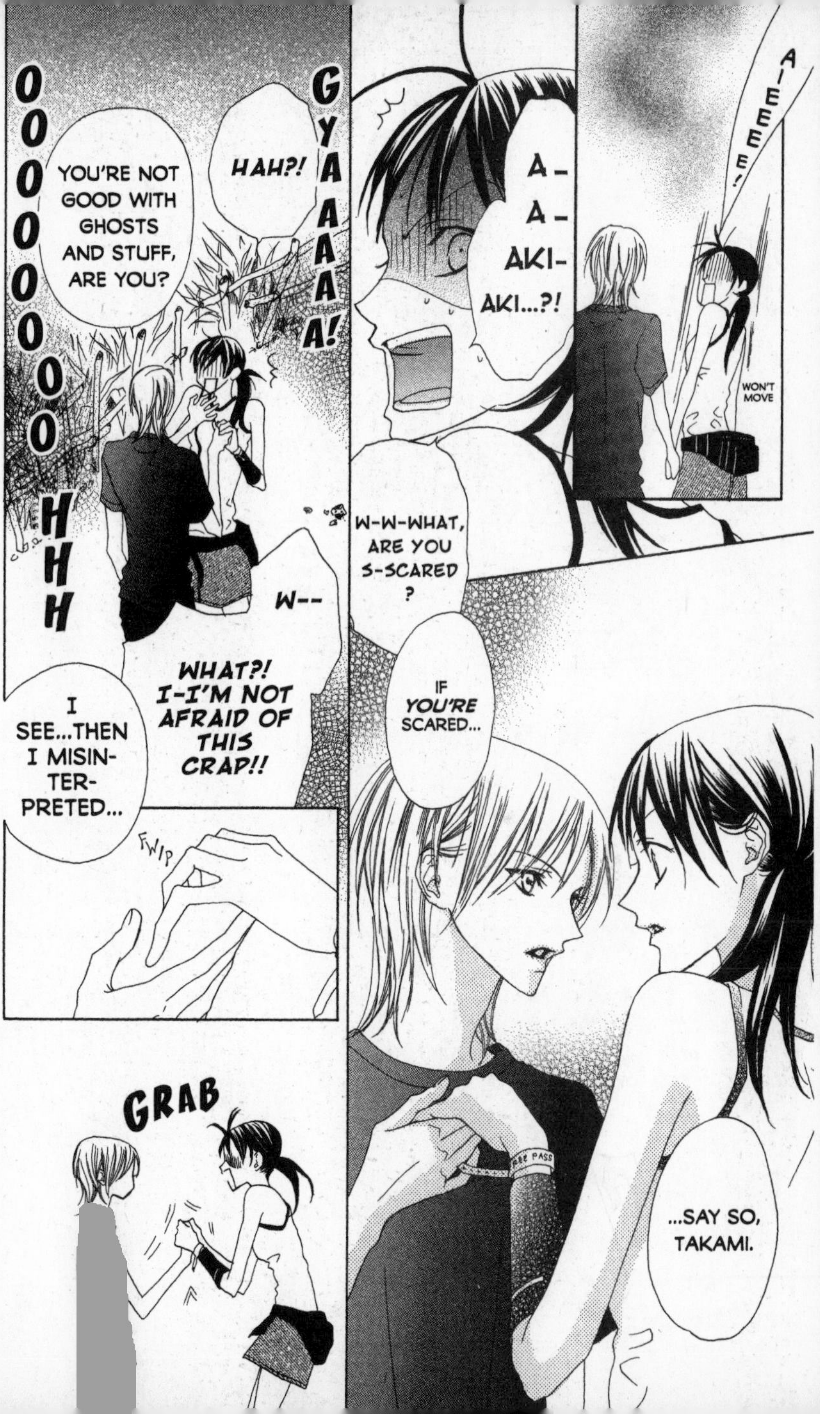
GYAAAAA!
OOOOOOOOOHHH
YOU'RE NOT GOOD WITH GHOSTS AND STUFF, ARE YOU?
HAH?!
W--
WHAT?! I-I'M NOT AFRAID OF THIS CRAP!!
I SEE...THEN I MISINTERPRETED...
FWIP
GRAB
AIEEEE!
WON'T MOVE
A- A- AKI- AKI...?!
W-W-WHAT, ARE YOU S-SCARED?
IF YOU'RE SCARED...
...SAY SO, TAKAMI.

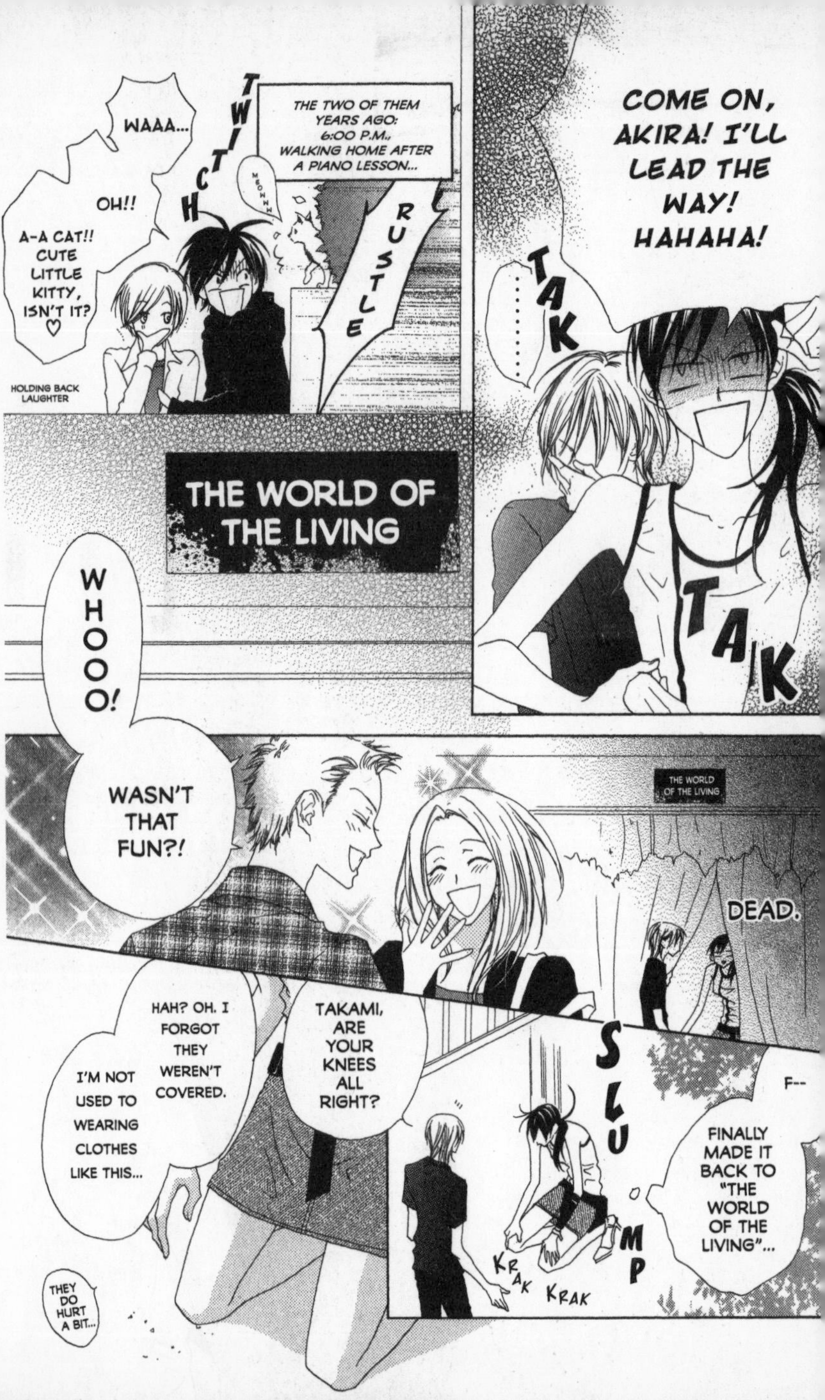
COME ON, AKIRA! I'LL LEAD THE WAY! HAHAHA!
TAK TAK
...
TAK TAK
THE TWO OF THEM YEARS AGO: 6:00 P.M., WALKING HOME AFTER A PIANO LESSON...
RUSTLE
MEOWWW
TWITCH
WAAA...
OH!!
A-A CAT!! CUTE LITTLE KITTY, ISN'T IT? ♡
HOLDING BACK LAUGHTER
THE WORLD OF THE LIVING
WHOOO!
THE WORLD OF THE LIVING
WASN'T THAT FUN?!
DEAD.
SLUMP
F--
FINALLY MADE IT BACK TO "THE WORLD OF THE LIVING"...
KRAK KRAK
TAKAMI, ARE YOUR KNEES ALL RIGHT?
HAH? OH. I FORGOT THEY WEREN'T COVERED.
I'M NOT USED TO WEARING CLOTHES LIKE THIS...
THEY DO HURT A BIT...

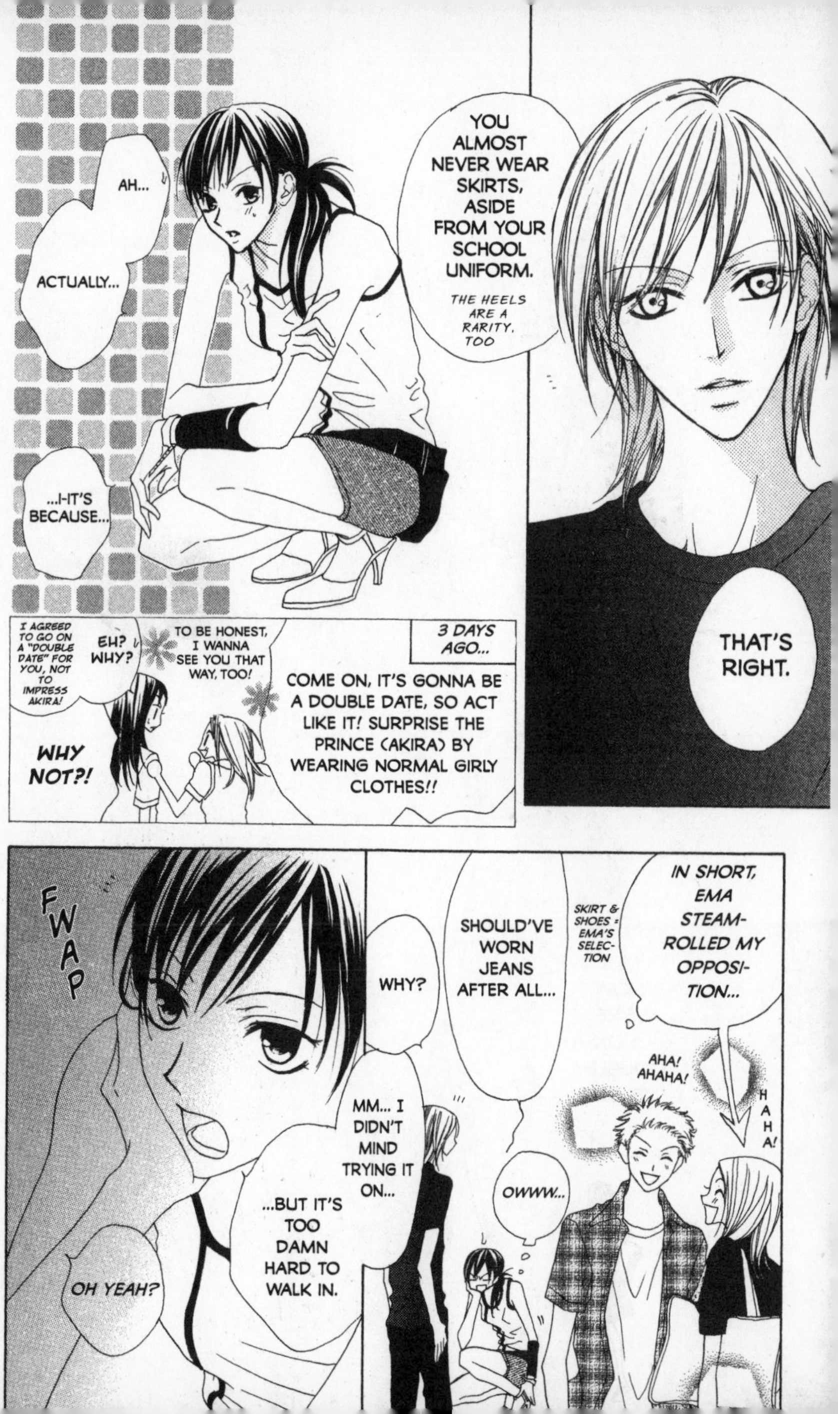
YOU ALMOST NEVER WEAR SKIRTS, ASIDE FROM YOUR SCHOOL UNIFORM.
THE HEELS ARE A RARITY, TOO
THAT'S RIGHT.
AH...
ACTUALLY...
...I-IT'S BECAUSE...
3 DAYS AGO...
COME ON, IT'S GONNA BE A DOUBLE DATE, SO ACT LIKE IT! SURPRISE THE PRINCE (AKIRA) BY WEARING NORMAL GIRLY CLOTHES!!
TO BE HONEST, I WANNA SEE YOU THAT WAY, TOO!
EH? WHY?
I AGREED TO GO ON A "DOUBLE DATE" FOR YOU, NOT TO IMPRESS AKIRA!
WHY NOT?!
IN SHORT, EMA STEAM-ROLLED MY OPPOSITION...
SKIRT & SHOES = EMA'S SELECTION
SHOULD'VE WORN JEANS AFTER ALL...
AHA! AHAHA!
HAHA!
OWWW...
WHY?
MM... I DIDN'T MIND TRYING IT ON...
...BUT IT'S TOO DAMN HARD TO WALK IN.
FWAP
OH YEAH?

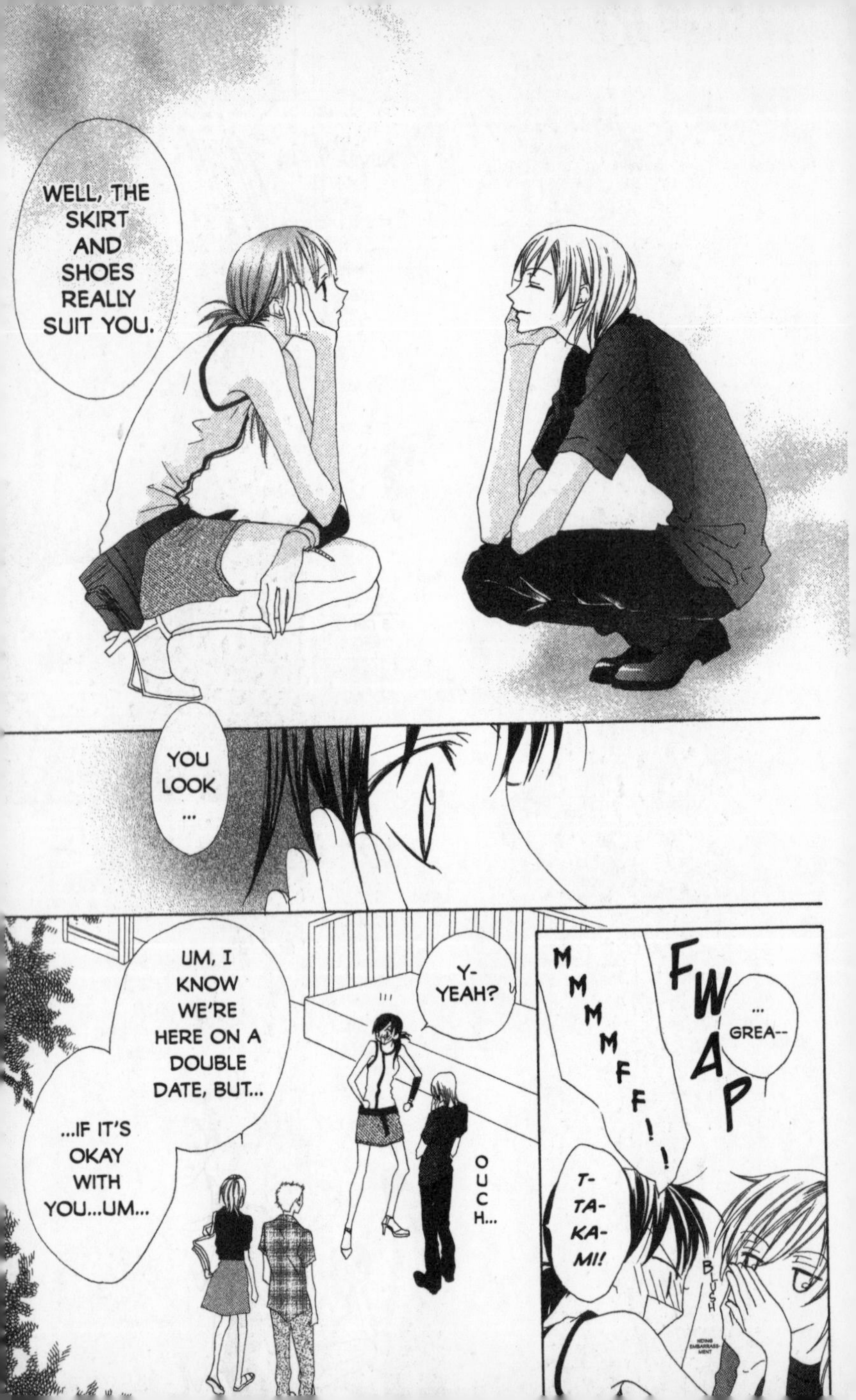

WELL, THE SKIRT AND SHOES REALLY SUIT YOU.
YOU LOOK ...
... GREA--
FWAP
MMMMFF!!
T-TA-KA-MI!
BLUSH
UM, I KNOW WE'RE HERE ON A DOUBLE DATE, BUT...
Y-YEAH?
...IF IT'S OKAY WITH YOU...UM...
OUCH...

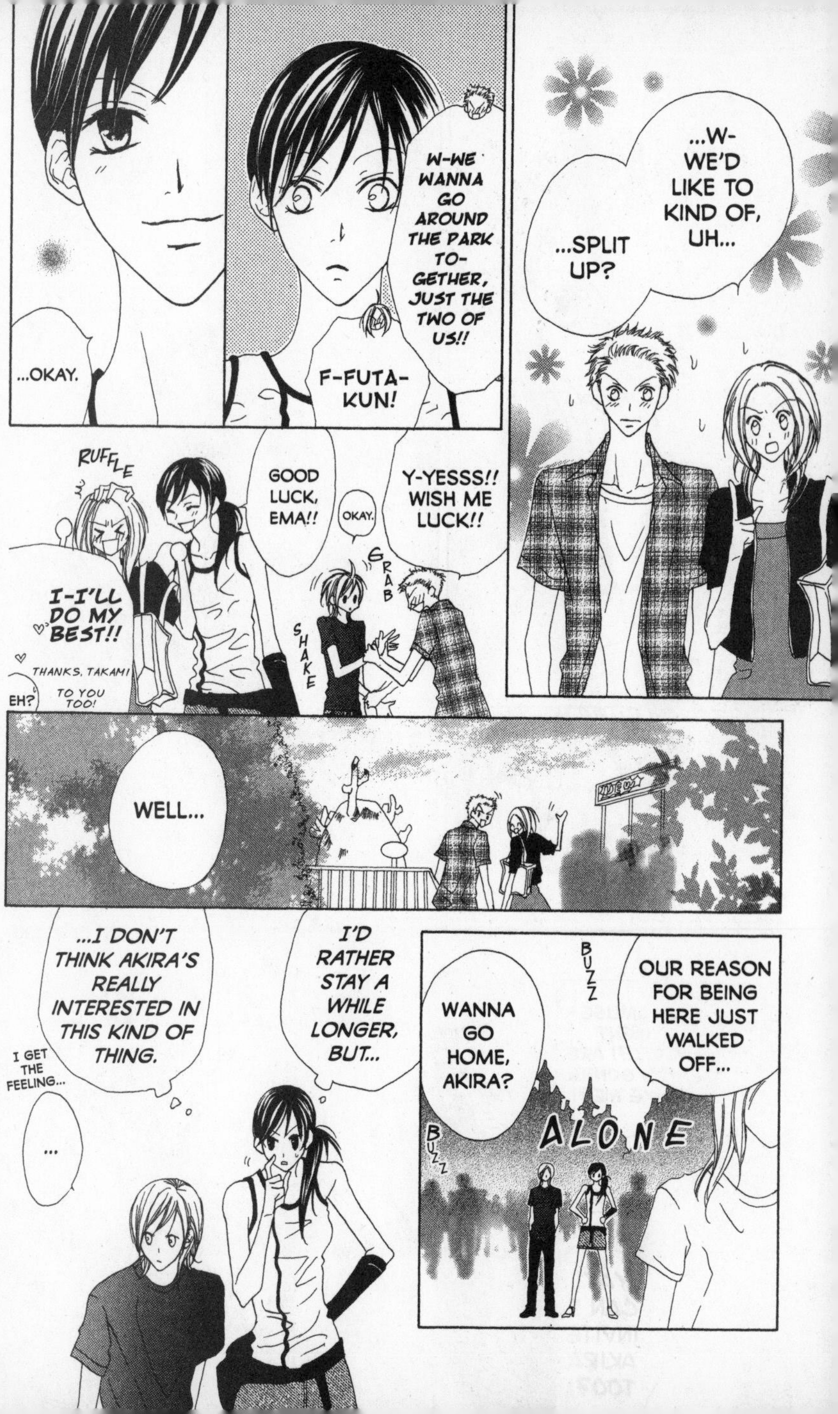
...W- WE'D LIKE TO KIND OF, UH...
...SPLIT UP?
W-WE WANNA GO AROUND THE PARK TO-GETHER, JUST THE TWO OF US!!
F-FUTA-KUN!
...OKAY.
Y-YESSS!! WISH ME LUCK!!
GOOD LUCK, EMA!!
OKAY.
GRAB
SHAKE
RUFFLE
I-I'LL DO MY BEST!!
THANKS, TAKAMI
TO YOU TOO!
EH?
WELL...
OUR REASON FOR BEING HERE JUST WALKED OFF...
BUZZ
WANNA GO HOME, AKIRA?
ALONE
BUZZ
I'D RATHER STAY A WHILE LONGER, BUT...
...I DON'T THINK AKIRA'S REALLY INTERESTED IN THIS KIND OF THING.
I GET THE FEELING...
...

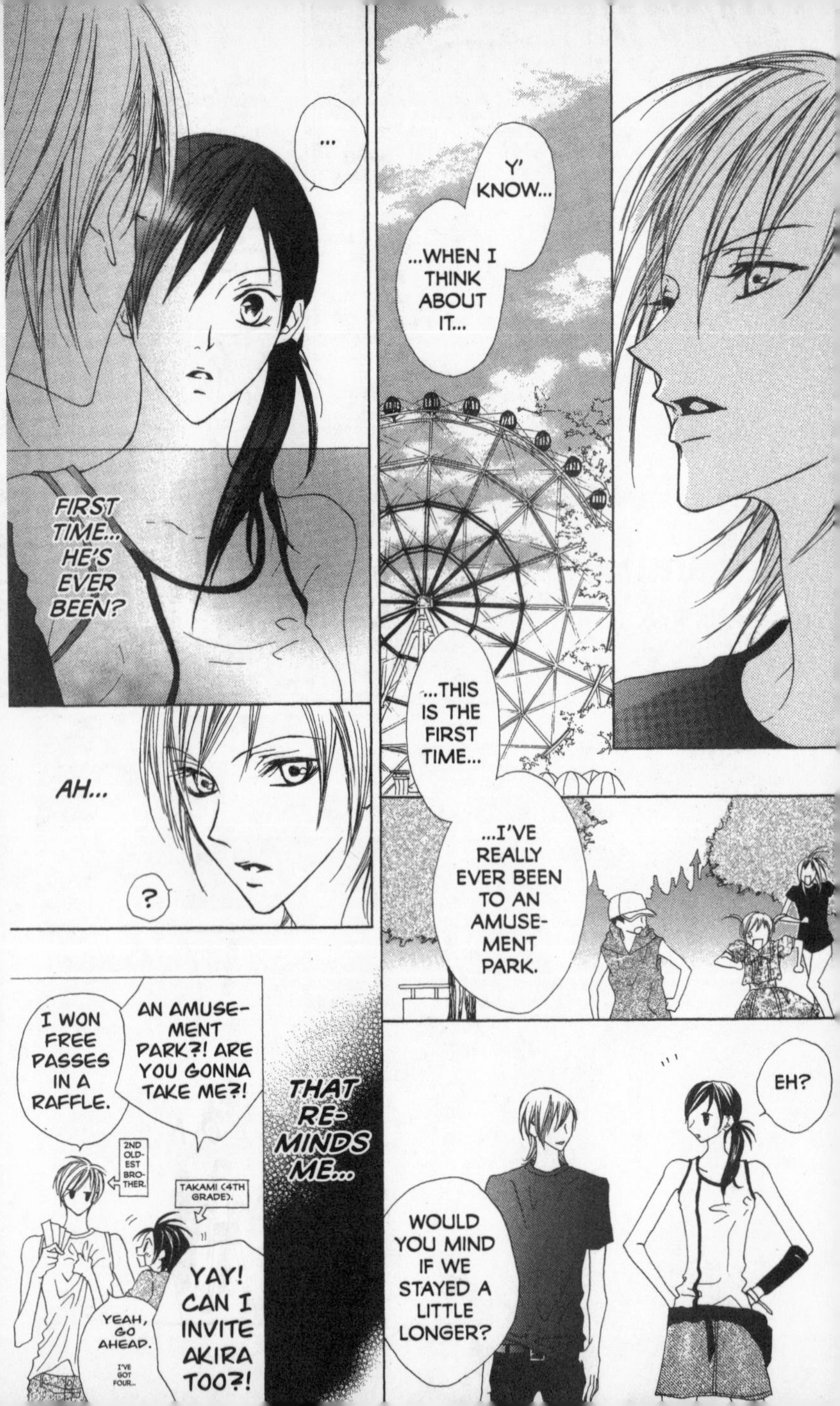
Y' KNOW...
...WHEN I THINK ABOUT IT...
...THIS IS THE FIRST TIME...
...I'VE REALLY EVER BEEN TO AN AMUSEMENT PARK.
EH?
WOULD YOU MIND IF WE STAYED A LITTLE LONGER?
...
FIRST TIME... HE'S EVER BEEN?
AH...
?
THAT REMINDS ME...
AN AMUSEMENT PARK?! ARE YOU GONNA TAKE ME?!
I WON FREE PASSES IN A RAFFLE.
2ND OLDEST BROTHER.
TAKAMI (4TH GRADE).
YAY! CAN I INVITE AKIRA TOO?!
YEAH, GO AHEAD.
I'VE GOT FOUR...

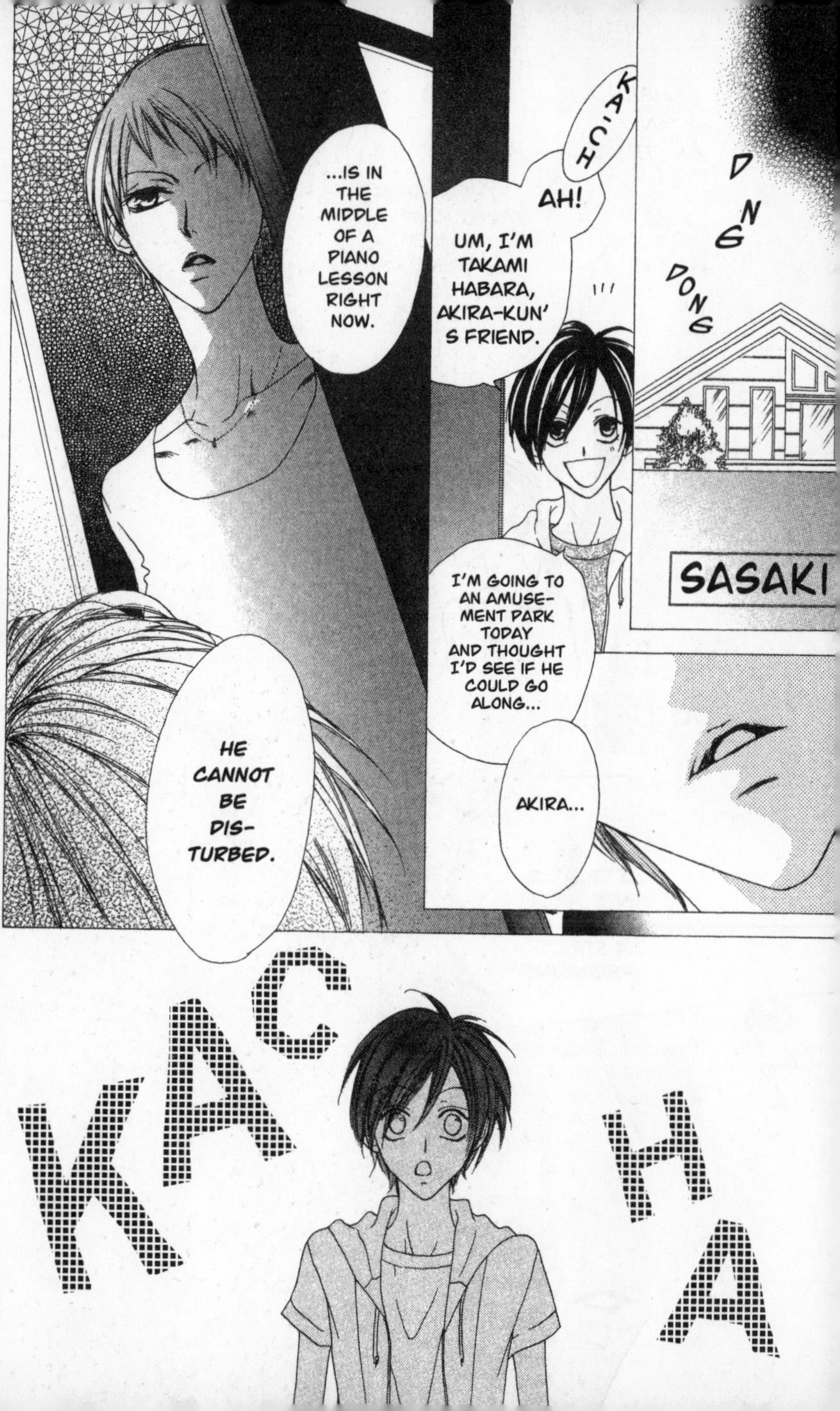
DING DONG
SASAKI
KA'CH
AH!
UM, I'M TAKAMI HABARA, AKIRA-KUN'S FRIEND.
I'M GOING TO AN AMUSEMENT PARK TODAY AND THOUGHT I'D SEE IF HE COULD GO ALONG...
AKIRA...
...IS IN THE MIDDLE OF A PIANO LESSON RIGHT NOW.
HE CANNOT BE DIS-TURBED.
KACHA

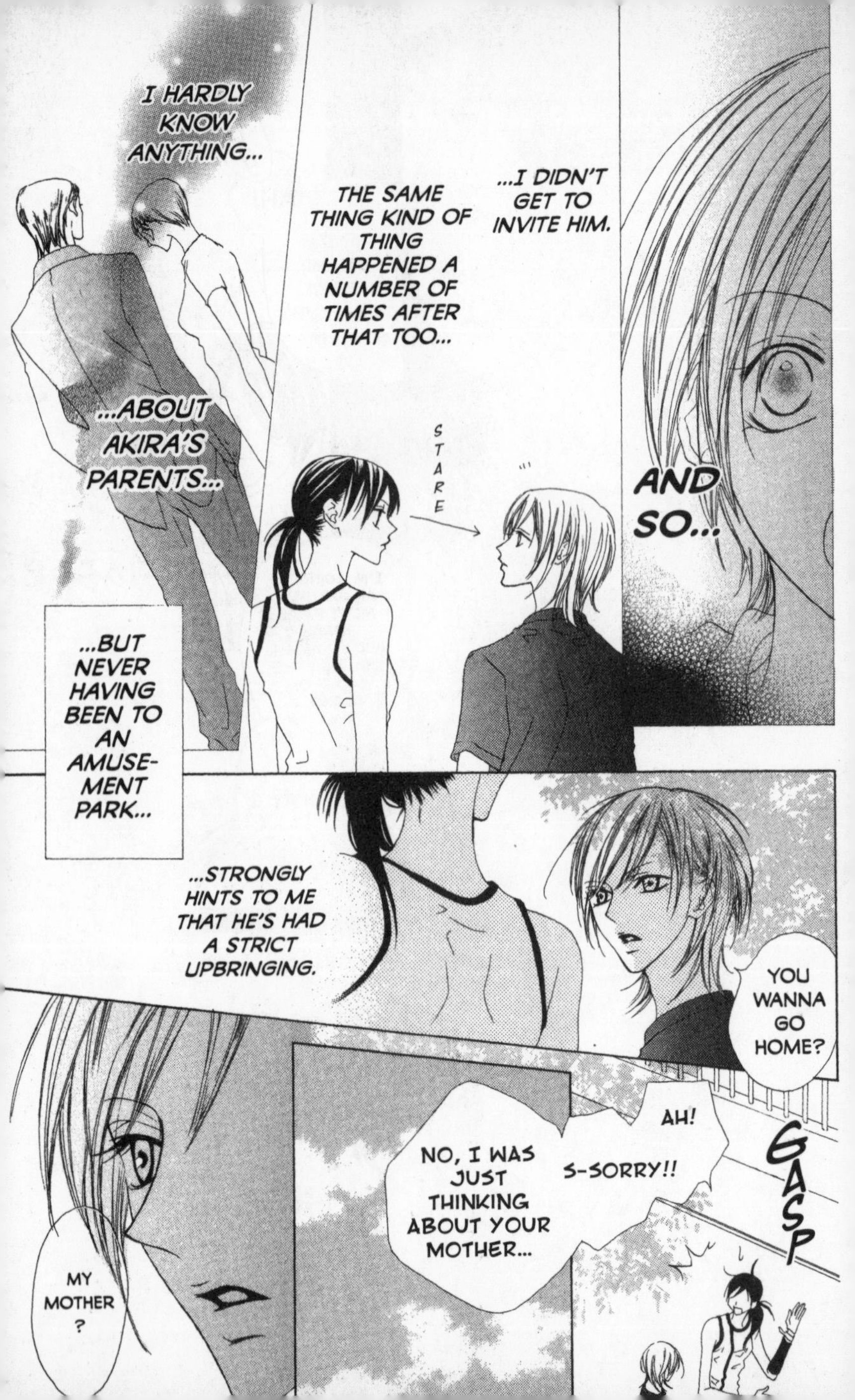
AND SO...
...I DIDN'T GET TO INVITE HIM.
THE SAME THING KIND OF THING HAPPENED A NUMBER OF TIMES AFTER THAT TOO...
STARE
I HARDLY KNOW ANYTHING...
...ABOUT AKIRA'S PARENTS...
YOU WANNA GO HOME?
...STRONGLY HINTS TO ME THAT HE'S HAD A STRICT UPBRINGING.
...BUT NEVER HAVING BEEN TO AN AMUSEMENT PARK...
GASP
AH!
S-SORRY!!
NO, I WAS JUST THINKING ABOUT YOUR MOTHER...
MY MOTHER ?

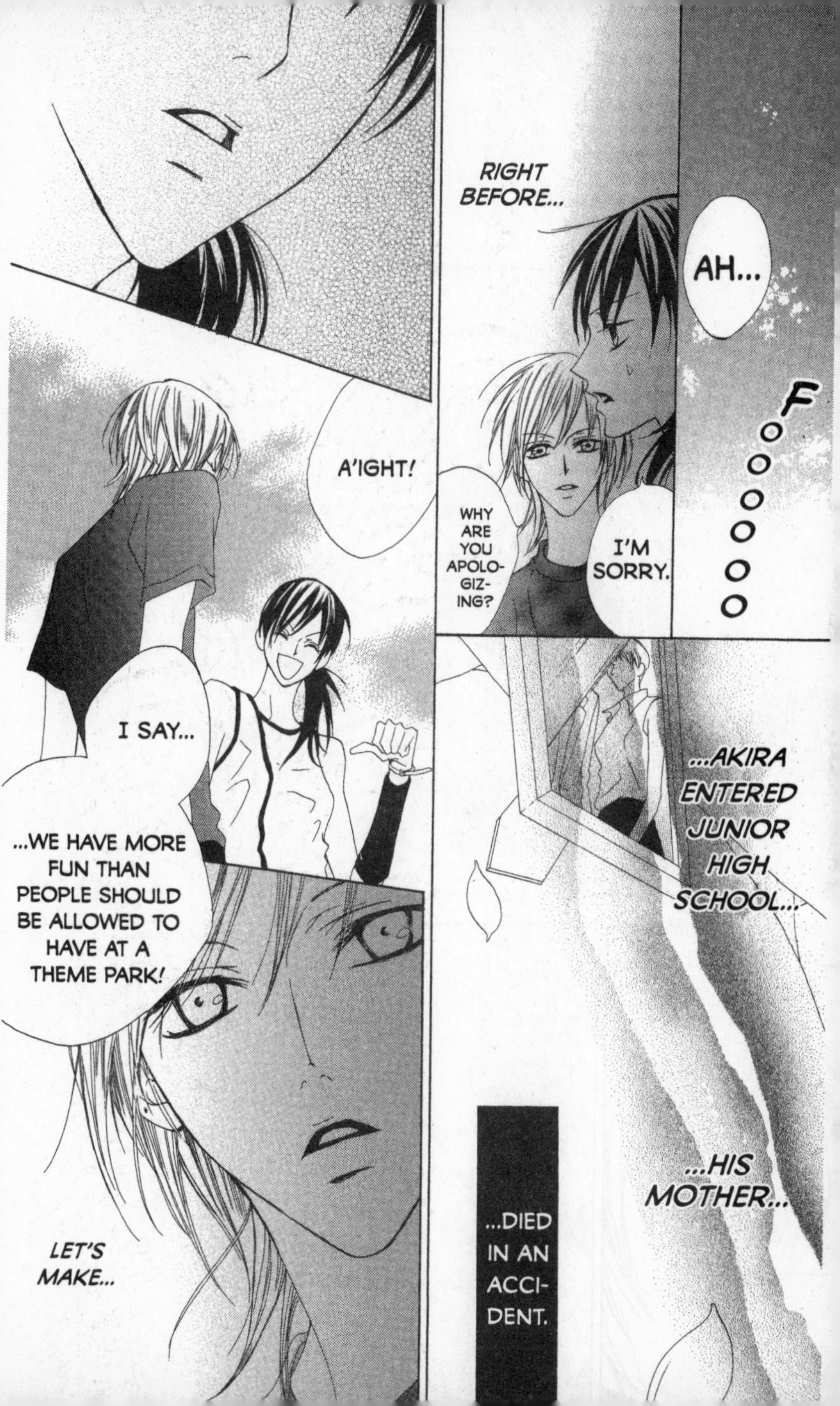
AH...
FOOOOOO
RIGHT BEFORE...
I'M SORRY.
WHY ARE YOU APOLOGIZING?
...AKIRA ENTERED JUNIOR HIGH SCHOOL...
...HIS MOTHER...
...DIED IN AN ACCIDENT.
A'IGHT!
I SAY...
...WE HAVE MORE FUN THAN PEOPLE SHOULD BE ALLOWED TO HAVE AT A THEME PARK!
LET'S MAKE...

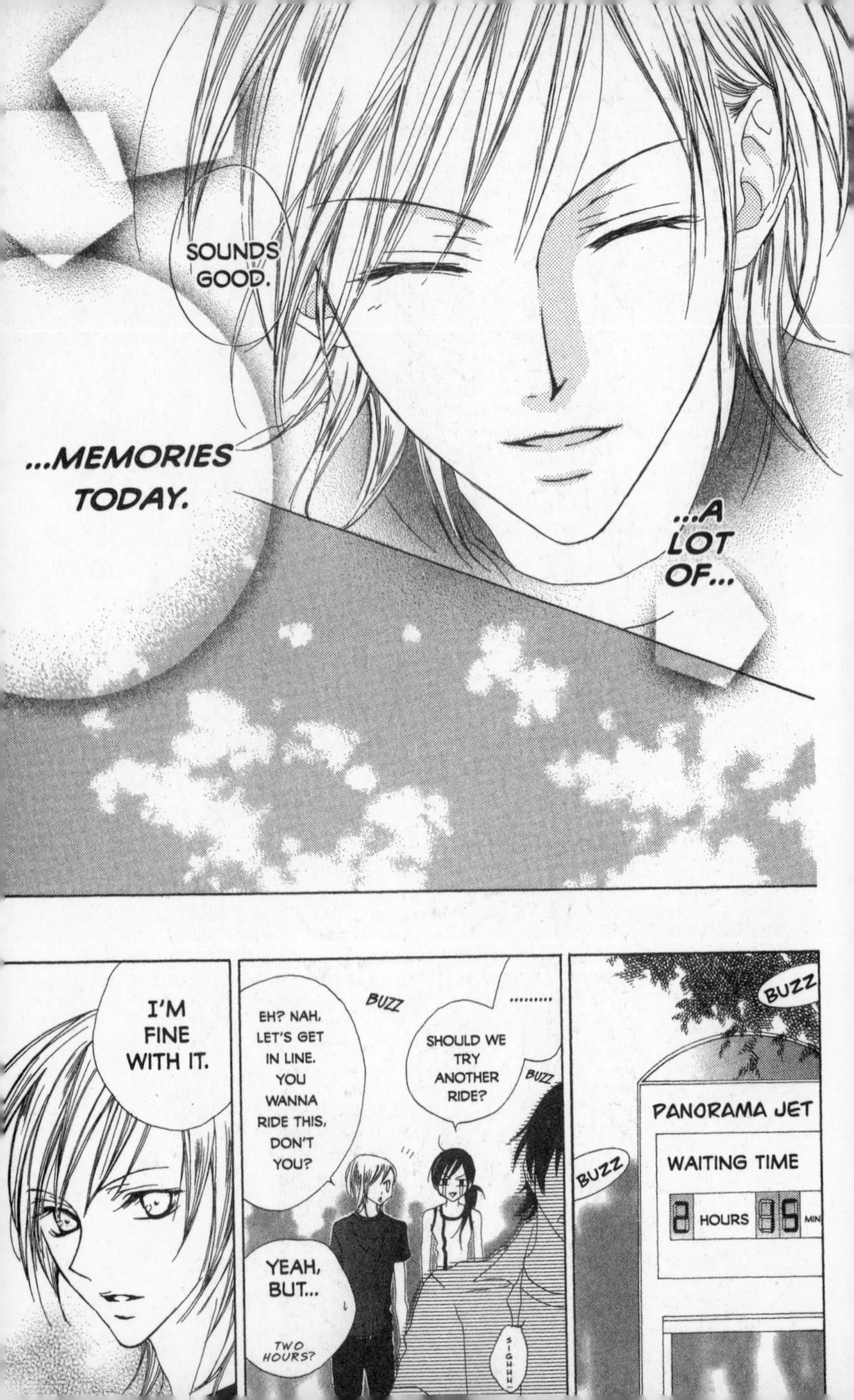
...A LOT OF...
...MEMORIES TODAY.
SOUNDS GOOD.
BUZZ
PANORAMA JET
WAITING TIME
2 HOURS 15 MIN
BUZZ
....
SHOULD WE TRY ANOTHER RIDE?
BUZZ
BUZZ
EH? NAH, LET'S GET IN LINE. YOU WANNA RIDE THIS, DON'T YOU?
YEAH, BUT...
TWO HOURS?
SIGHHH...
I'M FINE WITH IT.

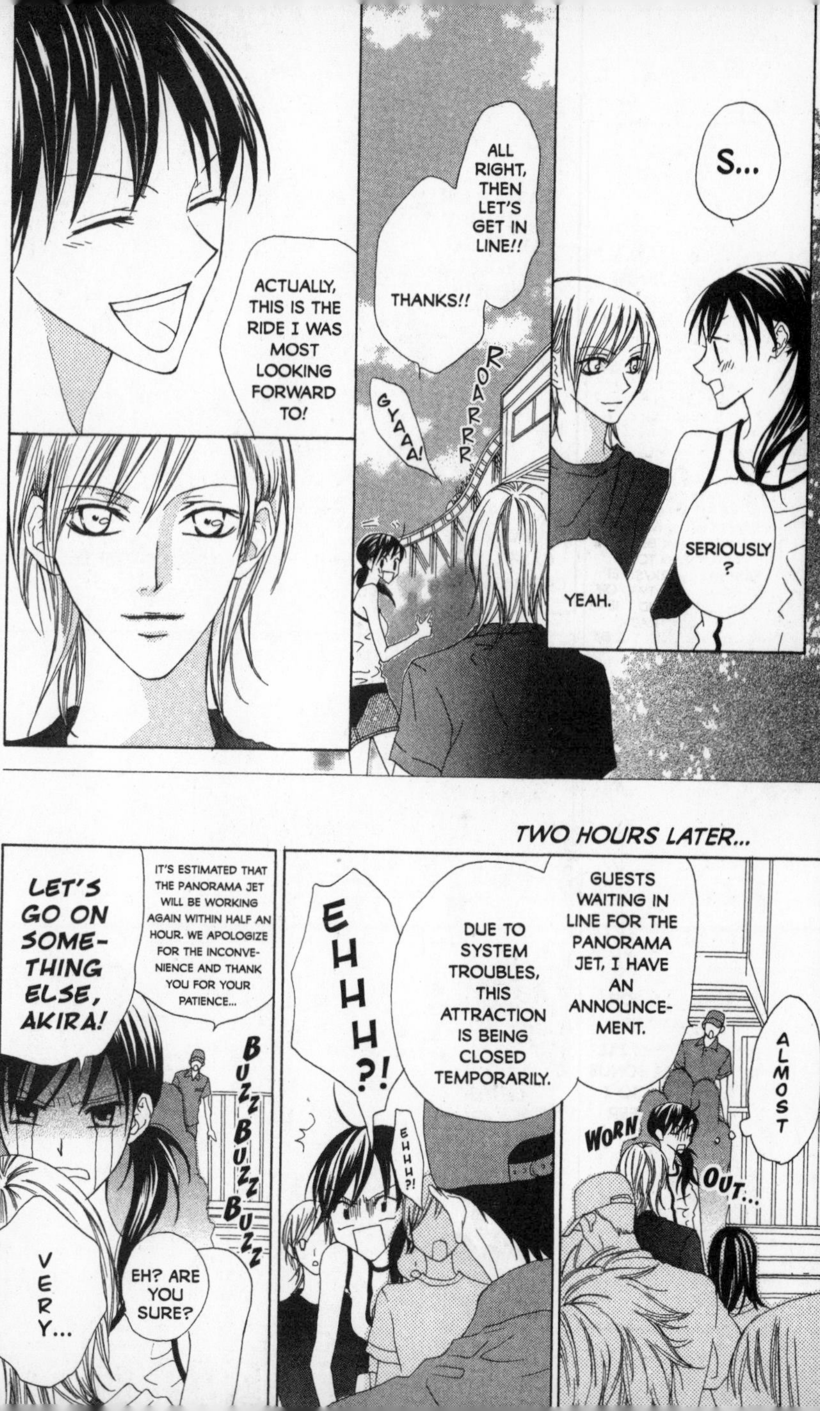
S...
SERIOUSLY?
YEAH.
ALL RIGHT, THEN LET'S GET IN LINE!!
THANKS!!
ROARRRR
GYAAA!
ACTUALLY, THIS IS THE RIDE I WAS MOST LOOKING FORWARD TO!
TWO HOURS LATER...
ALMOST
WORN OUT...
GUESTS WAITING IN LINE FOR THE PANORAMA JET, I HAVE AN ANNOUNCEMENT.
DUE TO SYSTEM TROUBLES, THIS ATTRACTION IS BEING CLOSED TEMPORARILY.
EHHHH?!
EHHH?!
IT'S ESTIMATED THAT THE PANORAMA JET WILL BE WORKING AGAIN WITHIN HALF AN HOUR. WE APOLOGIZE FOR THE INCONVENIENCE AND THANK YOU FOR YOUR PATIENCE...
LET'S GO ON SOMETHING ELSE, AKIRA!
BUZZ BUZZ BUZZ
EH? ARE YOU SURE?
VERY...

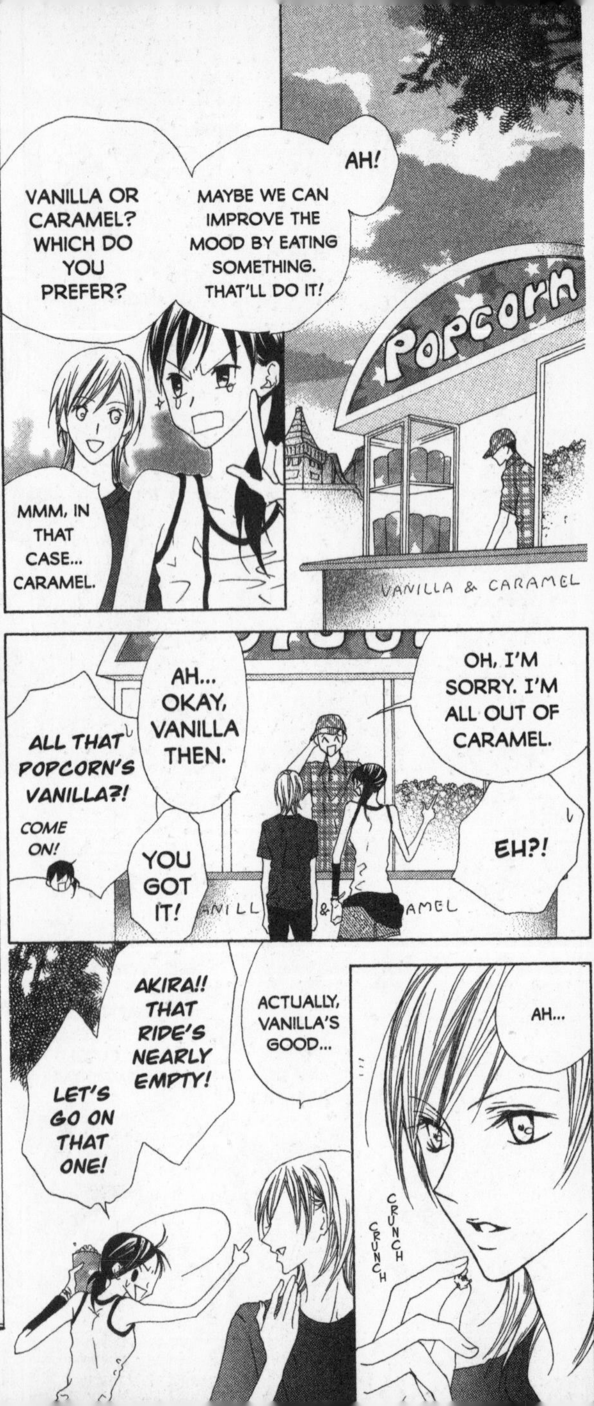
AH!
MAYBE WE CAN IMPROVE THE MOOD BY EATING SOMETHING. THAT'LL DO IT!
VANILLA OR CARAMEL? WHICH DO YOU PREFER?
POPCORN
MMM, IN THAT CASE... CARAMEL.
VANILLA & CARAMEL
OH, I'M SORRY. I'M ALL OUT OF CARAMEL.
EH?!
AH... OKAY, VANILLA THEN.
YOU GOT IT!
ALL THAT POPCORN'S VANILLA?!
COME ON!
AH...
ACTUALLY, VANILLA'S GOOD...
CRUNCH CRUNCH
AKIRA!! THAT RIDE'S NEARLY EMPTY!
LET'S GO ON THAT ONE!

5

THIS IS THE LAST 1/4 COLUMN IN THIS VOLUME.

THE DAWN IS BREAKING AS I WRITE THIS. RECENTLY, MY MORNINGS AND NIGHTS HAVE BEEN GETTING MIXED UP. TOTALLY THROWING OFF MY CIRCADIAN RHYTHM. HAVING A REGULAR SCHEDULE IS HEALTHIER, I KNOW, SO I'M GONNA TRY TO GET BACK TO A MORE NORMAL PATTERN...IS WHAT I ALWAYS THINK BEFORE RETURNING TO A NORMAL WORK/SLEEP SCHEDULE FOR TWO OR THREE DAYS...AND THEN I GET OFF TRACK AGAIN. THIS TIME, I'LL BE CAREFUL.
BY THE WAY, THE ALARMS OF THE PEOPLE IN MY FAMILY GO OFF AROUND NOW AND THE NOISE THEY MAKE IS INCREDIBLE.

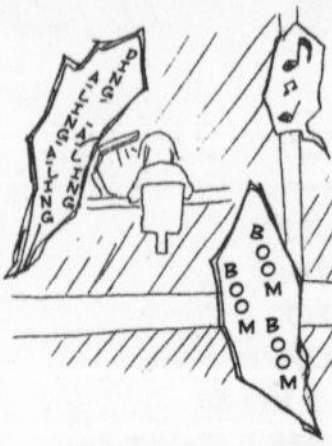
BOOM BOOM BOOM BOOM

THANK YOU FOR READING THIS.
NEXT VOLUME, I'LL PUT IN SOME BONUS STUFF, TOO, SO I HOPE YOU KEEP READING.

MY CAT

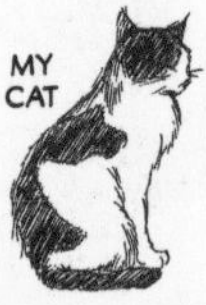

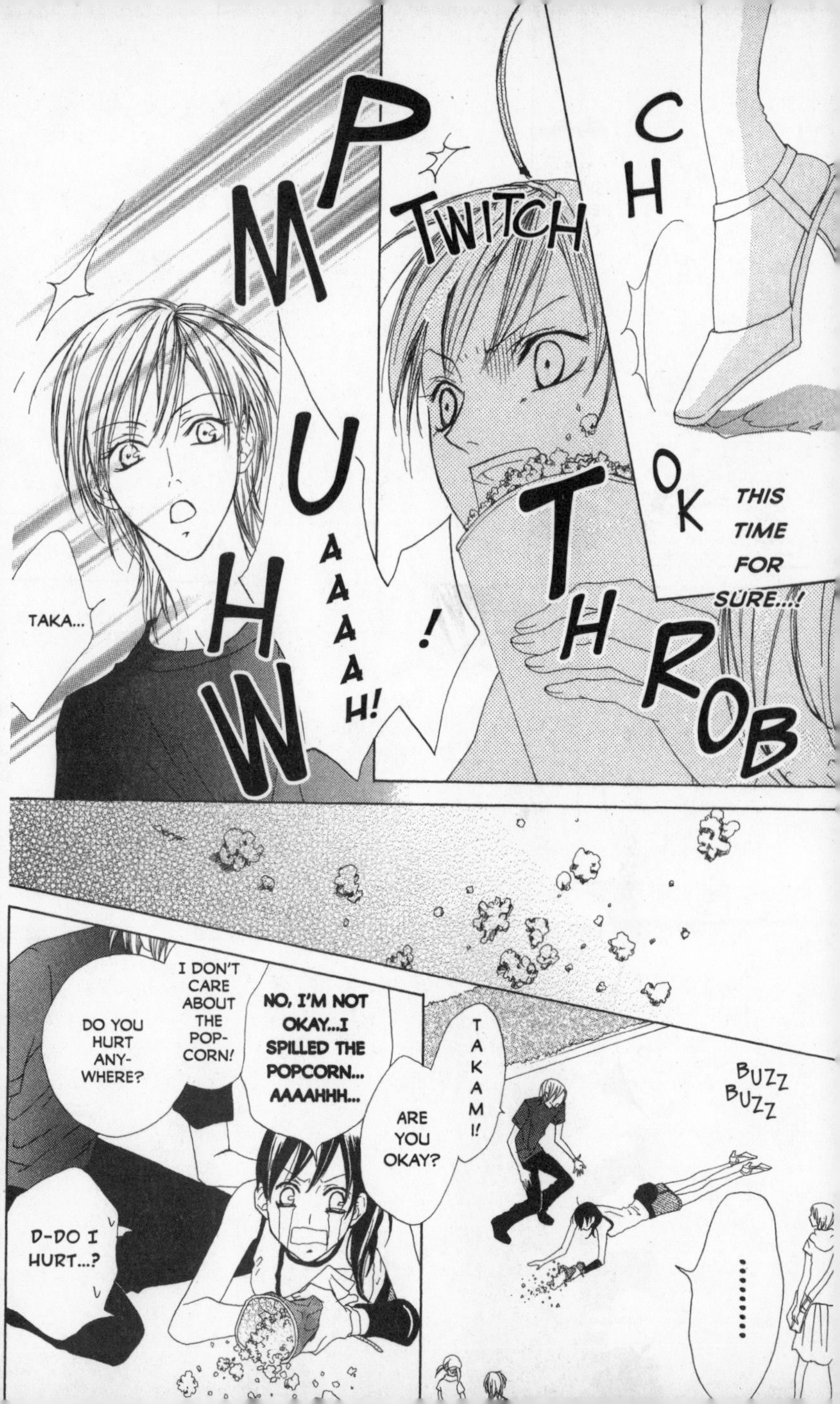

THIS TIME FOR SURE...!
CHOK
TWITCH
THROB
WHUMP
AAAAAH!
TAKA...
BUZZ BUZZ
......
TAKAMI!
ARE YOU OKAY?
NO, I'M NOT OKAY...I SPILLED THE POPCORN... AAAAHHH...
I DON'T CARE ABOUT THE POPCORN!
DO YOU HURT ANYWHERE?
D-DO I HURT...?

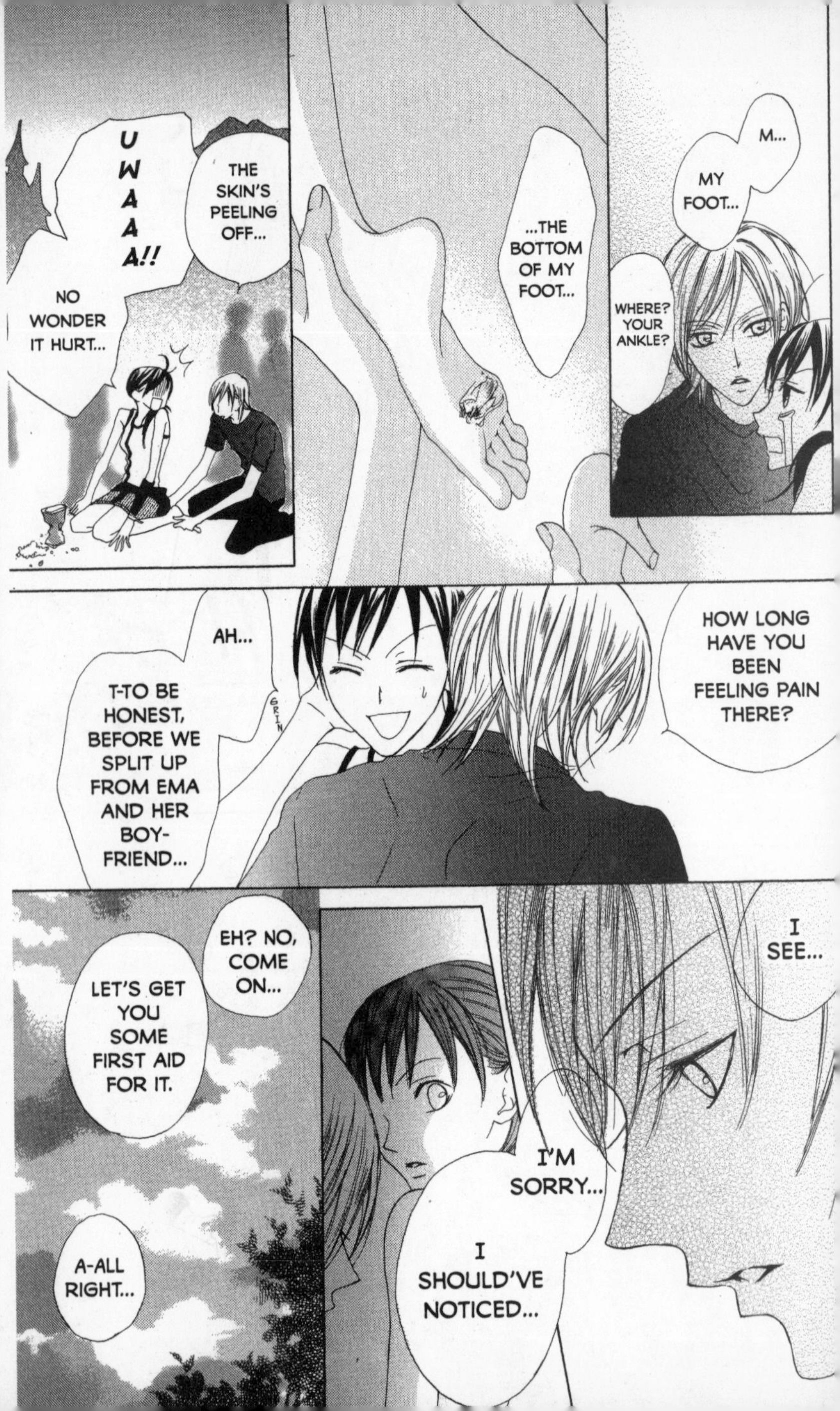
M...
MY FOOT...
WHERE? YOUR ANKLE?
...THE BOTTOM OF MY FOOT...
THE SKIN'S PEELING OFF...
UWAAAA!!
NO WONDER IT HURT...
HOW LONG HAVE YOU BEEN FEELING PAIN THERE?
AH...
GRIN
T-TO BE HONEST, BEFORE WE SPLIT UP FROM EMA AND HER BOY-FRIEND...
I SEE...
I'M SORRY...
I SHOULD'VE NOTICED...
EH? NO, COME ON...
LET'S GET YOU SOME FIRST AID FOR IT.
A-ALL RIGHT...

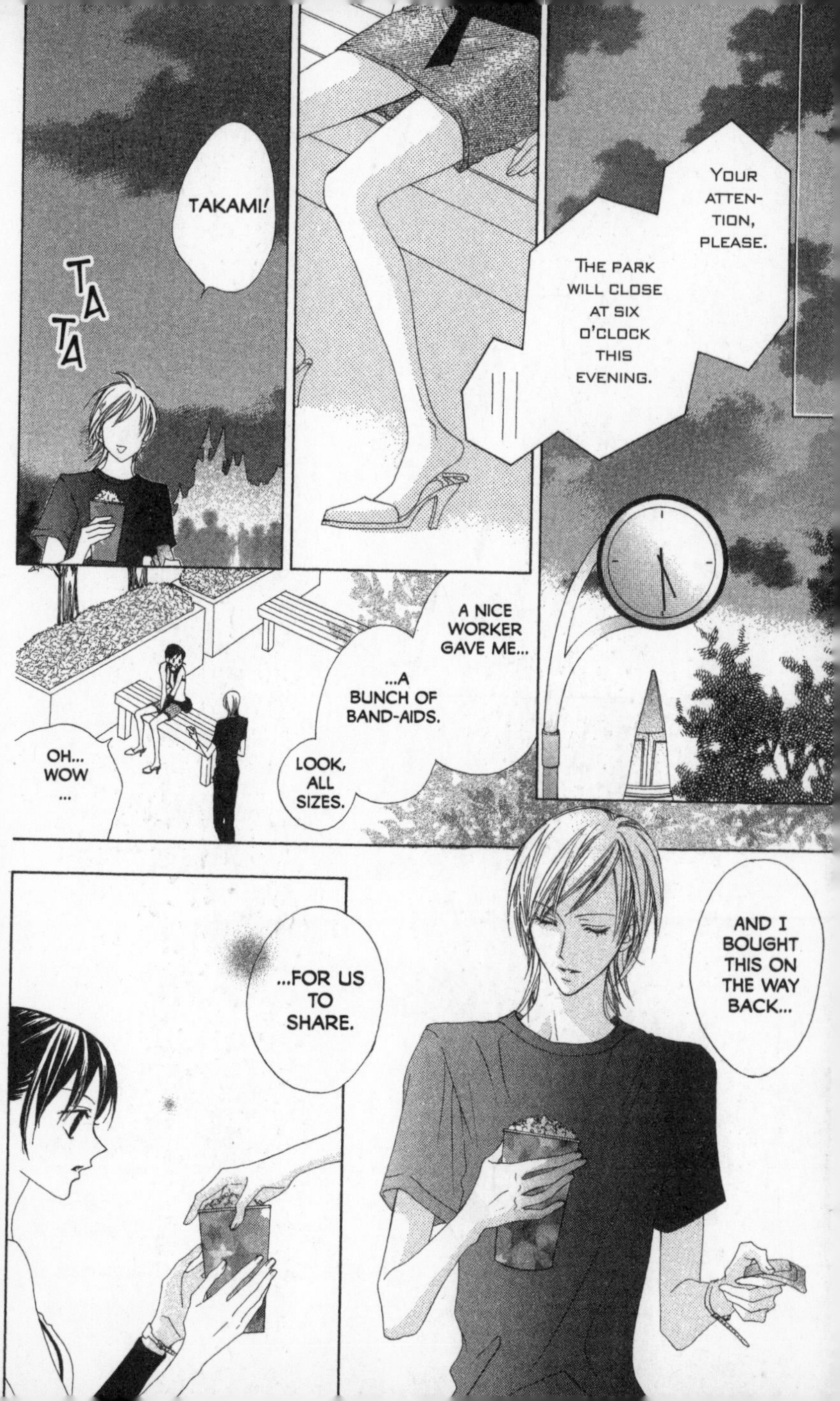
YOUR ATTENTION, PLEASE.
THE PARK WILL CLOSE AT SIX O'CLOCK THIS EVENING.
TAKAMI!
TA TA
A NICE WORKER GAVE ME...
...A BUNCH OF BAND-AIDS.
LOOK, ALL SIZES.
OH... WOW ...
AND I BOUGHT THIS ON THE WAY BACK...
...FOR US TO SHARE.

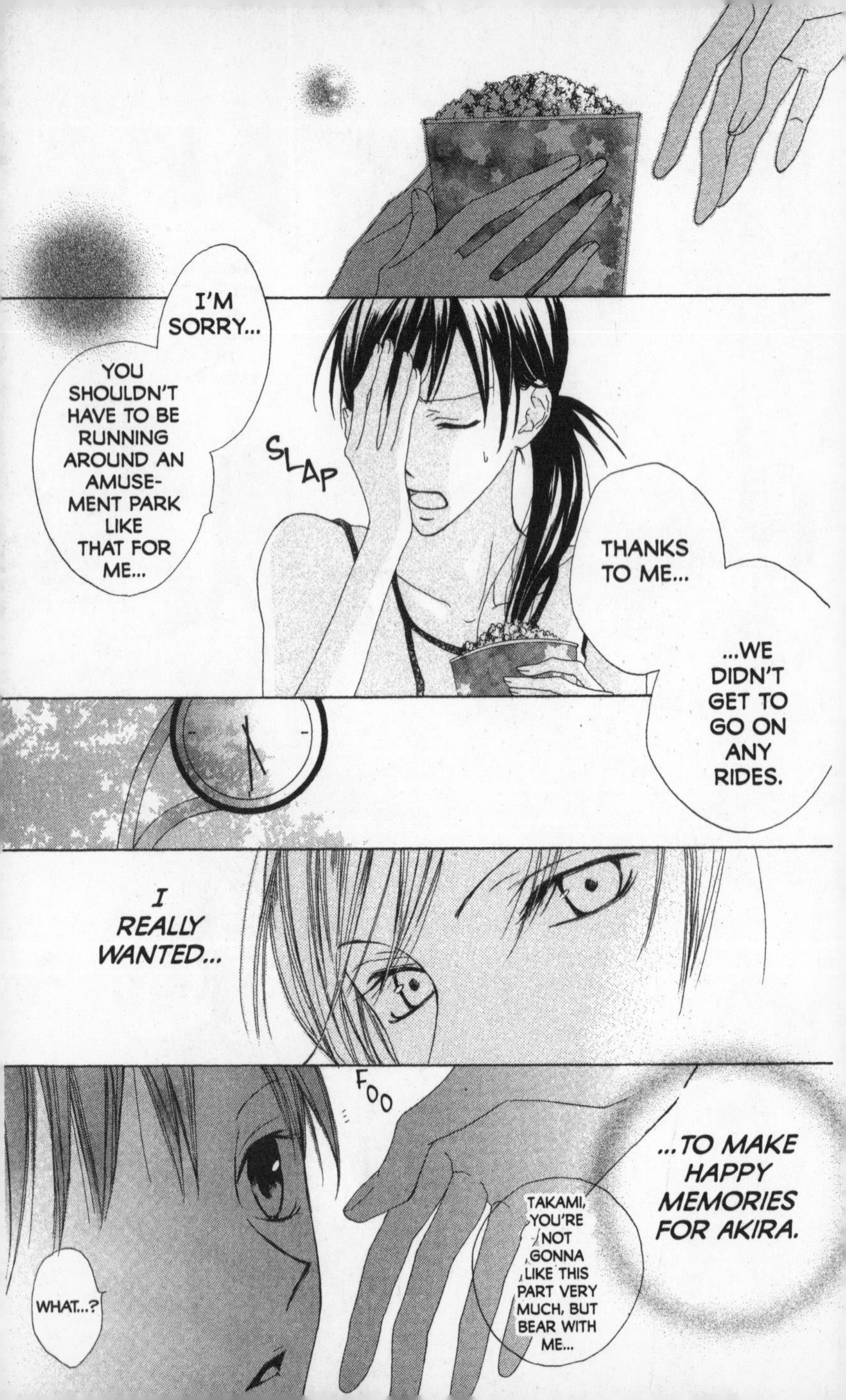
I'M SORRY...
YOU SHOULDN'T HAVE TO BE RUNNING AROUND AN AMUSE-MENT PARK LIKE THAT FOR ME...
SLAP
THANKS TO ME...
...WE DIDN'T GET TO GO ON ANY RIDES.
I REALLY WANTED...
...TO MAKE HAPPY MEMORIES FOR AKIRA.
FOO
TAKAMI, YOU'RE NOT GONNA LIKE THIS PART VERY MUCH, BUT BEAR WITH ME...
WHAT...?

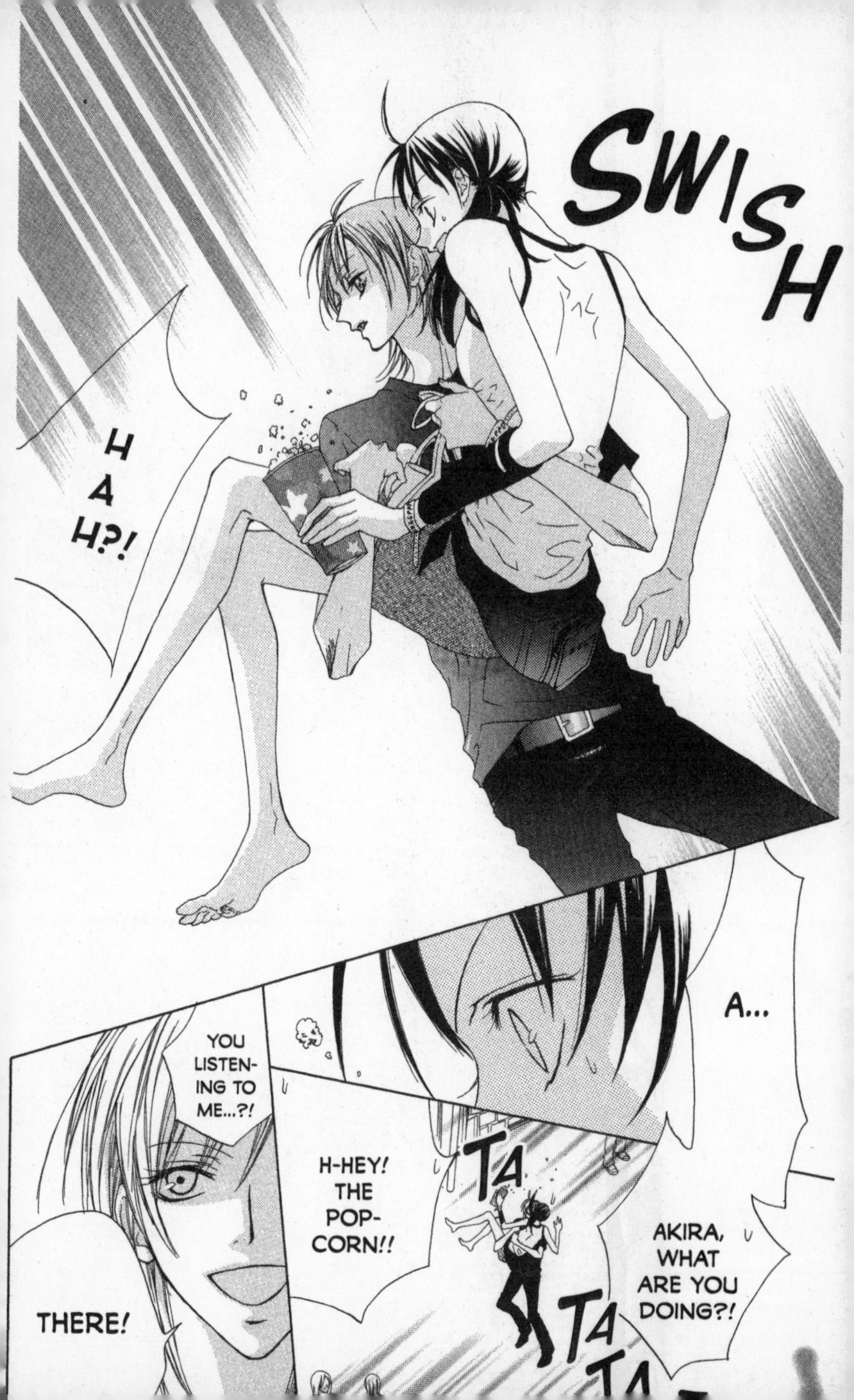
SWISH
HAH?!
A...
AKIRA, WHAT ARE YOU DOING?!
TA
TA
TA
H-HEY! THE POPCORN!!
YOU LISTENING TO ME...?!
THERE!

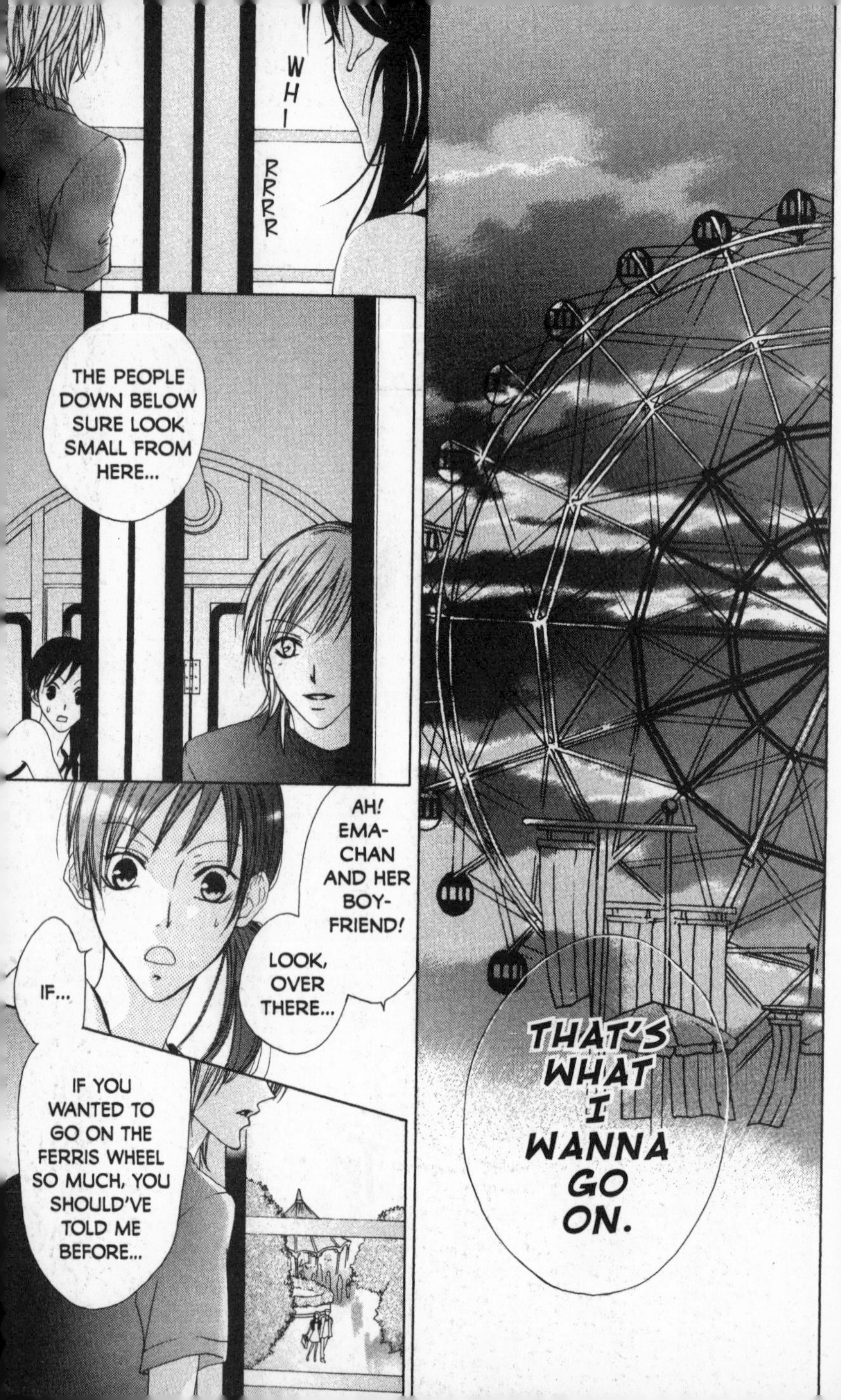
THAT'S WHAT I WANNA GO ON.
WHIRRRR
THE PEOPLE DOWN BELOW SURE LOOK SMALL FROM HERE...
AH! EMA-CHAN AND HER BOY-FRIEND!
LOOK, OVER THERE...
IF...
IF YOU WANTED TO GO ON THE FERRIS WHEEL SO MUCH, YOU SHOULD'VE TOLD ME BEFORE...

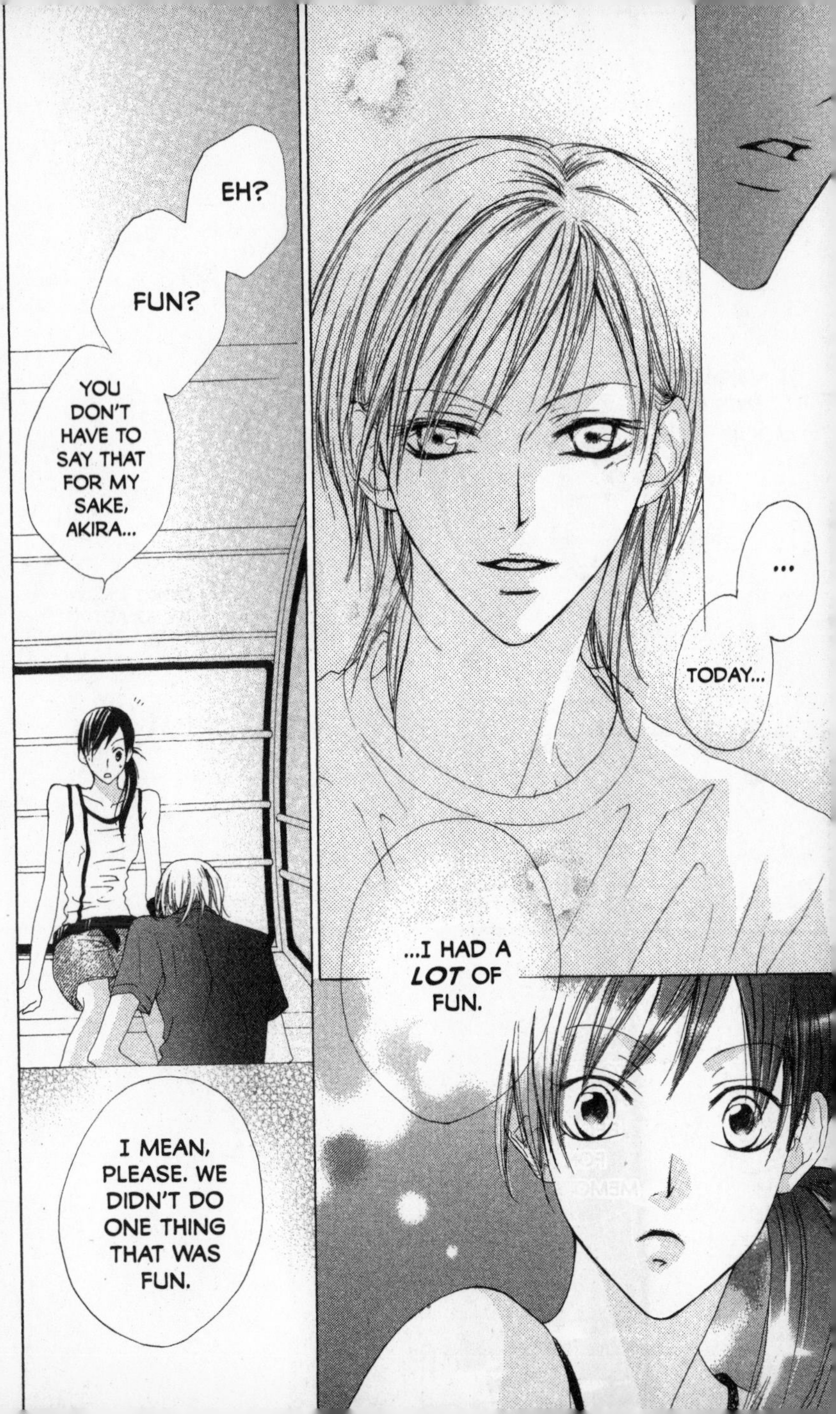
...
TODAY...
...I HAD A *LOT* OF FUN.
EH?
FUN?
YOU DON'T HAVE TO SAY THAT FOR MY SAKE, AKIRA...
I MEAN, PLEASE. WE DIDN'T DO ONE THING THAT WAS FUN.

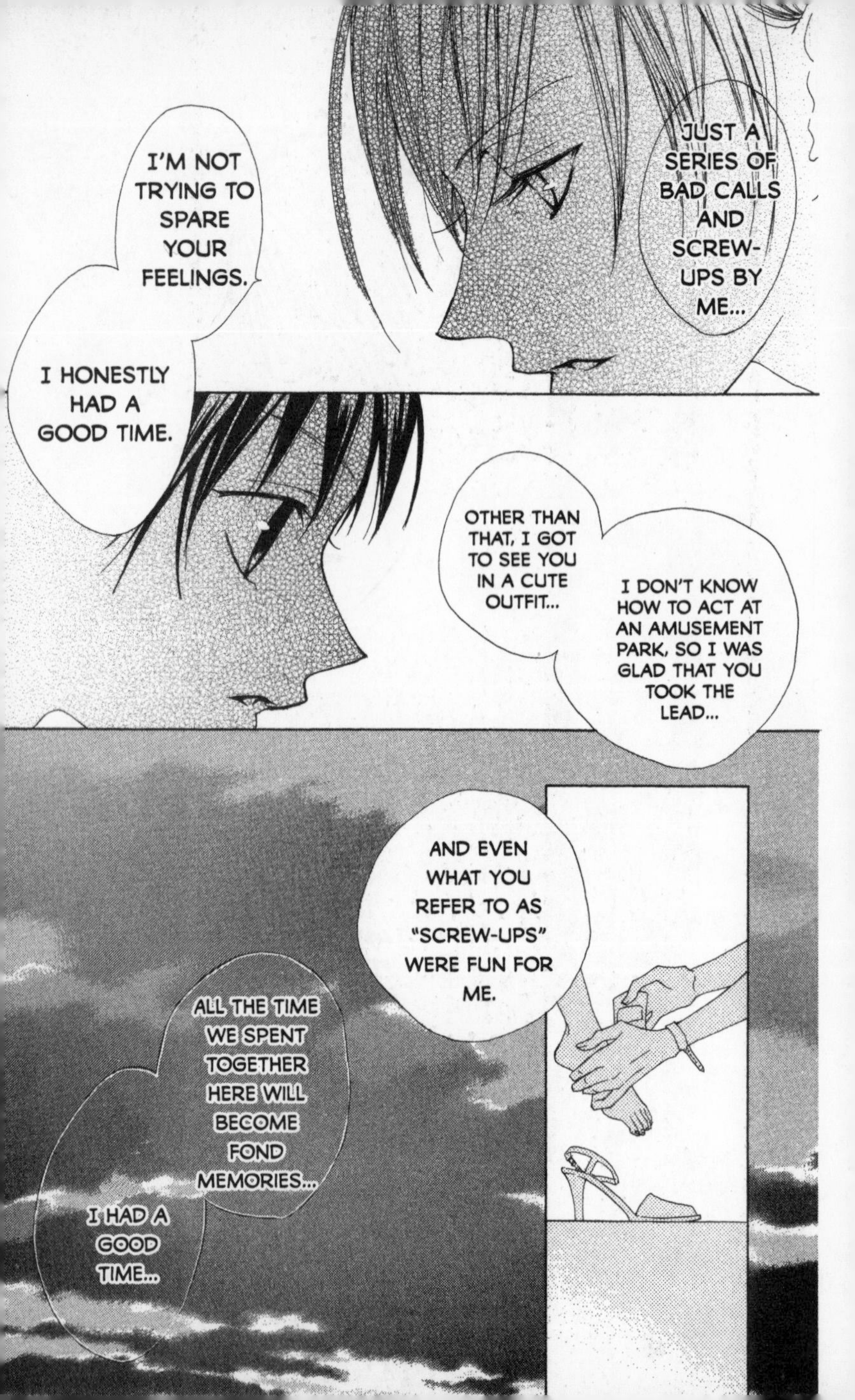
JUST A SERIES OF BAD CALLS AND SCREW-UPS BY ME...
I'M NOT TRYING TO SPARE YOUR FEELINGS.
I HONESTLY HAD A GOOD TIME.
OTHER THAN THAT, I GOT TO SEE YOU IN A CUTE OUTFIT...
I DON'T KNOW HOW TO ACT AT AN AMUSEMENT PARK, SO I WAS GLAD THAT YOU TOOK THE LEAD...
AND EVEN WHAT YOU REFER TO AS "SCREW-UPS" WERE FUN FOR ME.
ALL THE TIME WE SPENT TOGETHER HERE WILL BECOME FOND MEMORIES...
I HAD A GOOD TIME...

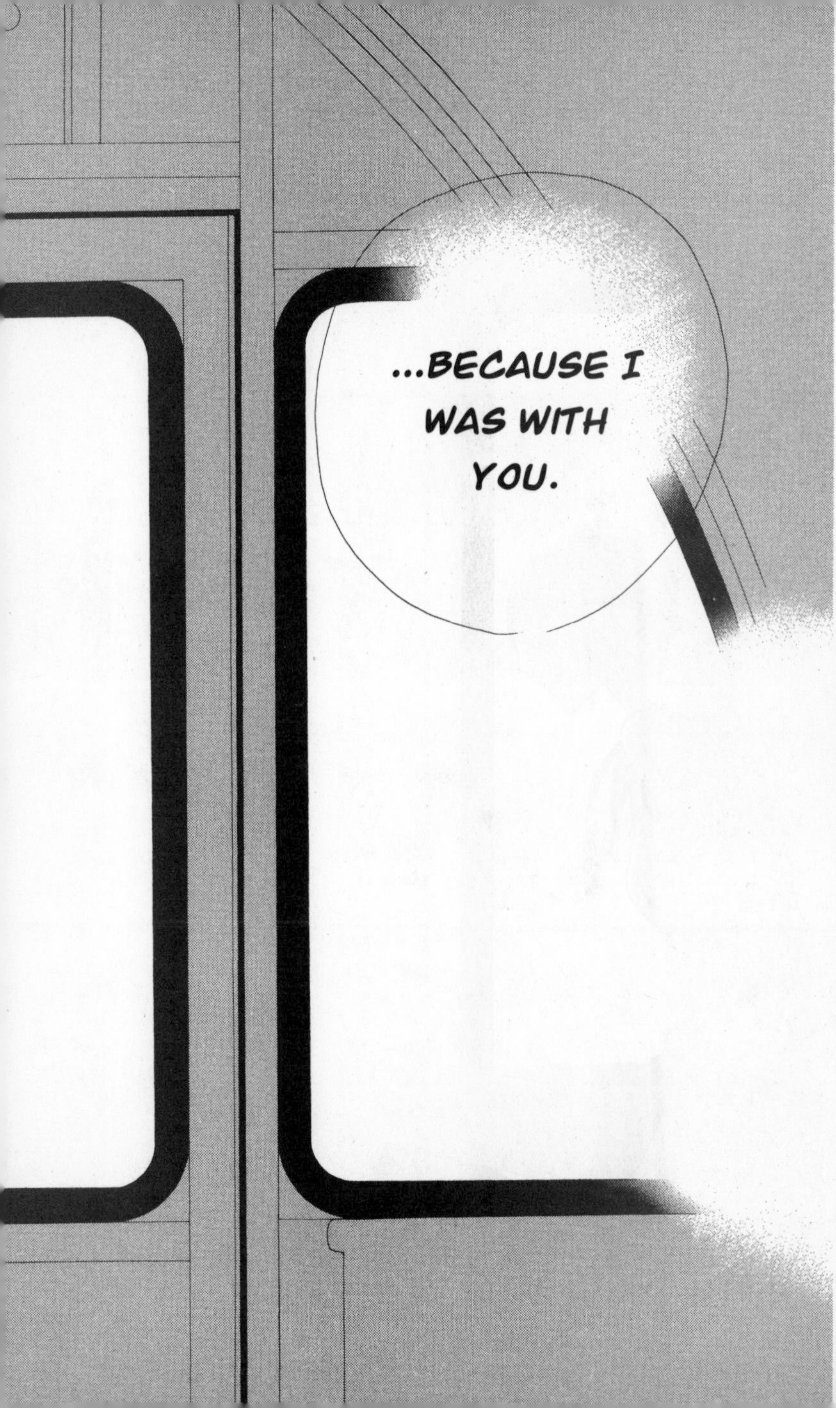
...BECAUSE I WAS WITH YOU.

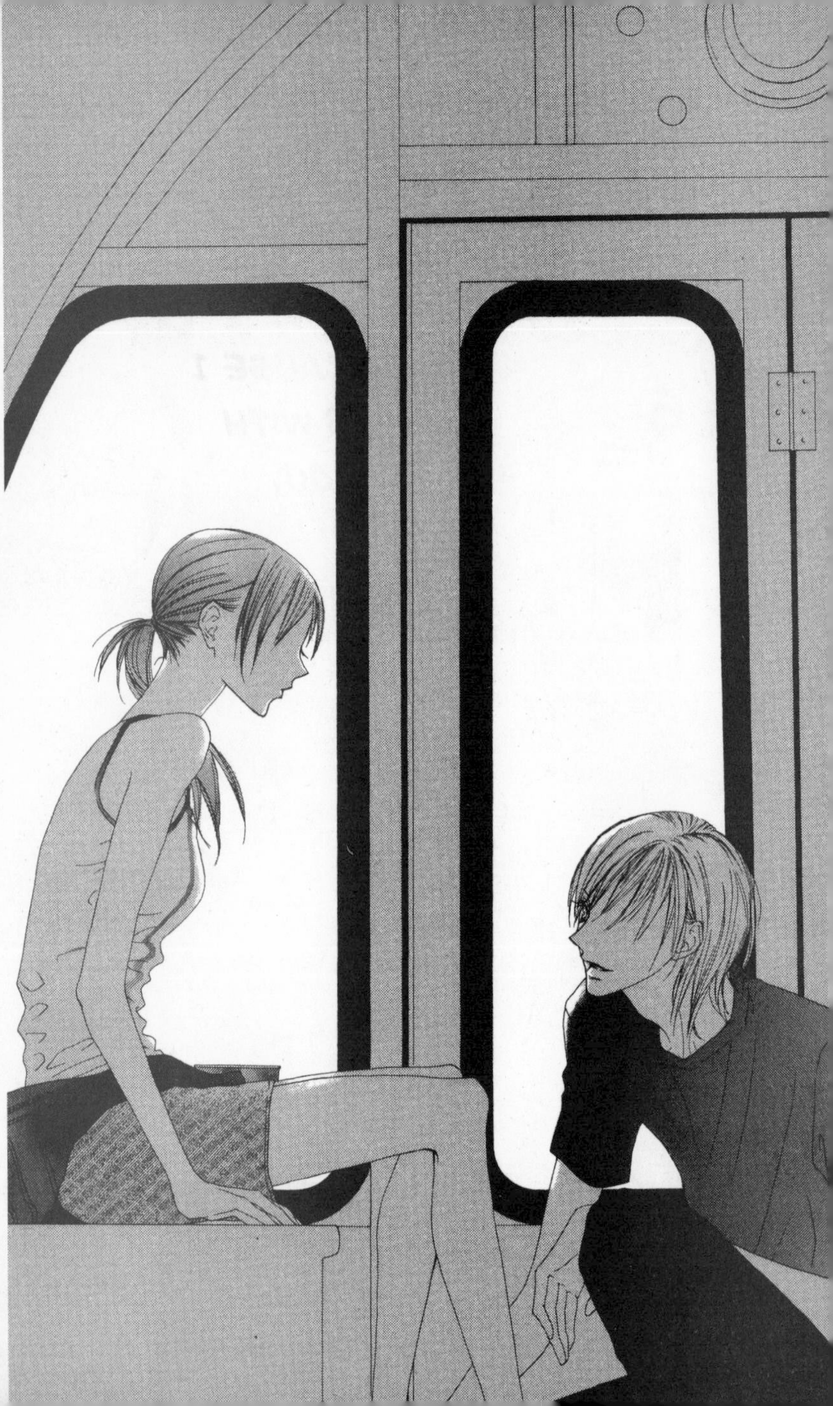

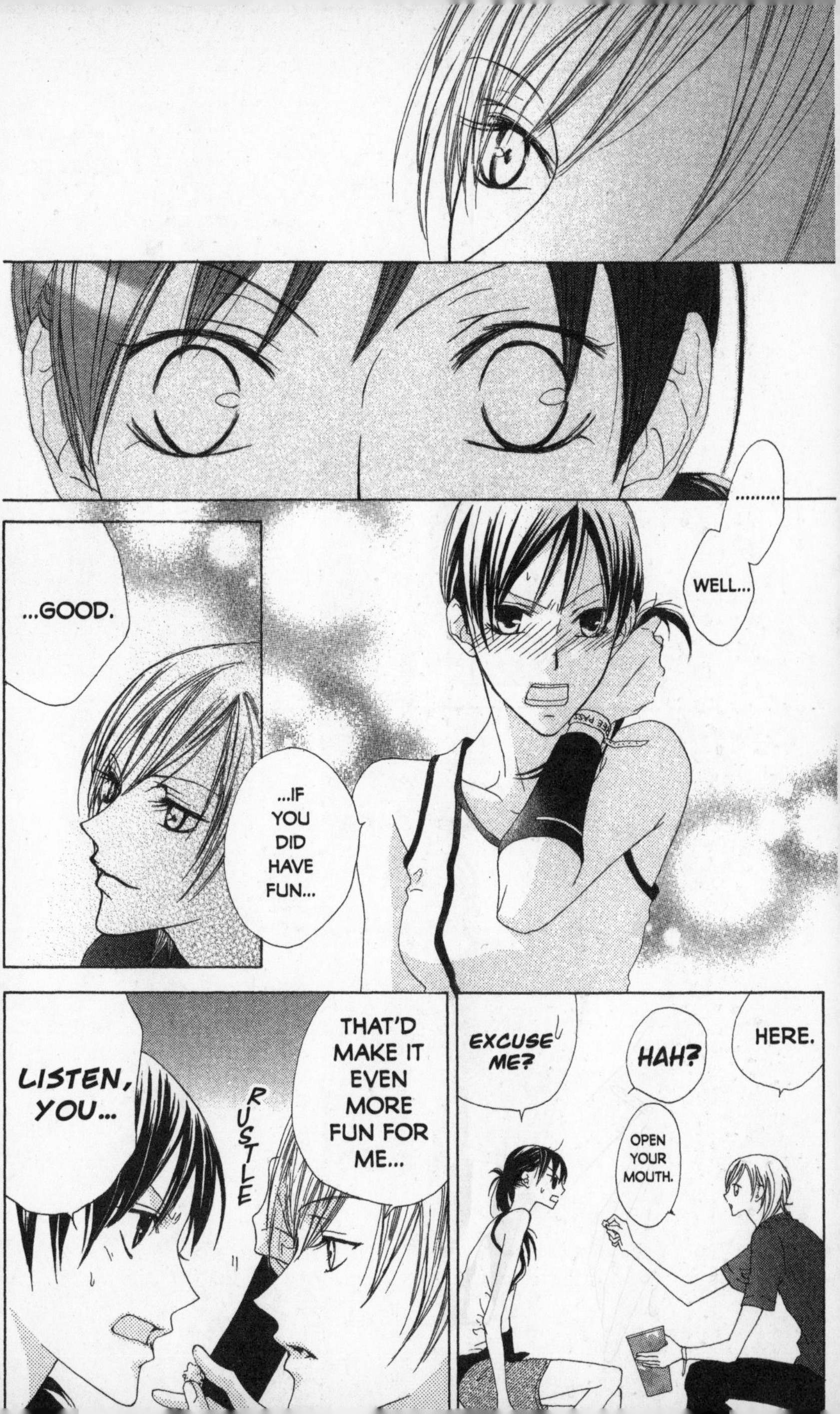
....
WELL...
...GOOD.
...IF YOU DID HAVE FUN...
HERE.
HAH?
EXCUSE ME?
OPEN YOUR MOUTH.
THAT'D MAKE IT EVEN MORE FUN FOR ME...
RUSTLE
LISTEN, YOU...

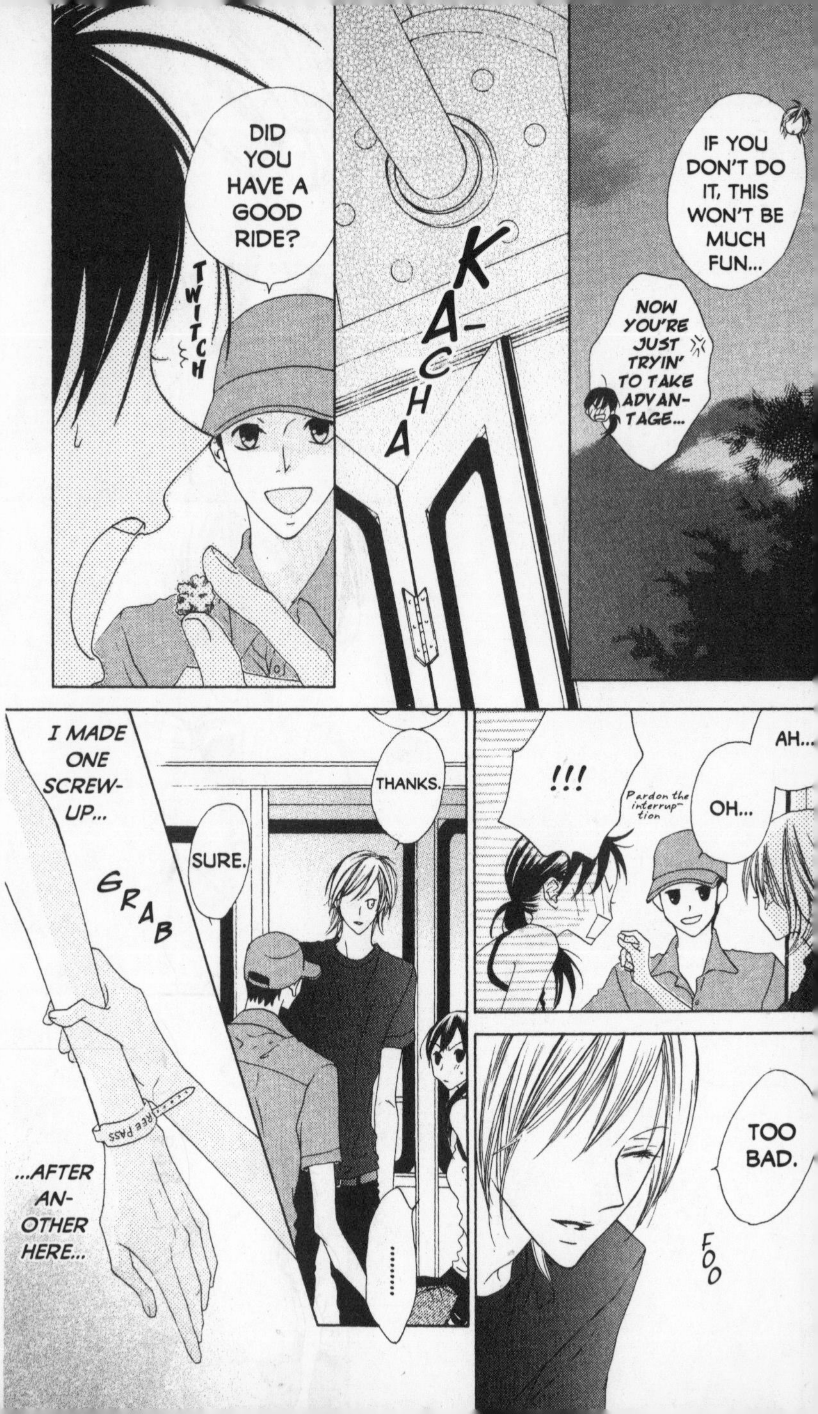

IF YOU DON'T DO IT, THIS WON'T BE MUCH FUN...
NOW YOU'RE JUST TRYIN' TO TAKE ADVANTAGE...
KA-CHA
DID YOU HAVE A GOOD RIDE?
TWITCH
AH...
OH...
!!!
Pardon the interruption
TOO BAD.
FOO
THANKS.
SURE.
......
I MADE ONE SCREW-UP...
GRAB
...AFTER ANOTHER HERE...

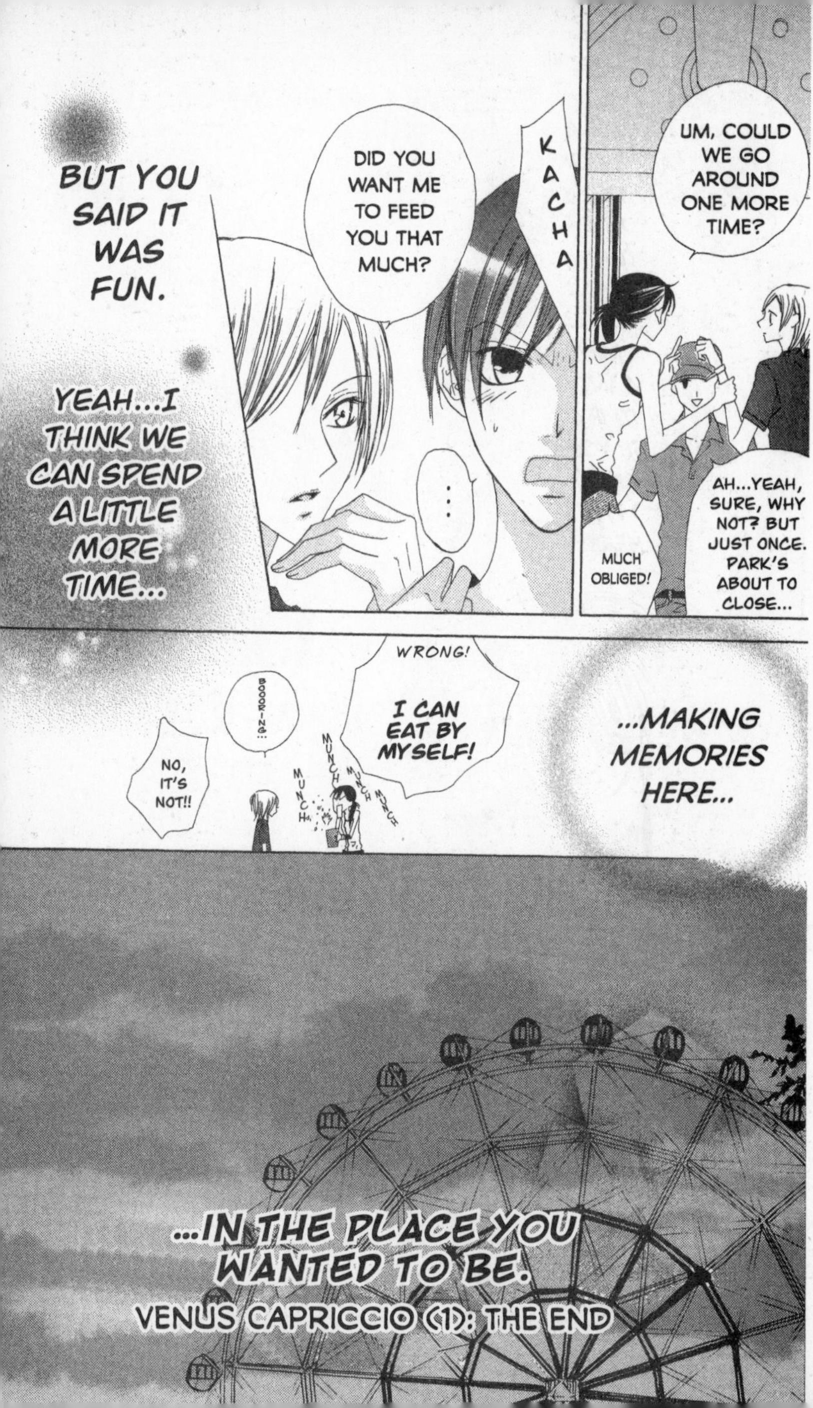

UM, COULD WE GO AROUND ONE MORE TIME?
AH...YEAH, SURE, WHY NOT? BUT JUST ONCE. PARK'S ABOUT TO CLOSE...
MUCH OBLIGED!
KACHA
DID YOU WANT ME TO FEED YOU THAT MUCH?
...
BUT YOU SAID IT WAS FUN.
YEAH...I THINK WE CAN SPEND A LITTLE MORE TIME...
...MAKING MEMORIES HERE...
WRONG!
I CAN EAT BY MYSELF!
MUNCH MUNCH MUNCH MUNCH
BOOORING...
NO, IT'S NOT!!
...IN THE PLACE YOU WANTED TO BE.
VENUS CAPRICCIO (1): THE END

BONUS PAGES

THERE'S A STRANGE BONUS MINI-STORY ON THE NEXT PAGE (FEATURING AKIRA). I HONESTLY DON'T MIND IF YOU WANT TO SKIP IT; IF SO, CLOSE YOUR EYES AND FLIP TWO PAGES AHEAD.

← GO

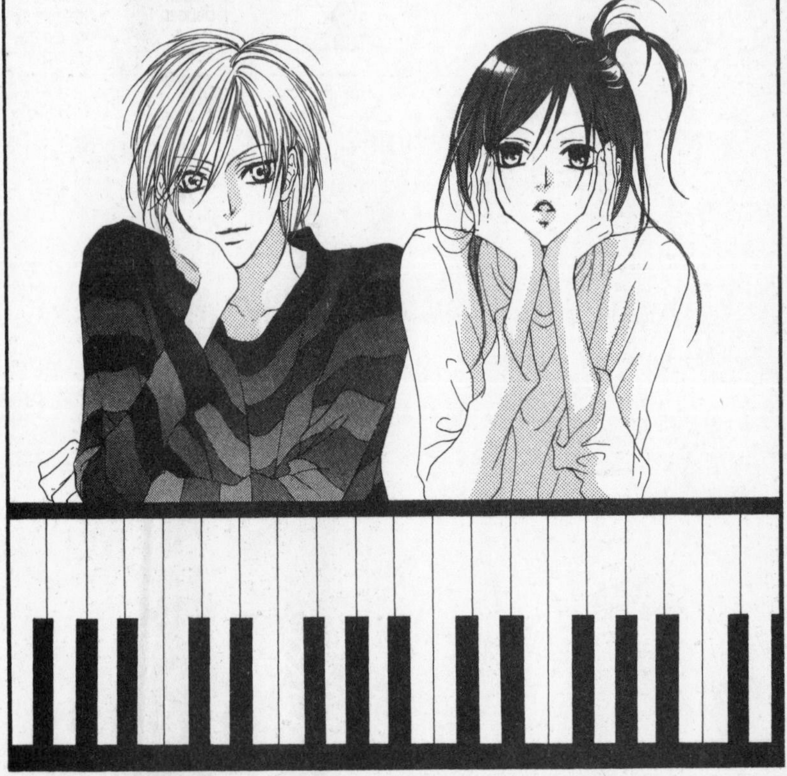

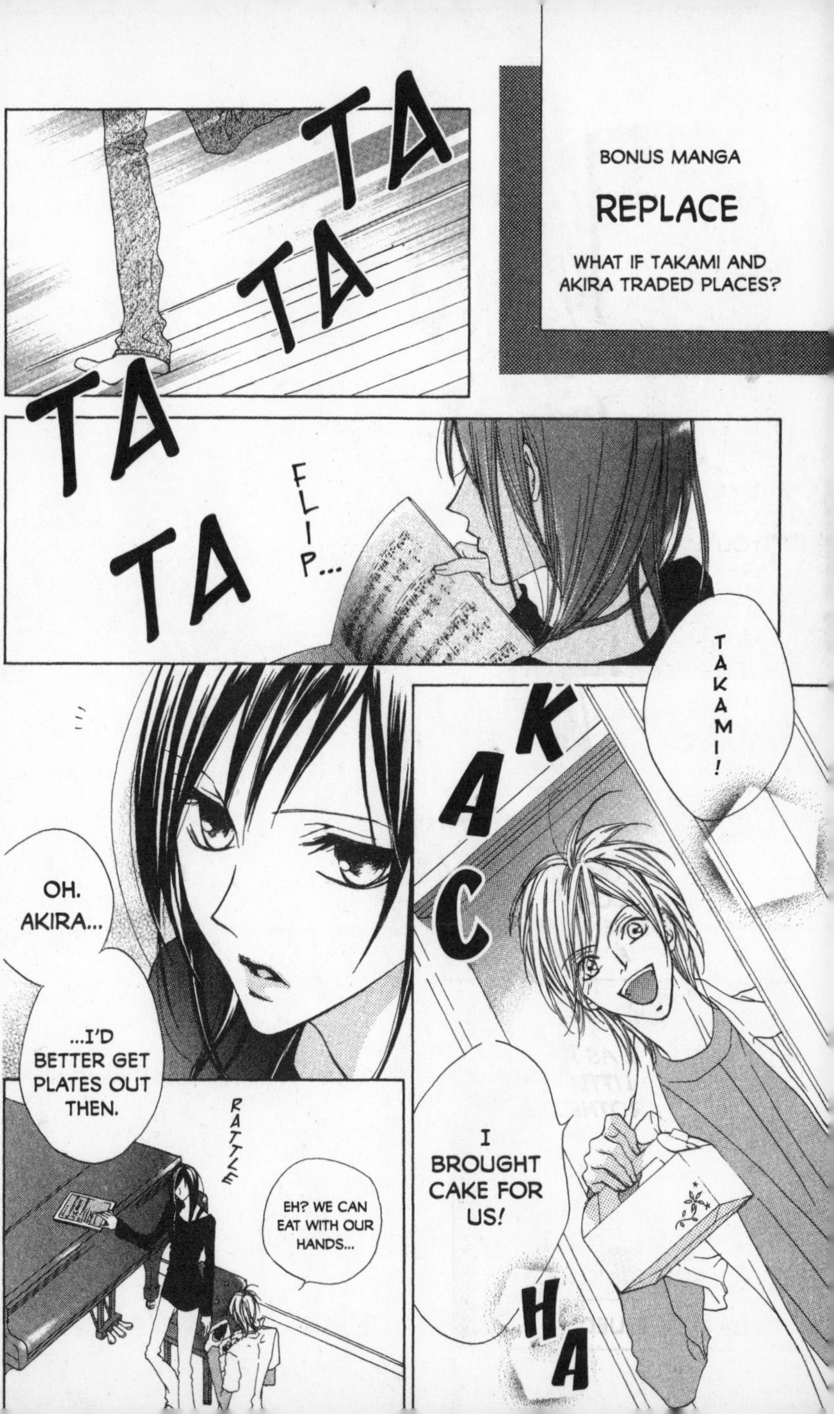
BONUS MANGA
REPLACE
WHAT IF TAKAMI AND AKIRA TRADED PLACES?
TA TA TA
TA
FLIP...
TAKAMI!
KACHA
I BROUGHT CAKE FOR US!
OH. AKIRA...
...I'D BETTER GET PLATES OUT THEN.
RATTLE
EH? WE CAN EAT WITH OUR HANDS...

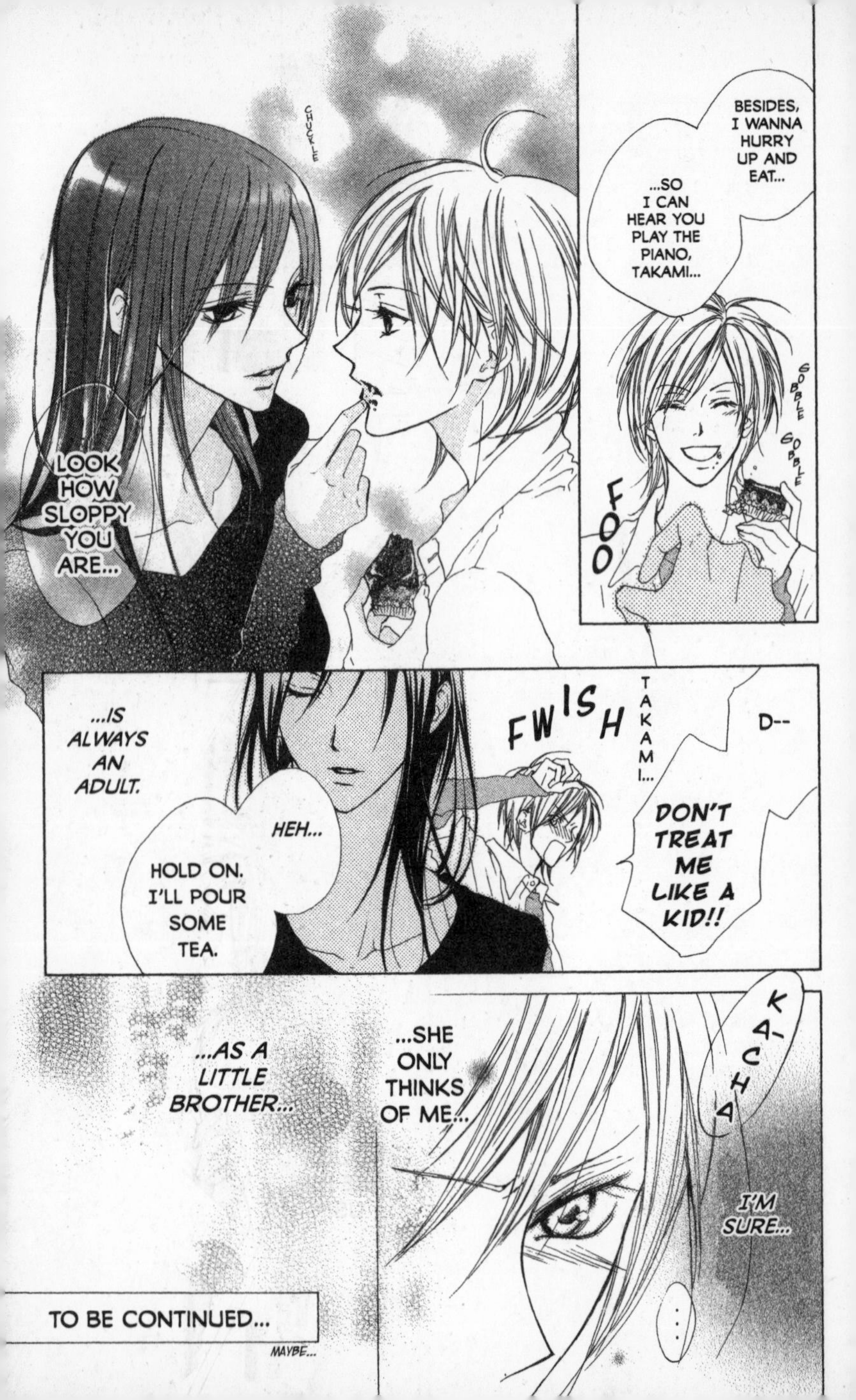
BESIDES, I WANNA HURRY UP AND EAT...
...SO I CAN HEAR YOU PLAY THE PIANO, TAKAMI...
GOBBLE GOBBLE
FOO
CHUCKLE
LOOK HOW SLOPPY YOU ARE...
D--
DON'T TREAT ME LIKE A KID!!
TAKAMI...
FWISH
HEH...
HOLD ON. I'LL POUR SOME TEA.
...IS ALWAYS AN ADULT.
KA-CHA
I'M SURE...
...
...SHE ONLY THINKS OF ME...
...AS A LITTLE BROTHER...
TO BE CONTINUED...
MAYBE...

TAKAMI HABARA.

HEIGHT: 5' 8 1/2"
BIRTHDAY: 8/30

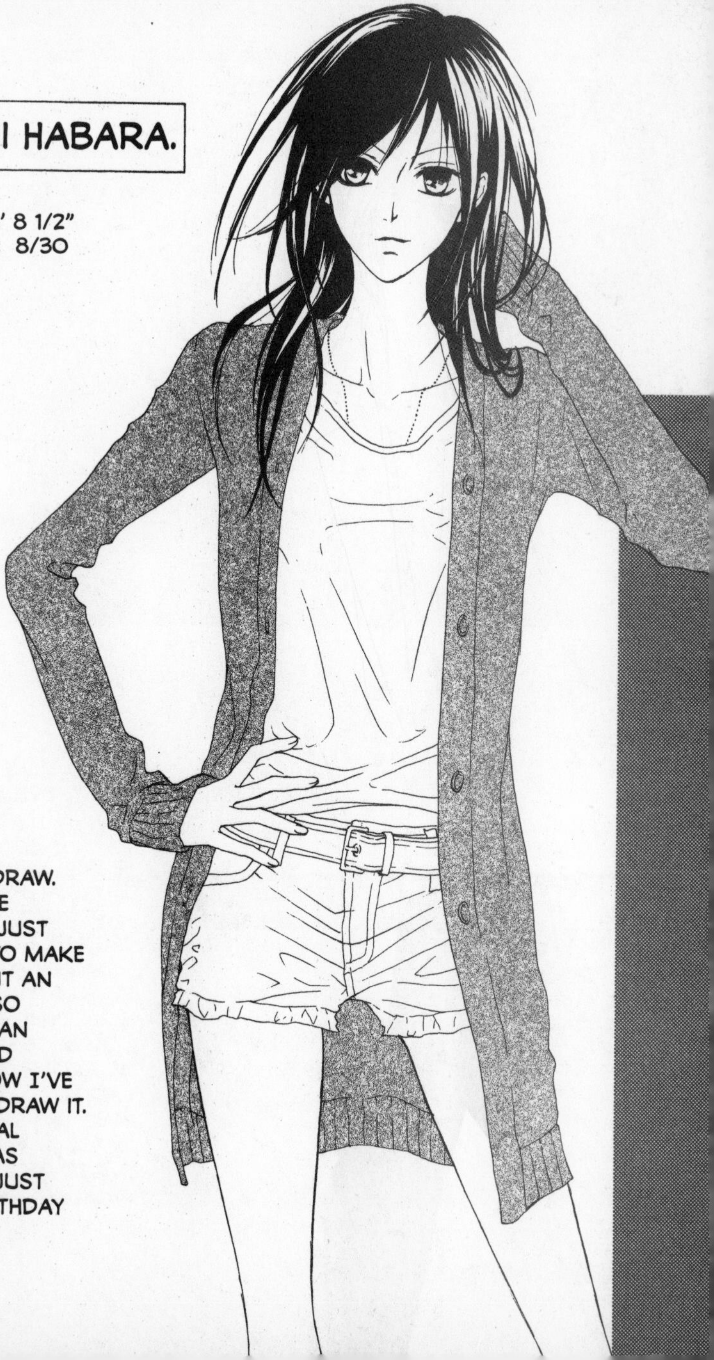

EASY TO DRAW. ABOUT THE HEIGHT, I JUST WANTED TO MAKE HER ABOUT AN INCH OR SO TALLER THAN AKIRA, AND THAT'S HOW I'VE TRIED TO DRAW IT. THE ACTUAL HEIGHT WAS DECIDED JUST NOW (BIRTHDAY TOO).

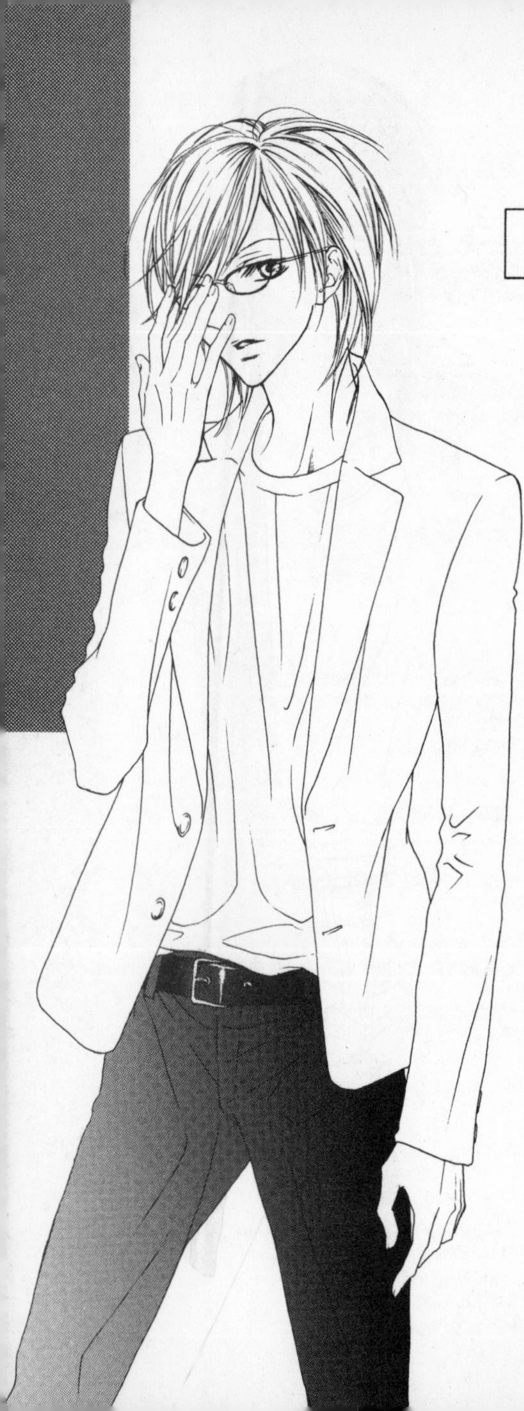

AKIRA SASAKI.

HEIGHT: 5' 7"
BIRTHDAY: 3/30

HE WAS HARD TO DRAW AT FIRST, BUT HAS GOTTEN EASIER OVER TIME.
IT'S DIFFICULT TO MAKE HIS HAIR BLONDE FOR THE COLORED CUTS.
TAKAMI DESCRIBES HIM AS HAVING GOLDEN HAIR AND LIGHT BLUE EYES, BUT I THINK THE SHADE IS A BIT DARKER.
I JUST DECIDED AKIRA'S HEIGHT NOW TOO.

AFTERWORD

GOOD JOB, READING ALL THE
WAY TO THE END!

I THINK MY INEXPERIENCE SHOWS
THROUGH ANY WAY YOU LOOK AT IT, BUT
I'M THRILLED TO HAVE MY FIRST VOLUME
EVER PUBLISHED.

THANK YOU SO MUCH TO EVERYONE
WHO READ THIS, BOUGHT THIS,
WROTE ME A LETTER AND CHEERED
ME ON!

I APPRECIATE YOU ALL,
FROM THE BOTTOM OF MY
HEART.

SPECIAL THANKS!!
MY EDITOR, S-SAMA, WHOM I'M INDEBTED TO...
ALL OF MY FRIENDS AND ACQUAINTANCES
WHO ENCOURAGED ME...
MY FAMILY, WHO SUPPORTED ME...
TSUKADA-SENSEI!

DUG-SAMA, WHO HELPED ME WITH
RESEARCH...
ACE HELPER AI-CHAN...
EVERYONE WHO PLAYED A PART IN GETTING
THIS BOOK PUBLISHED!

IF YOU HAVE ANY THOUGHTS, OPINIONS, ETC.
YOU'D LIKE TO SHARE ABOUT THIS TITLE, PLEASE
SEND THEM TO ME AT:
(THEY'LL BE SLOW IN COMING, BUT I PROMISE
TO RESPOND TO EVERY LETTER!)

MAI NISHIKATA/VENUS CAPRICCIO
CMX
888 PROSPECT STREET
SUITE 240
LA JOLLA, CA 92037

I HOPE WE CAN MEET AGAIN
SOMEWHERE.
THIS HAS BEEN MAI
NISHIKATA!
OCT. 2006